ACADEMIC LIVES

ACADEMIC LIVES

Memoir, Cultural Theory, and the University Today

CYNTHIA G. FRANKLIN

THE UNIVERSITY OF GEORGIA PRESS

ATHENS & LONDON

© 2009 by the University of Georgia Press
Athens, Georgia 30602
www.ugapress.org
All rights reserved

Set in New Caledonia by BookComp, Inc.
Printed digitally in the United States of America

Library of Congress Cataloging-in-Publication Data

Franklin, Cynthia G.
Academic lives : memoir, cultural theory, and the
university today / Cynthia G. Franklin.
        p. cm.
Includes bibliographical references and index.
ISBN-13: 978-0-8203-3342-7 (cloth : alk. paper)
ISBN-13: 0-8203-3342-5 (cloth : alk. paper)
ISBN-10: 978-0-8203-3343-4 (pbk. : alk. paper)
ISBN-10: 0-8203-3343-3 (pbk. : alk. paper)
1. College teachers—United States—Biography.
2. College teachers as authors—United States.
3. Autobiography—Authorship. I. Title.
LB1778.2.F73 2009
378.0092'2—dc22   2008049647

British Library Cataloging-in-Publication Data available

For Jesse

CONTENTS

ACKNOWLEDGMENTS

If in this book on academic memoir there is any place where I most directly write my own, it is here, in this space set aside to acknowledge my own institutional location and the experiences and the deep attachments without which this book would not exist.

My dean, Joe O'Mealy, has been the source not only of a superb wit but also of funding, and I thank him for supporting me with research and travel money. This project has been strengthened by responses from audiences at the following conferences: the American Studies Association (ASA), the Association for Asian American Studies (AAAS), the International Narrative Conference, the Modern Language Association (MLA), the Society for the Study of Multi-Ethnic Literature (MELUS), the Pacific Rim Conference on Disabilities, and by audiences at the University of Hawai'i (in particular the International Cultural Studies Certificate Program and the Women's Studies Colloquium Series). So, too, students in graduate courses in American studies, cultural studies, and in my graduate and upper-division courses on memoir have helped me formulate ideas that appear in this book; I'd particularly like to thank Carlo Arreglo, Donna Tanigawa, and Allison Yap.

This project has spanned the life of two writing groups whose contributions have been immeasurable. Andrea Feeser, Laura Lyons, and Beth Tobin provided crucial guidance and encouragement through the beginning stages of this project, and Andrea and Beth have continued to be wonderful—and sorely missed and much loved—long-distance friends and colleagues. It is fitting that I was able to spend time with Beth and Joe Tobin in New York City while completing the final revisions to this book, where an unexpected gift of that visit was their expert editorial advice. The later stages of this project owe much to the collective and individual energies and insights of Monisha Das Gupta, Linda Lierheimer, Laura Lyons, Kieko Matteson, Naoko Shibusawa (first in her embodied presence and then, when calling from Providence, as an intrepid voice emanating from the speaker phone, surrounded by strawberries), and Mari Yoshihara. That the intellectual pleasure of these groups has been seamless with the friendship and nourishment that they have offered is one of the profound pleasures of academic life and *Academic Lives*.

Other friends, colleagues, and mentors have been invaluable interlocutors, and have provided insightful responses to the manuscript or to ideas in it: my thanks to Elizabeth Abel, Hosam Aboul-Ela, Gloria Anzaldúa, S. Charusheela, Tom Couser, Ann Cvetkovich, Marcus Daniel, Candace Fujikane, Anne Goldman, Sian Hunter, AnaLouise Keating, Satya Mohanty, Lauren Muller, Robert Perkinson, M. S. S. Pandian, Francesca Royster, Ann Russo, Susan Schweik, Theresa Tensuan, Pam Thoma, Gillian Whitlock, Rob Wilson, Jean Wyatt, and readers whose reports on the manuscript have been anonymous but extremely helpful.

I could not ask for a better or more supportive editor than Erika Stevens, and I thank her for her enthusiasm and for her exacting eye. Working with her, Jon Davies, David Des Jardines, Jennifer Reichlin, and the other staff at the University of Georgia Press has been a true pleasure. This book also has benefited enormously from Deborah Oliver's scrupulous copyediting.

A number of friends deserve particular mention for sustaining me and my scholarship in often daily ways that cannot be disentangled. At *Biography*, Miriam Fuchs, Craig Howes, and Stan Schab not only have been a joy to work with, but also a constant source of encouragement, and their faith in this project has been of tremendous importance to me. Monica Ghosh was a source of pleasure and support as we walked the rises and falls of Mānoa Valley during a difficult year. Juliana Spahr responded to significant portions of this manuscript with insight and intelligence, and I thank her more generally for letting me know where the bottom line is in all things and also for assuring me that I will survive the experience and even manage to find it funny. My gratitude goes to Irene Tucker (Ms. Tuck) for a long and deep friendship, for loyalty and, on all the right occasions, outrage! I formulated many of the ideas put forth here—and received rejuvenating perspectives and friendship—hiking the 'Aihualama Trail with Paul Lyons. I also have profited from his rapidly delivered, sometimes cranky, but always constructive and copious queries, generously given in response to so many sections of this manuscript. I am deeply grateful for love and support of all kinds from my fierce friend Monisha Das Gupta—be it home-cooked meals (often enriched by Rich Rath's culinary skills and his weirdly compelling musical creations), loyally aimed scowls and growls, or always on-target feedback on big chunks of this manuscript.

Discussions about Said, humanism, and academic culture with S. Shankar are woven throughout this manuscript, and I am indebted to him for his steady encouragement and confidence in this book, and, more particularly, for the book's title, for his careful and often multiple readings of every section of the manuscript, and especially for his persistent insistence that I raise the stakes. In addition to his contributions to *Academic Lives*, my own life has been made richer by Shankar's presence, and I thank him for being my always-friend.

Vrinda Dalmiya's love and friendship mean more to me than she will ever know; I experience both, along with her shining brilliance and extraordinary kindness, as the most precious of gifts. And our discussions, especially about disability studies, care ethics, and empathy have been hugely helpful to me in writing this book, as have her responses to significant portions of the manuscript. I have come to depend as well on our Bollywood nights and on evenings spent witnessing Vrinda, and Arindam and Bhasha Chakrabarti engage in philosophical debate with my indefatigable young Republican.

For wise and loving counsel on this manuscript as well as on all matters of life, I am immeasurably grateful to Jacqueline Shea Murphy, who through over 20 years of friendship continues to know what I am doing better than I know it myself, and who never fails to make me feel a sense of home in her own as she, Kenny, Casey—and now Katara and Rickie—Shea Dinkin continue to surround me with music, food, and superheroes!

In addition to having the unenviable knack of being present for every manner of crisis, Cristina Bacchilega has served as the smartest mentor and Chair imaginable, one whose protean and awe-inspiring intelligence rises to every occasion. Our Sunday morning ocean walks from Kaimana Beach to the Kahala Mandarin these past several years have kept me anchored to this island and have contributed in direct ways to this book's existence. So, too, Cristina's comments on the manuscript and all the documents that go into getting a book published have been invaluable. Plus, Cristina knows when to tickle my young solipsist while John Rieder feeds him Marx and lamb, and I thank them both, and Bruna Rieder, for being a second family to Jesse and me.

Since coming to Hawai'i in 1994, Laura Lyons has been the very best best friend I ever could ask for: she has been a constant source of intellectual inspiration, concrete advice, rare friendship, and love that leaves me without adequate words with which to express my gratitude. My collaborator in other writing projects, Laura is also responsible for so much of what is right about this book—many ideas here are the result of conversations with and lessons learned from her. So, too, John Zuern's feedback on sections of this manuscript has been breathtakingly smart, witty, and a constant reminder of his creativity and of the capaciousness and compassion of his heart and mind. Laura and John, together with the delightful, theatrical, and sometimes diabolical Sam, have given me a sense of family even as my own has been an ocean away, and for this I am truly grateful.

Others who have not passed their pens over this project's pages but who have supported me in various ways during the writing of it include: Fran Acoba, Jean Adair-Leland, Scott Anderson, Erica Benson, the Comparativism and Translation in Literary and Cultural Studies gang, Lance Collins, Kim Drake, Jane Garrity, Richard Gibson, Theo Gonzalves, Mark Heberle, John Henry, Pensri Ho and Roy Gal, Lisa Jaffe, RaeDeen Keahiolalo Karasuda, Anne Kennedy, Mamo Kim, Karen and Eiko Kosasa, R. Zamora Linmark, Andy Lohmeier, Mary Lucasse and the Baker Boys, Nancy Luckie, Nephtaly Lugo, Bill Luoma, Robin Martin, Maria Mehr, Jeff Mexia, Kalawaia Moore, Rodney Morales and Holly Yamada, Caroline Mulder, Robert Sullivan, Glen Tomita, Haunani-Kay Trask, Val Wayne, Charles Weigl, Reina Whaitiri and Al Wendt, John R. Wilkins (one of the world's funniest men), and Kimball Fenn. In the Bay Area, Sherry and Scott Haber and Anne Jennings and Andy and Sam Stacklin have repeatedly shared their home with me. In Hawai'i, Burt Gordon deserves special mention for being such a good phone companion and for coming up with the most perfect albeit deadly metaphors to describe my scholarship. And I have particularly treasured my nearly careening-out-of-control pizza-and-movie nights with Ujjayan Siddhartha and Samuel Aidan Lyons Zuern.

Finally, I wish to thank my family who, despite the great geographical distance between us, has been so present for me. They have been an enormous support to me during the writing of this book, even as its contents have remained for the most part a mystery to them. My mother, Elaine Franklin, is a source of unconditional love and generosity, and I especially appreciate her and Jerry Miller taking such good care of Jesse, and also for opening their home by the lake to me and giving me a space of solitude and peace to write during a summer when I really needed it. My father, Sheldon Franklin, carries with him a passion, tenacity (stubbornness?), creativity, and interest in ideas that have been my inheritance and that have helped me in the writing of this book. I thank him as well for his love and support and am deeply grateful as well for the arrival of Juvy Reyes and for her steady loving presence. My sister, Julie Franklin, has healing powers that extend across an ocean, and her loving spirit and daily phone calls are essential to my survival. Thanks, as well, to Mark Follansbee for his care, his teasing, and his patient good humor; and to the delightful and funny Ayla and Jasper! I thank my brother, Bob Franklin, for his unfailing love and kindness to me and to Jesse and for his off-beat sense of humor. I especially appreciate his and Jessica Pitt's warm hospitality, and I thank them profusely for taking such good care of Jesse for extended periods of time, even with the fabulous arrival of the frenetically busy Ivan (the Terrible) Alexander (the Great)! Thanks as well to Marc Murdock, for undertaking the project of parenting with such a loving heart when no one gave us a handbook for it; to Racine and Gerry Murdock; to Susan, Randy, Jackie, and Daniel Klueger; and to the Landy and Leon families. My Aunt Diane deserves special mention—I cherish our phone calls and lunch dates. Catalina Nieves and Diane Alpert have become family members these past several years as they extended the life of my grandmother, Elsie Franklin, keeping her not only healthy but happy. My grandmother died shortly before this book's publication and I miss her sorely, but her larger-than-life spirit continues to serve me as a source of inspiration.

Jesse Franklin-Murdock has lived with this book for much of his life and has derived from it a precocious impatience with academe. I thank him both for his patience with me and for his perspective-granting if at times arrogant exasperation with academe, and I stand in awe of his relentless intellect, his inimitable spirit, and his bravery. With love, gratitude, and hopes that someday it will help to dispel more of his perceptions than it will confirm about the strange lives of professors, I dedicate this book to him.

A version of material from chapter 2 is published as "Recollecting *This Bridge* in an Anti-Affirmative Action Era: Literary Anthologies, Academic Memoir, and Institutional Autobiography," in *This Bridge We Call Home: Radical Visions for Transformation*, eds. Gloria Anzaldúa and AnaLouise Keating (New York: Routledge, 2002), 415–33. A portion of chapter 3 appears as "Turning Japanese/Returning to America: Gender, Class and Nation in David Mura's Use of Memoir," *LIT (Literature, Interpretation, Theory)* 13 (Oct. 2001): 235–65.

ACADEMIC LIVES

CHAPTER 1   The Academic Memoir Movement

Humanist Returns and the Currency of Academic Memoirs

In this book I explore the insights that contemporary academic memoirs provide into the humanities as an intellectual and institutional formation. Since the early 1990s and continuing into the present, humanities professors, many of them working in English departments, have been writing their memoirs in unprecedented numbers. As David Simpson caustically remarks in *The Academic Postmodern and the Rule of Literature*, "the award of tenure now seems to bring with it a contract for one's autobiography" (24).[1] By partaking in this "memoir movement," academics participate in what journalist James Atlas has dubbed "the Age of the Literary Memoir," or what Nancy Miller speculates "may emerge as a master form in the twenty-first century" ("The Entangled Self" 545). They also contribute to the burgeoning field of life writing in the U.S. academy. Although the memoir phenomenon has been much remarked on and studies of memoirs have flourished within the rapidly developing life writing field, academic memoirs have escaped scrutiny.[2] *Academic Lives* considers why so many professors choose to write their memoirs and why these memoirs claim so much cultural capital.

Even as academic memoirs constitute a widely noted phenomenon for the most part, literary and cultural critics have overlooked their cultural significance, giving them only cursory readings in articles or individual chapters before dismissing or celebrating them. A number of critics have read academic memoirs as evidencing a reaction against postmodernism or a fatigue with poststructuralist theory (Simpson), as unfortunate by-products of the academic star system (David Shumway), or as the self-indulgent products of middle-aged academics experiencing identity crises (Adam Begley). Other critics have been more welcoming, championing memoir for its "crossover" appeal (Michael Bérubé), its democratizing capacities (Jill Ker Conway), and its feminist realization of the personal as political (Nancy Miller).[3] *Academic Lives* complicates these claims, for even if there is some measure of truth to each of them, they do not capture the complex story that accounts of individual professors' lives have to tell about the current cultural and political climate in the academy. One of this book's central contentions is that memoirs afford crucial insights into the academy because, in offering spaces that are more musing and pliable than those afforded by theory, they can display contradictions between the personal and political without having to reconcile them.

The free play and seeming frivolity that accompanies the genre constitutes not grounds for its critical dismissal but engagement: academic memoirs provide not only an index of scholars' lives and why they matter, but also unparalleled ways to catch the currents that define the U.S. academy. I believe that, in part, academic memoirs have not received sustained critical analysis on the grounds that they are seen as simply affording "private," or prurient and indulgent, sometimes embarrassing, glimpses into an often well-known academic's life—like their now-defunct contemporary, *Lingua Franca* (the *People* magazine of academe), they seemingly constitute reading "on the side."[4] Memoirs enable academics working in the humanities to escape *from* the self-reflexivity that the increasingly politicized realm of literary studies has come to demand. In other words, memoirs too often have become a means by which those working in the academy can speak "only" personally, and hence unassailably; in some cases they have functioned to give academics a haven from criticism and its rigors. Indeed, to hold academic memoirs to the scholarly standard of critical books or essays can seem like a trivial undertaking, if not a form of voyeurism or foul play. Academic memoirs potentially offer a criticism-free zone: as memoirists perform public confessions and address readers in intimate terms, readers implicitly are asked to forgive authors their shortcomings and love them anyway. And yet, even as memoirs are received as existing apart from a professor's "real" work, this reception paradoxically depends on the author's academic credentials and other publications. Authors' critical achievements endow their memoirs with an often unspoken context and a form of social legitimation. Moreover, memoirs are public documents; therefore, their autobiographical nature and intimate address should not foreclose rigorous critique, perhaps especially when they come from academics well-versed in identity politics or other theories of subjectivity. Indeed, the blind spots memoirs often exhibit regarding their practitioners' institutional privilege and the contradictions they frequently pose to authors' theoretical writings can unmask the workings of the academy during a time when it is under attack.

Taken together as an epiphenomenon, academic memoirs serve as a barometer for the state of the humanities during a period of crisis, including the recent return to humanism by some of the academy's most prominent scholars. A number of competing and sometimes contradictory factors have contributed to this crisis in the past few decades. These include external conditions, such as reduced public subsidizing and increasing corporatization of universities; the commodification of knowledge; the professionalization of graduate studies; the call for national standardized curricula; the ongoing purchase of individualism and the antidote it provides to the supposed takeover of affirmative action and "p.c." politics; the withdrawal of public support due to a perception of the university's failed humanist mission; general anti-intellectualism; and, most recently, attacks on academic freedom. Challenges from within universities that have brought the humanities to a crossroads include the disenchantment with high theory and its erasure of agency; the strength of—and unhappiness with—the academic star system and the concurrent and increasing reliance on an underpaid temporary, or adjunct, labor force; a sense of uncertainty about the purposes and content of a humanities education; and an increase in student passivity. So, too, technology and the digital revolution have changed the game of scholarship in ways that threaten the "human" and utterly devalue certain kinds of labor and research skills.[5] Exploring how these different circumstances contribute to the turn to memoir writing is the focus of this book.

As I argue for a serious consideration of the subgenre of contemporary academic memoir, I am especially interested in how academic memoirs anticipate and impact contemporary considerations of humanism and the state of the humanities. Humanism is being rehabilitated through academic memoir in reactive and transformative ways after having fallen out of favor with poststructuralist and postcolonial theorists, who saw it as exclusionary, as bound to the largely white male Enlightenment canon. The turn back toward humanism effected in contemporary academic memoirs, I claim, includes surreptitious or frankly nostalgic "returns" to humanism. Other memoirs I discuss posit a wide-reaching humanism that insistently seeks not to transcend, but rather to make use of and transform the academic and other institutions in which we are all unequally located. Thus, rather than signaling a retreat from the professional and political concerns that characterize the humanities, these memoirs are harbingers for the critical turn to explore the interrelations among humanism, the humanities, and human-rights struggles. In particular, I consider in the following chapters how memoirs and their humanist engagements crucially articulate with—and offer insights into—an ongoing preoccupation with subjectivity (despite the supposed "death of the subject") and with other concerns that have centrally defined the humanities from the 1990s into the present: identity politics, postcolonial studies, feminism, and disability studies.

Although I rely heavily on close textual analysis of memoirs by well-known academic personalities (i.e., Michael Bérubé, Cathy Davidson, Jane Gallop, bell hooks, Edward Said, Eve Sedgwick, and Jane Tompkins), my intent is not to focus on the individual strengths and limitations of these particular authors. Rather, I seek to understand the ways that the memoir's foundations in the Enlightenment, and its ideologies of autonomous individualism and exclusionary humanism, can present problems even for scholars who demonstrate in their other work their investment in a progressive politics and structural analyses of power. By focusing on genre and by asking how and why it is being used by academics today, I show how the memoir enacts the contradictions and allure that reinstantiating humanism holds for many poststructuralist critics. I investigate how such tensions provide insights into the difficulties we have in contemporary academic culture with negotiating not only the crisis in the humanities, but also the personal and the professional or political, the experiential and the theoretical, and the individual and the institutional. At the same time, I explore memoirs as a site for forging a progressive humanism that enables the crossing of these divides and others—particularly those of race, gender, nation, and ability.

Full-length memoirs by academics pose a particular set of questions. Whereas most autobiographies and memoirs give voice to experiences or identities that are in some way extraordinary or underrepresented, most academic memoirs take as their subject those identities and experiences that are not remarkable. In this way they differ from memoirs published in the 1970s and 1980s by those challenging or at the margins of the academy (i.e., Gloria Anzaldúa, Angela Davis, and Cherríe Moraga).[6] In contrast, academics who wrote their memoirs in the 1990s usually led "lives of the mind" that were not exceptionally eventful, and if some achieved stardom within academic contexts, only rarely did this stature extend more broadly. And while some of these memoirs (those, for example by Alvin Kernan or William Pritchard) may share qualities with memoirs written by public intellectuals of the 1950s reflecting on their careers, most academics in the 1990s wrote their memoirs at around the age of fifty, after they became full professors and established a national reputation. Academic memoirs also must be differentiated from, even as they are importantly connected to, less sustained forms of contemporary autobiographical writing such as personal criticism, autocritography, Web sites, blogging, the confessional or autobiographical essay, and the personal narrative that occurs in books alongside or mixed in with more traditional scholarly writing. Book-length memoirs evidence an intense focus inward and a more marked departure from these genres that employ elements of autobiography. In this book I explore why academics devote themselves to book-length projects that ostensibly stand apart from their usual academic writings; why mainstream and university presses publish these memoirs; and what they tell us about the contemporary political and cultural milieu.

I also am interested in how these memoirs relate to personal writing from the 1980s, in the heyday of identity politics. Regardless of their various political and theoretical orientations, with their centering of the individual (however split and fragmented), academic memoirs often seem to forgo the collective and activist vision that fuels earlier practices of identity politics. In my book *Writing Women's Communities: The Politics and Poetics of Contemporary Multi-Genre Anthologies* I looked at the 1980s and early 1990s as a period during which groups of women were together creating and participating in identity-based multigenre anthologies. I argue there that anthologies such as *This Bridge Called My Back*, *Home Girls*, *Nice Jewish Girls*, *Making Waves*, and *Making Face, Making Soul* theorize and enact identity-based models of women's communities. These anthologies constitute an important part of a new literary and social movement aimed at reaching nonacademic audiences *and* clearing a space in universities for women of color and genres of writing usually excluded from the realm of the literary. By contrast, some academic memoirs signal their authors' retreat from or a rejection of a politicized approach to literature and the adoption of an intense individualism. As David Shumway argues, "In marginalized fields, autobiography is used to establish communal identity, whereas now it seeks to distinguish the author from everyone else" (97). In *English Papers* (1995), William Pritchard illustrates this emphasis on an individualism opposed to identity politics when he proclaims his response to pressures to diversify Amherst's predominantly white male faculty, "I had thought that *I* was different from 'us'!" (173). Or, in *The Edge of Night*, Frank Lentricchia reviles identity politics even as he muses on the unique particularity of his identity as an Italian American. From an entirely different, earnest rather than satirical, angle, in her memoir Jane Tompkins also repudiates a political agenda. When Jeffrey Williams interviewed her about *A Life in School*, she explained, "I used to be interested in politics," but "my own interests have evolved from institutional polemics to personal development and exploration" (163). However, not all academics link their memoir writing to an embrace of the individual and a rejection of the political. Participating in the same interview, Cathy Davidson insists that her memoir, *Thirty-six Views of Mount Fuji*, is "informed by a constellation of my own personal politics, antiracist politics, multicultural politics, feminist politics" (172). And as indicated by its title, Paula Rothenberg's *Invisible Privilege: A Memoir about Race, Class, and Gender* also maintains a political commitment to identity-based explorations of privilege and oppression, as does Dalton Conley's memoir *Honky*. As these few examples suggest, no one agenda characterizes academic memoirs, and they resist generalizations in terms of purpose, style, and subject matter. A central question that animates my interest in academic memoir, then, is whether the genre can sustain a politics that is not primarily focused on the individual self. Must a focus on the individual happen at the expense of larger, potentially revolutionary, social and political identities and concerns that challenged the academy in the 1980s?

As I argue throughout *Academic Lives*, when academic memoirs focus on feelings or experiences of marginalization without investigating how these feelings and experiences are socially situated and constructed, their form and content often combine to mask (however inadvertently) structural privilege, institutional hierarchies, and an individualism that reinforces the status quo.[7] Such memoirs expose the limitations of reigning theories in the humanities that pertain to race, class, gender, and nation, and they provide insights into how critics—and the institutions in which they work—often remain entrenched in the very structures of oppression that contemporary cultural theory opposes. By contrast, when memoirs explore the violence, allure, contradictions, or constructed nature of dominant identities and feelings, and the difficulties of finding alternatives to them, they can carry with them a collective politics. Moreover, enabled by their formal qualities, memoirs can convey cultural theories to a crossover audience, thus bringing together a critical humanism, the humanities, and the struggle for human rights. In short, as they invest in their life stories, academics reap a variety of humanist returns, some of which allow them entry into a wider public sphere to make a case for the humanities during a time when it is in crisis.

Accounting for Academic Memoirs

Academics' engagements with personal writing can, as critics have noted, be read in relation to the concurrent development of the academic star system that developed in the 1980s and reached its apex in the 1990s. David Shumway attributes the rise of the star system in literary studies to a host of factors that includes the ascendancy of theory that, even as it contributes to the demise of the author, highlights the theorist (95). Condemning the star system, Shumway finds that it leads to an impoverished sense of community, and also that it has reduced the discipline's legitimacy in the culture at large, casting academic stars as curiosities rather than as public intellectuals. Rachel Brownstein issues a similar critique when she reads *Lingua Franca*'s existence as a sign of the times' excessive, obsessive concern with personalities and the merely personal, and she connects personal writing to the cult of the personality (32, 36). Aram Veeser, who capitalizes on the star system with his 1996 collection *Confessions of the Critics*, more optimistically assesses the celebrity status of academics and their turn to the first person, announcing that "critics want, rightly, to make themselves objects of desire, interest, public fascination" (xxi).

As is indicated by the demise in 2001 of *Lingua Franca* and fanzines like the one on "Judy" Butler, the fin de siècle saw the last gasps of the star system. The publication of academic memoirs, however, continues, and if fuelled in part by the star system, the relationship is not a simple one, nor do all memoirs come from academic celebrities. The genre is also utilized by those who document academic "failure" (for example, Don Snyder's 1997 *The Cliff Walk: A Memoir of a Job Lost and a Life Found*) or the start of an academic career (James Lang's 2005 *Life on the Tenure Track*). Thus, even as I posit memoirs as commodity effects of the academic star system, I look to how and why writers inhabit the genre in ways that can disrupt as well as support institutional hierarchies.

The development of the academic memoir movement has dovetailed with a renewed attention in the United States to the status and nature of the public intellectual—a concern that is linked to but distinguishable from the "star system." Although definitions of the "public intellectual" are subject to debate, most would draw a distinction between the public intellectual and the more recent phenomenon of the academic star, even as some academics—including a number of African Americans who occupy both positions as they participate in a long history of African Americans who have served as public intellectuals (for example, Mary McLeod Bethune, Frederick Douglass, W. E. B. Du Bois, Ida B. Wells. Angela Davis, Henry Louis Gates Jr., bell hooks, Toni Morrison, Anna Deveare Smith, Cornell West, and Patricia Williams) fulfill both roles, as do Noam Chomsky, the late Edward Said, Haunani-Kay Trask, and Howard Zinn. Although some of these figures have written their memoirs (including hooks and Said, both of whom I address in this book), I contend that, despite arguments to the contrary, memoirs cannot be taken as sufficient evidence of academics' success during the 1990s in reaching a general public in their roles as intellectuals. Throughout the culture wars of the 1980s, academics maintained a public voice (however controversial), and in our post–September 11 era, professors receive media attention for their perceived threat to national security. However, I believe that in the 1990s an aporia existed. During this era, when noticed at all, humanities scholars appear in the mainstream media largely as public curiosities, fleetingly noteworthy for their obscure language (e.g., the widespread coverage in 1999 of *Philosophy and Literature*'s annual Bad Writing Contest), or for their bizarre interests and outlandish wardrobes (e.g., the *NYT Magazine*'s annual satirizing of MLA Convention session titles and outfits). Although a few academic memoirs have sold in significant numbers or been seriously reviewed in nonacademic venues (Alice Kaplan's *French Lessons*, Said's *Out of Place*, Tompkins's *A Life in School*), most often they enter the mainstream as occasionally noticed curiosities.

Thus, rather than evidence professors' importance, memoirs might instead emerge from academics' struggles with the tenuousness of their status in the public sphere and that, more generally, of the university's. Commenting on the media's "sniping at the University," Bill Readings locates the causes for such bad press in a "general uncertainty as to the role of the University" (1). According to Readings, "the grand narrative of the University, centered on the production of a liberal, reasoning, subject, is no longer readily available to us" (9). Because "*Bildung* will no longer fuse the subjective and the objective," Readings contends that academics "need to find out another way of understanding how what we say about culture participates in culture" (103). Readings argues that academics face yet another problem that compounds their crisis in definition: "the sense that the general public may not exist" (140). Considered within these contexts, memoirs cannot be presumed to signify academics' ability to bask in the bright public light cast by their "stardom." Instead, memoirs in the 1990s may stand as academics' assertions of singularity or individuality in the face of their uncertain institutional position; as attempts to reclaim the power of the *Bildung* or reproduce the "liberal, reasoning, subject" that is under siege; as a means to prove the continuing relevance of the humanities; and as efforts to achieve purchase over a public that appears unreachable.

In making such assertions I depart from those who assume memoir's crossover appeal. Academic memoirists and critics who have taken academic memoirs seriously frequently champion them for how they open channels of what Michael Bérubé calls "public access." Jill Ker Conway, for example, claims that unlike modern disciplines including literary criticism and history, autobiography tackles questions "in language a nonspecialist can read with ease" (17). As Nancy Miller notes, Jeffrey Williams has "recently recast the vogue of personal criticism as the 'new belletrism,'" one that "represents a *journalization* of academic criticism'" ("'But Enough about Me'" 421–22).[8] Such arguments are supported by the fact that academic memoirs are sometimes published by commercial presses (e.g., *Out of Place, Teacher, Honky, The Cliff Walk, Thirty-six Views of Mount Fuji*). And yet, these analyses too quickly equate accessible language and a popular genre with public access. Academics' use of a popular genre guarantees neither that their language and concerns will be accessible nor, even if they are, that the memoirs will be taken up by a mainstream readership.[9]

When making claims to academic memoirs' crossover appeal, critics often diminish not only the difficulties of reaching a broad public but also the extent to which academic memoirs are products of institutional privilege. As discussed above, most who engage in memoir writing are not only tenured, usually in top-tier universities, but also have achieved some level of "fame," if only within the world of academe. Even as the memoirs evidence this privilege, their authors often fail to acknowledge it, or the academic nature of their concerns. For those few academics who do situate their memoirs in relation to the institutions in which they work, for reasons I explore in the following chapters, it can prove difficult for them to acknowledge, let alone reflect on, their institutional privilege and power. More frequently, academics instead identify writing autobiography as a daring enterprise. However, as Adam Begley points out, this "rebellion" against the academy is illusory: he wryly notes that not only have most members of the Duke University English department written their memoirs in the 1990s, but also that among Duke's eminent memoirists, "mass resignations are not imminent" (55).[10] In "The Long Goodbye: Against Personal Testimony or, an Infant Grifter Grows Up," a lacerating but at times reductive and racially insensitive attack on "personal testimony," Linda S. Kauffman links the use of the personal voice to academics' "tendency to be hermetically sealed . . . in academic obsessions." She continues, "the allure of personal testimony makes it easy to conflate the feminist with the academic perspective" (138). Certainly some—though by no means all—memoirs bear out Kauffman's critiques. James Phelan's *Beyond the Tenure Track*, for example, reads like a cross between a newsy Christmas card, an application for promotion, and a confession to a therapist regarding his job-related angst and insecurities. Or, in *Life on the Tenure Track*, James Lang describes an unexpected fight at a faculty meeting over the kind of assistance junior faculty should receive during the tenure process as "the worst thirty minutes of my life, to this very day" (134). And yet other memoirs, such as Arlene Avakian's *Lion Woman's Legacy* or Shirley Geok-lin Lim's *Among the White Moon Faces,* employ the personal to give voice to feminist commitments and assessments of academe. Nonetheless, because the academic memoir phenomenon is underwritten by the star system with its hierarchies and academic preoccupations, celebrations of it as the success of a democratic form of writing or as a realization of the feminist proclamation that "the personal is political" require critique and qualification. So, too, critics need to consider the causes—and effects—of memoir's practitioners so seldom addressing their institutional privilege and position. As I make clear over the course of this book, my own investments lie in memoirs that address institutional privilege head-on, and that engage lived experiences as a way to expose, grapple with, and sometimes even provide solutions to complexities, impasses, and contradictions that riddle contemporary cultural theorists struggling to make the university and the wider culture places that are more just.

Although they are markers of institutional privilege and success, memoirs frequently register, even if only indirectly, critics' discontent with the academy, their sense that, as Toril Moi puts it, "The poststructuralist paradigm is now exhausted. We are living through an era of 'crisis,' as Thomas Kuhn would call it, an era in which the old is dying and the new has not yet been born" (1735). In this regard memoirs are very much products of their place and time. They stand alongside collections such as Paul Bové's *In the Wake of Theory*, Terry Eagleton's *After Theory*, and Michael Payne and John Schad's edited collection *Life after Theory* as symptoms of literary critics' disenchantment with their profession's reigning discursive mode. That Eagleton published a boyhood memoir *The Gatekeeper* (2001) just a few years before *After Theory* (2003) provides support for this connection, one that Begley remarks on when he contends that the memoirs by Duke University's "'Moi' Critics" result from their fatigue with academe and its dominant critical idiom. David Simpson also reads "speaking personally" as symptomatic of a dissatisfaction with contemporary theory ("Speaking Personally" 87). In *The Academic Postmodern*, Simpson claims that "the return of the storyteller" and their "small narratives" allow "the tellers of little tales to smuggle back . . . precisely the most uncritical and traditional formations of self and subject" (30). As I demonstrate, many memoirs explicitly or implicitly support Begley's and Simpson's contentions.

That said, memoirs do not uniformly stand in opposition to theory. Indeed, as I argue, at times they extend academics' theoretical work—although sometimes in ways that expose liberal or humanist tenets that the theory itself conceals. In contrast to Simpson, Timothy Brennan finds that contemporary theory has not rejected, but rather disguises its investments in, identitarian politics and liberal narratives of self and subject. In *Wars of Position*, Brennan argues that, despite its claims to the contrary, contemporary theory is "a secret sharer with American liberalism" that is supportive of "the middle way" (10). Although Brennan does not address the memoir phenomenon, it follows from his line of attack that memoirs are continuous with contemporary theory's investments in an identitarian politics and the status quo rather than, as Simpson claims, narratives that repudiate postmodern theory's key components.

Departing from both Simpson's and Brennan's lines of thought, I argue that employing liberal genres or formations of self and subject need not—though they often do—support the political status quo. By countering postmodernism's diminishment and, at times, evacuation of individual agency and its dismissal of the importance of individual experiences and emotions, memoirs can *at times* rework rather than reinscribe what Simpson calls "the unacknowledged grand narratives that surreptitiously maintain them" (*Academic Postmodern* 30).[11] To revisit Moi's contentions that poststructuralism is exhausted and that new paradigms have yet to be born, I believe that it is possible to read in some memoirs the search for new paradigms that will reinvigorate the humanities and address its crisis in subjectivity. In delineating this crisis, Nick Mansfield finds that contemporary theories of subjectivity contain competing impulses.

Poststructuralists' claims to the contrary, Mansfield establishes how contemporary theorists do not break with the Enlightenment's emphasis on the individual subject or self, even as they question individual autonomy and uniqueness (3). Despite the supposed death of the subject, Mansfield observes that the "focus on the self as the centre both of lived experience and of discernible meaning has become one of the—if not *the*—defining issues of modern and postmodern cultures" (1). As proliferating accounts of subjectivity so amply indicate, far from being theorized out of existence, the self is hyperpresent and as unresolved in its status in the academy as it is in the mainstream culture.

In considering memoirs that reflect an unease with theory, I argue that their authors are in part responding to tenets of contemporary theory that have led them into a poststructuralist trap, one that delegitimates assertions of individual subjectivity or explorations of how individual experiences and intimate relationships are not completely institutionally determined. Rather than address these problems within theory *through* theory, some critics instead shift to the genre of memoir. In doing so, these critics sometimes allow for the return of "human" elements that poststructuralist theory has repressed or insufficiently repudiated, and at other times they leave their theoretical work behind in a way that creates an unsettling but productive dissonance between their theoretical and their autobiographical writing. At yet other times, memoirs carry forth a critic's theoretical work in ways that illuminate covert investments in Enlightenment conceptualizations of the self. Thus the memoirs provide ways to track academics' contemporary struggles with the purpose and definition of subjectivity and with other theories that centrally define the humanities during the 1990s and into the twenty-first century.

In their efforts to realize the potential of contemporary theory or to counter or escape its limitations, memoirs articulate particularly closely with work being done under the rubric of cultural studies. An interdisciplinary field of study that has transformed the humanities over the past few decades, cultural studies was well established by the time academics began to write their memoirs, and most academics who write memoirs also have standing as cultural studies critics.[12] At first glance memoir and cultural studies scholarship seem to be at odds: whereas the former takes an individualist and traditionally literary form, the latter is expressly political and collective in its aims and is often accused of devaluing the aesthetic. And yet, in ways I analyze throughout this book, academic memoirs are neither aberrations nor departures from cultural studies scholarship. Indeed, the two have important points of connection. Although diverse and difficult to define, cultural studies scholarship, like academic memoir, has as its hallmarks an ambivalence about the academy, the desire to reach a broadly defined public, and a commitment to giving voice to the here and now.

Moreover, the failures of cultural studies to achieve hoped-for transformations in the public sphere can be causally linked to the emergence of academic memoirs. Accompanying cultural studies scholars' calls for widespread and progressive cultural and political change are expressions of blighted hope about the potency of cultural studies. For example, in his attack on contemporary theory, Brennan subjects cultural studies work to particularly harsh critique. In a scathing denouncement of those who publish in cultural studies journals, Brennan opines, "There one need not suffer guilt for exploiting others, since one's body ventures nowhere, takes responsibility only for itself, and allows each subject to enjoy that happy antinomy of universal experience in a particular being" (*Wars of Position* 151). This state of affairs, Brennan claims, "is bolstered by a convergence, on the one hand, of a forbidding poststructuralist armature and, on the other, of a rather lazy American individualism" (151). My analyses of memoirs at times support Brennan's argument as I find that some memoirs' self-absorbed individualism turns out to be continuous with and revealing of their authors' cultural studies scholarship. And yet, counter to Brennan's wholesale dismissal, I do not think that all cultural theory—or, by extension, all memoirs by cultural studies critics—can be characterized by a self-serving solipsism. I believe that cultural studies theory includes progressive, even radically transformative, possibilities, even as, during the 1990s, its institutionalization and the university's estrangement from a wider public have blunted these possibilities. For cultural studies critics, writing a memoir can serve not only as a retreat in the face of failed political and collectively minded imperatives, but also as a means to advance cultural studies' objectives in a form that appeals to nonacademic audiences. Neither inherently conservative nor counterhegemonic, memoirs reflect in multiple and complex ways on the place of cultural studies in the academy, and if they register cultural studies scholars' estrangement from a public sphere, they also provide academics with a possible means to make cultural theory matter beyond the confines of the academy.

Emotions and Ideology

As *Academic Lives* tracks why some critics turn away from the genre of theoretical writing, it considers the social import of memoirs that encompass a range of personal expressions, even including those that might seem frivolous, mundane, and self-involved. Working under the assumption that the most personal expressions often mask (however inadvertently) structural privilege and social hierarchies, I pay attention to precisely what the most personal effects enable as well as foreclose, and what forms personal disclosure takes. Rachel Brownstein presents an argument *against* taking such expressions seriously: she claims that if "intruding the body, the banal, the bit of familiar scandal, or the merely personal was once a useful political strategy . . . it now threatens to foreclose thought. It also contributes to the political atmosphere of invasiveness, staged confession, and 'outing'" (37). Rather than dismiss the "purely personal" on these grounds, I instead read personal moments as a rhetorical effect that results when a memoirist—however well-versed in social constructionism—ignores ways feelings are socially situated and constructed. I approach those moments as places to examine some of the most deeply seated ideologies that underwrite academic culture today.

My analyses of memoirs are based on my understanding that the most private feelings and emotions cannot be cordoned off from the public sphere. Raymond Williams has argued that "the psychological" serves as a "'great modern ideological system' that, with the advent of industrial capitalism, began to assume prodigious cultural authority to 'assemble and generalize'—and to provide forms for the structuring of—'subjectivity'" (128–29). Cultural anthropologists, psychologists, and, more recently, literary critics have been building on Williams's insights.[13] Kathleen Woodward notes that "historicizing the emotions, or forms of feeling, is itself as important a history as is the social and cultural history in which it is intertwined" (182). Such analysis challenges the still dominant perception that construes emotions as purely psychological rather than socially constructed. According to Catherine Lutz, the association of emotions with the "precultural" (70) or the "private property of the self" (72) is an ideology that derives from the Romantic tradition, where "the natural (including emotion) is depicted as synonymous with the uncorrupted, the pure, the honest, the original" (68). Such a perception of emotions plays a role in maintaining existing hegemonies. As Ann Cvetkovich explains, "the construction of affect as natural might well be part of the discursive apparatus that performs the work of what Foucault has described as the disciplining of the body" (24–25). Feelings and affect, in other words, comprise important, socially constructed forms of knowledge, or ideologies, that are all the more powerful for passing as natural. Thus, precisely because they often serve as "free zones" in which academics record their personal experiences and feelings, memoirs constitute rich texts through which to analyze academic and other institutional structures. Whether used by critics as a refuge from theory, or to explore the complexly constructed nature of individual identity and experiences, academic memoirs offer insights into the knottiest, most recalcitrant, and accepted ideologies in the academy and in the broader U.S. culture.

In subjecting academics' feelings and experiences to analysis, I draw not only on historians of the emotions but also on the theory of "postpositivist realism" developed by Satya Mohanty and other scholars including Paula Moya, Michael Hames-García, and Linda Martín Alcoff. These theorists have provided important insights into how "'personal experience' is socially and 'theoretically' constructed" (Mohanty 33). As Mohanty explains, "our access to our remotest personal feelings is dependent on social narratives, paradigms, and even ideologies" (35). Building on Mohanty's views, I assume that personal experiences and feelings are thoroughly saturated in the social and theoretical, and I read memoirs as cultural touchstones for the present-day academy.

As I analyze moments that appear to be "purely personal," I attend to how the *genre* of memoir structures the emotions represented. Martha Nussbaum addresses the relationship between form and feeling when she states, "narratives contain emotions in their very structure; so their form stands in need of the same sort of scrutiny that we give to emotions represented within it. . . . Narratives are constructs that respond to certain patterns of living and shape them in their turn. So we must always ask what content the literary forms themselves express, what structures of desire they represent and evoke" ("Narrative Emotions" 310).[14] Although I agree with Nussbaum that genres carry history and emotions in their very form, I also am interested in how genres change over time, in large part because of the uses to which writers put them as they move within and against their formal structures and ideological currents. My approach to genre ideology is therefore both to historicize it and to analyze its various present-day uses, influences, and effects. My assumption is that a genre's uses and effects cannot be considered independently of a writer's historical and institutional location. Nor does use of one or another genre serve as a reliable index of a text's place on a political spectrum. Genres are of course political and deeply ideological, but not in ways that are fixed or predictable. In making this argument I do not wish to endorse ambivalence and indeterminacy. Rather I wish to posit the political possibilities not only of transgressing institutional borders and boundaries of genre, but also of reinhabiting traditionally conservative genres (in this case, memoir) so as to imagine new possibilities for them, particularly in relation to interrelated conceptualizations of individualism, liberalism, and humanism.

Individualism, Liberalism, and Humanism

Thinking through the form of contemporary academic memoirs and their structures of desire requires attention to the longer history of autobiography, one in which individualism—and related discourses of liberalism and humanism—figures prominently. Individualism has regularly been associated with traditional western autobiography, a genre that arose concomitantly with and helped to construct ideologies of individualism.[15] In their historical overview, Sidonie Smith and Julia Watson explain that autobiography is a genre rooted in the Enlightenment that "celebrates the autonomous individual and the universalizing life story" (3–4). Although critics widely agree that traditional autobiography is based on a radical individualism that privileges a white, male, property-owning subject (in U.S. contexts, the prototype has been the self-made-man narrative), many, especially those working from postcolonial or feminist perspectives, have looked to how writers have departed from the exclusionary biases that characterize the form from its inception.

Despite autobiography's origins, contemporary autobiographies—and memoir—constitute a diverse body of work, and much of it, especially by groups rendered invisible by self-made-man narratives, works actively against its individualist origins. Moreover, critics often posit memoir and autobiography as distinct forms of life writing, even as the two terms are often used interchangeably and in many cases cannot be decisively differentiated from one another. In general, though, critics distinguish memoir from autobiography for its attention, through a historically situated account of the author's perceptions and experiences, to a social environment, one peopled by individuals with whom the author interacts. For Lee Quinby, for example, the "I" in memoir is externalized and dialogical (S. Smith and Watson 198); for Nancy Miller, "memoir is fashionably postmodern, since it hesitates to define the boundaries between private and public, subject and object" (*Bequest and Betrayal* 43).[16] Even granting these definitions that emphasize memoir's social situatedness and outward gaze, it is nonetheless a genre that highlights the feelings, impressions, and experiences of a singular narrator, and as such, it remains an individualist genre as well as an established and traditionally literary one.

In *Academic Lives* I argue that personal narrative, even when embodied in one of its most conventional genres, need not simply reproduce American ideologies of individualism, although some practitioners surely and symptomatically use memoir to this effect. With this position I depart from a number of critics who make the case that revolutionary messages cannot be conveyed through conventional forms, ranging from Audre Lorde with her assertion that "the master's tools will never dismantle the master's house" (110) to critics such as Linda Kauffman. Addressing the particular issue of feminists' use of personal testimony, Kauffman contends that "writing about yourself does not liberate you, it just shows how ingrained the ideology of freedom through self-expression is in our thinking" (134). Kauffman's implication is that contemporary personal narratives, and, for the purposes of this book, academic memoirs, inevitably end up supporting individualistic agendas, or what I refer to as "bourgeois individualism," "autonomous individualism," "Western individualism," or "liberal individualism."[17] Rather than accept such conclusions wholesale, I interrogate the degree to which contemporary U.S. academic memoirs retain traditional U.S. autobiography's implications in an exclusionary individualism that is tied to practices of a whole range of what have come to be known as "isms." Exploring this issue throughout *Academic Lives* provides a means to assess how entrenched the humanities remains in dominant social hierarchies. For example, my analysis of memoirs by Jane Tompkins and Jane Gallop suggests the persistence in the humanities of ideologies of individualism, even in feminist quarters. By contrast, I claim that memoirs by Edward Said and Michael Bérubé counter such ideologies. Because memoir's familiar form—as with Said's and Bérubé's memoirs—appeals to a broad liberal readership, it can enable academics to expose the limitations of and reach beyond an American civil-rights framework, which defines the humanity of U.S. citizens against those who fall outside the parameters of citizenship. These memoirs exemplify how scholars make use of humanism not to reinstate traditional conceptions of the humanities and bourgeois individualism, but rather to broadcast the conviction that conjoining humanism and human rights should be at the center of the humanities.

Individualism cannot be considered in its U.S. contexts apart from liberalism, and both ideologies are foundational not only to a U.S. (and a Western) identity, but also to the genre of autobiography. Thus, in addition to individualism, a questioning of liberalism runs through *Academic Lives*. Liberalism arose with Enlightenment beliefs in humanity's unity and common nature. As articulated by the classically liberal intellectuals Alexis de Tocqueville, John Stuart Mill, and John Locke, liberalism carries with it the assumption that one man's vantage point can be universal, and that those who are enlightened have the moral responsibility to bring knowledge to the ignorant and fight evil with good. Because in liberal thinking the individual rather than the community constitutes the measure of value, and the rational and therefore right way of life can be embodied by one man, the formal properties of autobiography serve it well. Liberal thought, as many postcolonial critics have noted, is imbricated not only in individualism, but also in colonialism.[18] Liberalism has undergone a number of changes since the Enlightenment, including liberal pluralism's and liberal multiculturalism's seeming tolerance for cultural choices and differences. And yet, as contemporary critics have found, liberalism and, in its more recent guise, neoliberalism, have successfully maintained the political and economic hierarchies liberalism's proponents have given lip service to overturning, and colonialist agendas and human-rights violations continue unchecked.

As they go on to write their memoirs, some of the very critics of colonialism and of related forms of oppression invest in a genre with classically liberal as well as individualist roots. When they do so without attention to their own institutional locations or the social hierarchies that structure their identities and experiences, these academics expose the conservative underpinnings of some of the academy's reigning theoretical work. The humanities' continuing investments in liberalism do not, however, uniformly suggest the counterfeit nature of—or run counter to—cultural theory. As I argue, some memoirs, particularly by academics who attend to their institutional privilege or center subjects who regularly fall outside exclusionary definitions of "the human," demonstrate how the humanities can employ tenets of liberalism to support and develop contemporary theory's critiques of social and political injustices.

In tandem with liberalism, the concept of humanism has been at the heart of the humanities, and many authors I consider came of age as academics when humanism occupied a central place in U.S. universities. Broadly speaking, humanism is a system of thought that affirms human beings' dignity and worth and seeks to advance universal morals and values through humankind's capacity for rational thinking and self-determination. Although its origins can be traced back to the time of Gautama Buddha and Confucius, "humanism" as it most commonly circulates today is associated with philosophy that became popular in the West during the Renaissance and especially the Enlightenment. Its present-day associations in the humanities date back to 1808, when the term was coined by German educator J. J. Neithammer "'to express the emphasis on the Greek and Latin classics in secondary education, as against the rising demands for a practical and more scientific education'" (quoted in Torrance 164). The discourse of humanism dominant in the academy from the 1950s through the 1980s—one with its emphasis on the classics and with a faith in universality—was associated with exclusionary forms of canon building and maintenance, and the reification of high culture that contributed to defining the human subject as white, male, and propertied.[19]

Humanism's history, however, allows for a wider range of meanings. A concept saturated in debate, humanism has existed in many forms, including, for example, Arnoldian, romantic, Marxist, liberal, civic, existential, pragmatic, naturalistic, scientific, phenomenological, Protestant, and socialist humanisms.[20] Although every version shares a belief in the centrality of the human, the lack of precision with which the term "humanism" circulates—and the way humanism, and the concept of the human itself, have long operated as moving targets—are the conditions of its hegemonic power rather than its emptiness.[21] As Tony Davies observes, the contested and elusive nature of the meaning of humanism provides it with political force; as he explains, "The problem of meaning . . . belongs not to semantics but to politics" (129).

The 1980s and 1990s saw a range of attacks on humanism. In the 1980s academy a determination to overturn an exclusionary "humanism" was an integral part of the "culture wars" and the drive to revolutionize humanities curricula, opening the university to feminist, multicultural and postcolonial perspectives and literatures. In attacking the reigning cold-war humanism that often went, however imprecisely, under the names of "Arnoldian humanism," "Western humanism," "traditional humanism," "bourgeois humanism," "liberal humanism," or "humanist individualism," critics zeroed in on its entrenchment in race, class, and gender oppression, and on how "enlightenment pretensions toward universality were punctured from the moment of their conception in the womb of colonial space" (Gilroy 65). As Abdul JanMohamed and David Lloyd argue in "Introduction: Minority Discourse," a seminal article that sets forth the arguments fuelling the academic Left's opposition to humanism and a traditional humanities education, the traditional humanist intellectual's function has been to legitimate sets of discriminations which economic and social domination requires. JanMohamed and Lloyd contend that humanism's claim to universality is annulled by the developmental schema of world history, that actual exploitation is legitimated from the perspective of perpetually deferred universality (12). In the 1990s postcolonial and cultural studies theorists continued to develop such critiques. By the time he writes his 1997 survey of humanisms, Tony Davies is able to state authoritatively, "All humanisms, until now, have been imperial. . . . It is almost impossible to think of a crime that has not been committed in the name of humanity" (131). Postcolonial critiques of humanism coincided and sometimes overlapped with the poststructuralist dismantling of the human subject (Barthes, Derrida, Foucault, Lacan) and identity politics' efforts to make a place in the humanities for identities, traditions and texts excluded from the humanities and the Western humanist canon (Moraga and Anzaldúa, Barbara Christian, Barbara Smith).[22] Also contributing to the turning away from humanism were critics in the 1990s who announced the dawning of a posthumanist age that they either attributed to human-rights abuses of the modern and postmodern eras (Robert Torrance) or linked to technological advances of the late twentieth century (Torrance, Donna Haraway).

If the 1990s seemed to sound the death knell for humanism in the humanities, in the late 1990s and especially the post–September 11 era, interest in a rehabilitated humanism is everywhere in the air.[23] Conferences, journals, and books are once again headlining humanism, often in conjunction with the humanities and sometimes human rights as well. In the prestigious journal *differences*, Jacques Lezra analyzes "the resurgence of interest in 'humanism'" (75). The *PMLA*, a barometer for what has achieved currency in the humanities, published nearly 150 pages of proceedings from a 2005 conference convened by Judith Butler and MLA President Domna C. Stanton titled the Humanities in Human Rights: Critique, Language, Politics. In the foreword Stanton revises recent critical accounts of humanism when she states that "connections between the humanities and human rights have existed historically and conceptually in the West through the mediation of humanism" (1518).[24]

She announces that the essays in the *PMLA* collection "see the task of the humanities as asking how the human is constituted and how its meanings can be rethought in human rights" (1521).

Especially in the post–September 11 era, humanities scholars are thinking hard about how humanism can and does engage human-rights issues. Gilroy, for example, calls in *Against Race* for a "pragmatic, planetary humanism" that "exhibits a primary concern with the forms of human dignity that race-thinking strips away" (17). Edward Said, who castigates literary critics, stating, "Our bankruptcy on the once glamorous question of human rights alone is enough to strip us of our title to humanism" (*World, the Text, and the Critic* 172), contends nonetheless that humanism can and must be squared with a more humane tradition, a topic he pursues in depth in his posthumously published *Humanism and Democratic Criticism* (2004).[25] In *Humanism of the Other*, Emmanuel Levinas strives to reclaim humanism by making an ethical argument for the necessity of understanding one's humanity through recognition of the suffering and humanity of others.[26] Despite their significant differences, these theorists all attempt to reconcile humanism with the humanities in order to achieve a more inclusive sense of and regard for humans across races, religions, classes, cultures, genders, and other differences—a project that seems particularly pressing in the U.S. academy given the increase in violence-inducing religious fundamentalisms and the escalation of a U.S. imperialism that is accompanied by the government's flagrant defense of torture and other human-rights violations.

Memoirs of the 1990s evidence humanist investments that in many cases predate—and anticipate—this renewed critical interest in humanism, sometimes in exciting ways. In this book I explore the historical location of the memoirs and consider how their returns to humanism both presage current critical directions in the humanities as well as offer nostalgic retreats to a prepolitical academy.[27] Those writing the memoirs considered here have participated in various and significant ways—in their literary criticism and in their teaching and administrative work—in challenging what in effect were exclusionary models of humanism. By the time they write their memoirs, some of the memoirists seem to be returning to the very humanism they played a part in dismantling. In his interview with the Duke writing group, when Jeffrey Williams asks if their memoir writing is "a return to a humanistic or belletristic ethos?" (168), Jane Tompkins readily agrees that her memoir constitutes a "return" to literature and by extension humanism, and in my reading of her memoir—and in others especially in chapters 4 and 5—I account for the present-day appeals of, but also the problems with, unselfconscious returns to humanistic valorizations of art and the artist. At the same time, I am interested in tracking how the belletristic and political need not be at odds, but in fact can be powerfully yoked together as they are, for example, in Edward Said's memoir. Whereas some critics I study here do not endorse humanism even as they reinhabit different forms of humanism, Said, as does Michael Bérubé, writes a memoir that complements the call in his criticism for a nonexclusionary humanism.[28] In chapter 5 I look to the possibilities memoirs that engage disability studies afford for thinking about ways to reconceive humanism in potentially transformative ways. As I address the many humanist returns effected in *Academic Lives*, I attempt to answer the question posed by Gayatri Chakravorty Spivak in *Death of a Discipline*: "Who slips into the place of the 'human' of 'humanism' at the end of the day?" (26). In thinking through this question in relation to contemporary academic memoirs, I arrive at not one but many answers, all of which are crucial to the definition and direction of the humanities today.

If humanism in multiple, complex, and sometimes contradictory ways underwrites the form of autobiography and is traceable as a presence in all of the memoirs under consideration here, sometimes the humanist returns evidenced in the memoirs are nostalgic and steeped in an imperial politics, whereas at other times (sometimes in the same memoir), they are more progressive and directed toward a nonexclusionary universalism. My exploration confirms Levinas's conviction that "humanity is neither an essence nor an end, but a continuous and precarious process of becoming human, a process that entails the inescapable recognition that our humanity is on loan from others, to precisely the extent that we acknowledge it in them" (Davies 132). In *Academic Lives*, as I analyze different subsets of academic memoirs, I argue that tracking their takes on the "precarious process of becoming human" affords a richly detailed mapping not only of individual human experiences and desires, but also of their intersections with academic culture and the debates that define the humanities today.

Organization

The chapters of this book put academic memoirs into dialogue with fields of study that have instigated debates and that define the humanities

today: identity politics and whiteness studies, postcolonial studies, pedagogy and feminist theory, and disability studies. Each chapter analyzes
individual memoirs that, taken together, comment on the uses and impact of these fields of study, and on the contemporary poetics and politics
of the memoir genre. In chapters 2 through 4 I am especially interested
in how memoir both depends on institutional privilege and can render
it invisible. In chapter 5 I explore how disability studies creates a paradigm for memoir writing that enables writers to reconfigure radically the
genre's grounding in forms of individualism and humanism that are defined through exceptional intelligence and ability. Not all of the memoirs
I discuss work deliberately within the theoretical frameworks through
which I read them. Nevertheless, I am interested in how these memoirs
are informed by, help shape, and sometimes exist in meaningful contradiction to the theories and fields of study with which they intersect, and
in what these intersections tell us about academic culture of the 1990s
into the present.

By focusing each chapter on a central problematic, I hope to counter
the individualism that inheres in my reading method. Because I rely on
sustained textual analysis of memoirs by influential cultural critics, my
methodology exists, at times, in tension with my central argument. Although I frequently critique memoirists for individualism, my reading
methodology keeps attention firmly on the authors themselves, all the
more so because the memoir genre makes it impossible to disentangle
discussions of author and text. The close readings, however, are not meant
to limn these authors' individual strengths and limitations. By discussing
the memoirs in each topical chapter I hope to provide counterweight to
the focus on individual authors, and instead foreground my structural
analysis of key components of contemporary academic culture.

I further develop my institutional analysis by framing each chapter
with discussion that places academic memoir in relation to a set of pressing political issues and cultural conditions in the academy and beyond.
Each part begins with, and later returns to, accounts of events situated
in Hawai'i—at the department and university levels, at talks and conferences, and in other institutional settings. These narrative interludes
introduce each chapter's concerns and, as I explore articulations between
the Hawai'i-based stories and the memoirs I analyze, I mean to ground
and foreground the importance of location and of specific institutional
contexts to textual production, interpretation, and political intervention.
This interstitial material attempts to suggest the necessity of speaking

from a location that is clearly marked institutionally and geographically as well as in terms of the more typical subject positions of race, class, gender, and sexual orientation. These interludes are reminders that the academy is made up of diverse institutions with their own complicated local histories that articulate more global professional debates about education in quite specific ways. Rather than have the interludes stand as the "solution" to the problems of the memoirs I examine, I hope that they will enable readers to consider the significance of the shortcomings as well as possibilities that arise from my own particular vantage point, as they also allow me to reflect on what I have come to understand about the multiple demands placed on the writer of academic memoir. At the same time, the interludes attempt to put into practice my claim that sometimes, personal writing can address complexities and contradictions that escape even the most nuanced theoretical formulations. Thus, I aim in these interludes to theorize, in ways that complement my readings of the memoirs, the interrelations that exist among the personal, the professional, and the political in the U.S. academy today, and also to provide insights into the articulations and stimulating as well as limiting divergences that exist between contemporary theory and academic memoir.

Before I outline the remaining chapters, it is important to note that my structure could have taken a distinctly different shape and considered a different set of academic memoirs. Other obvious groupings I do not consider include memoirs about parents; aging; childhood; adoption or parenting, especially in mixed-race families; sexuality, in particular, accounts of claiming a GLBT identity; home (an especially prevalent theme among African American academics); Buddhism; memory; and photography.[29] Memoirs considered in *Academic Lives* could fit into some of these or other categories; many memoirs can be viewed through multiple frames (and indeed, I consider the same memoirs by bell hooks and Edward Said in two chapters). I also could have extended my analysis beyond the United States, and to a more diverse array of disciplines.[30] However, rather than strive for the widest possible sampling, I chose memoirs and categories that I believe intersect most directly with debates that are central to the U.S. academy, and to contemporary crises in the humanities.

Through analyses of memoirs by white feminist academics, chapter 2, "Whiteness Studies and Institutional Autobiography," explores how whiteness studies has developed in the 1990s as both a field that builds on the antiracist and feminist identity politics advanced by women of color in the 1980s, and, given the time and conditions of its emergence, can contribute to the recentering of whiteness. Analyses of memoirs by Marianne Hirsch, Marianna Torgovnick, Maureen Reddy, and Jane Lazarre present the opportunity to think about how feminists' expansive uses of the genre and their explorations of white ethnicity in the 1990s can both further—and undermine—earlier, counterhegemonic practices of identity politics. As identity politics has entered into the mainstream of the academy at the same time as affirmative action is under siege, I speculate about the need for writings that challenge institutional practices and politics without ignoring the significance of the personal. I suggest that in the contemporary academy, language that is impersonal, even legalistic, can paradoxically have the most impact personally, and in a way that can be transformative politically.

In chapter 3, "Postcolonial Studies and Memoirs of Travel, Diaspora, and Exile," I read memoirs by Cathy Davidson, David Mura, and Edward Said to map the impact of postcolonial and related fields of studies on the humanities. As these authors translate their various theoretical and political commitments to the memoir genre, they afford key insights into postcolonial studies' possibilities and limitations in thinking through questions of race, culture, and nation that are at the forefront of not only the academy's but America's political consciousness—and unconscious. Framed by sections analyzing Doris Duke's Honolulu home, Shangri La, and House Resolution 3077, Part Two posits identity, home, and autobiography as complexly constructed and interconnected social spaces. Reading the East-West crossings and representations of travel—and home—in Davidson's *Thirty-six Views of Mount Fuji*, Mura's *Turning Japanese*, and Said's *Out of Place*, I explore the economics that structure and sustain personal fantasies and ideological investments. In reading memoirs' most intimate disclosures, I am especially interested in accounting for the persistence of, as well as the resistance to, Orientalism and exclusionary frameworks for cosmopolitanism and humanism. What particularly interests me is how memoirs' most intimate disclosures often reveal forms of Orientalism or exclusionary humanisms or cosmopolitanisms that persist despite their authors' critical awareness of and opposition to these dominant ideologies. I argue that personal narratives uncover, whereas theory often masks, how postcolonial studies remains implicated in colonial ways of knowing. At the same time, as attention to Said's *Out of Place* demonstrates, perhaps especially when they defy the categories of the theoretical and the political, memoirs present academics with possibilities for disseminating postcolonial ways of seeing beyond the parameters of the academy.

In chapter 4, "Feminist Studies and the Academic Star System," I argue that prominent feminists write pedagogy memoirs to negotiate the anxieties that attend the institutionalization of feminism, particularly as it is accompanied by the academic star system, the underfunding of the university, and the devaluation of the humanities. Through analyses of Jane Gallop's *Feminist Accused of Sexual Harassment* and Jane Tompkins's *A Life in School: What the Teacher Learned*, I investigate feminist pedagogies that claim to level student-teacher power imbalances, whether it be through spectacle (Gallop) or efforts to overturn student-teacher hierarchies (Tompkins). As Gallop attempts through her feminist pedagogy to transgress—but reinstates—institutional roles and rules, she suggests the difficulties for feminists of maintaining an oppositional politics when feminism has achieved institutional power. Tompkins, on the other hand, attempts a purely experiential and emotional approach to learning that predates life in school. I argue that this "radical" pedagogy both returns Tompkins to the exclusionary humanism that she formerly rejected as it also reinforces her institutional power. These memoirs evidence the difficulties of performing institutional critiques of authority through the genre of memoir, and exemplify the challenges that feminists face in the academy today. They also provide insights into ways reigning theories can be fueled by personal investments and how failures in emotional intelligence can both expose limitations in cultural theories *and* the difficulties of accounting for institutional privilege and power. Chapter 4 concludes with a consideration of bell hooks's *Teaching to Transgress*, and relates it to hooks's use of memoir. I argue that hooks's career trajectory is suggestive not only of the seductions of academic stardom, but also of how the shift in the academy from a culture of ideas to one of personality is, paradoxically, impoverishing emotionally as well as intellectually.

Chapter 5, "Disability Studies and Institutional Interventions," focuses on disability studies' potential to answer questions humanities scholars are asking with some urgency about how academics can bring together the humanities and human rights' struggles. Through readings of memoirs by bell hooks, Edward Said, Eve Sedgwick, and Michael Bérubé, I contend that memoirs about disability by academics can productively occupy the genre's contradictions in order to revalue not only the meaning of binaries including independence and dependence, intelligence and retardation, mind and body, health and illness, and ability and disability, but also the relations between individuals and academic and other institutions. Although disability studies has been relegated to the sidelines in the academy, I argue for the importance of viewing this disciplinary formation as a location that affords a place from which to establish and analyze connections among disability and other forms of oppression in order to transform the institutions and histories that engender and sustain them. Memoirs by academics that engage disability studies provide a particularly good vehicle for this work because they can convey to a crossover readership the personal effects of—and thus the need to resist—forms of oppression that other genres can represent as abstractions. I argue that memoirs that engage a disability studies framework can demonstrate the power of the connections between emotional or empathic intelligence and institutional analysis. During a time in the academy when traditional exclusionary humanisms are returning in new guises, disability studies can combine with memoir to reinvigorate cultural theory, embodying the possibility of an expansive, inclusive humanism, and making a case in the wider culture for the humanities' value as a carrier of human rights.

CHAPTER 2

Whiteness Studies and
Institutional Autobiography

From Activist Anthology to Academic Memoir

Toward the end of the 1997–98 school year, the English Department at
the University of Hawai'i was in the final rounds of a three-year struggle
over the revision of the undergraduate major. After a tense department
meeting—one during which many assistant professors called the present curriculum colonialist and irrelevant to Hawai'i students—a senior
colleague (white, male) e-mailed a "campaign document" to the department's sixty full-time faculty members. In it he announced his interest
in serving on the hiring committee. He promised, if elected, to screen
for and oppose any job candidate whose application materials included
terms such as "of color" or "colonial," or who otherwise evidenced signs
that she (his hypothetical applicant was a "she") or her work was politically motivated. A barrage of department-wide e-mails followed: one expression of support; several admonishments to the writer for disrespect-
ing junior colleagues; an incisive analysis of the "campaign document's"
racism and sexism by one of the faculty's four women of color; memos
calling the whole set of exchanges "silly"; and a few assertions from the
campaigning colleague stating that his target was "jargon" and "cultural
studies imperialism," not people.

This bit of departmental history and the related writings and events
that I discuss in this chapter interest me because such stories constitute
concrete ways that affirmative action is being rolled back in universities
in informal and incremental as well as official and more clearly docu-
mented ways. They also point to a crisis during the 1990s in the relationship in the academy between the personal and the political, and provide a
way to think about the role that identity politics and emotionally charged
narratives about individuals play in shaping institutional politics.

Working from the insight that "the personal is political," women of
color gave expression in the 1980s to collective forms of identity politics,
often in the form of multigenre anthologies. Among the first and the most
influential of these was *This Bridge Called My Back* (1981), edited by
Cherríe Moraga and Gloria Anzaldúa. *This Bridge* was instrumental in

creating a paradigm shift in the academy, one that enabled wide-ranging critiques of the academy's discrimination against disempowered groups and progressive institutional and curricular reforms. In the late 1990s, however, a backlash occurred. Expressions of racism and sexism were often cloaked as intellectual arguments against theoretical language ("jargon") and the politicization of the academy ("cultural studies imperialism"). Furthermore, racist and sexist attacks often articulated with reactionary institutional practices that are supposedly politically neutral. At the same time, explicitly political positions—especially those premised on identity politics—were regularly dismissed on the grounds that they were either *merely* personal or only represented the interests of a "narrow" group. Such dismissals depended on seeing identity politics as a strictly personal rather than political formation, one interchangeable with any assertions of identity. Thus, in the 1990s and continuing well into the first decade of the twenty-first century, the meaning of "the personal is political" has become complex, various, and confused. Furthermore, as I explain below, my campaigning colleague's e-mails indicate how the language of marginalization can be co-opted when affirmative action is under attack. Indeed, personal narratives based on identity politics deployed in anthologies such as *This Bridge* are even being used to perpetuate the individual acts of racism and the discriminatory institutional practices that these anthologies powerfully oppose. At the same time, as explored in this chapter through analyses of memoirs by white feminist academics, whiteness studies emerged in the 1990s as both a field that, in marking and historicizing whiteness, builds on the antiracist and feminist identity politics advanced by women of color in the 1980s, and, given the time and conditions of its emergence, can contribute to the recentering of whiteness that is evidenced by the departmental history discussed here.

In one of his later missives, my colleague quoted a passage from Gloria Anzaldúa from a Norton anthology. In the passage Anzaldúa describes the rituals that she undergoes to begin writing. These include "wash[ing] the dishes or my underthings, tak[ing] a bath, or mop[ping] the kitchen floor." My colleague used this passage—initially published in *Borderlands/La Frontera*—to denounce the proposed curriculum's cultural studies component and to justify his "campaign document."[1] Noting that D. H. Lawrence, whom he described as "the whitest of the white and the malest of the male," expressed in his letters an affinity for jam making and floor mopping, this colleague expressed disappointment that Anzaldúa showed no sign of having read Lawrence's letters.

The Norton's inclusion of Anzaldúa removed her work from its specifically Chicana, feminist, and activist contexts and recontextualized it as a part of the literary canon. My colleague, reading this work in its new context, tried to further contain—and indeed discredit—Anzaldúa's aesthetic innovations and the identity politics integral to them. The relevant antecedents for this passage become not Anzaldúa's lived experiences as a feminist, working-class Chicana, but literary, and canonically so. This substitution itself depends on ignoring Lawrence's working-class background and the significance that he discloses his domestic proclivities in his private letters. Thus Anzaldúa's writing becomes the unwitting emulation of the "minor" work of a dead white man of letters, rather than a political intervention into the elitist realm of Western literature. As this analysis makes Anzaldúa into a second-rate rather than a revolutionary writer, it undermines the literary and political claims of her writing by leveling the material differences between her and "the whitest of the white, the malest of the male"—if white guys as well as women of color can (and do) mop floors, it is, apparently, only white guys who can really write.

In his efforts not simply to invalidate Anzaldúa's politics but to depoliticize her work altogether, my colleague bespeaks his desire for a clear separation between literature and identity politics. He also registers the threat that Anzaldúa's work poses to this split. His use of Lawrence signals his desire for white men's continued control over the domain of literature and his covert or unconscious investments in a hegemonic form of identity politics—one that affirms the need for the whiteness studies that emerged in the 1990s. Moreover, the uses to which he puts Anzaldúa's work indicates that a relationship exists between Anzaldúa's writing and curricular reform and between this writing and the hiring of women of color.

Rather than dignify his "campaign documents" with a direct response, some junior faculty members instead forwarded them to the university's sex equity specialist and to the civil-rights counselor, along with an expression of concern that department culture made possible such public outpourings.

This decision not to enter directly into department debate changed, however, when our campaigning colleague received fourteen of forty-four votes cast and made the final rounds of the hiring committee election. At this point, some women, myself included, cosigned a letter to the department. We stressed that "to implement a policy of active discrimination against people on the basis of their race, gender or politics was in fact illegal." We circulated this memo on e-mail and in hard copy on departmental stationery, highlighting in yellow the printed line at the bottom advertising the University of Hawaiʻi as an equal opportunity/affirmative action institution. Four of us signed this memo—three of us untenured at the time; two, women of color.

Colleagues responded to our memo with disapproval, even outrage. We received some angry and some sadly chastising responses to our "lack of collegiality" and "unjustified accusations of racism." Even those expressing agreement with our position stated discomfort with our recourse to references to the law, or our use of "threats" and "intimidation." In the next round of elections our colleague received eighteen of fifty-five votes cast—enough to require yet another round of voting, although he ultimately was not elected. The following academic year, the four of us who had signed the equal-opportunity letter were relieved of our heavy committee loads and advised to lay low.

Although this event has become largely forgotten in departmental history, what struck me about it was the anger and disruption our letter's references to the law occasioned, and how this contrasted with the relative ease with which discourses of identity politics were circulating.

I believe that even as writing such as Anzaldúa's—particularly in its communal contexts and commitments—continues to inspire change in the academy, academic institutions have limited the oppositional force and revolutionary energy that this writing can continue to engender. The Norton anthology is at the center of literary canon making and is emblematic of the individualism and elitist humanism that Anzaldúa challenges in *Borderlands* and in *This Bridge Called My Back*, with coeditor Cherríe Moraga and the other contributors. The Norton's incorporation of Anzaldúa's work—and the board's selection of a chapter from her individually authored book rather than one from *This Bridge* or *Making Face, Making Soul*—suggests how academic institutions can co-opt, neutralize, and individualize oppositional forms of writing. Indeed, it is unsurprising that the Norton includes Anzaldúa's *Borderlands* essay "Tlilli, Tlapalli, the Path of the Red and Black Ink" rather than, for example, "Speaking in Tongues: A Letter to Third World Women Writers," a piece in *This Bridge* that takes up similar issues about writing from a more explicitly collective and activist perspective.[2] The Norton's inclusion of Anzaldúa's writing from *Borderlands* obscures *Borderlands'* connection to *This Bridge* and instead situates it as part of the literary canon. The

movement of this writing into the mainstream of academe and my colleague's anxiety regarding Anzaldúa's inclusion and his subsequent moves
to contain her writing's transformative possibilities signal to me not that
the war waged by Anzaldúa and other *This Bridge* contributors was won
as it entered the literary mainstream in the 1990s, but rather the need
to adopt new forms of oppositional writing from this place of often embattled and ambivalent arrival.

In saying this, I in no way mean to discount the importance that *This
Bridge, Borderlands*, and their successors continue to have for students,
particularly as models for politicization and self-empowerment of women
of color. As contributors to Anzaldúa and AnaLouise Keating's follow-up
to *This Bridge Called My Back*, their *This Bridge We Call Home: Radical
Visions for Transformation* (2002), so eloquently indicate, these works
have played a crucial role in challenging the biases of what constitutes
literature and theory in the humanities, and in making a place for women
of color in the academy. Multigenre anthologies such as *This Bridge
Called My Back* have been transformative with their collective format;
their stress on community coupled with an insistence that feminism and
women's community must be founded on difference; and in their attention to how structures of racism, sexism, classism, and homophobia inform the everyday lives of women of color. Especially in the classroom I
continue to be moved by the revolutionary fervor of anthologies such as
This Bridge, and by the passionate and politically powerful student writings that their practices of identity politics elicit. Furthermore, Norton's
canonization of Anzaldúa brings identity politics and multicultural and
feminist studies to a broad readership.

And yet these identity-based writings from the 1980s do not necessarily cause the disruptions they once did in an academy still sorely in need
of antiracist and feminist transformation. As happens with all radical art
forms, over time their oppositional edge has been blunted. For teachers
of ethnic and women's literature, this writing by now constitutes a familiar
genre. And it has become commonplace in composition classes to ask students to explore their marginalized identities. This acceptance limits the
challenges this writing poses to those in dominant positions in the academy, even as its success demonstrates identity politics' effectiveness.

For students today, however relevant the writings in *This Bridge* and
its successors remain, this writing appears as a part of literary history,
particularly if students are introduced to it by a professor or a Norton
headnote. Most students will have been born after the publication of

This Bridge and will first read Anzaldúa after her passing, encountering contributors not as contemporaries but rather as figures in history. And as happens with all literature, some of *This Bridge*'s most powerful innovations and insights have become naturalized over time. Given their place within literary history, then, they can inspire—but perhaps no longer provide a direct model for—writing that will engender community and transform the academy.

Viewing Anzaldúa's work in its different contexts serves as a reminder that its transformative power was not only bound to the genres it utilizes but also to its moment of production. Norton's recontextualization of Anzaldúa's work illuminates the extent to which transgression is temporally bound. As Anzaldúa herself writes, reflecting on *This Bridge* in her preface to *This Bridge We Call Home*, "no bridge lasts forever" (1). Generic strategies that work at one time will do a different kind of work at another time. Therefore, without discounting the connections between the politicization of students and the transformation of academic institutions, I would, nonetheless, argue that in the decades since its 1981 publication, *This Bridge Called My Back* and its successors have become less directly transformative for academic institutions than they continue to be for individual students. The need, then, exists for new forms of writings that can challenge the structural foundations of the academy. And if the challenge in the early 1980s was how to write from a position marginal to or outside the academy, the task in the 1990s became one of how those located within the academy, however tenuously, can engage in practices to transform it.

In considering what forms of writing can serve oppositional purposes in an era when expressions of identity politics have become assimilated into the academy, I have been thinking about the heated intradepartmental reactions to the letter regarding our department's hiring practices and what they reveal about the relationship between the personal and the political. I am struck by how explosive our memo proved to be and by how personally our colleagues took it. In some ways, differences between our missive and our campaigning colleague's were leveled—both were perceived as troublesome and mean spirited. However, our colleague's attacks were attributed to his individual idiosyncrasies and dismissed. In contrast, our collectively authored letter, placing department members in relation to institutional laws and regulations, proved more incendiary and less forgivable. Paradoxically, it was precisely this letter's impersonal nature that made it so threatening to our colleagues on a personal level.

Their responses to the equal-opportunity letter suggested to me the importance of institutional structures and the strength of faculty desires to view departmental relations and decisions apart from those structures. Our department, in particular, prides itself on its collegiality and often has moved against change on the grounds that it will cause hurt feelings. One exasperated colleague has dubbed this "the politics of hurt feelings."[3] The perception that untenured or newly tenured professors are not only invulnerable to insult but also are "threatening" and "intimidating" to senior colleagues revealed to me how unmindful faculty members can be of factors of institutional power and also the extent to which language about marginalization can be co-opted and cut free of material groundings. In the University of Hawai'i's English Department and in English departments more generally, the language of oppression that has come with identity politics has been appropriated since the early 1990s to describe anything from the neglect of medieval poetics to the condition of full professors who oppose literary theory. In *The University in Ruins*, Bill Readings remarks on this phenomenon when he observes, "in order to speak in today's academy one is constrained to assume a position of marginality." Readings wonders, "What can it mean that [even] those who speak *for the center* need to claim to be marginalized?" (112). One possible answer to Readings's question is that much dissonance can exist between faculty members' personal feelings of marginalization and their institutional power. More importantly, Readings's analysis indicates both the influence that identity politics has achieved in the university, and also how much work remains to be done. Often reduced to a rhetoric that can be marshaled to obfuscate and perpetuate the material realities it sought to name and to change, the vocabulary of oppression introduced by identity politics is regularly used to suture over the divide between personal feelings and institutional privilege, and the inequities among those in the academy with differing degrees of power. With the transformations to and co-optation of discourses of 1980s identity politics, legitimate claims to marginalization are often dismissed or emptied of meaning as they coexist alongside trivial or unjustified ones.

Given this state of affairs, language that is most impersonal, even legalistic, can hit hardest on a personal as well as political level, in part because it refuses those in institutionally privileged positions the right to feelings of being marginalized, and instead highlights the often uncomfortable responsibilities of institutional location. When people with institutional authority become skilled at using language of disenfranchisement to enforce discriminatory politics, to fight this discrimination requires changes in strategy. Rather than employing the language of marginaliza- tion or a personal framework, it can be effective, especially for those with any degree of institutional privilege, to lay claim to institutional au- thority—or "the Master's tools"—in order to uphold the civil rights that still exist and to work to make the laws and structures governing the academy more just. (And this need is arguably even more urgent in the post–September 11 era.) For students or for those lacking institutional privilege, however, personal narratives based on a politics of identity can retain their oppositional edge; I return to this point in the conclusion to this chapter.

To account for the transformations in the academy of the relationship between the personal and the political, it is instructive to examine the academic memoir as a form of personal writing that is a successor to *This Bridge* and other multigenre identity-based publications. Academic memoirs—like my colleague's e-mails—demonstrate an important way that identity politics, as it has been assimilated into the academy, has been taken up by those in positions of privilege. Memoirs of the 1990s that engage identity politics exhibit possibilities as well as limitations that accompanied the institutionalization of work done by feminists of color in the 1980s; the movement from multigenre, identity-based anthologies by women in contested relationships to the academy, to single-authored, more conventionally literary autobiographies by tenured academics fol- lows no one clear trajectory. This movement can signal a retreat from, or a giving up on—or even an opposition to—a form of identity politics that is collective and explicitly activist. And yet, the memoir movement also offers the possibility for academics to cross over into the wider public sphere. Moving in a trajectory that reverses the one taken by contribu- tors to the 1980s anthologies—from a secured place within the academy to reach an audience outside academe—some professors writing their memoirs carry on the antiracist and feminist efforts of contributors to the anthologies, and their strivings to bridge academic and nonacademic communities.

Of those professors who repudiate identity politics in their memoirs, many express a sense of how such a politics has left them feeling dis- placed or alienated. One such example is Frank Lentricchia, in *The Edge of Night*. Lentricchia renounces his former political, Marxist approach to literature in "Last Confessions of a Literary Critic"—a *Lingua Franca* article from which my campaigning colleague quotes approvingly in the paragraph preceding his critique of Anzaldúa. In his memoir as well as in "Last Confessions," Lentricchia attacks identity politics, even as his portrayals of himself as Italian American and working class are animated by identity politics. Other memoirs also express hostility or defensiveness in response to the changes brought on by identity politics. In *English Papers* (1995), William Pritchard looks back nostalgically to the period preceding the entry of feminism and multiculturalism into the humanities; he laments that in the wake of the Vietnam War era, "A historical moment in American education at a small college had come to its end. . . . Nor could it have existed without a homogeneous climate of white male idealism and privilege" (154). In his memoir *In Plato's Cave*, Alvin Kernan similarly bemoans how, in the 1990s, "politics was substituted for education" (214). In *The Cliff Walk: A Memoir of a Job Lost and a Life Found* (1997), former English professor Don Snyder blames his expulsion from academe on the impact of identity politics. As he searches for a new job in the 1990s, "The only thing I allowed to dampen my enthusiasm was the faint acknowledgment that the reason I'd been rejected by twenty-one colleges in the fifteen months since Colgate fired me was because I was not a woman or a minority applicant" (51). Although different in their objectives and in their authors' academic stature, what these memoirs share is the campaign document's repudiation of identity politics, and an unwillingness to think about the racial and gender power that white men continue to possess in the academy.

By contrast, other academic memoirs, including a number by white feminists, embrace and build on the identity politics forwarded by women of color in the 1980s.[4] And yet, as I argue, despite their significant differences from my colleague and memoirists hostile to identity politics, when these critics collapse, as they sometimes do, individual feelings and institutional structures, they demonstrate how this convergence can have the same conservative effects as trying to prize apart the personal and the political. Furthermore, the canonical literary form of memoir and its grounding in bourgeois individualism—particularly when used by tenured faculty members with racial privilege—can prove to be at odds with and to subsume politically progressive agendas found in the identity-based anthologies on which contemporary academic memoirs depend in significant ways. Thus, these memoirs are more limited than *This Bridge* in the challenges they pose to ideologies of individualism and definitions of literature and theory. And yet, when memoirs subject dominant identities to rigorous forms of institutional analysis and explore the complex interplay between personal feelings of marginalization and institutional forms of privilege, they can serve as apt vehicles to carry on the work of anthologies such as *This Bridge*. Within the contexts of humanities departments, such memoirs can extend *This Bridge*'s vision of a "theory in the flesh," one where, as Moraga and Anzaldúa explain in their introduction, "the physical realities of our lives . . . all fuse to create a politic born of necessity" (23). And whereas the multigenre anthologies crossed from a position outside the academy to one within it, memoirs by academics possess the potential to carry transformative theories of race and gender from the academy to a wider liberal readership.

I am particularly interested here in the insights that memoirs by white feminist academics offer in regard to whiteness studies, an interdisciplinary field of study that emerged in response to the arrival of identity politics in the academy. Along with feminist studies, whiteness studies has emerged as an academic arena in which issues of identity politics are being importantly negotiated in the 1990s, and feminist practices of whiteness studies provide a way to assess the impact that practices of identity politics by women of color have had in the humanities. Memoirs, in particular, provide vehicles for white feminists to struggle with and embody—and sometimes anxiously evade and at other times overcome—challenges, limitations, impasses, and inadequacies of identity politics as practiced in the 1990s academy. As individual endeavors premised on forms of feminist community and institutional privilege, these memoirs present the opportunity to think about how well-established white academic feminists can use their institutional power in progressive and collectively minded ways. And because *This Bridge* has such iconic value for how women of color practiced identity politics and made a place for themselves in the academy in the 1980s, I am particularly interested in tracing its influence on the memoirs I analyze in the sections that follow. Doing so enables me to theorize connections among academic memoirs of the 1990s and the anthologies of the 1980s, and to consider ways that feminists' deployments of whiteness studies can combine with their expansive uses of memoir to help to mobilize a politics located within the academy in keeping with *This Bridge*'s revolutionary agenda.

Whiteness Studies and Academic Memoirs

In the 1980s Jenny Bourne remarked that "identity politics is all the rage" (1). The same can be said for whiteness studies in the 1990s. The centrality "whiteness studies" came to assume in literary and cultural studies is evidenced by the special journal issues on the topic (e.g., the *Minnesota Review*'s "The White Issue," 1996); the many books with titles such as *White Trash, Off-White, Displacing Whiteness, How the Irish Became White, The Social Construction of Whiteness*, or *Whiteness*; and the renewed scholarly attention to Jewish Americans, Italian Americans, and other white ethnic groups.[5] As scholars seek to understand the constructedness of whiteness, they often work to expose and undermine white supremacy, or to challenge the perception that whiteness automatically entails privilege or an absence of ethnicity.

On the one hand, such attention has been crucial. As AnaLouise Keating notes, "'whiteness' has played a central role in maintaining and naturalizing a hierarchical social system" ("Interrogating" 908), and discourses racializing whiteness that expose its ideological force and function are precisely what some scholars committed to fighting racism have been calling for. I am thinking here of people such as Hazel Carby, bell hooks, or Toni Morrison, who express impatience with the term "people of color" for the way it leaves whiteness unmarked, and who have long urged white critics to investigate it.[6] Furthermore, attention to the ethnic identities of white people can disrupt the hegemonic force of whiteness. Such scholarship can challenge the homogeneity and naturalness of whiteness, open up possibilities for cross-racial alliances, and elucidate how some ethnic groups have achieved "whiteness" at the expense of others.[7]

At the same time, the 1990s saw a proliferation of studies that focus on white ethnic groups without attention to structures of racism. Such studies are licensed by and often merge with whiteness studies, even as they may contribute to the privileging of whiteness that whiteness studies was founded to challenge. All of this attention to whiteness—especially given the slippage between whiteness studies and white ethnic studies—can result in a recentering of whiteness that is all the more disturbing given contemporary racial politics. Commenting on these dynamics, particularly on the divide between an embrace of multiculturalism and setbacks to adjudicating historically sedimented forms of racism, Timothy Brennan notes, "Multiculturalism came into its own at just the time that affirmative action was suffering its first serious defeats" (*Wars of Position* 31). As the 1998 *PMLA* special issue on ethnicity indicates, explorations of "whiteness" in literature departments in the 1990s too often were accompanied by diminishing attention to the decreasing numbers of racial minorities in universities, not to mention their increasing oppression in an era characterized by anti–affirmative action, anti-immigration legislation, and an exponential growth in what Angela Davis calls the prison industrial complex, which criminalizes the poor and people of color.[8] When a focus on the complexity of whiteness and white ethnic groups replaces attention to racial minorities and their cultural production, or when such studies place white ethnic texts in relation to those by racial minorities without engaging questions of institutional racism and unequal power relations, then I think that despite the excellence and integrity of much whiteness studies scholarship, as a movement it can reinscribe rather than undermine the hegemony of whiteness.[9]

Memoirs factor into this mix in telling ways. Although they have not been read as such, memoirs importantly contribute to whiteness studies at the same time that they are underwritten by it. Furthermore, in their explorations of racial and ethnic identity—and how these identities articulate with those of gender, class, and sexuality—both whiteness studies and academic memoirs are indebted to the identity-based anthologies of the 1980s. White feminists, among them some of the profession's most influential scholars, draw extensively on discourses developed in these activist anthologies in order to write individual memoirs in which they render visible and explore their feelings of marginality or ethnic difference. Some of these memoirs focus more on ethnicity or culture than race—for example, Marjorie Perloff's *The Vienna Paradox*, Marianne Hirsch's *Family Frames*, Alice Kaplan's *French Lessons*—whereas others focus more on race, or on race in combination with ethnicity—Arlene Avakian's *Lion Woman's Legacy*, Maureen Reddy's *Crossing the Color Line*, Jane Lazarre's *Beyond the Whiteness of Whiteness*, Paula Rothenberg's *Invisible Privilege*, Marianna Torgovnick's *Crossing Ocean Parkway*. These memoirs provide apt sites to assess both the impact of the anthologies as well as the possibilities and limitations that accompany the institutionalization of identity politics, and, more particularly, whiteness studies, a movement that, in contrast to women's anthologizing practices in the 1980s, originates from within, and has not traveled in any easily recognizable ways beyond, the academy. Throughout the rest of this chapter, through attention to a representative sampling of these memoirs, I analyze ways that feminists with institutional as well as racial privilege explore questions of race, ethnicity, and gender in a traditionally literary and individualist form. I am particularly interested in the significance these memoirs carry during an era in which the institutionalization of whiteness and feminist studies, and celebrations of multiculturalism and ethnic "difference," have been accompanied by attacks on affirmative action and worsening conditions in the academy for women and racial minorities.

The memoirs by white academic feminists analyzed here evidence an engagement with whiteness studies and a politics influenced by women of color in the 1980s and their anthologies. The texts I focus on by Marianne Hirsch, Marianna Torgovnick, Maureen Reddy, and Jane Lazarre not only represent a spectrum of influential feminist approaches to whiteness studies, but they also represent the memoir genre as it was employed in the 1990s. I concentrate on moments in these works in which their racial politics come most sharply into focus. My readings do not attempt to do full justice to each author's use of memoir or to the various important uses to which they put the genre. Nevertheless, these readings exemplify some of the past decade's recurring problems with whiteness studies and memoirs, as well as the intersections between them, and what they reveal about the place of identity politics in contemporary academic culture. Together, albeit to varying degrees, these memoirs, with their focus on how *individuals* experience their dominant racial identities in complex and contradictory ways, indicate ways that the institutionalization of identity politics in the academy, especially in the form of whiteness studies, can displace and elide the need for work that engages institutional forms of racism in the United States. At the same time, they evidence the genre's flexibility and its possibilities for bringing whiteness studies to readers located outside the academy.

Reframing Whiteness

As a work that combines theory, criticism, and autobiography in order to expose and contest the ideological power of family photographs in the postmodern moment, Marianne Hirsch's *Family Frames: Photography, Narrative, and Postmemory* (1997) is in many ways peripheral to both whiteness studies and the memoir movement. In fact, only one chapter, "Pictures of a Displaced Girlhood," addresses ethnicity within U.S. contexts, and in some respects that chapter indicates the need for, rather than constitutes a part of, whiteness studies. Moreover, although "Pictures of a Displaced Girlhood" clearly conforms to the memoir genre, others, which brilliantly mix textual analysis with family memories to formulate Hirsch's groundbreaking theory of postmemory, do not. However, throughout *Family Frames*, Hirsch explores her family history, including her sense of displacement as a white Jew whose parents escaped Czernowitz (now Chernivtsi, Ukraine) to Romania (where Hirsch was born) after World War II, before going to Vienna and then to Rhode Island. In this way her book both contributes to and is also underwritten by whiteness studies and the memoir movement. Furthermore, as I discuss below, Hirsch's use of Anzaldúa in "Pictures of a Displaced Girlhood," the book's best-known chapter, is indicative of how extensively theorizing by feminists of color in the 1980s has shaped white feminists' approach to ethnicity. In "Pictures," Hirsch's fleeting use of Anzaldúa puts into relief problems feminists face in combining studies of white ethnicity and memoir without supporting the academy's recently institutionalized version of identity politics and its elision of structural differences in the United States between being white or a racial minority. Because *Family Frames* otherwise evidences an innovative use of memoir that challenges forms of liberalism that often characterize the humanities and its traditional versions of humanism, I read the limitations resulting from its convergence of identity politics and memoir as symptomatic of the problems with how they come together in the 1990s academy.

Hirsch's work also holds representative value owing to her importance in feminist and literary studies. A professor of English and comparative literature at Columbia University, a Guggenheim recipient, and the current editor of the *PMLA*, Hirsch is a renowned feminist cultural critic whose wide-ranging interests anticipate the newest directions in cultural criticism. In the 1980s and early 1990s Hirsch established her reputation as a leading feminist psychoanalytic critic: she wrote *The Mother/Daughter Plot: Narrative, Psychoanalysis, Feminism* (1989), *Choice's* Outstanding academic book of the year, and coedited the landmark collections *The Voyage In: Fictions of Female Development* (1983) and *Conflicts in Feminism* (1990). In *Family Frames*, Hirsch maintains her interest in ideologies of family and gender while developing an expertise in Holocaust studies, World War II literature, visual culture, photography, cultural memory, and testimony; *Family Frames* also put Hirsch on the map for her theory of postmemory.

In *Family Frames*, Hirsch takes a multigenre approach to a narrative about family that counters as it shows the power of the nostalgia, idealization, and universalizing qualities that often characterize family memoirs—and dominant forms of humanism. Hirsch mixes textual criticism, theory, and autobiography as she analyzes family photographs and an impressive range of "imagetexts" (photographs accompanied by text) to "expose and resist the conventions of family photographs and hegemonic family ideologies" (8). Stating that she views *Family Frames* as "an album in itself," Hirsch self-reflexively and creatively interweaves different modes of writing, explaining, "I offer them all as different forms of narrative, as a set of stories—narrative snapshots—about family photography" (12, 15). Taken together these stories allow Hirsch to trace the "intersection of private and public history" (13). Mixing modes enables her to curb and comment on the excesses of each. She explains that she needs family photos "to counterbalance my critical voice. But in the personal mode, the balance between nostalgia and critique is not easily achieved. Often exposure seems unseemly, excessive, charged with a familial ideology I would like to but cannot always resist" (149). Through its genre shifts, *Family Frames* is able to expose not simply what Hirsch takes to be her "unseemly" investments in family ideologies, but also the contradictions that so often exist between a feminist's critical awareness and her feelings and lived experiences.

Hirsch also resists succumbing to family ideologies—and models of exclusionary humanism—by employing a model of identity and difference that, like her mixed-genre approach, implicitly draws on the identity politics conceived of by women of color in anthologies such as *This Bridge*. This model, premised on asserting connections and identifications across differences, counters white feminist models of the 1970s–80s and traditional humanism, both of which base community bonds and identifications on sameness. In "Reframing the Human Family Romance," a chapter on the 1955 Museum of Modern Art exhibition *The Family of Man*, Hirsch analyzes the ethnocentrism and universalizing tenets of this exhibit's humanist vision (69). Although noting that ideologies of family have become less monolithic than in the 1950s, Hirsch posits the family in the postmodern era as the site of new and alluring humanisms that *Family Frames* opposes (71). However, as Hirsch reads Jamaica Kincaid's novel *Lucy* and considers her own family history in order to challenge humanist ideologies, this does not happen at the expense of dismissing familial bonds, but rather to advocate for a way of looking that "insists on difference *and* interconnection, on conflict *and* commonality. It still invokes a familial gaze, but one that . . . has radically reframed and opened up its boundaries" (77). While resisting how the family romance falsely promises a universalizing liberal humanism that denies hierarchies and divisions, through its mix of family photos, analysis, and autobiographical narrative, *Family Frames* also affirms the love and the ties that exist among family members and humans more generally. By positing a model of family based on difference rather than sameness, and by using a mix of genres to theorize this model, Hirsch implicitly builds on the model of community forwarded in the identity-based anthologies of the 1980s as she also opens the possibility for precisely the kind of nonexclusionary humanism humanities scholars are calling for early in the twenty-first century.

As she elaborates the complex relationship between self and other and explores the articulations among autobiography and other genres, Hirsch forwards in *Family Frames* a theory of postmemory that provides an un-stated but nuanced extension and revision of the identity politics of the 1980s. Hirsch sets up in *Family Frames* an opposition between autobi-ography and criticism, only to self-reflexively and dialectically undo it, in a way that is key to her theory of postmemory. For example, Hirsch explains how she initially found *The Mother/Daughter Plot* to be "a kind of autobiographical act" only insofar as its cover features a photograph of her grandmother and aunt (82). However, as she continues to muse on her relationship to this scholarly work, she recognizes it as "a complicated form of self-portraiture which reveals the self as necessarily relational and familial, as well as fragmented and dispersed" (83). *Family Frames'* formal experimentation embodies this understanding of the self, and the theory of postmemory that is integral to it. Hirsch defines postmemory as that which "characterizes the experience of those who grow up domi-nated by narratives that preceded their birth, whose own belated sto-ries are evacuated by the stories of the previous generation shaped by traumatic events that can be neither understood nor recreated" (22). Al-though she primarily addresses the Holocaust to investigate postmemory, Hirsch's theory holds implications for how literary criticism and life ex-periences intermingle for her. Throughout *Family Frames*, Hirsch shows how instrumental the thoughts, memories, and experiences of others are to her sense of self and to her perceptions of family. Thus the boundaries between autobiography and others' texts, and between her work as a lit-erary critic and her experiences as a family member, become blurred, as does the line between personal experience and history. The conclusion to *Family Frames* captures these intermixings. Musing on how to access her lost past, Hirsch realizes that to do so most probably will not involve travel to her parents' birthplace, but rather dwelling on family archives and on the imagetexts that have been the subject of *Family Frames*. For

Hirsch these imagetexts become her way to map her world and constitute her sense of self. As autobiographical and nonautobiographical texts
comingle to shape her imagination, her desires, and her experiences, the
line between them is both maintained and undone. The effect is a sophisticated reworking of an identity politics—one in which what constitutes
the personal, and one's experiences, broadens to encompass more than
that which is directly experienced, and yet not in a way that makes all
texts and experiences equally available to all people.

In this reworking of identity politics Hirsch scrupulously avoids claiming others' narratives or pasts as her own. *Family Frames*' opening and
closing chapters consider how the Holocaust has left a legacy of cultural
dislocation for herself and for others without firsthand memories of it.
These chapters, groundbreaking in Holocaust and autobiography studies,
explore how our memories are made up by others' experiences that we
both can and cannot own, and they address the dangers and possibilities
of empathy and identification. Only once in *Family Frames* does Hirsch
claim another story as her own without qualification, and she marks this
experience as at odds with her critical approach. Registering her discomfort with her immediate identification with Eva Hoffman's memoir
Lost in Translation, she states, "Eva Hoffman's story is my story, and
the only lens through which I can read it is an utterly unreconstructed
form of identification—a response quite disconcerting to someone who
has been studying and teaching literature for twenty-five years, and one
which makes me uneasy" (219). It is fitting that Hirsch explores her intense identification with Hoffman in "Pictures of a Displaced Girlhood,"
Family Frames' most straightforwardly autobiographical chapter. And
yet Hirsch ultimately subjects to analysis her "unreconstructed" identification with *Lost in Translation*: by the chapter's end, Hirsch has established how her strategies for surviving cultural dislocation differ from
Hoffman's. Hirsch concludes "Pictures" this way: "Thus, I do not shuttle
between the surface control and the internal rage that define the sides of
Hoffman's Archimedean triangle. Instead, I invest my psychic energies in
a series of (dis) and (re) locations that allow me to live in this 'permanent
sojourn in the wilderness,' this 'alien element,' which is, and always has
been, 'not comfortable but home'" (240). Even in this most unmediated
chapter of memoir, Hirsch comes to understand her own experiences
through engagement with others' memoirs, and even here she resists collapsing another's history into her own, although her immediate impulse
is to do so. Ultimately, Hirsch uses Hoffman's memoir as a framework

through which to analyze and represent her own experiences. This process involves questioning her visceral response to Hoffman's narrative and attending closely to how Hoffman's life does and does not translate into her own.

A striking exception to Hirsch's nuanced exploration of the relationship between self and other occurs in this same chapter. Although anomalous (indeed perhaps *because* it is), Hirsch's use of Anzaldúa in "Pictures of a Displaced Girlhood" is suggestive of the extent to which 1980s theories of identity politics by women of color (here, borderlands theory) structure white feminists' perceptions and sense of self in the 1990s, and it exposes difficulties that white feminists encounter when they use these theories to explore their ethnic identity. Hirsch introduces "Pictures of a Displaced Girlhood" with epigraphs by Mark Krupnick, Anzaldúa, and Hoffman. Then, in the chapter's concluding sentence (cited above), she returns to the Anzaldúa epigraph, which reads: "Borderlands are physically present wherever two or more cultures edge each other. . . . Living on borders and in margins, keeping intact one's shifting multiple identity and integrity, is like trying to swim in a new element, an 'alien' element . . . not comfortable but home" (217). As Hirsch cites Anzaldúa in her epigraph to support her own experience of cultural dislocation and to differentiate it from Hoffman's, her use of ellipses empties Anzaldúa's account of its historical and cultural specificity. Anzaldúa's statement that "Borderlands are physically present wherever two or more cultures edge each other" continues, "where people of different races occupy the same territory, where under, lower, middle and upper classes touch, where the space between the individuals shrinks with intimacy" (*Borderlands* vii). These considerations of race and class, at the heart of *Borderlands*, are those that not only Hirsch's epigraph but also the chapter itself elides. Throughout "Pictures," as Hirsch analyzes photographs of her girlhood and marks forms of cultural displacement not visible in the photos themselves, she posits ethnic difference as something that becomes visible only through personal narrative.[10] Although the epigraph by Anzaldúa helps structure Hirsch's exploration of cultural displacement, in sharp contrast to Hirsch's historically precise and detailed reading of Hoffman's *Lost in Translation*, the chapter includes no overt reference to the epigraph or to Anzaldúa until its final sentence, when Hirsch describes how she lives in an "'alien element,' which is, and always has been, 'not comfortable but home'" (240). Although the quote marks signal Anzaldúa's presence, Anzaldúa remains unnamed, and the reader must recall the epigraph to catch Hirsch's reference. The familiarity Hirsch assumes her readers have with Anzaldúa, and her own reliance on borderlands theory to provide a vocabulary through which to address ethnicity, evidence the powerful ways in which this theory has shaped white feminist approaches to ethnicity and experiences of marginalization. Hirsch's use of Anzaldúa also shows how in a U.S. context, white feminists' autobiographical accounts of ethnicity can, as they draw on theories of identity by women of color, gloss over key historical and political differences, particularly those pertaining to race and class.

Whereas Anzaldúa's identity politics, with its insights into constructions of race, class and nation, unfixes rather than supports U.S. geopolitical borders and hegemonic forms of national definition, Hirsch's reinforces them in a way that her evocation of Anzaldúa's model masks. Through Hirsch's focus on her own and Hoffman's experiences as immigrants in "Pictures of a Displaced Girlhood," U.S. identity and culture are homogenized and the significance of Hirsch's class and race privilege is diminished. Thus, the model for being an outsider in the United States becomes—in a return to an older model of ethnicity—that of the white, ethnic immigrant. Hirsch discloses, "At the end of ninth grade I know enough English to write a composition about what it is like to lose one's country—to be located nowhere, and have no cultural identity. I express the pain and nostalgia of homelessness so eloquently and describe so feelingly patriotic feelings that have no *patria* to which to attach themselves that I am asked to read it at a school assembly. Some people weep, and I get much praise, but I am a bit embarrassed by the nostalgia I have been able to evoke and which I cultivate so as to remain on the border" (231). Despite Hirsch's discomfort even at the time with her nostalgia-evoking performance, "Pictures of a Displaced Girlhood" does a similar kind of work insofar as it employs contemporary discourse on "borderlands" not to challenge but rather to return to ideologies of ethnicity and models for U.S. citizenship that center the white ethnic immigrant. Such models were prevalent when Hirsch was in ninth grade, but not when she writes "Pictures." On the one hand, Hirsch seems to bring a contemporary theoretical perspective to her childhood experience. On the other hand, Hirsch's memory of this moment lacks a "post" perspective insofar as she does not put her childhood perspective into dialogue with a present-day perspective on ethnicity, one in which factors of race and racism figure prominently.[11] By contrast, the opening and closing chapters—discussions of how the Holocaust has left a legacy of cultural dislocation even for those of Hirsch's generation who have no firsthand memories of it—make compelling and original arguments concerning ethnicity and culture that preserve past and present time frames and the different perspectives that each carries. Through the contrast between these chapters and "Pictures," *Family Frames* suggests how explorations of white ethnicity that build on work by Anzaldúa and other women of color—especially autobiographical accounts focused on a single subject—that do not attend to white racism's history and forms can effect and conceal a return to older models of ethnicity.

Other moments in this chapter undermine Hirsch's concept of post-memory as they further evidence the problems that can attend white feminists accounting for their ethnicity by drawing on theories of identity politics that originated from women of color in the 1980s. *Family Frames* evidences how doing so without attention to racial hierarchies can end up reinforcing work by first-wave white feminists. In "Pictures," Hirsch critiques as well as extends Carol Gilligan's *In A Different Voice* (1982) when she highlights the importance of cultural differences among girls. Building on Gilligan's work Hirsch likens the transition to female adulthood to the experience of emigration. She then states, "But if for American girls the move into adolescence feels like emigrating to a foreign culture . . . , what additional pressures confront girls like Hoffman and me who, in addition to learning the language of patriarchy, literally had to learn the English language and American culture?" (221–22). In comparison to her contemporaries, she describes herself and Hoffman as "doubly displaced, doubly dispossessed, doubly at risk" (222). Such descriptions—along with Hirsch's assertion that her comparative literature major is "the academic counterpart of the borderland" (xx)—are informed by theorists such as Anzaldúa who provide a vocabulary with which to discuss multiple, interlocking forms of oppression. At the same time, in distinction to these theorists of identity politics, what such statements in "Pictures" ignore is the significance that many girls—especially racial minorities—born in the United States also experience displacement and, moreover, that unlike Hirsch, their borderland existence is visually marked, externally enforced, and often silenced or punished. That Hirsch does not adequately address the significance of her structural privilege in relation to her feelings of dislocation can be partially attributed to the fact that she is describing her experience during an era when such considerations coming from a white girl would be extraordinary. At the same time, her failure to attend to race exists in tension with and is masked by her contemporary academic discourse about her ethnic identity and her present-day reflection on her past. This unresolved tension limits *Family Frames'* analysis of gender and race; in addition, in the chapter's flattening of how different generations come to understand the formation of ethnic identity, *Family Frame's* theory of postmemory is undercut.

Throughout "Pictures," Hirsch shows how it is possible to reintroduce older models of feminism and ethnicity in new feminist and multicultural, or whiteness studies, packaging. The problems that attend how Hirsch juggles different discourses and models of ethnicity are perhaps especially evident when readers compare her description of a photograph from her junior-high graduation to the photo itself. Hirsch says of herself and her friend, "our hair is teased just the right amount, we smile just like the other girls, and we fold our hands on our laps with just the right modesty: we pass" (231). Here, as throughout *Family Frames*, Hirsch explores with sensitivity how experiences of marginalization can be psychically felt even as they are physically invisible. What she addresses less rigorously is the significance of the disparity between marked and unmarked forms of dislocation—a difference that should be available to Hirsch the literary critic if not Hirsch the teenager. In the photo itself, Hirsch and her friend do not merely pass, but arguably set the standard to which the girls are expected to aspire—they sit center front, are among the few girls smiling, and embody conventional standards of beauty. By contrast, sitting next to Hirsch's friend is the only black girl in the picture who, though her self-presentation matches the other girls', does not pass. Attention to this girl from a 1990s perspective would complicate Hirsch's account of being doubly displaced. However, with Hirsch's exclusive focus on her own past experience, the importance of race drops from consideration, even as her vocabulary suggests that her approach to her past is a contemporary one. In effect, Hirsch's use of identity politics and a "borderlands" discourse to mark her ethnic identity render her racial privilege doubly invisible—both from a past and present-day perspective. *Family Frames* is thus suggestive of how studies of white ethnicity and memoir can combine to erase, even as they seem to build on, the contributions made by theorists of color in the 1980s.[12]

So, too, given its firm location in the academy, *Family Frames* departs in its experiments with genre from the 1980s anthologies' use of the multigenre format. *This Bridge* contributors, located either outside or at the margins of the academy, brought together diary entries, conversations, journal entries, and other "extraliterary" forms to contest exclusionary definitions of literature and theory, and boundaries between academic and nonacademic communities. By contrast, Hirsch's genre experimentation is not directed toward defining literature or theory more inclusively, and the acts of resistance in which *Family Frames* invests are those of writing, making pictures, and reading (215). Moreover, Hirsch addresses a primarily academic readership: she frequently employs the discourse of psychoanalysis and analyzes difficult, highly regarded literary or theoretical texts. Hirsch's academic focus is also reflected in her description of her comparative literature major as "the academic counterpart of the borderland" (xx). As her use of Anzaldúa's border theory reterritorializes it, Hirsch overrides its investments in critiquing geopolitical borders and elitist social hierarchies. Thus, as *Family Frames* registers the influence of Anzaldúa and other theorists who, during the 1980s, experiment with genre to transgress the boundaries of academe, it shows how works situated within the academy can continue the anthologies' genre experimentation without continuing to dismantle academic hierarchies, and in a way that arguably contains the anthologies' revolutionary strivings.

In its departures from as well as its continuities with anthologies of the 1980s, *Family Frames* renders visible some of the challenges of exploring white ethnicity through memoir. The book provides evidence of the inroads feminists of color have made into academe and also suggests the domesticating forces that can accompany the institutionalization of identity politics, and the discipline of whiteness studies. And yet, in its genre experimentation and its theory of postmemory, *Family Frames* works from within its academic contexts to invent new ways for humanities scholars to approach dispossession and trauma, the relationship between self and other, and personal and public histories. Through its strengths and limitations, *Family Frames* evidences the possibilities and challenges that face white feminists in the 1990s as they build on an identity politics that has become a part of academic culture.

Black Frames and White Studies

A work that more fully partakes in the movement in the 1990s to explore white ethnic identity is Marianna Torgovnick's *Crossing Ocean Parkway: Readings by an Italian American Daughter* (1994). Like *Family Frames*, this American Book Award winner, particularly its widely anthologized autobiographical chapter titled "On Being White," reveals the feelings of marginalization that those in positions of institutional success and racial privilege can experience. Although such accounts can provide insights into feelings and experiences that white privilege and institutional stature render invisible, as the following reading of *Crossing Ocean Parkway* underlines, even when they include discussions of race and racism, enabled by the memoir genre, these accounts can subsume in symptomatic ways the disparities between personal feelings and institutional or societal structures.

In *Crossing Ocean Parkway*, Torgovnick draws on the identity politics and the genre experiments of the 1980s anthologies in order to explore her identity as an Italian American woman and professor from Bensonhurst in Brooklyn, and also to take up more general questions of race and ethnicity. As does Hirsch, Torgovnick brings together cultural criticism and memoir: although part 1 of *Crossing Ocean Parkway* is memoir and part 2 is cultural criticism, Torgovnick explains that "a central contention of this book is the crossing between personal history and intellectual life. So that the autobiographical essays are also about American society and autobiography erupts more and more into the readings of U.S. culture" (xi). Like *Family Frames*, *Crossing Ocean Parkway* redefines what, particularly for a literary critic, constitutes autobiography: one of the crossings that Torgovnick stages is between autobiography and cultural criticism. Thus, in part 2 she draws on her own upbringing to critique Camille Paglia's gender politics, and in a chapter on *The Godfather* she relates characters' experiences to her own (104, 117). Like Hirsch, Torgovnick writes as an established academic who insists on the autobiographical investments of cultural criticism. These works reveal how, in the 1990s, not only is the personal political for the feminist literary critic, but so, too, is the personal professional.

What differentiates Torgovnick's approach from Hirsch's is how *Crossing Ocean Parkway*, in its chatty tone and everyday language, targets a mainstream readership. Torgovnick, a professor of English at Duke University and the author of seven books, is a well-known cultural critic with a long-standing interest in reaching a broad readership: she has published in the *New York Times* and *Partisan Review* as well as in academic venues, and her critically acclaimed books, *Gone Primitive* and its sequel, *Primitive Passions*, explore for crossover audiences how a spiritual hunger fuels the western fascination with the primitive. In *Crossing Ocean Parkway*, Torgovnick's creative mix of memoir and literary criticism provides the possibility of bringing ethnic and feminist studies to a broad readership.

However, in *Crossing Ocean Parkway*, even as the personal approach allows for a wide audience, as happens in *Family Frames*, this element at times undoes rather than expands the work's cultural criticism: its version of identity politics supports rather than challenges liberalism's inability to address racism at a structural rather than individual level, and brings out problems with combining whiteness studies and memoir. The first chapter, "On Being White, Female, and Born in Bensonhurst"—which, as its title indicates, explicitly engages a whiteness studies framework—makes these problems particularly evident. Moreover, "On Being White" not only has been anthologized in at least a dozen introductory reading and writing textbooks and in anthologies that thematize multiculturalism, but it also was a prize-winning essay in *Best American Essays 1991*, a book whose target audience is primarily nonacademic. As such it is representative of how ethnicity and memoir are packaged and taught in the 1990s, and it offers a way to calculate how whiteness studies is being disseminated in the academy and to a more general readership.

In "On Being White" the focus rapidly shifts from race to gender in a practice of identity politics that proves to be highly individualistic: although the chapter begins with a discussion of the racially motivated murder in Bensonhurst of Yusef Hawkins, and of African American and Italian American relations, it almost immediately turns to Torgovnick's ongoing gendered struggles with the Italian American working-class community into which she was born and which through class ascension she has left behind. Not until the last line of "On Being White" does Torgovnick circle back to the introductory discussion of the murder. Torgovnick has just narrated her search for a Cremolata at the wrong time of day (in town because her father is sick, Torgovnick wants this Italian delicacy before returning to Duke University that afternoon). Her quest takes her to a men's club, which she enters, emboldened by her class privilege and professional clout. Exiting the men's club with her Italian ice in hand, Torgovnick reflects on her position as an assertive, professional, Italian American woman who refuses to play by Bensonhurst rules. She states, "I shake hands with my discreetly rebellious past, still an outsider walking through the neighborhood, marked and insulted—though unlikely to be shot" (18). Even as this ending gestures back to the racial killing at the chapter's start, it—and the chapter itself—turns out to be more about Torgovnick's spunk in resisting her community's prescribed gender and class identities. Although Torgovnick here wryly underscores the differing degrees of danger that she and young black men face from being in the wrong place at the wrong time, the chapter does not ultimately illuminate white racism and its interconnections with sexism, nor is Torgovnick's feminist assertion made in solidarity with black men. Instead, by the chapter's end, white Italians' racist violence against African American men becomes weakly analogous to the community's discrimination against Torgovnick as an Italian American woman.[13] Torgovnick's entry into the men's club constitutes a feminist disruption of the gendered order of the Bensonhurst community (if not one that will help other women, especially those without class privilege), but not an antiracist intervention.

Moreover, noteworthy here is the individualism of this feminist assertion. In striking contrast to the collectivity of *This Bridge*, this individualism often characterizes academic memoir's practices of identity politics. When Torgovnick closes with the description of herself "shaking hands with her discreetly rebellious past" over the purchase of her Italian ice, she provides an apt image for this bourgeois individualism and its version of "the personal is political." Here a handshake does not form a bridge to or a connection with others, but to one's former self and, at a safe vantage point, to previous acts of low-stakes rebellion (enacted through consumption) or states of marginalization.

Throughout *Crossing Ocean Parkway*, concerns with race and a larger cultural canvas or collectivity often fall away with the focus on Torgovnick's individual experiences as an Italian American woman. With a structure similar to *Family Frames*, in which theorizations of ethnicity frame but for the most part do not centrally inform the analysis of family photos, in *Crossing Ocean Parkway*, personal narratives about gender, class ascension, and Italian and Jewish identity are packaged as, but are largely untouched by, broader analyses of black-white relations. The second chapter, "Crossing Ocean Parkway," opens with the 1991 racial conflict in Crown Heights between Hasidic Jews and African Americans, but only as a lead-in to an exploration of how Torgovnick routed her desires for upward mobility and education through association with Jews. Concerns of race disappear almost entirely as the book progresses and as Torgovnick works more concentratedly from within a white ethnic framework. In the final chapter of part 1, "The College Way," as Torgovnick vividly details the cruelties of the small-town college in which she was an assistant professor, whiteness is assumed and uninterrogated in the chapter as well as in the town. In essays in part 2 on Dr. Doolittle, Camille Paglia, *The Godfather*, and Lionel Trilling, Torgovnick's readings are inflected by her perspective as an Italian American woman, but without consideration of how racial privilege informs experiences of ethnic marginalization.

The book obscures the ways that Torgovnick's explorations of her ethnic and gender identity and her genre crossings relate to autobiographical and theoretical writings by women of color, even as *Crossing's* failures to mark whiteness undermine that work's identity politics. As Torgovnick continually contrasts the rarity of accounts of Italian American life to the many such Jewish ones, she ignores the structural differences between ethnic white women and women of color. She also fails to consider how the lack of an intellectual space that is "marked Italian American and female" (150) registers the possibility (or at least the appearance) of assimilation—and therefore white privilege; the fact that Torgovnick first includes her Italian maiden name, "De Marco," on a publication only after she has become a full professor at Duke University attests to this racial privilege. As Andrijka Kwasny notes in a review of *Crossing Ocean Parkway* and Lentricchia's *The Edge of Night*, Torgovnick's timing in marking her ethnicity is not idiosyncratic. Rather, it is representative of how professors can claim and write about their ethnic identities only after leaving these identities—and a working-class background—behind in order to become university professors. If the pressure not to disclose one's ethnicity indicates the presence of prejudice, the ability to conceal ethnicity is a product of racial privilege. Whereas *This Bridge* contributors highlighted their marginalized identities as a reason for their systemic exclusion from the university, once identity politics becomes institutionalized, the proclamation of an ethnic or racial identity then becomes an act of individual assertion and a register of arrival.

In part, then, *Crossing Ocean Parkway's* neglect of structures of racism results from and also signals a slippage between equating personal feelings with larger structural realities—from a compromised practice of identity politics. In the preface Torgovnick states, "I have a strong attraction to powerful (largely male), upper- and upper-middle-class American culture. I want to feel privileged and entitled. At the same time, I identify, *I like to identify*, with outsiders" (x, original emphasis). Here, as Torgovnick's identification as an outsider is expressed as a *desire* rather than a *material reality*, desiring to be in the position of an outsider is collapsed into actually being in that outside position. Like Hirsch's, Torgovnick's position as outsider is one that must be made visible through language and, as sometimes happens with Hirsch, Torgovnick conflates the differences between feeling like an outsider and being subjected to the material conditions of marginalization. This conflation is symptomatic of the white privilege that can govern approaches to identity politics in the contemporary academy, and it emerges with particular clarity in memoirs, given their foregrounding of their authors' feelings and desires.

Furthermore, as Torgovnick seeks to illustrate for readers the humanity of members of her Bensonhurst community, *Crossing Ocean Parkway* suggests how a focus on personal feelings can override structural analyses or realities in a way that undermines counterhegemonic practices of identity politics. Torgovnick often ignores the material conditions that govern personal relationships and her personal focus often limits rather than furthers *Crossing Ocean Parkway*'s insights into interracial relations. In this way *Crossing Ocean Parkway* demonstrates the difficulty of using memoir, especially when it includes accounts about loved ones, as a way to analyze race relations from a position of privilege. For example, in "On Being White," Torgovnick relays that her father, after commenting on the wrongness of the racial violence against the three black men in Bensonhurst, remarked, "'yeah, but what were they *doing* there. They didn't belong'" (8). Despite this comment Torgovnick maintains that her father, because "he has no trouble acknowledging the wrongness of the death," is not a racist (8). As its epilogue makes poignantly clear, *Crossing Ocean Parkway* is in part a tribute to and a book of mourning for her father. Indeed, "Crossing Back" stands as epilogue both for her father's life and for the book. In "On Being White," love, grief, and family loyalty render the gentleness of Torgovnick's critique of her father—who is dying of lung cancer when she writes it—not only understandable but also moving. Indeed, one of the contributions of *Crossing Ocean Parkway* is how powerfully this chapter and "The College Way," which deals with her colleagues' insensitivity to her devastating loss of her child, speak to how racial and institutional privilege cannot protect against experiences of personal loss. However, to conclude that in "On Being White" Torgovnick's father is not racist simply because he finds racially motivated murder wrong reinforces the understanding of racism as simply a prejudicial feeling. It is precisely this hegemonic definition that enables white individuals not to take responsibility for the racist social conditions that made the Bensonhurst shootings possible. Moreover, such an understanding of how the personal is political takes the oppositional edge out of identity politics.

Crossing Ocean Parkway illuminates how practices of identity politics that humanize individuals implicated in racist structures (a group that includes all white Americans) can support forms of liberal humanism that impede antiracist critique.[14] In "On Being White," Torgovnick asks, "Why did I need to write about this killing in Bensonhurst, but not in the manner of a news account or a statistical sociological analysis? Within days of hearing the news, I began to plan this essay, to tell the world what I knew, though I stopped midway, worried that my parents or their neighbors would hear about it" (9). As this statement reveals, a challenge to Torgovnick's neighborhood—the scene of the racist killing—is not a desired effect of the essay; rather, Torgovnick sets out to explain this violence to the world outside Bensonhurst. Torgovnick's use here of the personal counters the identity politics found in the multigenre anthologies, where it is precisely the most personal relationships that become the place to create political change: as Cherríe Moraga urges the women who constitute her community in *This Bridge*, "if it takes head-on collisions, let's do it: this polite timidity is killing us" ("La Güera" 34). Furthermore, as Torgovnick's explanation complicates readers' understandings of Italian Americans in Bensonhurst and elicits readers' sympathies on behalf of this community, the structural realities conveyed by "statistical sociological analysis" are not deepened so much as buried. Although this might protect Torgovnick's family and provide insight into how white Americans' racism grows out of their own experiences of marginalization, such compassion, unattended by structural analysis, can inadvertently support rather than counter the hegemony of whiteness.[15]

On its own and as part of *Crossing Ocean Parkway*, "On Being White" can be read as symptomatic of how, in the 1990s, identity politics circulates in and beyond the academy in a new "whiteness studies" packaging, one that gestures toward but does not deeply engage interracial relations or antiracist politics and one that, in its bourgeois individualism as well as its liberal racial politics, can effect a return to first-wave feminism and exclusionary forms of humanism. In particular the anthologizing of "On Being White" suggests how easily a structural approach to the harsh realities of racism drops out when identity politics, whiteness studies, and multiculturalism become institutionalized, especially in the form of autobiographical accounts of white ethnicity.

Recalling First-Wave Feminism

Together with *Family Frames*, *Crossing Ocean Parkway* signals not only some problems with the intersections of memoir, explorations of white ethnicity, and identity politics, but also how the popularization of whiteness studies can disguise the return in the 1990s academy to first-wave feminism's inattention to race. Nancy Miller's 1997 "Public Statements, Private Lives: Academic Memoirs for the Nineties," a review of more than a dozen memoirs, brings this point out with particular clarity. In this article Miller, both a critic and a writer of memoir, reads memoirs as an expression of feminism by women of her generation. She frames her analysis with a reading of Shirley Geok-lin Lim's *Among the White Moon Faces*. As she makes Lim's memoir paradigmatic and stresses points of commonality among the memoirs under review, Miller neglects important differences, particularly those involving race and histories of colonialism. For example, Miller addresses Lim's account of leaving Malaysia to attend graduate school at Brandeis University, after the racial uprisings in Malaysia drive out non-Malaysians such as herself. Arriving in Boston in wintertime, with no place to live and less than a hundred dollars, Lim experiences isolation, hunger, culture shock, and severe depression. Another graduate student recognizes her distress and takes her to a crisis intervention center, where a woman named Dr. Helda helps her. Miller summarizes this period in Lim's life this way: "Lim describes her lonely graduate student days in the Northeast. 'There is no pain as the pain of isolation,' she writes, until finally a new friend brings her to the Crisis Intervention Center. Lim learns from Dr. Helda what her mother had missed teaching her" (989). Miller recounts this lesson, and then contends, "In some ways, this is also the lesson [Jane] Tompkins learns [in *A Life in School*]" (989). Linking Lim's and Tompkins's unhappiness to her own, Miller concludes: "It is this tracking back and forth between girl with longings and woman with doubts that makes itself felt in so many of these memoirs. I was THAT unhappy girl (how many of us weren't?). And now these/we women of some achievement with books and students of their own, look back and reconstruct that other story of becoming . . . a professor. At what cost? Can I be happy now?" (990). Miller's autobiographical reading, in which all girls become the same girl, who becomes Miller herself, disregards the significance of Lim's experiences of racism, deracination, and poverty.[16] Whereas for first-wave feminists all the women were white and middle class, the 1990s finds Miller highlighting the work of a woman of color. And yet Miller retains a model premised on sameness and identification, one that, as she folds in women of color, remains predominantly white and middle-class, and inattentive to how racism structures people's lives in the United States.

Miller's multiculturalism requires the repression of the significant challenges issued to white feminists by women of color deploying identity politics in the 1980s. These challenges, which center around race and which transformed academic feminism in the mid-1980s, are ones that Miller herself takes up with Hirsch and Jane Gallop in the conversation that concludes the influential 1990 collection *Conflicts in Feminism.* Therefore, when Miller concludes in "Public Statements, Private Lives," "In recent years, no doubt as an effect of feminism, the favorite other has been the mother" (999), this statement—and her article as a whole—are striking in their neglect of considerations of racial otherness. Perhaps this is because Miller believes that feminism has overcome racism. And yet, her inattention to race and racism, even as she explores memoirs centrally concerned with these matters and highlights themes of "otherness," demonstrates the ongoing need for a feminist politics that rigorously interrogates its relations to race and racism.

Also troubling is the smallness of the stakes that Miller assigns to the acts of reading and writing memoir—a smallness that diminishes the understanding of the way in which the personal is political. As her comment, "I was THAT unhappy girl" suggests, Miller's emphasis is on finding points of identification as ends in and of themselves. She explains, "My literary critic self shows the places where she (that readerly self) stops or starts with recognition, saying 'me too.' That's my story you're telling" (982). In Miller's understanding of autobiography, what disappears are the political stakes of recognition and identification, and the impetus to establish activist communities found in anthologies such as *This Bridge.*

What also drops out is a sense of community that goes beyond a one-to-one relation between reader and text. I find this especially striking since of the fifteen memoirs Miller discusses in "Public Statements, Private Lives," six had not yet been published, and others are by women with whom Miller has collaborated (i.e., Hirsch and Gallop). Although Miller remarks on the personal nature of her interest in the memoirs she considers, she does not address her personal relationships to the writers. As the experience of identification creates for Miller a sought-after bond of intimacy that is insistently textual, extratextual connections among writers remain largely a closed circuit to which most readers are denied access. I raise this point not to condemn academic feminists for networking, but rather to consider the effect of not theorizing such connections in an article concerned with the question "Can a woman, more precisely, *how* can a woman be at home in the university? Or can't she?" (983). Addressing interrelations among those partaking in the memoir movement would disrupt Miller's privileging of solitary moments of recognition and identification between reader and text, and open up a space to explore the collective work that feminists writing autobiographies are accomplishing. For example: What are the "memoir movement's" possibilities and limitations for helping to create a home for women in the university? What can this movement offer to those more marginally positioned in the university, or excluded from it altogether? Writing a few years later, in 2000, and defending the genre against what she calls its "critical disrepute," Miller attributes the inordinate "rhetorical abuse" that she says memoir inspires to "the predominance of women in the memoir bizz" ("'But Enough about Me'" 430). What Miller here neglects is the privilege that attends being able to publish a memoir, and how the memoir phenomenon might register feminists' successful inroads into the academy. One of the running themes of *Academic Lives* concerns the difficulties—and the importance—of using memoirs to address their authors' forms of privilege (not only racial, but also institutional) as well as their marginalized forms of identity.

In an interview with Jeffrey Williams about the writing group they formed while colleagues and friends at Duke University, Torgovnick, Cathy Davidson, Alice Kaplan, and Jane Tompkins provide a rare discussion of the community that exists among established academic feminists and that fuels the academic memoir movement. Their discussion suggests the difficulties of tying memoir and institutional privilege to a collectivist politics. In their group interview Torgovnick responds to Williams's question as to whether the group could be called a salon: "I don't have any problem with being in a circle. I think we probably do represent a movement, and we are passing up a power-move in not naming it" (169–70). Torgovnick's feminist analysis does not extend to what the group writes; acknowledging the success group members have achieved, Torgovnick states, "I think that the project now has moved from reaching a wider audience to simply being ourselves as writers" (162). Davidson, too, stresses the importance—and frankly and refreshingly acknowledges the privilege—of writing for oneself: "I think that we feel secure enough to take risks now, to try things that might not bring glory. That's a privilege, to be able to do writing without the goal of reaching a large audience, or of impressing anyone in your profession" (163). With Torgovnick's and other members' focus on self-expression and writerly freedom, what drops from consideration is how the individualized focus of memoir can end up depoliticizing a feminist politics, atomizing practices of identity politics and, especially in the present-day contexts, masking the erosion of civil liberties. Along with Miller's "Public Statements, Private Lives," Williams's interview suggests the need to rethink how the personal is political, and to see if academic memoirs can productively reinvigorate rather than circumscribe a politics of identity, and in a way that takes account of the racial and institutional privileges of its feminist practitioners.

The bourgeois individualism and inattention to race that attend Miller's review (and the Duke group's interview) are not simply functions of the way Miller reads, but characterize many of the memoirs themselves, particularly those by white feminists that take their authors' ethnicity as their subject. Such problems, however, are not inevitable. As memoirs by two of the most recognized proponents of whiteness studies, *Crossing the Color Line: Race, Parenting, and Culture* by Maureen Reddy and *Beyond the Whiteness of Whiteness: Memoir of a White Mother of Black Sons* by Jane Lazarre, demonstrate, memoir and whiteness studies can come together in ways that are resolutely antiracist and attuned to how structures of race inform our most intimate relationships and everyday experiences. At the same time, in ways the next two sections explore, these memoirs raise questions about the work that memoirs coming from academic locations can do, and about potential limitations, especially when it comes to addressing historical injustices that continue to impact hiring practices and other institutional inequities that structure university life, of an antiracist, feminist politics of identity premised on personal feelings and relationships.

The Travels of This Bridge Called My Back

The 1994 memoir *Crossing the Color Line* centrally engages a whiteness studies framework as in it Maureen T. Reddy describes how her experience marrying a black man and bringing up black sons transforms her understanding of whiteness and race relations, and her identity as a mother, a teacher, a literary critic, a white American, and a community member. Reddy finds her way to memoir not as an "academic star" but rather through the personal approach she has taken to her long-standing interests in African American and women's studies. An English professor at Rhode Island College, Reddy is the author of *Everyday Acts against*

Racism (1996); of books on crime fiction and its relation to race and feminism; and of volumes on race and maternity, including the 1994 coedited
collection *Mother Journeys: Feminists Write about Mothering*, for which
her own contribution was nominated for a 1995 Pushcart Prize. Over
the course of her career, Reddy's role as a mother to black sons both informs and has been informed by her immersion in African American and
women's studies and her sense of how to live ethically as a white person
in the United States.

Although Reddy's textual engagements in *Crossing the Color Line* are
with African American literature and theory and her model for race relations is a black-white one, her memoir formally and thematically registers the enormous influence of *This Bridge Called My Back*. In its use
of bridge imagery, in its identity politics, and in the challenges it poses
to mind-body dualisms, *Crossing the Color Line* provides a way to trace
continuities between *This Bridge* and both the later developments of
whiteness studies and the 1990s memoir movement. That *This Bridge*'s
impact is a largely unmarked one for Reddy speaks to the pervasiveness
of its influence, and the extent to which its insights on race, ethnicity, and
gender have become naturalized by the mid 1990s. Moreover, Reddy's
use of bridge imagery—starting with the word "crossing" in her title—as
it builds on *This Bridge*'s conceptualization of "a theory in the flesh,"
demonstrates ways that memoir and whiteness studies can extend the
work of *This Bridge*.

Along with identity politics, bridge imagery plays a complex and crucial role in Reddy's memoir. The memoir opens with an account of a
panic attack Reddy experienced when crossing the Tappan Zee Bridge.
The rest of part 1, "On Lines and Bridges," details the development of
Reddy's bridge phobia during the mid-1980s, and her subsequent discovery, during a conversation with a friend, of its origins. Reflecting on her
relationship to her black husband and sons, she explains, "I think I stand
on the color line itself, not on one side of it. Or maybe I'm like a bridge,
stretching across the line, touching both sides, but mostly in the middle
somewhere.' As I say this, I have a visual image of my body as a bridge that
strikes me with the force of an epiphany: *that's* the source of the bridge
panic, I realize with a strange elation. The panic is not about heights or
speed or water, but about metaphor and race" (5–6, original emphasis).
With this discovery that her panic results not from elemental but socially
structured fears, she realizes, "It was not the Tappan Zee that was in
danger of falling apart in 1985, but me. . . . Driving across that bridge

literalized my metaphoric position, which was becoming more complicated and stressful than it ever had been before, and I panicked. Identifying the source of the panic also helped explain why the phobia had waned
so much in recent months, as I had finally become comfortable with my
own racial position, in particular with the multiple, ever-evolving meanings of being the white mother of black children" (6). At this point in her
memoir Reddy footnotes *This Bridge*, albeit only to observe that Moraga
and Anzaldúa "employ the bridge metaphor differently. Although I was
familiar with this text at the time of my bridge panic, I did not see the
racial analogy in my own life until years later" (176). Through the course
of the memoir, as Reddy analyzes her emotions and theorizes from her
experiences as wife and mother to black men, her bridge phobia evolves
into a structuring metaphor. Her description of the process of overcoming this phobia and her use of bridge imagery double as an account of her
growing insights into how interracial relationships provide a necessary
means of overcoming fatal forms of white racism.

To develop her bridge metaphor, although Reddy builds on W. E. B.
Du Bois's concept of the color line, both her phobia and her account of
it dramatically illustrate *This Bridge's* impact on white feminists in the
1990s. Reddy concludes her memoir with the argument that "White people cannot become black, but we can reject the privileges of whiteness,
calling them what they are, and in that choice build a bridge across the
color line, beginning the journey away from white essentialist attitudes
that support racism and that undermine our humanity. Feminists should
be in the vanguard of this bridge building. All of our lives depend on
that bridge; without it we will surely drown" (173). Reddy's emphatically
feminist and antiracist statement not only draws consciously on Du Bois,
but also forges a bridge between her memoir and whiteness studies, and
the project and language of *This Bridge*. The influence of *This Bridge* on
Crossing the Color Line is arguably all the more powerful for not being
consciously articulated. That this bridge metaphor—that widely circulated among feminists in the 1980s—structures not only Reddy's development of a whiteness studies analysis in her 1994 memoir but also her
deepest and most unconscious fears in the 1980s, suggests its profound
influence.

Of particular significance is how Reddy's account of her bridge phobia
develops *This Bridge's* formulation of a "theory in the flesh." *This Bridge*
contributors combated the assumption in the academy in the early 1980s
that theory is objective and impartial by emphasizing how it emerges from

one's bodily experiences. *Crossing the Color Line* builds on this form of identity politics and its concomitant belief that the personal is political with statements such as this: "With Sean's birth, I felt a more intensely personal stake in racial issues. . . . From the very beginning, mothering Sean shifted my position in the world, giving me a new standpoint and a new angle of vision" (40). Such expressions bringing together the personal and the political were very familiar by the 1990s, but *Crossing the Color Line* develops how the two are interrelated. Through Reddy's account of her bridge phobia, she extends the notion of a theory in the flesh by illuminating how even the most visceral feelings can be socially constructed and shaped by theory and political beliefs. In this way Reddy's memoir supports the contention made by history of emotions scholars Jeff Goodwin, James M. Jasper, and Francesca Polletta that "there are no emotions without ideas . . . and no ideas without emotions" (176). In its version of identity politics, her memoir furthers Moraga and Anzaldúa's refusal of binary oppositions between theory and experience, the personal and the political, and the mind and the body through its demonstration not only of how experiences shape theory, but also of how bodily emotions can result from reading theory.

Reddy's representation of her bridge phobia suggests the possibilities of memoir as a genre from which to map complex crossings that undo reigning binaries. *This Bridge* contributors used the multigenre format to challenge binary oppositions, particularly those that delegitimated them as writers and intellectuals and denied them entry to the academy. Utilizing a more conventionally literary form fifteen years later, and situated as a tenured professor who teaches in the by-now institutionalized fields of African American literature and women's studies, Reddy works with a different, more established, set of contexts and concerns. As is true for Hirsch and Torgovnick, literature as well as life experiences form the texts that Reddy reads. In these readings Reddy moves in and out of academic discourses and more everyday language, effecting crossings between the two. Her memoir contains interpretations, for example, of James Weldon Johnson's *The Autobiography of an Ex-Coloured Man* that simultaneously serve as literary criticism and personal meditation on her family life and experiences as a white woman teaching African American literature. As she seamlessly interweaves discussions of African American novels and theory into her memoir, the lines she blurs are between those of fiction and life, theory and experience, the personal and the professional, the professional and the political, the personal and the political.

Literary criticism and theorizing become as intensely personal as her autobiographical narrative is theoretical and political. Firmly ensconced within the academy—in terms of her own location, and that of her subject matter and her genre choices—Reddy is able to effect crossings that continue the work of *This Bridge*.

Reddy's model of activism also articulates with as it departs from *This Bridge*'s. *This Bridge* contributors utilize a horizontal, or sororal, model of community, one in which they insist on working through differences. Reddy also claims the importance of basing a politics and community on difference, but her model is maternal. Building on her own experiences as a mother, and also on Patricia Hill Collins's "othermother" model (caring for children who are not one's own by either blood or law), Reddy espouses her belief that "by committing herself to a particular child (or children) for reasons other than bourgeois individualism, a woman commits herself to the future and strikes a blow against a social system that tries to push us all into rigidly bounded nuclear families that compete against each other for ever scarcer rewards" (155). Reddy justifies her focus on the maternal role by explaining that "the one role in the family through which women might form enduring cross-racial alliances is the role of the mother. Mothers are committed to preservation and to the future in ways that sisters are not, or at least do not have to be" (168). Women's common interests and commitments as mothers serve, for Reddy, as the basis for their comradeship and cross-racial alliances: "one area in which black and white women sometimes seem able to form coalitions for working together is that concerning children, our own and others. This suggests to me that although the sororal model of feminism may not be workable across racial lines, an 'othermother' model . . . might be more fruitful. Black women have often reached out to my children through me or to me through my children" (154). By reflecting on her own experiences and through her readings of comothering in contemporary African American novels, she arrives at the conclusion that "black and white women need to be each other's comrades, a kind of political friendship that recognizes difference and works *because* of them, not in spite of them" (169). This model for building political community, or comradeship, through recognition of differences is one that directly resonates with that found in *This Bridge*, even as Reddy's privileging of the mother-child relationship as the basis for her politics distinguishes her vision from *This Bridge*'s model of sisterhood. *Crossing the Color Line* exists in implicit dialogue with *This Bridge*, and it is a work that

registers how deeply *This Bridge* informs the feelings and conscious-
nesses of white feminists committed to antiracist work founded on an
identity politics.

Through its focus on how Reddy's identity as a white mother of black
sons determines her everyday interactions, her politics, and her emotional responses, *Crossing the Color Line* demonstrates how memoir
and whiteness studies can come together to develop *This Bridge*'s formulation of a "theory in the flesh," its challenges to a host of mind-body
dualisms, and its understanding that "the revolution begins at home."
That it accomplishes these things evidences how the institutionalization
of feminism and identity politics (in the form of whiteness studies) need
not forgo the transformative energies and political commitments that
these movements had prior to their assimilation into the academy. At
the same time, however, what remains unaddressed is how her maternal
model operates in more institutional, impersonal contexts. Reddy's autobiographical approach leaves unanswered questions not only about how
those who do not wish to adopt the role of mother can make use of her
model, but also how this maternal model can and cannot effect change in
institutional or academic contexts, where interrelations are not governed
by love and empathy, or even friendship. At the same time as *Crossing
the Color Line* performs acute analyses of race and racism and offers a
vigorous understanding of how the personal is political, a question remains concerning the limits of an antiracist and feminist politics based
on familial intimacy.

The Limits of Empathy and Identification

Jane Lazarre's 1996 *Beyond the Whiteness of Whiteness: Memoir of
a White Mother of Black Sons* provides some possible answers to this
question. Like *Crossing the Color Line, Beyond the Whiteness of Whiteness* is a memoir that fully partakes in whiteness studies, and, as its title
announces, it too bases its antiracist politics on a maternal model that
emerges from Lazarre's experiences as a white mother of black sons. Indeed, as acknowledgments in each book make clear, Reddy and Lazarre
see their projects as closely intertwined, and they take inspiration from
each other's life and work. Lazarre's interest in writing autobiography predates academic fashion (Lazarre is primarily known for her memoirs, as
well as for her novels and essays), and autobiographical writing is central
to her teaching and research—she wrote her first memoir, *The Mother*

Knot, in the mid-1970s. Like Reddy, Lazarre—director of the Writing Program and professor of Writing and Literature at Eugene Lang College, at the New School for Social Research—does not come to memoir as an academic star, but rather she uses memoir as an accessible way to execute her long-standing conviction as a feminist that the personal is political. In distinction to Reddy in *Crossing the Color Line*, in *Beyond the Whiteness of Whiteness*, Lazarre puts her maternal model into play in interactions that are not among friends or family members, thus providing a way to assess the possibilities and limitations of basing a politics on intimacy and empathy when the contexts are institutional.

Like Reddy, Lazarre uses memoir not as a covert return to individualism, but rather as a vehicle for transcending the self in order to "speak out against even the smallest injustice" (134). Indeed, her commitment to social justice, and particularly to an antiracist politics, fuels her interest in writing and teaching memoir. Whereas many white academics write memoirs in the 1990s in order to claim unmarked white ethnic identities or to assert other experiences of marginalization, Lazarre's focus is not on complicating whiteness, but rather on moving beyond "the whiteness of whiteness" that "is the blindness of willful innocence" (49). For Lazarre whiteness cannot be understood independently of blackness, and awareness of race is both ever present and part of every decision she makes about her sons' lives (47).

Lazarre consistently refuses a perspective unmediated by historical analysis, and her memoir foregrounds U.S. history as important but not all-determining of personal relationships. In the first chapter, "The Richmond Museum of the Confederacy," Lazarre tells of viewing a slavery exhibit, where she realizes that "without understanding slavery, we cannot understand the United States of America. And from that perspective it was clear to me that I would have to revisit the story of my life in a Black family" (20). The story Lazarre tells insists on the ongoing significance of race in the United States, even as she posits racism not as inevitable but rather as something to resist and overcome.

Lazarre's struggle against racism and her identity as a writer are based on her model of mothering. Her role as white mother of black sons informs her perspective in all arenas of her life. For Lazarre mothering means empathizing and identifying with her sons, and using her white privilege only when it can help them. Learning to see through her sons' eyes is "not only an aspect of narrative and aesthetic technique, but has an important ethical dimension as well" (71). Identification with them leads to what Lazarre calls "passing over" into blackness, to moments during which "I became my sons, Black Americans" (5).

As Lazarre chronicles the process of "passing over," she maintains the tension between having white skin and rejecting whiteness as a social identity. Nevertheless, the memoir increasingly focuses on how Lazarre passes beyond whiteness and comes to view her identity as "hidden" by her white skin (49). Lazarre traces the paradox of how "learning the depth and dimension of my whiteness—which I can no more easily throw off than I can the social definitions of my gender— . . . leads to the realization that I am not really white at all" (56). As Lazarre comes to disidentify with whiteness, blackness achieves an ever greater reality for her: "In my long journey of escape from the whiteness of whiteness, I have come upon a piece of understanding of the blackness of Blackness after all" (97). By the memoir's conclusion Lazarre presents her journey beyond whiteness as nearly complete; she explains that when she is among black and white people who do not know her, "I am always comforted by this thought: I am no longer white. However I may appear to others, I am a person of color now" (135). To support this claim Lazarre relies on a metaphor, one that cuts race free of its material groundings: she likens her color to that of a multicolored piece of thread that makes up a tapestry. Although, unlike Torgovnick, she draws attention to the difference between her own perceptions or desires and material conditions, for reasons I discuss later her claim is nonetheless problematic; her resort to metaphor also marks her shift here from a rigorous identity politics framework to a more liberal humanist literary register.[17]

Lazarre's disidentification with whiteness is not simply a move made through metaphor, but is one enabled by the memoir's structure—its settings become increasingly intimate and familial and so do not require the abdication of an identity politics. Whereas the first chapter is set at a slavery exhibit and the next two detail a mix of institutional and domestic contexts, chapter 4, "Reunions, Retellings, Refrains," concerns Lazarre's experiences at her husband's family reunions, where she is surrounded by black people who love and accept her. Although Lazarre at no time abandons attention to structures of race, by "Reunions," her full identification with a black vantage point and her simultaneous maintenance of an identity politics is made possible by the chapter's intimate domestic settings.

In Lazarre's memoir the political becomes based on relationships that are increasingly personal. Successfully utilizing the genre of memoir,

Lazarre sets forth what is in many ways a radical politics, one based on overcoming racism through empathy, love, and identification. And yet the memoir's focus on familial relationships and its increasingly domestic settings often gloss over the limitations of such a model when the setting is institutional or impersonal. One moment in the memoir gestures toward these limitations. When Lazarre relays her experience serving on a faculty hiring committee, she suggests how her model can fail her personally and politically in an institutional context. Lazarre's account stands out because it is the memoir's least processed and most vexed one; indeed, Lazarre describes the experience as one "accompanied by a confusion so powerful I know it is a signal of depth" (90).

The section in question follows an account of Lazarre's discovery of her son's vulnerability as a black male when a white hospital staff mistakes his fear for violence. Lazarre next describes being on an almost all-white hiring committee conducting a search for a scholar in African American history. When "Suzanne," a black, middle-aged finalist comes for a campus visit, Lazarre describes her as follows: "She has an impressive resume, including a privileged education, world travel, honors, and degrees. Yet, she seems held back professionally, somehow trapped. Her work, our resident historians worry, is characterized by the same curious inhibition or restraint as her life seems to be" (91). During the interview Lazarre notes the frayed T-shirt beneath the candidate's silk jacket, and observes that "She pauses for long moments before she answers questions, speaks low, and if someone disagrees with her she neither presses her point nor changes her mind; she remains silent. The only Black person on our committee, G., tells us he believes she is scared" (91–92). Describing to the reader her own response to Suzanne, Lazarre confesses to "a confusing ambivalence toward her which has nothing to do with her academic work or credentials. . . . I feel intimidated, yet I can see she is doing nothing intimidating" (92). Observing this candidate's performance with the student committee, Lazarre notes that "she is warmly engaged with them, sounding confident in her own purposes and attitudes about teaching" (92). That evening, when the committee takes Suzanne to a poetry reading, Lazarre is overcome by a desire to go home: *Something about her vulnerability—the clothes, the braids, the fear*"—"She makes me think about my fear of rejection" (92, original emphasis). Lazarre presses the candidate, whom she is supposed to accompany to a cab, to leave; Suzanne responds to Lazarre with cold dignity and Lazarre says, "in this passing moment of her anger, I sense her strength and feel relief"

(93). Lazarre explains that when the committee reconvenes, "In terms of objective standards, the key members of the committee decide, we cannot hire her. We need leaders on this faculty. If she were stronger, more brave . . ." (93).

Several nights later, Lazarre has a dream:

> I am walking after an elegant tall woman who is turning around every so often to talk to me over her shoulder. As she does so, I feel small, tolerated, and exposed, like a young child on one of those leashes people attach to toddlers as if they were dogs. The tall woman is self-confident, secure; *she has her nerve*. She wears her clothes well . . . . She is looking down on me and I am not measuring up.
>
> I wake up thinking about Suzanne's braids, the frayed neckline of her T-shirt beneath the silk jacket. (93, original emphasis)

As she again identifies with Suzanne's vulnerability, musing on ways "we show up for interviews with old T-shirts visible beneath our new jackets," Lazarre recalls her relief in "finding armor that . . . enabled me to move around" (94). Her thoughts return to Suzanne, and she wonders, "If most of us had been Black, would she have seemed different, stronger, more free?" (94). These thoughts remind her of a blues lyric, which in turn reminds her of a moment of "musical intimacy" (94) during an Odetta concert, when the audience joined in to sing "Amazing Grace." Singing reawakens in Lazarre a sense of the awesome responsibility of mothering black sons and of their vulnerability.

Lazarre sandwiches her experience on the hiring committee between discussions of her sons' vulnerability as black males. Thus she implicitly posits the experience as part of a more general awakening about the vulnerability of being black in the United States, a discovery crucial to the process of "passing over" that the chapter chronicles. Only whereas Lazarre, in her role as mother at the hospital, is able to see her son's "violence" as fear and to comfort him, and whereas at a concert, she can merge her voice with African Americans' in an expression of community, the job search allows no such experience of "passing over." Lazarre neither knows what Suzanne is thinking, nor does Suzanne tell her—as a white professor with power over Suzanne's fate, Lazarre invites distrust, not identification or personal disclosures. Suzanne's aloofness intimidates Lazarre, and, combined with her age, strips Lazarre of her maternal role. Instead, Suzanne's response assigns to Lazarre the role of white oppressor, even as Lazarre's perception of Suzanne's vulnerability and her identification—via her sons and her own insecurities—with this feeling overwhelms her.

Suzanne catches Lazarre in the contradiction of occupying a white social identity while desiring and identifying with a black one. Lazarre's dream captures this contradiction. As the "I" who does not measure up, Lazarre registers her empathy with Suzanne's vulnerability and her inability to mother Suzanne (in the dream, stripped of her maternal authority, she feels like a young child). The dream also conveys her sense that it is she who is being judged—even infantilized—and found inadequate by Suzanne (that the tall woman is racially unmarked—an anomalous ambiguity for Lazarre—enables this interpretation). Moreover, by occupying the position of the powerless woman, Lazarre arguably expresses her wish to dissociate from her position of institutional authority.

Lazarre does a better job exposing her feelings of personal discomfort and failure than she does analyzing the failures of her politics during this job search. Although Lazarre asserts that "objective standards" dictate the decision not to hire Suzanne, the reasons for rejecting her seem questionable, at best. In addition to her impressive resume, Lazarre has noted that "her intelligence and passion for her work are unmistakable" (92). It is Suzanne's "restraint" that seems to be her downfall for "key members of the committee" (92). Lazarre, however, does not address whether "restraint" should be so defining, particularly when Suzanne's response to students—and to Lazarre at the poetry reading—suggests that it is situational. Nor does Lazarre consider how restraint seems to be less the problem than the discomfort it arouses, the reminder it gives Lazarre of her institutional power and whiteness. Moreover, in her focus on her own and Suzanne's emotional landscape, Lazarre does not disclose the role that she played in making the hiring decision, nor does she mention whether the committee ended up hiring someone else, and if so, on what grounds.

Lazarre's account leaves the fairness of the job search unaddressed, and the complexity of its racial politics largely unexplored. Lazarre's identification with Suzanne's vulnerability not only becomes unproductive in a situation in which this identification cannot be recognized, but in fact becomes politically problematic, since Suzanne's "failure" to see past committee members' institutional positions takes precedence over her qualifications. The professional arena remains intensely personal for Lazarre, and her politics are based on a maternal model that too exclusively depends on her feelings and her desire for recognition and intimacy. In the institutional, highly professionalized contexts of a job search, the problems become evident with basing a politics on a personalized, maternal model, especially one that privileges the family as a structure.

The inadequacies of Lazarre's response suggest the limits for white people of countering racism in the academy—one important manifestation of which is the lack of African American faculty members—through a maternal, or familial, model based on intimacy, love, and identification. The genre of memoir also suggests the limits of antiracist work, or a whiteness studies, that focuses too exclusively on individual consciousness, and on transforming feelings. Although absolutely crucial, this is not sufficient. This is perhaps important for those of us who, as academics particularly in an age of identity politics, have become practiced at identifying with and across categories of race, class, gender, and ethnicity in sometimes self-serving or nontransgressive ways and who are all too adept at analyzing ourselves in resistance to, rather than as part of, institutions.

Crossing Back, Moving Forward

This moment in Lazarre's memoir returns us to this chapter's starting point and contributes to an awareness of how contemporary understandings of the personal as political can articulate with reactionary practices and policies in universities. Although the political commitments of my colleague campaigning for the hiring committee—and his analysis of how the personal is political—could not be more opposed to Lazarre's, both their stories indicate the need to rethink this relationship between the personal and the political and to consider critically the ways that identity politics has entered into the mainstream of the academy. Their stories also suggest the importance of developing forms of writing that foreground institutional practices and politics without ignoring the significance of the personal.

What might such forms of writing look like? And how might *This Bridge Called My Back* and other activist anthologies of the 1980s serve as inspiration or provide the basis for such writing?

In teaching a graduate course on contemporary U.S. academic memoirs during the spring 1999 semester, I had the opportunity to think through these questions with class members. The class discussed ways academic memoirs of the 1990s are indebted to and depart from identity-based anthologies of the 1980s. The students, most of whom were already well-versed with *This Bridge* and its successors, found the 1980s

anthologies to be the semester's most compelling and inspirational reading. In contrast, they often responded to the memoirs with impatience
and, occasionally, outrage. From their perspectives as graduate students
and people of color, they provided incisive critiques of how authors of the
memoirs denied or took for granted their institutional privilege, or failed
to challenge academic structures.[18] While exploring the difficulties of using the conventionally literary genre of memoir to do oppositional work
in the academy, we focused on the pitfalls of tenured professors—especially but not exclusively white—writing *This Bridge*–inspired narratives
about their marginalization.

In their own writing projects, however, students evidenced ways that
autobiographical writing by women of color in the 1980s continues to
serve as an important model for combating discrimination. Their projects
suggested how personal narratives that employ identity politics continue
to issue important institutional critiques. Allison Yap, for example, wrote
"An Absence Ever Present," a beautifully lyrical autobiographical narrative that implicitly engages work by Moraga, Anzaldúa, and Hélène
Cixous. The biological daughter of a white mother and a Japanese father,
Yap grew up in Hawai'i with a Chinese father, a white mother, and a
white sister, also adopted. As she traces her family history, Yap effectively
critiques dominant cultural discourses about motherhood, adoption, and
racial identity. Following an exploration of birth certificates, census records, and birthmarks, she asks, "how do you mark belonging?" and goes
on to examine the complex ways that bloodlines, DNA, affectional bonds,
cultural discourses, and institutional structures and definitions pertaining to families, race, and adoption intersect (21). Another member of
the class, Donna Tsuyuko Tanigawa, has published a body of work that
both reflects the influence of women of color writing during the 1980s
and makes groundbreaking contributions to articulating issues of identity
that are distinctive to Hawai'i. For her final class project Tanigawa wrote
about trying to get pregnant as a local Japanese lesbian with limited economic resources. In this essay, "Premature Prologue," she writes, "I learn
what it means to be female in the most expected of places: the exam
table. There I was, naked from the waist down with only a paper blanket to cover me, when I caught on to what was going on with the men"
(6). Chronicling the doctors' overprescription of the fertility drug Clomid
and documenting the various invasive procedures she was subjected to
and their psychic as well as material costs, Tanigawa issues a scathing critique of the medical establishment, even as she preserves a sense of her

and her lover's strength and agency and a formulation of sexuality and reproductive powers that resist definition by this institution. These pieces both demonstrate how narratives premised on identity politics continue to serve counterhegemonic purposes for those who address state agencies and institutions in which they are not authorized or privileged.

That spring semester, class members also explored the importance—and indeed, for those located in the academy in provisional ways, the necessity—of finding alternatives to traditional and even small press publishing venues. As the book publishing industry has become increasingly constricted, technologies developed since *This Bridge*'s 1981 publication have made other means for reaching disparate audiences possible. Class members discussed how desktop publishing and the Internet can combat the elitism attached to book publishing and also can enable experimentation, collaboration, community, and freedom from academic conventions and marketplace pressures. Toward these ends, for his class project Carlo Arreglo started the print zine *Alibata*. As Arreglo explains in the inaugural issue, *Alibata* is the name of the indigenous Philippine script that "flourished before the evil Spanish empire colonized and brutalized the natives in their greedy quest for souls to convert and land to acquire." This first issue features an autobiographical narrative tracing the evolution of Arreglo's Filipino identity, his father's recipes for *mechado*, movie and CD reviews, a mock interview, and writings by friends that exist in sometimes contestatory dialogue with his own representation of Filipino identity. Having been inspired by anthologies of the 1980s, Arreglo emphasizes building community as a way to counter anti-Filipino racism in the U.S. academy. In addition to print zines such as *Alibata*, the blogosphere has become another alternative to the publishing system—and to the academic star system—that also serves as a kind of "memoir-on-the-go".

Shortly after teaching this class, when I received a letter from AnaLouise Keating and Gloria Anzaldúa soliciting work for a new publication to mark the twentieth anniversary of *This Bridge Called My Back*, I put these students in contact with the editors. Tanigawa's essay, "Premature," was published in the anthology that came to be called *This Bridge We Call Home: Radical Visions for Transformation*. Yap's piece, too, was selected, but the editors instead made plans to include it in a second book, one on telling stories and bearing witness, after Routledge insisted that the manuscript be drastically reduced from 1,300 to 850 pages.[19] Even as Anzaldúa's and Keating's negotiations with Routledge over the length of the book were symptomatic of the economic strictures of the academic publishing industry, the abundance of first-rate publishable pieces that encompassed a variety of themes illustrated the ongoing influence of *This Bridge Called My Back* and of a politics of identity.

This Bridge We Call Home evidences *This Bridge*'s arrival into the academy—one that carries new possibilities, and also restrictions. In part, this simultaneous gain and loss is symbolized by the change in publisher from the small but visionary Kitchen Table: Women of Color Press to Routledge—a press with cultural capital in the humanities and with the ability to market its books aggressively. Moreover, as Keating herself notes in her introduction to *This Bridge We Call Home*, the anthology includes far more pieces written in the language of theory, and these essays again suggest that contributors have achieved a location from which to continue their struggles—one that comes with the pitfalls and possibilities that legitimacy brings. Keating tells of her initial reaction of "astonishment, bewilderment, dismay, and concern" when she receives stacks of theoretical submissions by self-identified women of color: noting to Anzaldúa that *Bridge* "'has been repeatedly praised for its oppositional stance to the academy, . . . for its challenge to high theory,'" she wonders, "How could so many people respond to our call for papers . . . with such theoretical pieces? . . . [D]oes this use of theory indicate that they've been seduced by the academy, that they're 'white' academic clones/drones? Or is there something else going on here?" (12–13). Keating comes to the conclusion that theory cannot be equated with the desire "to achieve status within the academic system" (14), but that it can be used in "academic guerilla battles" (14). Sections in *This Bridge We Call Home* are structured to explore how contributors can use theory to wage war on the academy, to demand accountability of the institutions in which they are unequally located.

Such struggles were in my mind when formulating my own contribution to *This Bridge We Call Home* (a version of which appears in this chapter); so too was the first piece of writing that Donna Tanigawa wrote for my academic memoir class. That essay, titled "Interventions," has informed my thinking about how to build on 1980s identity-based writings in order to challenge the exclusions of contemporary academic culture; it also has informed the conceptualization of this chapter because it richly illuminates interrelations among different formulations of the personal as political. Tanigawa begins "Interventions" with personal narrative in a style reminiscent of *This Bridge*. Significantly, this narrative addresses—

and evidences the overcoming of—writer's block. Tanigawa details the personal costs of having published writing that breaks cultural and family silences, and also explores how graduate school curtailed her creativity and her sense of purpose in writing. Next, "Interventions" details a series of events in which women faculty (both white and of color) acted insensitively to local graduate students. This account includes excerpts from collectively authored e-mails in which Tanigawa and other graduate students called faculty members on misusing their institutional power. In contrast to the essay's wry and intimate first section, the e-mail excerpts and the accompanying commentary were at once impersonal in their institutional analysis and animated by anger.

The two sections of "Interventions" involved, for Tanigawa, different kinds of risks and breakthroughs, and a willingness to work from and through positions of discomfort. My interests here lie particularly with the second part of Tanigawa's essay and its departure from a focus on personal feelings and categories of identity (expected moves in an identity politics framework), to a less scripted exploration of institutional location and its intersections with racial, class, and gender identities. In the contexts of the academy, this shift—and Tanigawa's willingness to confront academic feminists with institutional power over her—felt particularly risky, productive, and important.[20] Indeed, "Interventions" served as the impetus for this chapter's opening account of departmental e-mail exchanges. Tanigawa's essay impressed on me the possibilities of circulating collectively written, local, ephemeral pieces of writing in a more formal and enduring format, one that allows for a wider audience and a different though related set of academic interventions.

Tanigawa's "Interventions" also prompted me to reflect on my own institutional identity. I found this reflection uncomfortable. As Tanigawa's narrative makes clear, my anxiety is not idiosyncratic. Although Tanigawa explains how the e-mail she sent was directed to only a few faculty members, she tells of how these faculty forwarded it to other women faculty, who in turn responded as if they were being personally criticized for upholding institutional structures that are oppressive to local graduate students. I attribute their—and my own—discomfort and defensiveness to my sense that although left-leaning academics have become accustomed to thinking through identities of race, gender, class, and sexuality, an identity politics that foregrounds institutional location feels not only more unfamiliar, but also more threatening. In ways that the next two chapters of *Academic Lives* explore in greater depth, not only are questions of institutional identity less theorized, but they also are more commonly disavowed or ignored. For academics whose work is premised on oppositional alliances or marginalized forms of identity, attention to our institutional identities can be a source of anxiety because—unlike other dominant identities—they are chosen ones that in various and complex ways position us as part of, rather than poise us against, a hegemonic institution. Tanigawa's "Interventions" is powerful in its demand that faculty members acknowledge and reflect on how responsibly we are using our institutional power, and on how our institutional identities relate to our political commitments, personal feelings, and experiences of and claims to marginalization.

Tanigawa's "Interventions" also suggests an important linkage between personal writings and those that are institutionally directed: in this essay, the institutional account follows the more personal one, even as the collective, institutionally aimed writings she describes enabled her return to the personal. I am not, then, positing a developmental narrative: both modes of expression are important and necessary, and each serves different purposes. Moreover, in their combination, something new happens to each. The two parts of "Interventions" exist in a dynamic relationship, one that reinvigorates and reopens questions of how the personal is political, and the political, personal.

If "Interventions" stages the tensions between the personal and the institutional, *This Bridge We Call Home* demarcates a different set of tensions, as its entries on identity politics exist alongside those that its editors define as instances of spiritual activism, or "spirituality for social change" (18). Remarking on these two trends, Keating notes, "What a contrast: while identity requires holding onto specific categories of identity, spiritual activism demands that we let them go" (18). Whereas the identity-based entries often take the form of both political protest and theoretical writing and urge specific institutional changes, the spiritually based entries manifest more as "ritual . . . prayer . . . blessing . . . for transformation," as "a port you moor to in all storms," and as a movement of inclusiveness that harms and excludes none, as Anzaldúa puts it in "Now Let Us Shift . . . the Path of Conocimiento . . . Inner Work, Public Acts," the piece that concludes *This Bridge We Call Home* (576, 572, 576). This spiritual expression is one of the most powerful currents that courses through the collection, and it encompasses a kind of knowing that takes place outside of institutions entirely, one for which there are no degrees awarded or jobs offered. (It is, I think, no accident that by the time that Anzaldúa coedits *This Bridge We Call Home* she has left academe, even as her work continues to be of profound importance to it.) Although Anzaldúa's "Now Let Us Shift" gets the final word in *This Bridge We Call Home*, this spiritually based writing and writing founded on an identity politics exist alongside one another, both powerfully present, with no easy resolution.

This Bridge We Call Home exists in a dynamic relationship to the memoirs explored in *Academic Lives*. Contributors to the 2002 anthology who continue to build on an identity politics respond, in part, precisely to what the shortcomings of the memoirs explored in this chapter reveal: that the inroads of identity politics into the academy—including the development of whiteness studies—have not obviated the need to continue to find ways to disrupt the operations of racist and other oppressive identity-based structures of power. At the same time, academics writing their memoirs, including those who are complicit in these structures, share some of the profound spiritual dissatisfactions that contributors to *This Bridge We Call Home* have with academe. *Academic Lives* takes up this topic from a variety of angles, along with a consideration as to whether, and how, those working from within the academy today can bridge the desires to feed spiritual hunger, with those to right social injustices and perform institutional analysis.

CHAPTER 3

Postcolonial Studies and Memoirs of Travel,
Diaspora, and Exile

Doris Duke's Shangri La and Architectures of Autobiography

In 2003, ten years after Doris Duke's death, portions of her Honolulu
home, Shangri La, were opened for public touring. The product of a
passion for Islamic art that Duke developed on her eight-month honeymoon when she visited the Taj Mahal, Shangri La houses the fifth-largest
collection of Islamic art in the United States. Before taking a museum
shuttle to this well-hidden, oceanfront home, visitors begin their tour
at the Honolulu Academy of Art with a video. In *Creating Shangri La*,
University of Hawai'i professor of architecture Kazi Ashraf states, "I see
the house as kind of an autobiography of Doris Duke. Some people write
diaries. Doris Duke built" (Noey).

Shangri La is an Orientalist fantasy as well as a kind of autobiography.
Although much of Islamic art is religious, Duke was not Muslim. And yet
Duke's investments in Islamic art cannot be dismissed as superficial: her
adult life was largely occupied by the study and acquisition of this art; she
oversaw every detail of the construction of Shangri La, a lifelong undertaking. Her control over its design ranged from its architectural layout
to the cleaning with cotton swabs of the entire grime-encrusted interior
of an eighteenth-century Syrian room that she purchased through New
York University. She put the objects to decidedly unconventional uses; for
example, the dining room table is made from a bed, and Duke fashioned
lamps by drilling holes through seventh-century vases. In the house's central courtyard, she achieved her desired "magical Arabian Nights quality"
by adhering strings of Christmas lights inside metal lamps so intricately
carved that they appear to be made of lace. She arranged other pieces
with equal disregard for tradition: mosaics are displayed like pictures in
a Western art gallery, and none of her several mihrabs, or prayer altars
used to orient Muslims in Saudi Arabia toward Mecca, face East. Moreover, although Duke archived every bill of sale, she did not consistently
document the time periods or origins of her 3,600 (and counting) art
pieces. She mixed and matched objects from different Islamic countries
and time periods with one another and with contemporary Western-style

furniture, including an enormous Baccharat chandelier originally made for the Islamic market. Duke's Shangri La is a highly personal and, as its name suggests, in many ways a Western vision, one without counterpart in any Islamic country.

A cultural hybrid, Shangri La not only combines East and West but also draws on its location in Hawai'i. The incongruous location for Duke's home and its major collection of Islamic art owes to Duke's honeymoon travels coupled with her attraction to surfing culture. A serious athlete, Duke settled in Hawai'i after visiting it as part of the same honeymoon that brought her before the Taj Mahal, and she consorted with world-class Hawaiian surfers including the Kahanamoku brothers, who gave her the Hawaiian name Lahilahi. With state-of-the-art technology, Shangri La features screened interiorized spaces that are a hallmark of Islamic architecture that transform with the touch of a button into Hawaiian-style outdoor spaces that open Shangri La to dramatic views of the ocean, the lush tropical landscaping, and the cooling trade winds. The living room reflects this cultural mixing as well as Duke's disregard for the spiritual meanings or histories of her art objects: what Duke called the house's "focal point," a mihrab made by a famous artisan in 1265 for an individual's tomb (and a piece for which Duke outbid the Metropolitan Museum of Art) occupies most of the western wall. This mihrab is counterbalanced with a striking view of Diamond Head Crater, O'ahu's eastern landmark. Floors made of polished coral or volcanic rock indigenize the Islamic practice of fashioning art from locally available materials. Thus the home draws eclectically on both Islamic and Hawaiian orientations, materials, and cultural traditions, creating not only disjunctions but also crossings and connections among different parts of the world as Duke's routes of travel, architectural assemblages, and art collecting also conjoin them.

Financed by the Duke family fortune to which Doris Duke was sole heir, the house is the product of unimaginable wealth. Enormous mosaics and entire ceilings were commissioned from around the world and shipped in, and 150 workers were employed full-time for two and a half years to build the house. Duke even called on President Franklin D. Roosevelt's assistance in order to trade six miles of her choice beachfront land across the island, in Kailua, to buy the land beneath the ocean contiguous with Shangri La (our tour guide speculates that she is the only Hawai'i resident with the capital and influence to have achieved such ownership). This extraordinary purchase enabled her to excavate the coral she wanted for her floors. In short, Shangri La is a heavily financed fantasy, one whose structure depends on capital derived from the Duke family tobacco fortune.

An idiosyncratic and autocratic woman with the means to build her fantasy home, Duke also had the power to insist that those allowed entry to Shangri La (and there were not many) conform to her carefully constructed world. She was famous, among other things, for firing anyone who failed to refer to her many dogs as children, and for terminating any employee caught smoking cigarettes on her property. The longtime head caretaker for Shangri La, Jin De Silva, who now shows Shangri La to visitors as part of his job, tells, however, of a time that he once challenged Duke on this rule, asking her how she would get her millions without smokers.

I introduce these details and anecdotes about Shangri La, which I will return to later, as a way to sound the keynotes of this chapter. If houses, like autobiographies or memoirs, can be social spaces in which one constructs one's identity, identity itself occupies a social space. As Linda Martín Alcoff explains, "To say that we have an identity is just to say that we have a location in social space, a hermeneutic horizon that is both grounded in a location and an opening or site from which we attempt to know the world" (335). In this chapter, considerations of Cathy Davidson's *Thirty-six Views of Mount Fuji: On Finding Myself in Japan* (1993), David Mura's *Turning Japanese: Memoirs of a Sansei* (1991), and Edward Said's *Out of Place: A Memoir* (1999) demonstrate identity, home, and autobiography to be complexly constructed and interconnected social spaces. As does Shangri La, these memoirs enable explorations of the interconnections among identity, home, travel, and Orientalism; the economics that, almost always invisibly, structure and sustain "personal" fantasies and ideological investments; and the connections among disparate colonial sites and East-West cultural crossings that can be structurally analyzed and accounted for even as individuals' experiences of them are neither predetermined nor predictable.

These memoirs also provide a window into how academics' insights central to postcolonial theory have shaped—as well as eluded—the most "private" of spaces. The memoirs I consider here participate in studies of diaspora, transnationalism, globalization, travel, and cosmopolitanism, all of which came into prominence in the humanities in the 1990s alongside postcolonial studies. Although each of these newly constituted fields has its own history and set of concerns, they form a constellation at the center of which is postcolonial studies. As I trace the footprint of postcolonial studies and related areas of study in memoirs not only by postcolonial scholars (Said) but also by those in fields influenced by postcolonial studies (Davidson and Mura), I am especially interested in accounting for the persistence of, as well as the resistance to, Orientalism and exclusionary forms of cosmopolitanism and humanism. I find that these memoirs reveal what theory often can mask: ways postcolonial studies remains implicated in colonial epistemologies and ideologies. At the same time, perhaps especially when they defy the categories of the theoretical and the political, I argue that memoirs present academics with possibilities for disseminating postcolonial ways of seeing beyond the parameters of the academy.

Academic memoirs focused on diaspora, colonialism, travel, or exile emerged as an important subgenre during the 1990s, reflecting humanities scholars' preoccupation with issues of racial and cultural alterity. A number of these memoirs come from Asian-born academics living in the United States—for example, Meena Alexander, *Fault Lines*; Amitava Kumar, *Passport Photos*; Shirley Lim, *Among the White Moon Faces*; and Sara Suleri, *Meatless Days*. Academics born on the African continent also employ memoir to consider experiences of diaspora or displacement and exile (André Aciman, *Out of Egypt*; Leila Ahmed, *A Border Passage*; Manthia Diawara, *In Search of Africa*). White academics, too, use the movement across national boundaries to investigate and sometimes unfix racial or national identity, as Davidson does in *Thirty-six Views*. Some of these academics are U.S. born (e.g., Alice Kaplan, in *French Lessons*, or John Whittier Treat, in *Great Mirrors Shattered: Homosexuality, Orientalism and Japan*), whereas others trace their relations to birthplaces that include South Africa (Rob Nixon, in *Dreambirds*), Austria (Marjorie Perloff, in *The Vienna Paradox*), or Bolivia (Leo Spitzer, in *Hotel Bolivia*). Despite their substantial differences, all of these authors use memoir to highlight movement across national borders in order to demonstrate the construction, complexity, and hybridity of identities that ethnic, racial, or national labels can simplify or essentialize.

No three memoirs could fully represent this diverse new body of work and its significance. However, because Davidson, Mura, and Said each occupy influential positions in the academy and hold different theoretical and experiential vantage points, taken together, their memoirs constitute apt case studies to gauge the inroads into the 1990s academy of postcolonial studies and related fields that engage racial and cultural otherness. Davidson, formerly a professor of English and now the vice provost for interdisciplinary studies at Duke University, is a leading scholar in the field of American studies. A recent president of the American Studies Association and one of the profession's most respected scholars, she writes and edits important academic books and journals that demonstrate keen awareness of the turn in American studies to questions of race, nation, and empire. Mura, best known as a poet, did graduate work in English and frequently teaches and gives readings at universities. Although as is true for many creative writers Mura is mobile and positioned both within and outside of academic institutions, he participates actively in the Association for Asian American Studies, often contributes to debates on multiculturalism and U.S. racial politics, and engages issues of cosmopolitanism and diasporic identity.[1] Until his death in 2003, Said, University Professor at Columbia, served as a relentless and preeminent critic of Western imperialism, as an eloquent spokesperson regarding the pains of exile, and as an advocate for Palestinians' claim to their homeland. Despite his contentious relationship to "postcolonial studies," Said is often described as having founded it with his 1978 book *Orientalism*. As these authors translate their various theoretical and political commitments to the memoir genre, they not only provide a way to map the impact on the humanities of postcolonial and related fields of studies, but they also afford key insights into these fields' possibilities and limitations in thinking through questions of race, culture, and nation that are at the forefront of both the academy's and America's political consciousness.

In particular, the memoirs reflect contemporary intellectuals' commitments to addressing problems of ethnocentrism and imperialism through a renewed interest in cosmopolitanism.[2] Timothy Brennan finds cosmopolitanism to be "the political ethic of the [contemporary] humanities intellectual" (*Wars of Position* 136). As Pheng Cheah explains, cosmopolitanism is "derived from . . . a composite of the Greek words for 'world' and 'citizen,'" and in its traditional meaning, it designates a "universal humanism" ("Introduction" 22). Most articulations of cosmopolitanism in the 1990s, however, respond to the related conditions of globalization and postcolonial migrancy and come from a poststructuralist perspective that disavows the possibility of a single universal humanism. At the same time, its critics, often working from a postcolonial studies perspective, have remarked on how celebrations of cosmopolitanism, or "world citizenship," ignore networks of power as they overemphasize feelings, rely in unacknowledged ways on the nation-state, and deny racial others membership in a cosmopolitan identity.

The memoirs analyzed in this chapter illuminate how contemporary conceptualizations of cosmopolitanism support as well as undermine a postcolonial (or anticolonial, antiracist) politics. In accounts of their travels to Japan in the 1980s in *Thirty-six Views* and *Turning Japanese*, as Davidson and Mura represent the crossing of national borders, they adopt a cosmopolitanism that at times results in a reinscription of a traditional humanism and Orientalism. Their memoirs' most "personal" disclosures reveal—in ways theory can mask—how cosmopolitanism remains a stubbornly Western concept, one rooted in the nation-state and a capitalist consumer economy. By contrast I argue that Said shows how memoir can be utilized, in combination with a postcolonial perspective, to put into circulation a more worldly viewpoint, one that maintains the interplay among different local, global, and national identities.

Said's memoir, together with Davidson's and Mura's, engages not only cosmopolitan studies but also the related and influential new field of diaspora studies, in especially telling ways. The 1990s saw an outpouring of scholarship theorizing diaspora as a response to present-day conditions of "decolonization, increased immigration, global communications, and transport" (Clifford 249). As Jana Evans Braziel and Anita Mannur observe in their 2003 reader, *Theorizing Diaspora*, "theorizations of diaspora have acquired an increasingly important space within critical discourse on race, ethnicity, nation, and identity" (5–6). At the same time, they observe, these theorizations "have been hotly contested and critiqued" (6). In addition to charges that diaspora theory is ahistorical, its critics also find that it often too quickly dismisses (its implications in) corporate globalization and nationalism.

Because memoirs that address experiences of diaspora are necessarily grounded in specific locations and histories, they sometimes have served as antidotes to theorizations of diaspora that are too abstract or generalizing, even as they, too, can justify or obscure the power of nation-states *and* the workings of transnational capital.[3] In *Cartographies of Diaspora*, Avtar Brah remarks on how autobiography has acted as a genre through which diasporic formulations of identity are at once given specific expression *and* require critical analysis. She claims that autobiographical accounts are important for "the way in which they reveal how the same geographical space comes to articulate different histories and meanings." At the same time she finds that autobiographies underscore "that diasporic or border positionality does not *in itself* assure a vantage point of privileged insight into and understanding of relations of power"

(207–8). As I look to memoirs by those who not only have lived experiences of diaspora but who also are immersed in theorizations of it, I argue that just as diasporic positionality does not guarantee a privileged vantage point, neither does being versed in theories of diaspora. Rather, academic memoirs reveal the various ways and the extent to which these theories have impacted academics' perceptions and representations of their experiences.

I am also interested in how the memoirs articulate with theorizations of travel writing—an area of exploration that emerges from postcolonial studies and that overlaps with studies of diaspora and cosmopolitanism. In the 1990s critics began addressing how travel writing, which has been "canonized in the form of autobiographical narrative" (Pratt 171), is thoroughly implicated in imperialist projects. In this chapter I investigate how academics writing memoirs are contributing to critiques of travel writing, and ways their memoirs also continue to participate in colonialist enterprises undaunted by third world decolonization struggles and chastisements issued from postcolonial critics.

In exploring memoirs by Davidson, Mura, and Said, one of my aims is to think about how and why they support as well as contradict, challenge, and provide alternatives to reigning theories about travel. More broadly speaking, analysis of these memoirs suggests the power of and possibilities for disseminating what can loosely be referred to as postcolonial ways of seeing, inside and outside the academy. While both Davidson and Mura point to the constructedness of national forms of identity that they question and sometimes disavow, they also represent Japan and the United States as distinct and often opposing nations. Both writers underline the existing power of national identities and, to varying degrees, explore ongoing forms of colonialism and Orientalism. In doing so they both resist the imperialist tendencies of much travel writing and, in keeping with some postcolonial theory, oppose theories of transnationalism and globalization that claim nation-states to be obsolete. However, as their memoirs support the connection among geopolitical sites, identity, and culture, this happens not only in self-conscious and oppositional ways but also in ways that are complicit with national narratives that depend on, even as they render invisible, forms of exclusion along lines of race, class, gender, and sexuality. Such moments frequently take place during particularly personal moments in the memoirs, and reinscribe forms of Orientalism and other oppressive discourses that the writers otherwise work to contravene. I find these moments significant for the questions that they raise: Why do writers with the academic training to challenge exclusionary forms of nationalism and Orientalism produce works that in some ways reestablish such discourses? And why does this happen when things get most personal? As I argue, often the genre of memoir does not merely allow for but in fact facilitates unproductive and often uncritical—if revealing—contradictions between the personal and the political. Such contradictions constitute a view into the political unconscious of postcolonial studies: memoirs offer places to track the affects of contemporary theories that pertain to race, nation, and culture, both in terms of their failings, and in terms of their success in transforming reigning ideologies. By concluding with a discussion that relates Said's *Out of Place* to Davidson's and Mura's memoirs, I explore how, as Said chronicles his forced exile from Palestine, his memoir serves as a reminder that theories of travel, cosmopolitanism, diaspora, exile and immigration cannot be collapsed even as they might take up related questions. I also look to how Said's "pre-political" and inward-looking perspective and his use of a genre based in Western forms of individualism and exclusionary humanism paradoxically enables him to advance the anti-imperialist teachings of postcolonial studies.

The Economics of Fantasy and Friendship

In "Flexible Citizenship among Chinese Cosmopolitans," Aihwa Ong tells how David Murdock, chairman and CEO of Dole Foods Company, delivered a keynote address in 1991 at a conference in Los Angeles on Asian Americans. Murdock, who Ong says "personifies corporate America," advocated that Asian Americans use their ties to Asia to "help Americans achieve political and business success" in Asia (154). As Ong notes, "by defining a role for Asian Americans as good citizens and trade ambassadors, Murdock's speech situated them in the wider narrative of the Oriental as trade enemy" (154).

Murdock's advice that Asian Americans serve as "trade ambassadors" follows from a direct line of arguments about immigration for Asians, and this formulation of ambassadorship is one that resonates with Cathy Davidson in *Thirty-six Views of Mount Fuji: On Finding Myself in Japan*, her memoir about her four trips to Japan in the 1980s.[4] In her introductory remarks Davidson explains that she liked to think of herself and the Japanese professor she was on exchange with during her initial year-long trip to Japan "as minor goodwill ambassadors" (8) who could work against the racial and cultural tensions between Japanese and American people that were running high in the 1980s, especially, as she notes, with the U.S. auto industry in crisis.[5] Her 1993 memoir seems to assume a similar function of goodwill ambassadorship, written as it was during a period when Japan bashing was becoming an all-too-frequent response by Americans to Japan's spectacular economic and technological successes and to a trade imbalance that stood about 50 billion dollars in Japan's favor.[6]

Clearly, Davidson's motives in proposing that she and her colleague serve as goodwill ambassadors differ from Murdock's urgings that Asian Americans take on the role of trade ambassadors: Davidson desires to promote intercultural harmony; whereas, Murdock wants Americans to regain their competitive edge over Asians and combat their trade deficit. At the same time Davidson, like Murdock, focuses on the importance of nation-states, and she positions individuals (herself and her Japanese colleague) as their representatives. In Murdock's formulation Asian Americans can, by virtue of their racial and cultural background, cross national lines in order to reassert them. In Davidson's example, race, nation, and culture align more neatly: because in *Thirty-six Views* Davidson alone stands in for America, whiteness lines up with Americanness, and Japanese racial and cultural identity line up with national identity. As a result of this representative schema (one naturalized by the individualist genre of memoir), Davidson's form of ambassadorship converges at times with Murdock's so that, however inadvertently, *Thirty-six Views* upholds as well as undermines forms of U.S. capitalism and nationalism that Murdock unabashedly supports. At the same time, Davidson's memoir reflects her immersion in cultural theories characterized by opposition to these hegemonic formations.[7] Davidson's conviction that the writer abroad can serve as cultural ambassador is accompanied by a critical orientation in keeping with contemporary cultural theories about race, gender, and nation—especially theories of travel and cosmopolitanism. As memoir enables Davidson to bring together these two approaches, it demonstrates how theories of travel and cosmopolitanism can dovetail in unexpected ways with ideologies that support global capitalism and nationalism. As memoir, *Thirty-six Views* is uniquely positioned to reveal—in a way that "pure" theory cannot—not only the failures of counterhegemonic theoretical positions (here, postcolonial critiques of travel) to effect transformations at the level of feelings rather than intellect, but also the limitations of basing theories (here, of cosmopolitanism) on sentiments without attention to structures of power.

Published by Plume, a trade house, Davidson's memoir constitutes part of her efforts to emotionally engage an audience that extends beyond the academy. In her 2004 introduction to the expanded edition of her groundbreaking 1986 book, *Revolution and the Word*, Davidson comments, "The ability to stir affect into action (individual or collective) has been a particular function of the artist" (27). As Davidson undertakes in the early 1990s the writing of memoir and a "coffee table" book that chronicles "the human cost of postindustrialism" (Bramberger and Davidson 222) through its history of a furniture company, she can be seen to be appealing to affect to promote social change. Although affective impact is difficult to gauge, *Thirty-six Views* received favorable reviews from venues including the *New York Times*, *Elle*, the *Washington Post*, *Book World*, and *Publishers Weekly*. It also reached an academic readership and continues to circulate among humanities scholars; Duke University Press reissued the book in 2006.

In *Thirty-six Views* Davidson carries out her role as "goodwill ambassador" by using often wry or humorous personal narrative to explain and attempt to diminish the nonessentialist nature of differences between Japanese and Americans. Implicitly drawing on poststructuralist theories of the constructed and fluid nature of cultural and racial differences, in *Thirty-six Views* Davidson explains these differences in order to lessen tensions and increase understanding between the United States and Japan. The memoir's opening chapter, "Seeing and Being Seen," is exemplary in this regard. Having just arrived in Japan where she will be teaching English at "Kansai University" (presumably Kobe Women's College), Davidson receives a memo requesting that she please go for a "health examination." Misinterpreting this suggestion as a requirement, Davidson enters an auditorium full of students for the exam. A focus of attention as the only white foreigner and professor, Davidson's discomfort peaks when she has to put a urine sample into a clear cup. Because she is on medication for a bladder infection, her urine is a brilliant blue. When she must walk her sample around the auditorium, she imagines that the staring students assume blue pee to be a white American phenomenon. At the same time as Davidson dramatizes the misconceptions that underwrite viewing racial, national, or cultural others as alien beings with different biological makeups, she establishes the learned cultural differences that distinguish her behavior from that of the Japanese women: as she watches them change from their clothes into hospital gowns without revealing any extra flesh, she realizes, "My American body didn't know how to do that Houdini bit with the underwear" (10). However, by the time she receives her chest X-ray, she has studied the girls' method, and the watching students applaud her newly acquired discretion. Here, as Davidson represents cultural differences as learned, she does not dismiss their importance because they are not "natural." Such moments quite literally embody ways those in postcolonial and related fields of study employ poststructuralist understandings of race, ethnicity, and culture without forgoing attention to their material effects.

Over a decade after the first publication of *Thirty-six Views*, Davidson's new afterword highlights the memoir's controlled playing out of cultural theory. When Davidson describes a 2005 visit to Japanese potter Naosaku Shogen, she recalls how, on her initial visit, she admired a vase with "smoky smudges and sprinkles of silver. . . . 'Frog pee,' he [Naosaku] said, and Maryvonne translated with glee" (236). In 2005 when Davidson buys another vase, she describes Naosaku's response: "'No frog pee,' he joked" (236). When concluding the afterword, Davidson tells of how a professor from Kansai Women's University agrees with her when she says, "'Everything has changed'" since she taught there. Then, he adds, "'Everything, that is, except for the school health exam'" (240). As the two reminisce about how students assumed that blue pee marked essential differences between Japanese and Americans, this bygone moment of cultural miscommunication contrasts both to the achieved understanding and affection between Davidson and her Japanese host, and also to the moment where exotically colored pee truly does demarcate interspecies difference.

As Davidson's memoir explores two-directional cultural miscommunications and foregrounds the importance—and difficulties as well as possibilities—of intercultural exchanges and communications, it departs from traditional travel narratives that scholars including Mary Louise Pratt have critiqued for positing a one-way gaze between the all-knowing and all-seeing writer ("the seeing-man") and his or her subject. By titling her first chapter "Seeing and Being Seen," Davidson signals awareness of studies of travel writing that are emerging when she writes her memoir, and *Thirty-six Views* counters practices scholars such as Pratt critique. However, Davidson does not entirely break free of conventions of travel writing and ethnography; her memoir exists in a complex relation to each. As the subtitle "*On Finding Myself in Japan*" suggests, the memoir is as much about self-discovery as it is about Japan. The subtitle's passive language also locates Davidson in Japan seemingly accidentally and without agency (a trope of conventional travel writing), thus high-lighting how *Thirty-six Views* as a memoir concerned with self-discovery can exist in tension with *Thirty-six Views* as travel writing that addresses the pitfalls and responsibilities of deliberately undertaken intercultural exploration. What the memoir makes manifest, in other words, is both the impact of contemporaneous theories of travel, and also, especially in its most "personal" moments, how persistent dominant ideologies that attend travel remain in the humanities, notwithstanding academics' criti-cal awareness.

In significant and self-reflexive ways Davidson uses memoir to embody alternatives to problems in travel writing that its critics have denounced. In the views that she provides of Japan, she underlines her own failures in communication, and works against "the belief that the entire world is equally available to be occupied or represented or identified by any subject" that Caren Kaplan finds "is just another manifestation of impe-rialism" (127). For example, the chapter title "Typical Japanese Women" evokes the methodology of traditional anthropology, only to assert the impossibility of delivering the information the title promises. In that chapter, as Davidson scrupulously counters scholarly claims and wide-spread assumptions in the United States that American gender roles are more liberatory than Japanese ones, she resists a tradition of nineteenth-century British women's travel writing which, in defining Western wom-en's freedom in opposition to Eastern women's oppression, supported English nationalism and imperialism.[8] Davidson's feminism works against this history of Orientalist travel writing and white liberal feminism.[9] In-stead, Davidson's memoir partakes in anticolonial feminist critiques of travel emerging in the 1990s by scholars such as Pratt, Inderpal Grewal, Mary Layoun, and Mari Yoshihara.

Through her use of Mount Fuji as a controlling metaphor, Davidson also calls up the conventions of travel writing, only to complicate them by emphasizing that the traveler's perspective is personal and partial. In *Imperial Eyes*, Pratt connects the attitudes of many contemporary travel writers to the imperialist ones of their predecessors. Noting that the end of colonial rule in much of Asia and Africa has not disrupted many travel writers' attempts to dominate the former colonies therein, Pratt com-ments, "lament as they might, these seeing-men do not relinquish their promontories and their sketch books" (220). On the one hand, Davidson's use in her title of Mount Fuji, noted in passing by Dorinne Kondo to be "the most hackneyed Orientalist image" of Japan, evokes Pratt's "seeing-man" and his sweeping view from above (*About Face* 77). On the other hand, Davidson uses Mount Fuji to express not domination but incomplete, partial, and subjective vision, and in the memoir she discloses having caught a glimpse of Mount Fuji only once, during her fourth visit to Japan.

And yet, with the discussions of Mount Fuji that frame the memoir, Davidson departs from, only to effect a return to, basic tenets of travel writing. As she explains in her preface, Davidson takes her title from a series of nineteenth-century wood-block prints by Katsushika Hokusai, and she includes illustrations from this series at the start of each chapter. She explains how the series "portrays the different, even contradictory, aspects of Japanese life. . . . The only constant is Mount Fuji, symbol of that which is permanent or unchanging in Japan. Hokusai does nothing to reconcile contradictions, but the presence of the mountain suggests that all of the views, taken together, make up Japan" (1). She further notes how Hokusai's woodcuts reinforce "the basic Buddhist (and quintessentially Japanese) idea that the person closest to a subject or event can never really see it. Sometimes it is the person passing through and at a remove who has the clearest view" (4). She concludes the preface by saying, "As an American writing about Japan, I'm hoping that Hokusai is right" (4). She circles back to this idea in her conclusion, followed by a teasing affirmation from a Japanese friend. She tells her friend Koichi, who is visiting her in North Carolina, that her current favorite of Hokusai's prints is "one where you can't see Mount Fuji because the pilgrims are actually on the mountain. I like the concept. How you can never really see what you're in the midst of, what you're closest to'" (288). In response Koichi jumps up and peers out of Davidson's window, delivering the memoir's last words with a sly twinkle in his eye: "'From here I cannot see Mount Fuji'" (288). As Koichi reminds Davidson that, her Japanese-style house notwithstanding, she is not in Japan (let alone standing on Mount Fuji!), he simultaneously affirms the clarity of her insights into Japan. Through her use of Hokusai's prints and his philosophy, Davidson avoids approaching Japan through a Western gaze. And yet Hokusai makes possible the memoir's claim to attaining wholeness through fragmented vision—something a Western postmodernist approach would not allow—and her Japanese friend serves to authorize this vision. Thus, through Hokusai and his Buddhist principles, and through intercultural friendship, Davidson reroutes "the seeing man's" mastery. Davidson's afterword in the 2006 edition, introduced by a woodcut that features a laborer using a brush to touch up a large circular structure set against a backdrop of a barely discernible Mount Fuji, further reinforces her memoir's vision, as it brings the book, its view of Japan, and Davidson herself full circle. The mastery (and its imperialist overtones) that the frame, both in 1993 and again in 2006, circuitously lays claim to works to contain the critiques it issues of travel writing.

The memoir articulates in similarly complex ways with attempts in the humanities to reclaim cosmopolitanism, and to reconcile it with patriotism. Martha Nussbaum, cosmopolitanism's best-known proponent in the 1990s academy, advocates in her hugely influential 1994 essay "Patriotism and Cosmopolitanism" the teaching of allegiance not to the nation in which one is situated but rather to a "moral community made up by the humanity of all human beings" (7). To achieve this vision of world citizenry—one that builds on the Stoic Diogenes as well as on Tagore and on Kant's ideal of "universal hospitality"—the American must be able, through imagination, to enter the lives of people from other nations. Nussbaum's call in this essay is one to which preeminent scholars in the humanities vigorously responded, first in the *Boston Review*, and then in the 1996 collection *For Love of Country?* Through the complex way she inhabits the role of "goodwill ambassador," Davidson enacts through memoir the cosmopolitan pedagogy that Nussbaum and some of the *For Love of Country?* respondents endorse. In Japan, as Davidson enters the lives of Japanese people, she represents America. However, in writing about her time in Japan, she represents Japan, extending to her U.S. readership imaginative entry into the lives of Japanese people. Through this double positioning, her "goodwill ambassadorship" is not one of allegiance to a single national identity, but instead positions her as a "world citizen." Davidson's new afterword develops this stance. Davidson begins by situating herself not in relation to September 11, 2001 (an increasingly standard move, especially for American studies scholars, and one that Nussbaum herself makes in the 2002 reissuing of *For Love of Country?*), but rather in relationship to the Great Hanshin Earthquake that hit Kobe in 1995. Working against nationalist lines of identification and alliance without disavowing her American identity, she describes feeling this event as keenly as she did September 11 and Hurricane Katrina (234). This account resonates with Nussbaum's cosmopolitan call in *For Love of Country?*, issued in the wake of September 11, for U.S. citizens to "renew our commitment to the equal worth of humanity, demanding media, and schools, that nourish and expand our imaginations by presenting non-American lives as deep, rich, and emotion-worthy" ("Introduction" xiv). Davidson's afterword develops her cosmopolitanism as more than a feeling as it depicts a world interconnected by globalization (one of cosmopolitan theory's key claims) when she tells of how a friend from Kyoto is able to reach her by telephone in North Carolina before being able to call other parts of Japan (234).

As Davidson adopts a cosmopolitan vision, she is clearly conscious of and works to counter the dangers that have attended previous models of cosmopolitanism—namely, false universalisms, ethnocentrism and Orientalism, and romanticizing other cultures, or cultural others. Instead, in her representations of intercultural exchange she often interrogates in nuanced ways her own fantasies about and attractions to Japan, as well as Japanese fantasies about America (and, in so doing, she supports Nussbaum's contention in "Patriotism" that "through cosmopolitan education, we learn more about ourselves" [11]). For example, she juxtaposes her stay in the "Practice House," a place where young women attending Kansai University go to learn to act the part of American wives to American diplomats or executives, with an account of her own commissioning of a "Japanese" house in Durham, North Carolina. Whereas the Practice House resembles a 1950s *Better Homes and Gardens* idealization (or nightmare) of America, Davidson's home in Durham is more purely "Japanese" than the hybridized urban spaces in which most Japanese people live. Davidson's discussions of the Practice House and her "Japanese" house foreground neither a world where national boundaries have been undone, nor one where cultures are static and pure, but rather, in keeping with more critical, contemporary articulations of cosmopolitanism, a world where cultural mixings and crossings reveal fantasies and desires that are inextricable from ongoing, if increasingly hybridized, national and cultural identities.

As Davidson excavates her own imaginings and desires, *Thirty-six Views* evidences—in ways that theoretical writings can mask—how formulations of cosmopolitanism that circulate in the 1990s humanities can fail to address cosmopolitanism's and the cosmopolitan academic's implications in a capitalist consumer economy. Although *Thirty-six Views* casts cultural purity as the product of fantasy in an increasingly globalized world, it renders visible neither how uneven economic and political relationships between the United States and Japan both differentiate and connect their fantasies of one another, nor where Davidson herself is located in relation to the countries' economies. Timothy Brennan remarks on the invisible consumer economy that often underwrites a cosmopolitan position when he contends that it regularly involves a "process by which one—benevolently, of course—expands his or her sensitivities toward the world while exporting a self-confident locality for consumption *as* the world" (*Wars of Position* 206–7). He remarks on academics' reluctance to reflect on the economics that govern their own cultural production as well as consumption: "cosmo-theory has been squeamish about analyzing the place of the researchers themselves in frameworks of interest. What is the economic function of the culturalist intellectual? . . . What relationship do we have to the state?" (*Wars of Position* 222). In its representations of the Practice House and the Japanese-style house that Davidson builds and furnishes, *Thirty-six Views* substantiates the claims that Brennan makes about academics' resistance to accounting for their own economic interests in relation to the United States.

When discussing the Practice House and her own house, although Davidson does not entirely neglect the material relations between Japan and the United States, her focus—facilitated by the memoir genre, but in keeping with contemporary cosmopolitanism theories—ultimately remains on psychic investments in a way that cuts them free of economic concerns. Initially Davidson's approach reflects her perspective as a cultural historian. Davidson explains that Practice House residency is being phased out, both because Japanese students already live in Westernized housing, and because faculty have protested the residency program as an "example of American colonialism" (255). Davidson also analyzes the impact that the Vietnam War, the women's movement, and the changing global economy might have had on the Practice House decor (259). However, when she considers the Practice House in relation to her own house, she forgoes this cultural analysis. She does not address the difference it makes that the Practice House is an institutional structure, one that suggests Japan's continuing embeddedness in Western forms of cultural domination, whereas Davidson's "Japanese" house is privately commissioned, predicated on Davidson's privileges as an American professional with enough capital to literally construct her fantasy. She does not consider that her ability to stay alone and practically rent-free in the Practice House depends on these economic conditions, nor does she subject her own construction of a Japanese house to economic and political analysis, even when she and her husband learn that the Practice House rent is half what they expected, and use their savings to buy Japanese furnishings for their Durham home. When Davidson tells of how, on seeing her fantasy house, her Japanese friend Kazue insists that she concede to being rich, Davidson shifts from an analysis of U.S.-Japan relations to a focus on feelings, confiding to her readers, "Oh god. I could be in therapy twenty years and not bring myself to say those words" (277). Instead of using the financial circuit that connects the two houses to reflect on cultural and economic differentials between the United States and Japan, the two houses stand in the memoir as mirror images. Economic conditions do not ultimately figure into its representation of the two houses as equivalent expressions of cross-cultural feelings and desires. This lack of analysis is particularly noteworthy given the central role Davidson's house plays in *Thirty-six Views'* construction: its importance is evidenced by the peculiar fact that in her acknowledgments, Davidson thanks her architect for creating a space (a Japan of one's own?) so conducive to the writing of her book. Thus, her home and her memoir both stand as cultural products, and embodiments of a cosmopolitan vision in which the economic investments and political economies on which they depend are left largely unexamined.

Davidson's version of cosmopolitanism derives neither from the particularities of the memoir genre nor from her individual proclivities, but rather resonates with prevalent approaches such as Anthony Appiah's, that modify cosmopolitanism as an ideology and instead endorse a "rooted cosmopolitanism" as a sentiment that "celebrates the fact that there are different local ways of being" ("Cosmopolitan Patriots" 25). Enabled by memoir's focus on feelings, *Thirty-six Views'* representation of cross-cultural borrowings and exchange provides a window into how the cosmopolitanism of the 1990s humanities often fails to reckon with the networks of power that sustain it. More than a feeling, this is a cosmopolitanism rooted in the existence of nation-states with global reach and power, and in the flow of capital and commodities that, like the privileged U.S. academic, can travel across national borders.

As she works within the memoir form, Davidson—as cosmopolitan subject and goodwill ambassador—presents the cultural exchanges between herself and the Japanese people she meets unmediated by each nation's history and the complications politics might pose to their exchanges. When her Japanese visitor Kazue, responding to Davidson's Japanese-style home in Durham, takes up complex questions that relate to Western privilege and hegemony, rather than address them, Davidson instead reflects on how a U.S. context allows for a more open exchange between herself and Kazue, and realizes anew "that Japan can never be my home. . . . We've created an imitation, an American version of Japan. This house is a replica and, like every replica, a fantasy. A moment captured under glass. Turn it upside down. Shake it. Little snowflakes come tumbling down" (280–81).[10] In closing the chapter with reflections on interpersonal relationships and on fantasy in the abstract, Davidson takes refuge in the memoir genre and does not interrogate the economic and political realities that structure Japanese and American fantasies, and the asymmetries that attend them.

In avoiding an investigation of these realities, even as Davidson pays tribute to her version of Japan, she potentially reinforces an Orientalist structure of thinking that makes possible the very forms of "Japan bashing" that she expressly wishes to resist. Masao Miyoshi observes that in both 1980s' American Japan bashing and Japanese American bashing, "a society, a culture, and a nation are all identified and defined as a pure abstract absolute that is sterilized from any interaction with other elements and forces in history. . . . Japan is; the Japanese are" (*Off Center* 72). This ahistorical purity, a hallmark of Orientalist thinking that Miyoshi and other postcolonial theorists critique, characterizes Davidson's idealized Japanese house in Durham and also her use of Mount Fuji as the memoir's "timeless" symbol for Japan. Davidson's fantasies—regardless of the fact that she marks them clearly as such—ultimately serve as an escape from economic and political realities, and depend on the same essentializing economy as the views of Japan that she sets out to challenge. And to understand Davidson's fantasizing as the flip side of Japan bashing is to see the Orientalism that can undergird contemporary cosmopolitan theory.

With its emphasis on the writer's fantasies, feelings, and individual experiences, academic memoir provides a particularly apt genre through which to view not only the persistence of Orientalist ideologies in cosmopolitan positions, but also how contemporary cosmopolitanism underestimates the power of nation-states and their ongoing histories of racism and imperialism. In *Thirty-six Views*, just as fantasies are sometimes divorced from their political and historical contexts, racism seems to result more from cultural misunderstandings than from institutionalized forms of discrimination. In contrast to the ways that the memoir insightfully addresses the significant problems of sexism within Japan and America, it renders race relations mainly as they exist between—and not within— these countries. Davidson's work as a "goodwill ambassador" assumes intercultural negotiations that posit Americans and Japanese as racially and culturally different but equal. Japan's phenomenal economic gains in the 1980s—as yet undiminished when Davidson writes *Thirty-six Views*—made such assumptions possible, if not entirely accurate given the United States' geopolitical power, and enable Davidson to evade difficulties that would come with writing about a nation in a more clearly disempowered relationship to the United States. As Davidson works within her own experiences to forward her vision of intercultural harmony and global citizenry, *Thirty-six Views* contains virtually no mention of U.S. colonialism or racism, and little emphasis on problems of Japanese racism and colonialism: Japan's invasion of China, its annexation of Korea, and its acts of aggression in other parts of Asia and the Pacific go largely unmentioned, as does discrimination against Korean Japanese people, the ethnically Japanese underclass, and other groups such as Brazilians.

Davidson's account of her trip to Okinawa constitutes the exception that proves the rule. Invited to lecture at the University of the Ryukyus on U.S. literature, Davidson describes seeing the devastation Okinawa suffered at the hands of the Japanese and U.S. governments. She also tells of learning about the discrimination Okinawans experienced—and continue to experience—from the Japanese who viewed them as "expendable," and who are largely responsible (along with the U.S. military) for killing tens of thousands of Okinawan civilians during World War II. From one of the Okinawan professors she learns that "an Okinawan nationalist movement now advocates separation from Japan just as an earlier movement sought independence and an end to the American postwar occupation" (118). He also tells her, "Okinawans are still discriminated against in mainland Japan. It's one reason . . . why Okinawa was ceded to the Americans, turned into a virtual military base for the United States from 1945 until 1972" (118). Davidson, conveying only the information told to her by her hosts (who perhaps out of politeness focus only on past acts of U.S. military colonialism), does not mention that over 20 percent of Okinawan land continues to be occupied by U.S. military bases, and that Okinawans must contend not only with Japanese colonialism but with the ongoing violence of the U.S. military, that includes the routine rape of local women and girls by U.S. servicemen and civilian deaths that occur during military training exercises.[11] Davidson's frequent references to the American style of the houses, and to the university's inclusion of American studies (hence Davidson's invitation) and faculty members (Christine, the American she meets, teaches English at the university), are divorced from a consideration of the United States' continuing involvement in Okinawa.

Rather than explore Japanese and U.S. colonialism and their ongoing effects, Davidson focuses instead on spiritual exchanges between herself and the women that she meets when Christine takes her to visit Mrs. Nishimae, an Okinawan priestess on Kudakajima, an island known as the world's last matriarchal communal place. From Mrs. Nishimae, Davidson learns of the Okinawan religion, and from Christine she learns the Kuda-kajima dance. In turn Davidson, using a dried eel as a cane, teaches Mrs. Nishimae the soft-shoe. The following morning, Mrs. Nishimae takes Davidson to the sacred grove, or *utaki*, that is at the very center of the Okinawan religion, and teaches her to identify the tiny altars that they encounter. When Davidson finally spots one on her own, she explains that Mrs. Nishimae "claps her hands, making a little tap step. I bow deeply, then move my hands in the motion I learned last night at the Kudakajima circle dance" (127). As throughout *Thirty-six Views*, good feelings trump bad histories: colonial legacies and power differentials are diminished in the interest of a cosmopolitan vision in which individuals from differ-ent nations can, in the spirit of "goodwill ambassadors"—or Nussbaum's world citizenry—learn from each other and communicate across their cultural differences.[12] As Immanuel Wallerstein incisively points out in regard to this concept of world citizenry, because "we occupy particular niches in an unequal world, . . . being disinterested and global on one hand and defending one's narrow interests on the other are not opposites but positions combined in complicated ways" (124). Encoded into mem-oir given the genre's attention to particular experiences, such a model of world citizenry masks, and so leaves in place, ongoing inequities that structure relations between nations.

The memoir's only view of North American race relations shows them to be governed by the same spirit of goodwill ambassadorship that struc-tures its representations of U.S.-Japanese relations, and in a way that further evidences how cosmopolitanism can carry on the work of the nationalism it seems to oppose. When Davidson goes to Calgary to be with her dying mother-in-law, as the family circles around her bedside, holding hands, Davidson muses, "Together we represent nine different ethnic groups and five different religious backgrounds, all in one room, a 'mosaic,' as they say in Canada. We grapple with the moment, trying to make sense from polyglot tradition" (227–28). This portrayal of the mul-ticultural family gathering serves to reinforce both *Thirty-six Views'* cos-mopolitanism and also the nationalist Canadian metaphor of the mosaic.

Davidson's description of her husband's brother-in-law threatens to—but doesn't—disrupt the rightness of this metaphor. She states, "Sykes has been watching out the window. He finds what he is after on the mauve horizon, an eagle soaring quietly there. Sykes is Metis, a descendant of Cree Indians who married early French settlers of Canada. . . . His mother was sixteen before she saw a white person. Although she's a devout Catholic, she's never found Catholicism a hindrance to her Native beliefs" (228). By providing this information on Sykes, Davidson represents this scene as one that holds cultural significance. Her description of Sykes's genealogy could serve to introduce into this intensely personal scene the history of colonialism that the state version of multiculturalism, with its mosaic metaphor, erases. However, in depicting this moment of grief Davidson reaches for a more comforting version of intercultural relations, one that seamlessly supports the state's as it simultaneously develops the memoir's vision of a cosmopolitanism that embraces cultural differences. Sykes whispers to his mother-in-law, "'Grandma, the eagle is here,' . . . giving her permission" (228). The eagle departs and the family members, holding onto one another, leave the room together. Sykes's native background, rather than disrupting or complicating the nationalist view of multiculturalism as mosaic and a complementary cosmopolitanism, instead enriches these mutually constitutive views: Sykes's mother's native beliefs coexist harmoniously with her Catholicism, and Sykes's intact traditions and native spirituality serve as solace to the family, whose ability to support each other is only enriched through their cultural differences.

As this scene intimately records grief and loss, it reveals problems with the memoir's ambassadorlike approach to intercultural relations wherein people's actions represent their country and its cultures. And yet this analysis of how a contemporary academic narrates the loss of a family member raises questions of collegiality and ethics in a way that a comparable fictional scene would not. In part I discuss this scene in order to confront these uncomfortable questions. As Terry Eagleton observes, the most emotionally laden moments are those that most powerfully convey ideology: ideology, he contends, is "less a question of ideas than of feelings, images, gut reactions" (*Ideology* 149). Intensely private moments are integral not only to *Thirty-six Views'* politics but also to the politics of memoirs in general, including those by writers who play out their agendas less consciously than Davidson.[13] In an academy dominated by often celebratory discourses of transnationalism, "denationalization," cosmopolitanism, globalization, and diaspora, *Thirty-six Views'* most personal moments underline both the ongoing power of nation-states, and also the need to think about what it means to be an American in both U.S. and international contexts.

In making these arguments I wish neither to praise nor to condemn Davidson or her memoir, but rather to understand better the cultural arena in which *Thirty-six Views*, and its theorizations of racial and cultural alterity, is situated.[14] *Thirty-six Views* illustrates ways that the humanities can contribute, sometimes through rather than in spite of its theories of cosmopolitanism and travel, to the nationalist narratives it sets out to oppose. As it partakes in "cosmo-theory's" optimism about bringing together patriotism and cosmopolitanism, *Thirty-six Views* embodies not so much the contradictions between the two, but rather their mutual dependencies on hegemonic Western forms of nationalism. Moreover, as Davidson's focus remains on interpersonal feelings and experiences, what drops from sight is the material forms racism takes on North American soil, and white Americans' complicity in, and responsibilities in relation to, this racism. Not only through their inattention to the power of nation-states and their ongoing histories of racism and imperialism, but also in their implications in Orientalism, *Thirty-six Views'* most intimate moments expose entrenched ideologies that can inhere in, but that often are covered up by, contemporary theories of cosmopolitanism and narratives about travel.

Thirty-six Views also enables insights of a more general nature. As the book enacts contemporary theories of cosmopolitanism based on sentiment—something memoir is uniquely suited to do—it highlights not only the possibilities for achieving cross-cultural connections through individual acts of goodwill, but also the limitations of basing a theory on feelings without accompanying attention to structural conditions. Conversely, the gaps between *Thirty-six Views'* self-reflexive response to postcolonial critiques of travel and Davidson's cross-cultural fantasies expose how theory cannot always account for, or address, recalcitrant feelings or deeply seated ideologies: the memoir's most troubling moments provide theorists with opportunities to consider emotional investments and ideologies with which postcolonial studies has not yet contended. *Thirty-six Views* suggests more generally, then, both the difficulties and the necessity for cultural theory to address the interplay between individuals and institutional structures, and between emotions and intellect.

Worldly Investments and Domestic Returns

Like Davidson's memoir, David Mura's 1991 memoir *Turning Japanese* offers telling insights into theories of diaspora and cosmopolitanism, as it also articulates with the 1990s "denationalization" of Asian American studies. Like Davidson, Mura focuses on his travels to Japan and how they refashion his understandings of racial and national identity. However, unlike Davidson, who leaves problems of U.S. racism behind in her transnational explorations, Mura goes to Japan and rediscovers and works to resist U.S. racism. In Japan Mura discovers his anger regarding the way whiteness operates as an unmarked norm in the United States and the alienation that comes with being Japanese American. In fact, despite its diasporic and cosmopolitan claims, the book is largely a meditation on Sansei identity situated within the context of U.S. identity politics. In *Turning Japanese*, Mura explains how being in Japan gives him a new vantage point on having grown up in a white Jewish middle-class suburb in the Midwest. Connecting his family's isolation from other Japanese Americans to the history of the World War II internment camps and the dispersal of West Coast Japanese American communities, Mura details his parents' deliberate forgetting of Japan as they struggled to assimilate into America. Understanding his parents' and his own response to the internment camps and to a more pervasive white racism as representative of their respective generations, Mura observes, "By assimilating, the Nisei shed what had made them guilty: their Japaneseness" and asks rhetorically, "is it any wonder that the next generation would inherit, instead of Japaneseness, a sense of shame?" (218). By adopting a diasporic Japanese identity and by taking hold of a cosmopolitan discourse, Mura is able to secure a more positive racial and ethnic identity and sense of belonging. Mura's pride in "turning Japanese" constitutes a rebellion against his Nisei parents' eschewal of Japanese culture and identity, a defiance of Nisei accommodation to white racism, and a refusal of the racial shame that has been passed onto him.[15] Along with cosmopolitanism, his reclamation of a Japanese identity is, as well, an oppositional response to the Japan-bashing of the 1980s that accompanied Japan's rise as an economic superpower.[16]

Contributing to a movement away from the cultural nationalism that characterizes Asian American literature during the 1970s and 1980s, *Turning Japanese* involves Mura simultaneously claiming a Japanese and a Japanese American identity. The title itself dramatizes the tension that

Mura sustains in the memoir between a diasporic, "denationalized" formulation of identity and one based on a practice of U.S. identity politics.
Both "Japanese" and a "Sansei," Mura enlists the title to position himself,
on the one hand, between nationalities. On the other hand, to the extent
that "Turning Japanese" references the Vapors' hit song, the contexts for
Mura's "turning Japanese" are distinctly American. (Although the Vapors
were an English New Wave band, "Turning Japanese" was hugely popular
in the United States, appearing, for example, in *Sixteen Candles*, a 1984
movie infamous for its anti-Asian racism). In this song about masturbating while obsessing over a white woman, the Vapors rapidly chant, "Everyone around me is a total stranger / Everyone avoids me like a cyclone
ranger / Everyone / That's why I'm turning Japanese I think I'm turning
Japanese I / really think so." With their equation of alienation, masturba-
tion (and its overtones of deviant and shameful sexuality), perverted and
voyeuristic obsession ("I asked the doctor to take your picture / so I can
look at you from the inside as well"), and Japanese identity (and here the
lack of distinction between Japanese and Japanese Americans is precisely
the point—both are equally alien), the Vapors deliver a condensed and
particularly clear articulation of racist U.S. stereotypes of Asian men. It
is these racialized and gendered stereotypes and their destructive effects
that Mura resists in his memoir, by putting claims to a cosmopolitan diasporic Japanese identity in the service of a distinctly American identity
politics.[17]

Mura refuses racist stereotypes that circulate in dominant U.S. culture through his claims, on the one hand, to a cosmopolitan identity, and,
on the other, through the process of identifying as Japanese and feeling
part of a majority in Japan. Whereas Davidson advances poststructuralist
ideas about the fluidity and performativity of cultural, racial, and national
identity, and as a white American crosses cultures and aligns herself
with a cosmopolitan identity through the study and adoption of specific
practices, Mura's diasporic blurring of national and cultural boundaries
sometimes reflects his investments in cosmopolitanism, and at other
times it derives from an essentialist racial identification. As I tease out
how Mura's diasporic claims to "Japaneseness" both support and exist
in tension with his cosmopolitanism and his practice of U.S. identity
politics, I investigate articulations among these theories of identity, and
how each can support hegemonic forms of nationalism and masculinity.
Moreover, as I look to how Mura uses memoir to confront race relations
in the United States and to chronicle his travels without "making the

humanist assumption that human beings are all alike beneath the skin" (*Turning Japanese* 41), I argue that his uncritical acceptance of this genre and his failure to address his privilege can override the activist impulses behind his deployment of identity politics and reinvest his memoir in the humanist assumptions that he challenges. In making these claims I am neither arguing that genre dictates these positions nor am I seeking to indict Mura. Rather, I am interested in ways his memoir, and its departures from and correspondences to Davidson's, make evident the ideological investments that persist in spite of, and in some cases as integral to, theories of race and alterity that are circulating in the 1990s humanities.

My discussion of Mura establishes diasporic and cosmopolitan formulations of identity and community as interrelated ones that often support forms of nationalism that they seem to oppose. Mura's memoir illustrates the contentions of postcolonial theorists such as Clifford and Brennan, who insist that diaspora and cosmopolitanism are neither inherently oppositional nor inherently assimilationist, and who urge the importance of considering the class and race politics that govern specific instances of each. Clifford, for example, cautions against a too-simple affirmation of the oppositional force of "diasporic subversions," especially in the Asia Pacific region, wherein exploitative labor regimes characterize Pacific Rim capitalism (257–58). As I discuss Mura's "diasporic subversions" and the cosmopolitanism that accompanies them, I investigate these stances in relation not only to Mura's class and race politics but also to his sexual and gender politics. As Mura routes his claims to masculinity through contemporary formulations of cosmopolitanism and diasporic identity, his memoir reveals how these theories can undermine as well as support not only hegemonic forms of nationalism but also the counterhegemonic aims of U.S. identity politics. Through these divergences and correspondences, Mura's memoir reveals the need in the academy to consider U.S. ethnic studies and postcolonial studies as intersecting rather than separate spheres.

As became increasingly common in the 1990s, in *Turning Japanese* Mura privileges diasporic Asian formulations of identity over national ones. Indeed, in her landmark article critiquing the "denationalization" of Asian American studies in the 1990s and its depoliticizing potentialities, Sau-ling Cynthia Wong turns her attention to *Turning Japanese* for its demonstration of "the alluring possibility of an ever-evolving never-resolved subjectivity, characterized by instability, endless movement, boundary transgressions, and multiple reference points" (11–12).[18]

Unlike Davidson, Mura destabilizes his identity as an American by fore-grounding racial continuity rather than cultural fluidity across national boundaries. Mura's discovery in Japan of a racial identity that supersedes national identity provides him with a comforting antidote to the alien-ation that he experienced growing up as a racial minority in a white Mid-western suburb. In Japan, Mura finds comfort in his physical likeness to those around him. When his Japanese teacher notes that Japanese people have small bladders, Mura thinks of his lifelong embarrassment regard-ing his frequent trips to the men's room and his short "performances" there, and he "heaved an enormous psychic sigh of relief. . . . I realized I wasn't a freak; I was simply Japanese" (47). Urination here marks for him an essential racial difference, not the misperception of difference, as in *Thirty-six Views*.[19] Mura also takes great pleasure in his ability to pass as Japanese. Living in Japan he feels he is "dwelling in some protective womb, this world of faces that looked like mine" (183). He explains his "joy in being part of the visual majority for the first time" (148). Although he acknowledges the superficiality of this fit, he counters this admission when he expresses an affinity for how "the Japanese place far more value on surface, on beauty and appearance, than the depth-seeking, psycho-logically and morally conscious Americans" (35). With these feelings of connection to Japan, Mura counteracts his marginalization in the United States.

In particular, Mura harnesses a Japanese diasporic identity to combat U.S. racism and gender stereotypes. He explains that whereas growing up "as an Asian male" in the United States he "was placed in a category of neutered sexuality" (149), in Japan he feels free of sexually demean-ing stereotypes. For the first time he experiences himself as "perfectly normal" (149) *and* finds heroic models of masculinity. In Butoh as well as Yukio Mishima and Mura's own samurai heritage, he discovers an ancient and specifically male tradition that seems untouched by—and thus offers an ennobling alternative to—the anti-Asian racism of Western gender roles. Mura connects his attraction to Butoh, which he sees as "muscular, ancient, dark" and "essential" in its Japaneseness, to his fascination with Mishima, whom he calls "the contemporary proponent of the samurai spirit" (66, 67); both provide Mura with a version of Japanese identity that enables him to defy racist stereotypes and take pride in his mascu-linity. These models of masculinity not only predate Western patriarchy but also give Mura claim to an ethos that defines him as masculine in Western terms.[20]

Through these claims Mura provides a way to understand why since the late 1990s theorists have been linking diasporic identity to racial purity and violent and exclusionary nationalisms. Clifford, for example, points out that, "Resistance to assimilation can take the form of reclaiming another nation that has been lost . . . , but that is powerful as a political formation here and now. . . . Indeed, some of the most violent articulations of purity and racial exclusivism come from diaspora populations" (251). Gayatri Gopinath, too, notes the reactionary force that often characterizes the diasporic imaginary; building on the insights of Stuart Hall, she remarks on the "violent effacements that produce the fictions of purity that lie at the heart of dominant nationalist and diasporic ideologies" (4). As Mura adopts a Japanese identity to shore up his masculinity, he embodies specific ways that racial essentialism, cultural purity, and nationalist and imperialist politics can underwrite forms of diasporic identity. Drawing on Mishima's writings and persona to bolster his masculinity, Mura ignores how these representations—and the masculinity he derives from them—are informed by Mishima's implications in Orientalism, and by oppressive uses of nationalism. Although he acknowledges Mishima's "fascist leanings," Mura describes how Mishima and the Butoh master, Ono, attract him for the challenge that they represent "to present-day Japan and to the increasing commercialization and trivialization of Japanese culture" (67). Going against majority opinion that Japan had "achieved" modern status, Mishima insisted on the "premodern" elements in Japanese society. In the 1960s Mishima worked to revive imperial sovereignty, which he thought would allow Japan to regain its cultural mastery.[21] As Mura formulates a diasporic Japanese identity via Mishima, he reifies aspects of Japanese high culture that serve Orientalist agendas in the West and conservative forms of nationalism in Japan, and reinforces dominant Western as well as Japanese masculinities. His memoir thus illustrates Gopinath's contention that "discourses of sexuality are inextricable from prior and continuing histories of colonialism, nationalism, racism and migration" (3). It also evidences how a diasporic positioning can perpetuate—and reveal continuities among—different national forms of patriarchy.

Mura looks not only to a "premodern" Japan to achieve a more powerful version of masculinity but also to the economic growth of a postmodern Japan, particularly as it is manifested through Japanese designer fashions and the sense of superior cool that they convey. With this vantage point, his memoir puts into relief not only diasporic identity's ties to nationalist discourse, but also ways class privilege and corporate capitalism are at the heart of diasporic identifications and disidentifications. Mura continually references the purchase of Japanese designer clothes (Kenzo in particular) and the pleasure he takes in window-shopping and walking among the well-dressed Tokyo crowds. As Mura himself realizes, his attraction to Japanese fashion is connected to the pride he takes in Japan's growing prosperity: "The fashions of Tokyo revealed not just a change in couture consciousness but a change in political power, a shifting of the economic ground; the rise of one country, Japan, and the decline of the other, America" (36). Mura remarks: "I was pleased by this conclusion. And surprised. It was as if I were cheering for the other side" (36). Mura's very selective portrayal of Japanese people as sleek, well-dressed Tokyo professionals illustrates his regional and class biases, and also the compatibility between global capitalism and nationalism.[22]

Mura's investments in Japanese fashion materialize Gopinath's insights into the "imbrication of diaspora and diasporic cultural forms with dominant nationalism on the one hand, and corporate globalization on the other" (9). With a pride born in reaction to his own experiences of U.S. racism, Mura includes a journal excerpt describing his response to white Americans: "*I think how out of place they look, . . . how pasty their skin looks, how splotchy; how loud, how coarse, how unfashionable, how 'uncool,' how un-Japanese they are*" (*Turning Japanese* 43, original emphasis). Mura's own feelings of being cool come from his Kenzo clothing, which proclaims his own class status as well as Japan's: Japanese fashion conveys wealth and erotic power. As Dorinne Kondo remarks, "in the early 1980s Japanese clothing design enabled a valorization and eroticizing of Asian bodies as stylish in a contemporary way, rather than merely exotic or an inadequate imitation of Western bodies" (*About Face* 16).[23] Kondo cites the Western adoption of loosely cut, black-on-black clothing of the sort that Mura sports on the cover of *Turning Japanese* as indicative of Japan's growing economic and political power. The fashion statement that Mura makes in his memoir not only aligns him with a Euro-American academic and urban "cool," but also a Japanese masculinity that depends on Japan's status as a world power. Purchasing masculinity comes, of course, with a cost greater than that of the clothes. To the extent that Mura bases his newfound claim to masculinity on his own buying power and on Japan's economic stature, his memoir partakes in a capitalist consumer culture that involves the exploitation of workers on global assembly lines (indeed, these workers are noticeably absent from

Mura's reflections on fashion), and it buys into forms of masculinity that are central to Japanese and American nationalism.

Mura's class politics and alignment with Japanese nationalism in *Turning Japanese* position him against those in Third World countries. In "Japan in the World," Miyoshi and H. D. Harootunian contend that "Japan's desire to present itself as a player among the leading First World nations has led to the establishment with Europe and the United States of a trilateral hegemony, which at the same time has resulted in distancing Japan from the Third World. This alienation from the non-West is based on Japan's refusal to articulate its relationship to the non-West, especially Asia, both in the past and in the present" (5). Mura's uncritical (if not unconscious) identification with Japan's desire to be "a player" has similar results: Mura expresses pride that "my genes linked me not to the poverty of the Third World but to a country as modern as, even more modern than, America" (17). At one point, when addressing Japan bashers' hypocritical complaints about the lack of a level playing field, Mura expresses fleeting sympathy for exploited workers in Taiwan and Korea but does not reflect on how Japan and the United States are linked in their transnational labor practices in Asia. Instead, Mura refutes the arguments of Japan bashers by noting that Japan is no *worse* than the United States, and he then confesses, "for me, Japan's changed economic status became part of its attraction, part of my desire to identify with the Japanese" (369).

A less self-conscious expression of Mura's desire to identify as Japanese highlights the exclusionary nature of his racial politics. Toward the memoir's conclusion, as Mura elaborates on his pride in Japanese power and privilege, to do so, he ignores and even participates in Japan's colonialist relationship to the Philippines: "When I think back to that year in Japan, what comes to mind . . . is the image from my trip to the Philippines, of me riding a jeepney in the mountainous region of northern Luzon" (362). When the jeepney driver picks up a Japanese tourist, Mura explains that "immediately the Japanese man and I began talking in Japanese, . . . and a circle formed between us, as there had been a circle between the driver and his friend. I was now grouped with the Japanese man, a compatriot of a sort. It was probably as close as I came that year to being Japanese" (363). Particularly given Mura's identification as an Asian American concerned with racial oppression, that Mura's most memorable experience of "turning Japanese" depends on his Othering of the Filipino who is serving him is disturbing.[24] Another such moment occurs a few pages later, when Mura concedes, "I realize that my feelings about my Japanese background would be less positive if I had returned to a less prosperous land of origin. Japan also possesses an incredibly well-preserved and complex indigenous culture" (369). As he contrasts Japan's cultural riches to those of the Philippines, he states, "the combined colonialism of the Spanish and the Americans has served to obliterate much of the native culture" (369). Here Mura makes no mention of the ongoing revolutionary struggles in the Philippines or its vital cultural production; instead, he uses his perception of Philippine cultural poverty to bolster his pride in Japanese power and privilege. Moreover, Mura makes no mention of Japan's role in colonizing the Philippines, and when lauding Japan's indigenous culture he glosses over Japan's colonization of its own indigenous people, the Ainu.

As he claims a diasporic Japanese identity, Mura unapologetically endorses a nationalist one and an Us-Them mentality that diaspora is meant to undermine. His memoir shows how diaspora, while seeming to unfix national identification, can keep national identities firmly in place but merely allow for the diasporic subject to "switch sides" without disrupting the logic of nation-states and nationalism. Indeed, Mura's pleasure in his majoritarian status in the context of Japan and its myths of racial homogeneity and exceptionalism supports a Japanese nationalism that exerts exclusionary force on, among others, Filipino, Okinawan, Ainu, Korean, and Chinese peoples. His diasporic positioning upholds the Japanese doctrine of *Nihonjinron*—the master narrative of cultural exceptionalism—through which, as Dorinne Kondo explains, "an ineffable Japanese essence inaccessible to foreigners grounds claims to Japanese economic and political superiority" (*About Face* 157–58).

Whereas at some moments, Mura, "turning Japanese," adopts a racially based diasporic identity, at other moments he blurs national boundaries to forge a cosmopolitan one that transcends racial identity. Mura's cosmopolitanism does not, however, counter the Us-Them mentality that inheres in his deployments of diaspora, and that most theorists of cosmopolitanism explicitly oppose.[25] Instead, although his cosmopolitanism exists at odds with his privileging of racial identity, it remains for the most part compatible with, and even dependent on, his elitist and divisive attitudes toward class and nation. Cosmopolitanism attracts Mura because, as it brackets differences of race and nation, it counters the racism and provincialism that Mura finds in the United States and also serves as a way to resolve his lack of identification with a Japanese culture that he ultimately finds "too cramped, too well defined, too rule-oriented, too polite, too circumscribed" (370). As Mura begins to see the profound differences that separate him from Japanese people, a cosmopolitan identity gains in appeal over a diasporic one, and he concludes, "either I was American or I was one of the homeless, one of the searchers for what John Berger calls a world culture. But I was not Japanese" (370).

Mura's attraction to Berger's world culture participates, in a different way than Davidson's goodwill ambassadorship, in the contemporary resurgence of interest in cosmopolitanism, and like *Thirty-six Views*, *Turning Japanese* illuminates problems embedded in its contemporary articulations. At first glance Mura's cosmopolitanism seems to be a perversion of contemporary academics' more socially progressive cosmopolitanism. Mura appears far less interested than many cultural critics in formulating a cosmopolitanism free of Eurocentrism, or in adopting cosmopolitanism as a way to empathically connect with cultural others or express what Nussbaum calls "allegiance to . . . the moral community made up by the humanity of all human beings" ("Patriotism" 7). In his cosmopolitanism Mura seems worlds away from Pheng Cheah, who states, "As a form of collective consciousness that erodes national parochialism and facilitates the arduous process of establishing a platform for transnational political regulation, cosmopolitanism can help to release human rights from their historical bondage to the instrumentality of sovereign national states" ("Humanity in the Field of Instrumentality" 1554). Mura's cosmopolitanism is blatantly self-interested and derives from his desire as a U.S. racial minority to have his own humanity recognized. Nevertheless, continuities exist between his stance and the cosmopolitanism of the contemporary U.S. academy, supporting suspicions voiced by some critics that current expressions of cosmopolitanism too often resemble older forms that are culturally and economically elitist, individualistic, and rooted in the West and its exclusionary versions of humanism and universalism.[26]

Despite its focus on Japan, the memoir's mapping of the world is distinctly Eurocentric. The epigraphs that begin each section portray the contours of Mura's cosmopolitanism. Mura establishes a pattern of engaging a culturally particular quotation in dialogue with a seemingly worldly one, with the latter perspective provided, with few exceptions, by revered male intellectuals, most of them European, such as Novalis, Michel Foucault, Roland Barthes, Octavio Paz, Franz Kafka, Walter Benjamin, and Claude Lévi-Strauss (Susan Sontag is the only woman, Frantz Fanon the only non-European). These epigraphs are frequently juxtaposed with epigraphs by white Americans in order to expose the provincialism and racism of the former. Mura's cosmopolitanism not only renders the United States a cultural wasteland but also grants Japan its cultured status only insofar as its own traditions intermingle with European ones. Mura discloses that when he won the fellowship that brought him to Japan, "part of me wished the prize was Paris, not Tokyo" (9). Though the memoir traces his increasing appreciation for Japan, Europe remains for him the center of knowledge and culture. The evidence that Mura provides of his Noh sensei's "sophistication" is not his deep knowledge of Noh as a long-standing intellectual art form, but that "he talked about Nietzsche and Heidegger and their relation to Japanese thought" (135). Similarly, his interest in Butoh is legitimated when, attending his first performance in the outskirts of Tokyo, he spots "a cartoon autographed with a greeting by Susan Sontag" (54). For Mura, even in Japan, intellectual value can only be assured through a tradition's associations to a European intellectual history that remains central to contemporary articulations of cosmopolitanism.

No one in *Turning Japanese* more clearly personifies cosmopolitanism than the German artist Gisela, whom Mura meets in Butoh class. Obsessed with Gisela's beauty, Mura remarks, "she looked English, but something in the way her nose turned up slightly betrayed what was German. No, it was her eyes, the slight curve at their edges, an Eastern European slant, a hint of Asia" (131). For Mura she represents the perfect mix: European with a dash of Asia. Her books, her travels throughout Europe and Asia, and her fluency in various European and Asian languages reflect this mix, and around Gisela Mura highlights his Japanese ancestry and his knowledge of European literature as he remains silent about a past that he "felt suddenly was much too provincial" (145). Although Mura becomes disenchanted with Gisela when she breaks off their sexually ambiguous relationship, *Turning Japanese* continues Mura's love affair with the cosmopolitanism that she embodies.

In its embrace of an international but predominantly European community and intellectual tradition, Mura's memoir evidences with particular clarity how, despite many theorists' claims to the contrary, contemporary expressions of cosmopolitanism remain Eurocentric and implicated in imperialism. In her 1997 *Questions of Travel*, Caren Kaplan establishes the continuities between the modernist expatriate and the postmodern cosmopolitan diasporic theorist. Both of these traveling subjects, she contends, exhibit individualism and a sophisticated ironizing that

floats free of political commitments and material engagements. Euro-
American modernist exiles' aesthetic preoccupations, Kaplan observes,
isolate them and free them "from the worldly locations of nation-states"
(30). She similarly finds that the postmodern theorist is "represented as
singular, unique, and existentially estranged or alienated from a 'home'
or point of origin." She explains: "The terms of that estrangement may
have shifted from modernist expatriation and exile to postmodern cosmopolitan diasporas, but the emphasis on dislocation or displacement as
an aesthetic or critical benefit remains" (103). Kaplan instead endorses a
perspective in which the "travel" of theory and theorists be "considered
as part of the legacy of imperialism" and as part of the politics of transnational and postmodern cultural production (103). As Kaplan identifies
interrelations among and imperialist underpinnings of theories of travel,
diaspora, and cosmopolitanism, she provides insights into their ties to
Euro-American modernist and postmodernist aesthetics.

Turning Japanese vividly illustrates not the progressive cosmopolitanism that Kaplan advocates but rather the stance of aesthetic distance—
and political conservatism—that she finds characteristic of Euro-American modernism and postmodern cosmopolitanism. In his introductory
chapter Mura mentions the political and economic transformations Japan
is undergoing, and its changing relationship to the United States. In striking contrast to Davidson, he then remarks, "But none of this had much to
do with me. After all, I was a poet" (8). Although tongue-in-cheek, Mura
maintains this separation between art and politics even as he narrates
the process of "turning Japanese." When Mura becomes provisionally
involved in the protest over the building of the airport in Narita, a project
that denied farmers access to their land and left people homeless, in his
constant ironizing and positioning of himself as an intellectual who stands
apart from "the people," he supports tenets of literary modernism. Mura,
accompanying his leftist friend Matsuo to the Narita protest, stands
through hours of speeches while dwelling on a John Berryman poem
about boredom (211) and relentlessly focusing on the protest's aesthetics.
He describes his discomfort when he discovers that, in his sports coat and
dress slacks, he stands out from the other protestors who "seem to belong
to the section in *Glamour* where those who have broken the fashion code
are pictured with their eyes blacked out like criminals" (206). Once he
has disguised himself with a hooded parka, a golf hat, gloves, and sun-
glasses, Mura jokes, "If the Japanese police don't arrest me, the fashion
police will" (208). Emphasizing his distance from the events even as they

unfold, Mura plays bored and petulant child—as helicopters begin tear-gassing protestors Mura's response is, "I am not having fun" (211, 213). Here, in the guise of self-ironizing "honesty," Mura's discomfort regarding his ignorance of Japanese forms of protest, and his distance from its stakes and those involved in it, results in a self-trivializing concern with style that ends up trivializing the protest as well.

The ironic detachment and self-absorption that Mura demonstrates in *Turning Japanese* as, claiming his "homelessness," he searches for membership in a "world culture," not only aligns him with literary modernists but puts into nearly parodic relief assessments of contemporary cosmopolitanism as individualistic and evidencing, according to Bruce Robbins, "a luxuriously free-floating view from above" (1). In *At Home in the World*, when he addresses cosmopolitanism's lack of sympathy for insurgent nationalisms, Brennan provides a particularly incisive critique of cosmopolitanism's complicity in maintaining Western forms of hegemony. He finds that even as cosmopolitanism is highly critical of imperialism, it "displays impatience, at times even hostility, to the legacy of decolonization and is filled with parodic or dismissive references to the exalted 'people' of the liberation movements" (39). Brennan further claims that cosmopolitanism maintains the status quo through its acceptance of "already established aesthetic criteria—chief among them being complexity, subtlety, irony, and understatement" (40). Attention to cosmopolitanism, Brennan believes, reveals its elusive and often unwitting upholding of imperialism, and the way it serves "to limit a necessary confrontation with alternative values implicit in the reception of the 'third world'" (310). Through its portrait of a disaffected artist, *Turning Japanese* embodies many of Brennan's contentions about the cosmopolitanism that circulates in the 1990s humanities: Mura is most at home among privileged intellectuals—unlike the Narita farmers, his claims to "homelessness" are clearly metaphoric—and although he expresses uneasiness regarding his detachment from political activism, the irony and ambiguities that attend even these expressions do not give rise to an alternative politics, nor does Mura recognize that his postmodernist affect and aesthetics maintain the political status quo.

Mura puts his politically conservative cosmopolitanism and his diasporic disavowal of national identity into the service of an Asian American identity politics. Although Mura often gestures toward "world citizenry" when meditating on his lack of belonging to the United States and to Japan, his alienation positions him not in the world at large but as consistently and specifically American: it is a place at the table of U.S. society that he seeks.[27] As does Davidson, in Japan Mura learns as much about being American as he does about Japanese identity, and as his memoir preserves distinctions between the two nations, Mura focuses on his relationship to America, even insofar as it is one of estrangement. "In Japan," he explains, "I saw how much I am not reflected in American culture, how much it is not my culture" (369). And yet, when Mura visits a class and reads his poetry, students' "reactions made me realize how American my themes were" (253). In *Turning Japanese*, Mura becomes increasingly attuned to how whiteness operates as an unmarked norm in the United States, and to how white racist structures invalidate and exclude him.

In issuing his critiques of U.S. racism, Mura explores race, gender, and sexuality as intersectional identities, espousing an identity politics that makes his memoir very much a product of its time. As Xiaojing Zhou eloquently argues, Mura offers insights into how white racist ideologies work to delimit the sexual and gender identities available for Asian American men. Although Mura does not reference the Vapors' song "Turning Japanese," his memoir responds to it; *Turning Japanese* provides an intimate exploration of the effects of white American stereotypes of Asian men as emasculated and sexually deviant.[28] Mura writes obsessively in *Turning Japanese* and other books about his wife, Susie, whom he describes as "beautiful, with long brown hair, a pale Wasp face, like Ali MacGraw" (149). He analyzes his desire for her in relation to the emasculation of Japanese American men and the Japanese American internment camps. When he notes Japanese men's attraction to her, he thinks, "She's like a prize to them. Immediately a voice inside echoed: 'And to you'" (119). Mura confesses his need, when younger, to sleep with as many white women as possible; he links his addictions to sex and pornography to the emasculation of Asian American men in U.S. culture. Reflecting on his many affairs, he asks, "How could I explain how the love I have for Susie was somehow mixed with a sense of inferiority and rage around my race and color?" (341).

In his exploration of intersecting categories of identity, Mura focuses on his oppression but remains blind to his privilege. When he explains his rage as a response to white U.S. racism, he fails to consider how his expressions of it demonstrate his need—and more importantly, his ability—to maintain gendered power over white women. Mura's love for Susie comingles with his need to visit on her the abuse that he himself has experienced, to punish her for the racism and sexual humiliation he has experienced. Although he narrates his mistreatment of Susie in the past tense, his extended flirtation with Gisela and the harsh light he casts on her once she ends their relationship, as well as his graphic reenactment of Susie's previous humiliation, suggest that his rage and sense of inferiority remain unresolved. Particularly cruel is his recounting of Susie's reaction when they were in college to his insistence that they have an open relationship because he desires to have sex with other women. He describes finding her in the basement bathroom of a dorm, retching vodka, and sobbing, "Go away, . . . I don't want you to see me like this" (150). Having made public a moment she wished to have kept private even from him, Mura does not appear to have considered how his need to confess his transgressions entails humiliating his wife. In focusing on how white U.S. racism has damaged and emasculated him, Mura ignores his own role in a cycle of abuse as he exercises gendered power in his relationships to Susie and other white women. As with cosmopolitan discourse, Mura takes up and, in instructive ways, misuses the discourse of identity politics that is so prevalent in the academy in the early 1990s: even as he engages categories of race, gender, and sexuality as intersecting, as he focuses so exclusively on his oppression and not his privilege, his memoir underlines the need to examine rigorously how power operates in multiple and sometimes competing ways.

Mura's intense dwelling on his experiences of marginalization as a Japanese American—a focus the memoir genre justifies—makes him unwilling, even unable, to see that people of Japanese descent can engage in, as well as be subjected to, racial or ethnic discrimination. Although the memoir genre does not necessarily demand such a singular vantage point, it can serve to naturalize or legitimate one. When Mura's Sansei friend Ken tells Mura that being in Japan makes him feel shame for being Japanese—"All that stuff about Japanese blood, all the prejudice against the Koreans, and no one sees it'"—Mura responds only that he feels more comfortable in Japan, since he is not an object of discrimination (269, 270). Because, even in Japan, Mura's focus remains on his own experiences of U.S. racism, he falls into the American provincialism he so despises, and then simultaneously becomes implicated in Japanese racism and colonialism.

Mura's confessional style, which often includes self-damning admissions, and his exclusive attention to his own experiences, are enabled by memoir and supported by his investments in a politics of identity. Identity politics, so influential in the 1990s academy, especially in literary, Asian American, ethnic and women's studies, underwrites Mura's conviction that his experiences and relationships with family and friends are symptomatic of U.S. race relations—as he explains, in his poems, his parents are "not just my parents, and I'm not just me. They're larger, more symptomatic and symbolic" (331). Likewise, in *Turning Japanese*, Mura presumably includes personal confessions for the more general insights that they provide into Sansei identity and U.S. racial politics—he asserts toward the memoir's conclusion, "identity is a political and economic matter, not just a personal matter" (370). However, Mura's use of confession often fits more readily into an individual therapeutic model than an activist or politicized one, in ways that suggest (as do memoirs in the previous chapter) the shortcomings of uncritically deploying the understanding so prevalent in the 1990s that "the personal is political." Representing his feelings and actions as symptomatic of U.S. race relations excuses Mura from individual agency or responsibility as it leaves some psychic motivations—and also privileges of class, gender, and nation that he enjoys—unexplored or justified, with the result that cycles of abuse and systems of oppression continue unquestioned. Mura's use of memoir, then, provides insights into identity politics' failure to disrupt the logic that maintains structures of oppression and its shortcomings in situating U.S. categories of identity in relation to global networks of power.

Mura's memoir also evidences problems with theories of diaspora and cosmopolitanism that are related to their privileging of personal experience. Theorists of diaspora frequently laud the autobiographical as a way to address the heterogeneity of different histories and regions; in studies of cosmopolitanism, theorists regularly employ anecdote or personal narrative to illustrate the transformative power of sentiment in undoing Us-Them distinctions, or, as Appiah puts it, in "learn[ing] about other people's situations, and then us[ing] our imaginations to walk a while in their moccasins" (*Cosmopolitanism* 63). What Mura's memoir reveals in different ways, but ways related to *Thirty-six Views*, are the limitations of basing a cosmopolitan politics on feelings and personal experiences. Particularly given Mura's absence of empathy, *Turning Japanese* evidences even more dramatically than *Thirty-six Views* and its goodwill ambassadorship how a cosmopolitanism based on individual feelings or consciousness can not only neglect but also perpetuate inequities that structure relationships between people in different countries and cultures. Mura's memoir bears out the objection that Elaine Scarry raises in regard to cosmopolitanism's reliance on empathic identification: *"The human capacity to injure other people is very great precisely because our capacity to imagine other people is very small"* (103, original emphasis). Moreover, as Mura takes up a diasporic perspective in *Turning Japanese*, his memoir, especially in its most intimate moments, reveals not only how personal accounts provide no assurance of privileged insights into specific geopolitical sites, but also ways in which—theorists' stated intentions to the contrary—formulations of diaspora remain implicated in national narratives that depend on, even as they render invisible, forms of exclusion along lines of race, class, gender, and sexuality.

Turning Japanese provides a way to assess not only limitations of identity politics and theories of cosmopolitanism and diaspora, but also, in its yoking together of these theories, problems with how knowledge is organized in the U.S. academy. As Mura, a traveler in Asian American and literary studies circles, deploys these theories to combat U.S. racism, he brings out tensions and contradictions within and among identity politics and theories of cosmopolitanism and diaspora. In the 1980s identity politics found an academic "home" in women's and ethnic studies, and theorists focused—and largely have continued to concentrate—on race, class, gender, and sexuality, most often within a U.S. context. Contemporary theorists of cosmopolitanism and diaspora have situated themselves in a more global or a postcolonial framework, and, although identity politics often underwrites these theorists' positioning (perhaps most obviously in the "denationalizing" field of Asian American studies), they highlight concerns of cultural hybridity, region, nation, empire, citizenship, and globalization. As Mura, in "turning Japanese," brings these discourses together, they butt up against each other in telling ways. When he brings an identity politics to Japan and subsumes cosmopolitan and diasporic positioning to a U.S. identity politics framework, he suggests the inability of identity politics to account adequately for international networks of power. His memoir also indicates the need for theorists of diaspora and cosmopolitanism to factor in categories of gender and sexuality and to attend more fully to the lessons of identity politics in thinking about identity as intersectional.[29] In part, then, the problem *Turning Japanese* points to seems to be one of unproductive divides among disparate discourses and fields. Mura's memoir suggests the need to consider ethnic studies and U.S. identity politics in relation to, rather than in a separate sphere from, studies of postcolonialism, diaspora, and cosmopolitanism.

At the same time, when Mura utilizes discourses of cosmopolitanism and diaspora for distinctly American purposes, the problem that emerges is not only that of U.S. identity politics' parochialism or ethnocentrism, nor does it simply result from Mura's individual failings or from a self-centeredness that sets him apart from those writing theory rather than memoir. Instead, Mura's memoir unmasks the distinctly U.S. identity of cosmopolitan and diaspora discourse. Contributors to the seminal collection *For Love of Country?* indicate just how American is the makeup of cosmopolitan thought, both in terms of theorists' own locations in the United States and also in terms of how many of them make their address to a U.S. readership, even in the course of advocating a lack of allegiance to the United States. Diaspora theorists, too, though often born in Asia or Africa, most often write from and to a U.S. readership. What differentiates Mura, then, from many theorists of diaspora and cosmopolitanism is not that he is speaking as an American and to a U.S readership, but rather that he is so unapologetically self-interested in how he does so.

In making these critiques my point is not to dismiss cosmopolitan or diaspora theory, any more than I am arguing in *Academic Lives* for the dismissal of humanism and human rights as exclusively Western concepts. Theorists such as Amartya Sen have vigorously—and I think rightly—rejected this position and looked to non-Western sources to resituate these discourses and argue for their political possibilities.[30] Edward Said does too, in ways I explore in the following section. Particularly given the juncture at which the U.S. academy finds itself, these claims to cosmopolitanism are of critical importance. On the one hand, U.S. universities (and university towns) are cosmopolitan places where people from different cultures come together, and where U.S. citizens learn about the world. On the other hand, universities produce knowledge largely for specifically nationalist projects, and when academics in the United States oppose American nationalism and imperialism, they meet with increasing governmental regulation and censure. In the post–September 11 era and in the midst of an open-ended "war on terror," working toward a cosmopolitan vision that is critical of U.S. imperialism and pushing, as diaspora theorists do, against the fixity of nation-states, are crucial moves in keeping sight of the university as a place of possibility as well as a state institution that produces national subjects and divides. And memoir, as

I argue in the rest of this chapter, provides not only a means to discern the difficulties of achieving such a vision, but also a place to imagine it into being.

Autobiographical Accidents

After completing an initial draft of this chapter, I went to a talk on area studies by Vicente Rafael. Anticipating a break from the subject of autobiography, this talk instead brought me once more face to face with it. Rafael addressed the importance of what he calls "the accidental" in area studies through readings of autobiographical moments in writing by Benedict Anderson and Arjun Appadurai. According to Rafael, academics' accounts of the accidental or serendipitous nature of their entry into their chosen area or "field" serve not simply as excuses for Orientalist fantasies, but also as ways those working in area studies resist its institutionalization. To support his argument, Rafael presented detailed biographical accounts of Anderson and Appadurai and anecdotes about other academics in area studies, as well. During the question-and-answer period, when asked if he wasn't ignoring institutional structures of power and privilege that made these scholars' personal experiences of finding their entry into area studies far from accidental, Rafael responded that while of course this was so, we all already know about structures of power, and that they are no longer interesting.[31]

After visiting Doris Duke's Shangri La, I recalled Rafael's talk and was struck by his emphasis on the individual's accidental or serendipitous entry into an institutionally mapped area of study (in this case, areas studies) and by his opposition of the individual or autobiographical and the institutional. His talk resonated for me with a moment in Aram Veeser's introduction to *Confessions of the Critics*, where he asks, "The anecdotes and the careers: an arbitrary connectedness? Or a causal chain?" (xix), and struck me as symptomatic of how theorists are ushering into their institutional analyses and poststructuralist theorizing a return to—and a longing for—the sense of individual agency and autonomy that characterizes bourgeois humanism. This desire also of course helps account for academics' turn to memoir, even as my readings of academic memoirs in *Academic Lives* indicate the extent to which individual accounts are imbricated in the institutional production and organization of knowledge.

Along with the analyses of *Thirty-six Views* and *Turning Japanese* in this chapter, the opening account of how Doris Duke came to build

Shangri La illustrates that the accidental and the autobiographical articulate with the institutional. If Duke's passion for Islamic art was unpredictable, the economic circuits that inaugurated this obsession by bringing her before the Taj Mahal on her extended honeymoon were not. Shangri La, formerly Duke's private fantasy world (this enormous house featured only two bedrooms as Duke rarely allowed houseguests) has with Duke's death become a museum and, on occasion, a place to hold Duke Foundation activities such as a Duke University symposium on Islamic Art. Also, although it is serendipitous for my analysis that both Cathy Davidson and Doris Duke built fantasy homes that constitute forms of autobiography, and although it is equally serendipitous that they share a connection to Duke University, just because such connections are not predetermined they do not exist outside of the logic and organization of institutions. Economics and other structures of power render these connections far from arbitrary (or without interest!) even if they are unpredictable.[32] Just as Doris Duke depended on the tobacco money that financed her honeymoon and the construction of Shangri La, the funding for Cathy Davidson's fantasy home can be traced back, albeit less directly, to the Duke family fortune that makes Duke one of the best-endowed universities in the United States. Thinking about Doris Duke and Davidson together suggests how institutional histories, economic circuits, and Orientalist fantasies can link different people and places in totally unexpected though not random ways.

In the next section I consider how even as Edward Said distinguishes *Out of Place* from his political and more scholarly writings, this deeply personal 1999 memoir anticipates the post–September 11 movement in the humanities to reclaim humanism in the name of a newly urgent interest in human-rights discourse. Said's ability to bring humanism and human-rights discourses into the humanities is no accident but results from the combination of his institutional location as an English professor and his personal experiences as a Palestinian who has a long-standing and firsthand history with human-rights violations. In the ways it engages theories of colonialism, Orientalism, cosmopolitanism, travel, and diaspora, *Out of Place* tells a story that, while particular to Said, suggests the possibilities and stakes of postcolonial studies. In this memoir that courts and resists fantasies of home, Said proffers a humanism that, as it builds on the insights of postcolonial theory, travels beyond the confines of Orientalist binaries and Western versions of cosmopolitanism and humanism, and also beyond the walls of academe.

Humanism and Human Rights

In *Out of Place*, Edward Said's diagnosis and experience of leukemia occasion his travel through memory to the places and times of his childhood. The political concerns and theoretical analysis that define Said's career and commitments as a public intellectual and as a crucial figure in postcolonial studies remain in the background, or else appear in highly personalized terms. Nor does the memoir highlight his accomplishments. One of the premier public intellectuals in the United States, Said achieved a remarkable level of influence and recognition, and his areas of accomplishment are many. From 1992 until his death in 2003, he held one of the eight university professorships at Columbia University, and he published over twenty books that have been translated into sixty-six languages. He delivered prestigious lecture series such as the Reith Lectures for the BBC and the Empson Lectures at Cambridge. He was a member of the executive board of PEN, and in 1999 he was president of the MLA. A music critic for the *Nation*, Said was also an opera critic and a pianist. He was awarded many honorary doctorates, and his groundbreaking book, *Orientalism*, a foundational text in cultural and postcolonial studies, was a runner-up for the National Book Critics Circle Award in 1979 and remains a key text for understanding racial and cultural alterity and the workings of colonialism.[33] In the 1970s Said became the de facto spokesperson in the West for the Palestinian cause. He worked for the Palestine National Council and testified before the U.S. Congressional Subcommittee on International Relations, and in 1998, he wrote and narrated a BBC documentary titled *Edward Said: A Very Personal View of Palestine*.[34] From September 11, 2001, until his death two years later, his essays denouncing U.S. and Israeli state-sponsored terrorism appeared widely in newspapers around the world, and were even more widely disseminated on the Internet. As Bill Ashcroft and Pal Ahluwalia note in their introduction to one of the many volumes that focus on Said's career, Said has "done more than any other person to place the plight of Palestine before a world audience" (1). Said's wide-ranging scholarly interests, political commitments, and accomplishments as a public intellectual are almost entirely absent from his boyhood memoir.

At first read *Out of Place* stands in dramatic contrast to Said's many writings on Palestine and the Middle East. The memoir, which Said describes as characterized by Virgilian sadness and which he likens in an interview to a Proustian meditation ("Interview" 420), is unapologetically nostalgic and traditionally literary in its themes and form. As the political recedes into the background, a psychoanalytic framework is paramount. Presented as a personal meditation on sleeplessness and death, Said casts his richly detailed and leisurely foray into his past as a way to counter a foreshortened future, as a means to triumph over time and the ravages of illness.[35] In an interview he describes the memoir's boyhood perspective as "pre-political" (Wicke and Sprinker 227), and in his preface to *Out of Place* he notes that his political and scholarly interests enter only "surreptitiously" (xi). At the forefront is Said's relationship to his parents and how they shape his sense of self, his relationships, his passions, and his grappling with his illness.

Such an intensely inward approach marks a departure for a public intellectual whose body of work emphatically insists on—and illustrates—the interconnections between literature and politics, and a scholar's life and theoretical positions. As Barbara Harlow notes, "From *Beginnings*, published in 1975 . . . Edward Said has argued in his writing for the intersection of culture and politics and the radical importance of narrative and of history in the elaboration of a critical place, an oppositional knowledge, and an alternative archival space" (190). These concerns are not simply academic: "his own place as an exiled Palestinian intellectual is constantly inflected in his work" (Ashcroft and Ahluwalia 1). Born to a wealthy Palestinian family in Jerusalem in 1935, Said was exiled from his home and homeland due to the calamitous events of 1948. He moved to the United States in 1951 and lived in New York City from 1963 onward. Reflecting on these conditions, Ashcroft and Ahluwalia assert that they "form the defining context for all his writing. His struggles with his dislocation, his recognition of the empowering potential of exile, his constant engagement with the link between textuality and the world, underlie the major directions of his theory" (5). Given how inseparable Said's passionate political commitments are from his life's story in his writings, their apparent absence in his memoir is striking.

And yet Said's theoretical and political concerns deeply inform *Out of Place*. Moustafa Bayoumi and Andrew Rubin note that "the pain of exile has been a grounding philosophy to all his work" (xii), and this holds true for his memoir. As it chronicles the various types of exile that Said undergoes as a boy, *Out of Place* advances Said's recurring themes, particularly his insistence on the importance of beginnings, his critiques of Orientalism and imperialism, his assertion of a non-Western humanism, his commitment to "worldliness," and his work on behalf of Palestinians' rights to their homeland. Although Said's theoretical positions enter his boyhood memoir only obliquely, they nonetheless are crucial. They enable him to remain within as he expands the possibilities of literary memoir in order to advance a humanism that can forward the human rights of the very people against whom Western humanism so often has defined itself. With its take on issues of identity, home, national belonging, diaspora, cosmopolitanism, humanism, Orientalism, and East-West binaries, *Out of Place* articulates the concerns of both *Thirty-six Views* and *Turning Japanese*, even as its departures from these memoirs suggest the possibilities that come with bringing a postcolonial perspective to bear on an individualist genre to produce a critical and wide-reaching humanism.

The story of Said's life that emerges in *Out of Place* shows him from an early age living a diasporic and cosmopolitan life, one that defies neat categories of national identity. Said was born an American in West Jerusalem because his Palestinian father, Wadie, had U.S. citizenship. His mother, Hilda, was born in Nazareth of Palestinian and Lebanese parents. Said was named Edward after the prince of Wales, and he was brought up in the Anglican Church. When he was two his family moved to Cairo, where his father ran a successful book and stationery business. His family's elite status gave them mobility, and the Saids regularly traveled back to the extended-family home in Jerusalem and, each summer, to the Lebanese resort Dhour el Schweir. In these various locations Said experienced religious diversity and complexity—he grew up amid Protestant, Greek Orthodox Christian, and Muslim practices. He attended private schools with boys of various nationalities and ethnicities, who defined themselves against the British administrators, not one another. As a teenager Said was sent to Mount Hermon School, a boarding school in Massachusetts, going on to Princeton University and then graduate school at Harvard.

Although Said's early years clearly can be read through his own and others' theories of racial and cultural alterity and colonialism, as Said recounts his history, what is paramount is a psychoanalytic framework that connects his memoir to much traditional twentieth-century Western autobiography. Said dwells on his self-consciously Oedipal relationship to his parents, and the memoir stops short of his politicization as a Palestinian and as a critic of imperialism. When considering why his father did not express himself to Said, Said reflects, "perhaps, for oedipal reasons, I had blocked him" (*Out of Place* 262). His musings on his mother support this Freudian approach. Accounting for their closeness before his departure to the United States, he confesses to "being pacified that she always referred to him as 'Daddy,' the two of us using the same name for husband and father" (221). The memoir itself can be read as Said's attempt to rival and to please his father, to resist and to conform to his father's desire that "I be directed by his script for me" (8). Said explains that his father, in giving his history, always "stuck to the story in its few episodes and details" (8). An obsessive photographer, his father took films that according to Said served as "my father's way of capturing as well as confirming the ordered family domain he had created and now ruled" (76). In response, as a boy, Said fantasizes about being a book "whose fate I took to be happily free of unwelcome changes, distortions of its shape, criticism of its looks" (76). As a book that represents Said's family domain in ways that capture as well as complicate his father's narrative, *Out of Place* reads as an Oedipal drama of homage and resistance.

To the extent that discourse about colonialism enters the memoir, it is to describe Said's intimate relationships. For example, Said asserts that in his family "there were bilateral relationships with my mother as colony to metropole" (60). Said attributes his sense of dislocation to his parents' disapproval of him as much as to historical conditions. The first chapter opens, "All families invent their parents and children. . . . There was always something wrong with how I was invented and meant to fit in with the world of my parents and four sisters. . . . The overriding sensation I had was of always being out of place" (3). As Said comes to affirm his separation from family and home as a "rupture" that is "fortunate" for the freedoms and intellectual insights it affords (294), he partakes in an intense individualism that he embraces as a metaphysical condition definitive of his very self. Such inward-looking uses of the memoir genre align *Out of Place* not with a postcolonial project but rather with twentieth-century autobiography and twentieth-century Western humanism, both of which have been critiqued for their Western biases, their individualism, and their racial and gendered exclusions.

The memoir engages Said's interest in beginnings in similarly individualistic ways. As a detailed account of his childhood years, the memoir lends itself to a psychological, privatized take on how Said theorizes beginnings. In *Beginnings: Intentions and Method*, Said states, "without at least a sense of a beginning, nothing can really be done, much less ended" (50). Said further claims, "a beginning gives us the chance to do work that compensates us for the tumbling disorder of brute reality that will not settle down" (50). For Said, "a major thesis of this book is that beginning is a consciously intentional, productive activity, and that, moreover, it is activity whose circumstances include a sense of loss" (372). Viewed as a response to his cancer, *Out of Place* can be read as Said's poignant effort to make sense of a present disordered by the cruel realities of his illness, and as an attempt to prepare for his life's ending by returning to his beginnings.

And yet, Said's focus on beginnings serves not only as a response to impending death but as a way to chronicle a history that is political and collective as well as personal and individual. In *Orientalism*, Said evokes Gramsci's statement that "the starting-point of critical elaboration is the consciousness of what one really is, and is 'knowing thyself' as a product of the historical process to date, which has deposited in you an infinity of traces, without leaving an inventory, therefore it is imperative at the outset to compile such an inventory."[36] For Said, *Orientalism* involves "an attempt to inventory the traces upon me, the Oriental subject, of the culture whose domination has been so powerful a factor in the life of all Orientals" (90). In *Out of Place*, Said's inventory of his beginnings underlines how his sense of self is constructed in response to personal circumstances that are also historical. Without positing his life as representative, Said's memoir delineates through "an infinity of traces" a people and a region that the Israeli-Palestinian conflict and an Orientalist perspective have rendered in rigid and ahistorical binaries.

As *Out of Place* serves collective as well as individual purposes, it shows how memoir can put humanism in the twenty-first century to work for human rights. Said's history, indeed his very existence, as a Palestinian has been subject to exclusions and wholesale erasure by those who espouse dominant forms of Western humanism. In *After the Last Sky*, Said asserts that "with the exception of a handful of literary works . . . the concrete human detail of Palestinian existence was sacrificed to big general ideas" (106–7). It is precisely this "concrete human detail" that *Out of Place* represents. Moreover, by making use of an established literary form, Said asserts a right to narrative that has been denied to Palestinians. As Said explains, "few people have given us the privilege even of having a narrative, much less of publicizing it; as outlaws we are always so censored and interdicted that we seem able only to get occasional messages through to an indifferent outside world" (*After the Last Sky* 10). In the context of this historical erasure, for Said to recover the personal ground of his boyhood constitutes an important political intervention. Use of the memoir genre allows Said to enact "the voyage in" that he describes in *Culture and Imperialism* as one in which "post-colonial writers take hold of the dominant modes of literary writing to expose their culture to a world audience" (quoted in Ashcroft and Ahluwalia 8). His success in this regard can be measured by his memoir receiving the New Yorker Book Award. *Out of Place* further supports Timothy Brennan's claim that Said demonstrates in his Eliot lectures that "in the United States . . . one can effectively be an organic intellectual of the poor and the disenfranchised by taking the traditional intellectual's high road." ("Places of Mind" 92). In his many *Al Ahram* articles as well as in books such as *After the Last Sky*, Said underscores the deadly implications of denying Palestinians their humanity (a call for human rights). In his memoir, by laying claim to and placing a Palestinian's individual story in a humanist literary tradition, Said forms a bridge between humanism and human-rights struggles, bearing out Joseph Slaughter's contention in 2006 that "human rights are a culture and a legal regime, as much a matter of literature as of legislation" (1419).

Given the suspicion with which postcolonial theorists in the 1990s viewed engagements with humanism, Said's 1999 memoir appears "out of place." However, as the memoir continues the anticolonial work of *Orientalism* in a humanist register, it offers possibilities to postcolonial and other humanities scholars such as Slaughter who, in the post–September 11 era, are looking for a way to reclaim humanism in the name of human rights. Using the memoir genre to tell a story that is systematically excluded from Western humanist representations of the world, in *Out of Place* Said undoes and reconfigures the "West-Rest" dichotomy on which much Western humanism—and its attendant forms of dehumanization—depends. As Said insists from *Orientalism* on, dehumanization depends on a clear Us-Them binary. And although Said finds Western liberalism bankrupt, he expresses the conviction that humanism can be squared with a more humane tradition. As Ashcroft and Ahluwalia note, Said has an "unfashionable belief in 'universal' values such as freedom from oppression, self-determination and peace" (135). Said's faith in universals is directly related to his equally unfashionable (at the time) belief in humanism. Rejecting charges by postcolonial critics in the 1980s and 1990s that humanism is a Western imperial concept, Said explains, "The only life that is possible for humanism is if it's revived in the interest of a universal concept" (Bayoumi and Rubin 433). Resistant to how universalism is usually tied to imperialism and the West, Said's endorsement of "universalism" is in the interest, he states, of "establishing and upholding 'a single standard' concerning 'freedom and justice'. This embrace of 'universal principles' is distinguished from 'the ideas of a universal norm of international behaviour [that] meant in effect the right of European power and European representations of other people to hold sway'" (*Representations of the Intellectual* 68–69).[37] Said relentlessly opposes imperialist uses of "universalism" and human-inhuman divides not only in his academic and journalistic writings, but also in his memoir.

While in the 1990s academy, attention to the crudeness of Us-Them ways of dividing the world seemed tired and dated, and a belief in universalism was "unfashionable," the "war on terror"—which includes the post–September 11 escalation of violence in the Middle East—demonstrates the ongoing need to expose, historicize, and overcome violent binaries, including "human-inhuman" divides.[38] Said's memoir does this work. His identity in *Out of Place* is a complexly drawn one that, through its details, disrupts the Israeli-Palestinian binary on which human-rights violations depend; his representation of his history also nuances the East-West opposition on which humanism and Orientalism traditionally rely, and which surface even in works informed by critiques of Orientalism, such as *Thirty-six Views* and *Turning Japanese*. As *Out of Place* so powerfully demonstrates, with its reliance on thick detail, memoir is uniquely situated both to complicate and to register the effects of binaries that are integral to Orientalism and that are foundational to postcolonial studies.

Through his individual story, as Said extends the work of *Orientalism*, he also conveys a corrective to Western forms of humanism in the form of a more supple humanism, one that allows for the humanity of those "othered" by such ideologies. As Ella Shohat contends, "one of the favored strategies used to discredit Edward Said has been systematically to associate him with the presumably irrational rage of the terrorist" (125). Shohat further observes that within academic contexts Said's political writings are "branded with rage and terrorism. Despite Said's intimacy with Western culture, then, the mere fact of his Arabness is used to disqualify his writing" (128). In *After the Last Sky*, Said looks at how the whole of the Palestinian people are similarly misrepresented, often with deadly results: "Especially in the West, particularly in the United States, Palestinians are not so much a people as a pretext for a call to arms. . . . To most people Palestinians are visible principally as fighters, terrorists, and lawless pariahs" (4). In narrating his prepolitical boyhood Said resists casting his previous actions as conscious forms of opposition to colonialism or as starting points for his activism. For example, Said describes the trouble he causes at his new school, Shubra, as boyhood pranks, though it would have been easy enough to claim a political motive for his acts of defiance (207). His refusal to read his past through a political lens disrupts Said's identity as "Professor of Terror" and, more generally, the equation of Palestinians with "terrorists." Nor is the "Edward" in *Out of Place* a preeminent expert on the Middle East, a distinguished professor, or a public intellectual, but rather an often lackluster student and politically naive boy whose beginnings are not marked by his later eminence or his righteous outrage regarding imperial practices (205). In his memoir, as Said records the processes and effects of Zionism and European colonialism, he maintains the complexity of Palestinian identity and the fullness of his own and others' humanity in a way that is consonant with his refusal of party lines, orthodoxies, or ideologies.[39]

Said's account of his education is especially important in challenging an East-West binary: the memoir inverts the hierarchized opposition between human and inhuman so that it is those with institutional power who are defined as the others against whom Said and his classmates define themselves. The British—present in the memoir primarily as administrators and teachers at the private schools that Said attends—appear as the other even as—indeed because—they dehumanize and define themselves against the ethnically, nationally, and religiously diverse groups of students who, in relation to them, become uniformly constituted as Arabs. These British teachers and administrators exert a disciplinary force against the children whom they inculcate with a Western humanist education. In Said's accounts of his education at Alexandria's Victoria College, or "the Eton of the Middle East," the British become other by virtue of their dehumanizing treatment of Said and his classmates.

Out of Place not only reverses the binaries that Said identifies in *Orientalism* but productively reconfigures them in ways that give him and other colonial subjects agency and ownership over a history and culture marked by incursions from the West. Because Said imbibes British and U.S. attitudes and cultures from an early age, his sense of self complicates any clear-cut East-West distinctions or ways of dividing the world. Said's sense of self, like his education, is complex. By virtue of the Middle Eastern location of the Anglo and U.S. educational institutions that Said attends, and because this education belongs to Said and his classmates, it is not simply Western. Even as Said develops his resistance to the British authorities, his mind is shaped by the tenets of a Western education that these authorities pass down. Moreover, Western literature and music come to hold an intensely private meaning for Said, constituting one of his deepest bonds with his mother. When his mother is ill with cancer, their worries go into abeyance when they attend a Shakespeare play in London. Said describes experiencing Shakespeare's lines "as if spoken in the accents of wartime Cairo, back in our little cocoon, the two of us very quiet and concentrated, sharing the language and communion despite the disparity in our ages and the fact that we were nevertheless mother and son, for the very last time" (*Out of Place* 53). As the Shakespeare performance bridges a generational rather than a national or cultural difference, Shakespeare's language becomes part of Said's personal landscape, one whose cadences and rhythms give him a rare experience of belonging.[40] While at Victoria College, Said contrasts his disengagement from school with "the complicated but mostly inarticulate inner life I cherished and lived through the emotions and sensations I derived from [Western] music, books, and memories intertwined with fantasies" (202). Here, as throughout the memoir, Said represents the humanist tradition as one that, above all, is a source of private sustenance and survival, separate from the colonizing force of educators and educational institutions. The empires of Britain, France, and the United States directly shape Said's educational experiences and identity in a way that shows just how intertwined the lines are between colonizer and colonized. Thus the memoir reflects Said's investments in a Western humanist tradition even as Said's representations of educational institutions support his critique of humanism's implications in imperial practices, his awareness of how it is used to further an imperial power's economic and social domination.[41]

In its representations of a Western humanist tradition, Said shows how memoir can nuance postcolonial theory in enabling ways. Leila Ahmed makes a similar move in *A Border Passage: From Cairo to America—A Woman's Journey*, a memoir that strongly resonates with *Out of Place*. Ahmed, a former schoolmate of Said's sister Jean and now a professor of women's studies and religion at Harvard Divinity School, represents a similarly complex view of the relationship she has to Western culture and colonialism; as she explores in her memoir how "we always embody in our multiple shifting consciousness a convergence of traditions, cultures, histories" (25), she represents not only the oppressiveness of Western institutions but also how the English language and literature have nourished and freed her imagination. As the memoir genre allows Ahmed to detail this relationship, it serves as a corrective to theory in general and to *Orientalism*'s binaries in particular. She notes, "No doubt it is part of the nature of grand, overarching theories, theories that redefine, as

Orientalism did, ways of seeing of an entire era, that they will overlook or erase particular terrains of experience" (240). By contrast, memoir affords her a way "to voice and to recognize the complexity of the field—and the world and experiences—with which we all struggled" (241). Published the same year as *A Border Passage*, *Out of Place* suggests memoir's importance for going places theory cannot, as the two memoirs also register the direction in postcolonial studies to nuance representations of Western culture and its humanist traditions without undercutting critiques of colonialism's violence.

Memoir serves as an equally productive site to carry on the work of diaspora theory. As Said's account of his family history—one that is worldly and diasporic—complicates, as does his account of his education, the East-West divides and the Orientalism that inhere in Western humanism, it also profoundly unsettles the unacknowledged ways that theories of diaspora remain tied to dominant forms of nationalism and to the West more generally. As *Out of Place* details Said's family history, it documents the heterogeneity of the region itself from 1935 until 1947, when Said and his family were driven out of Palestine. In the midst of political upheaval, the Saids lost all their property (though this loss was cushioned by the family's business in Egypt) and Said lost his childhood worlds of pre–civil war Lebanon and cosmopolitan Cairo as well as Palestine. In *Out of Place*, as Said dwells in the worldly and "amphibious" time that predates the 1948 establishment of the state of Israel—one characterized by what Said calls "a dancelike maze of personalities, modes of speech, backgrounds, religions, and nationalities" (190)—his foray into his beginnings serves as a reminder both of the constructed nature and historicity of nationalism and of nation-states in the Middle East, and also of their power and violence. In its unsettling of categories of national identity and East-West divides, *Out of Place* stands in contrast to *Thirty-six Views* and *Turning Japanese*, both of which are symptomatic of the humanities' reliance on and reification of national formations and related ethnic, racial, regional, and cultural binaries, even in poststructuralist mobilizations of diasporic identities.

If *Out of Place* shows national and diasporic identities to be products of a historical process, it also represents them as real—and often violently imposed, or withheld. Counter to Davidson and Mura, the stakes and often involuntary circumstances of Said's dislocations and relocations mean that neither the luxury of poststructuralist play nor embrace of a freely chosen diasporic identity are available to him. Said's memoir theorizes an identity that simultaneously emerges out of a sense of place, and from a lack of belonging to the places in which Said lives. Identity therefore derives from a dialectic of presence (or place) and absence (being out of place). Said describes first becoming politically aware of himself as Arab when he's at Princeton during the 1956 Suez crisis and the emergence of Arab nationalism under Egyptian president Gamal Nasser and then at Harvard during the Arab-Israeli Six-Day War of 1967. However, that Said doesn't arrive at an Arab or Palestinian identity until his adult years in the United States in no way undermines the reality of this identity.[42] Evidencing greater suspicion of reigning poststructuralist formulations of identity than do Davidson or Mura, Said's conception of identity paradoxically ends up being the most flexible and indeterminate, the most context-specific and insistent on identity as process grounded in particular experiences of family, culture, place, and time.[43] *Out of Place* documents the material reality and effects of national identities and borders constructed through the processes of colonialism, and the violence used to establish and maintain them. Moreover, Said's accounts of his and his family's experiences involve them being denied rather than defying national identity, and their mobility results not only from class privilege but also from necessity. Although the Said family has the economic means to travel between the Middle East and the United States, they are limited by the national identities available to them. Said's narrative about his mother's status as a "nonperson" after the fall of Palestine left her without passport or citizenship speaks to the ongoing force of national borders and identities. Said writes of how her visitor's visa ran out when she was comatose and dying of breast cancer in 1990 while in Maryland with Said's sister, Grace. As a result, "Grace, who was living with and selflessly caring for her, found herself involved in deportation hearings as my mother approached her very last days" (133). As this account makes painfully clear in ways diaspora theory often overlooks, a diasporic existence is not simply chosen but is violently regulated by nation-states.

In his memoir's descriptions of his family's movements across national borders, although Said does not utilize discourses of diaspora circulating in the 1990s academy, his memoir nonetheless articulates closely with—and advances—theories of diaspora. Through the density of his richly detailed narrative, Said posits in his memoir a complex formulation of diasporic experience that neither reifies nor denies the power of national boundaries. His memoir renders not just the freedoms afforded by mobility but also its liabilities when it is not chosen, and the constraints national boundaries and identities impose even for those with economic privilege. In this way his memoir makes a theoretical contribution to postcolonial and diaspora studies. As do other memoirs of the 1990s—for example Leila Ahmed's brilliant *A Border Passage*—*Out of Place* provides through its density of detail a way to resist the overgeneralizations of theory, to extend and develop theoretical insights through grounding them in specific times and places.

Through memoir Said similarly engages cosmopolitan discourse: in its thick account of historical realities, *Out of Place* offers a "worldliness" that serves as an alternative to how contemporary theorizations of cosmopolitanism retain Western biases and bolster dominant nationalisms. As Said represents what he calls in the memoir the "rich, teeming, historically dense metropolises, Jerusalem and Cairo" (235), this heterogeneity represents a cosmopolitanism that neither emanates from the West nor relies on the logic of nations.[44] From the various places that he lives as a child (Cairo, Jerusalem, Dhour el Schweir), Said experiences crisscrossings and convergences of people of various national, regional, racial, ethnic, and religious identities. Describing the family's Cairo friends, who are of mixed Lebanese, Egyptian, Armenian, and Turkish origins, Said observes, "we were all Shawam, amphibious Levantine creatures whose essential lostness was momentarily stayed by a kind of forgetfulness, a kind of daydream, that included elaborate catered dinner parties, outings to fashionable restaurants, the opera, ballet, and concerts" (195). The sophistication and heterogeneity of Said's Middle Eastern locales contrast dramatically to the United States that he first encounters as a student at Mount Hermon. In *Out of Place*, "middle America" appears as a landscape of "social vacancy" and "enforced desolation" (235); Mount Hermon consists for Said of "pristine woods, apple orchards, and the Connecticut River valley and hills stripped of their history" (235).[45] The fluidity of identities and borders that Said describes in the Middle East represents a rich "other worldliness" that not only serves as an alternative to a cosmopolitanism that radiates from the West, but that also unsettles and historicizes the seemingly timeless, and decidedly nationalist, Arab-Israeli binary (what Said calls in *Orientalism* the "timeless eternal") on which dehumanization of Palestinians and the delegitimation of their struggles for land and belonging depend.[46]

Counter to models of cosmopolitanism that circulate in the 1990s academy, "worldliness" in *Out of Place* is not primarily a feeling that enables a claim to world citizenship, but a complex state of identification and disidentification that emerges in response to a mix of historical and personal conditions. Said elsewhere has distinguished his endorsement of worldliness from cosmopolitanism: "When I talk about worldliness, I don't just mean a kind of cosmopolitanism or intellectual tourism. I'm talking about the kind of omnicompetent interest which a lot of us have that is anchored in a real struggle and a real social movement" (Wicke and Sprinker 242). Worldliness, in other words, is not just a state of mind, nor is it the ability to travel freely to and establish a sense of belonging in any given place. Instead, for Said, worldliness is a paradoxical condition that develops out of being at home with a lack of home or belonging. As Abdul JanMohamed notes, "Worldliness represents in Said's criticism . . . the critic's achieved freedom from loyalty and subordination to specific ideologies, cultures, systems, worlds. Seen in this way, worldliness is not opposed to homelessness, but is its complement. 'Worldliness-without-world' and 'homelessness-as-home' are different formulations privileging the same subject position: that of the specular border intellectual" (113). If through their cosmopolitanism (or "intellectual tourism") Mura and Davidson lay claim to the pleasures of belonging at home and abroad, Said is more interested in worldliness as a metaphysical and material position of displacement that one should embrace without romanticizing it or denying its loneliness and pain. His memoir advances this ethos and contributes to the work of postcolonial studies as it maps the material conditions out of which worldliness arises.

If *Out of Place* illustrates how worldliness—or what might in the academy more commonly go by the name cosmopolitanism—does not necessarily support or issue from nation-states, it also evidences nations' power to disrupt states of worldliness or cosmopolitanism and to extend or deny rights for which these states cannot compensate. In *Out of Place* the cosmopolitanism, or worldliness, of the "rich, teeming, historically dense metropolises" of pre-1948 Jerusalem and Cairo is affirmed, without forgoing the Palestinian identity that Said comes to through the very experience of national dispossession and delegitimation. The "family album" inserted midway through *Out of Place*—a chronologically ordered set of photographs that feature private Anglo and American schools, vacations, and affluent family affairs—ends with a photograph of Said's family's summer home in Dhour el Schweir. The caption under the photo of the home with a gaping hole reads, "A 1980 view of the summer house rented from 1946 to 1969 in Dhour el Schweir. The rocket hole made during the Lebanese Civil War went through the master bedroom" (n.p.).

This picture, which forecloses any utopian readings of the region's independence from concerns of nation, starkly portrays the inability to maintain a space of fluidity, a suspension of national and ethnic boundaries, in a region marked by violent boundary drawing.

Said's memoir also complicates assumptions that cosmopolitanism is tied to class privilege and consumption. The photograph at Dhour el Schweir serves as a poignant reminder that for Palestinians, wealth and a Western (or cosmopolitan) education might ease but in no way protect against one losing one's home. Palestinians, even those privileged to rent summer houses, intimately experience both the cultural rifts and discontinuities and the violence brought home by the establishment and enforcement of national boundaries that necessitate the development and strengthening of their own national identifications. Moreover, in ways also suggested by this photograph, the cosmopolitanism, or worldliness, represented in *Out of Place*, although related to class privilege, differs from the cosmopolitan formulations of the 1990s academy that are attached to consumption (expressed in Davidson's and Mura's memoirs through the buying of home furnishings or clothes).[47]

Thus the worldliness in *Out of Place* carries on the work of postcolonial studies as it offers an implicit critique of and an alternative to contemporary humanities scholars' theories of cosmopolitanism. Worldliness in Said's memoir accounts for the significance of ethos *and* depends on material conditions: *Out of Place* represents worldliness as not simply a sentiment or a free-floating state but as situated within economic and national structures. As it details the complexities of worldliness, the memoir neither justifies colonial violence nor endorses worldliness as compensation for the imposing and withholding of national identities. A metaphysical and a material condition, worldliness in *Out of Place*, like a diasporic existence, neither invalidates Palestinian identity nor mitigates the painful reality of displacement and exile. Worldliness serves, then, as a more supple and materially grounded cosmopolitanism that, like cosmopolitanism, carries a strong ethical imperative: worldliness allows one to think about how to live in a world divided into nations while neither wishing away national divisions nor succumbing to their logic as inevitable. In Said's hands, memoir accomplishes what theory is hard-pressed to do: an accomplice of theory, it serves as a way to map a worldliness that accounts for the delicate interrelations between affect and material conditions and to flesh out binary oppositions without dismissing their power.

Not only *Out of Place* itself, but also the attacks on it, provide a way to assess the contributions memoir can make to postcolonial studies, in the academy and in the wider public sphere. The 1999 attack on Said by Justus Reid Weiner, a U.S.-born scholar in residence at the Jerusalem Center for Public Affairs, is particularly telling. Weiner's article, published on the eve of *Out of Place*'s publication, shows the ongoing dependence of a Zionist politics on clear-cut binary oppositions, and the continuing relevance of Said's analysis in *Orientalism*. This article and its reception also suggest why Said's memoir makes important political interventions not despite, but because, it lingers on Said's prepolitical boyhood in ways that develop *Orientalism*'s insights and make them available to a broad readership. Weiner's article appeared in *Commentary*, a U.S.-based right-wing Jewish monthly that dubbed Said "the Professor of Terror" in the late 1980s. Insinuating that Said has no true claim to a Palestinian identity or to a history of forced exile, Weiner's article accuses Said of lying about having been born in a family home in Jerusalem and about having attended St. George's School Jerusalem. The mainstream media for the most part picked up and amplified Weiner's attack. The *New York Post* ran an editorial calling Said the "Palestinian Tawana Brawley"; the *Daily Telegraph*'s headline ran, "Past catches up with refugee from truth"; the *Wall Street Journal* labeled him "the false prophet of Palestine."[48]

Said's defenders moved on two fronts in this battle that has been likened to the one over Rigoberta Menchú's autobiography. They exposed the sloppiness of Weiner's research and the falsity of his claims, particularly the absurdity—and the megalomania—of his assertion that Said's memoir, begun in 1994 and completed in 1998, was written in response to Weiner's 1999 article. A *Salon* article by Christopher Hitchens also argues that defaming Said works "to heap insult on the injuries already suffered by the Palestinians, and to negate the work done by the Jewish and Israeli peace camp." Said made similar points in his written response; he positions Weiner's efforts to delegitimate him as "part of the attempt not to let us have a narrative" (quoted in Jaggi)—a charge that was supported when no major U.S. periodical published his rebuttal.

Conservative responses to Weiner's article also bear out Said's analysis, moving from a denunciation of Said for fraudulence to a discrediting of Palestinians' claims to be a people. These attacks depend on dehistoricizing and fixing national identities and borders and on charging academics on the Left with reductive thinking and self-righteous politics. On the one hand, Weiner's supporters insist that the "truths" that he uncovered render Said not really Palestinian and therefore unable to speak on behalf of Palestinians. On the other hand, these same critics read Said as representative of *all* Palestinians, and by delegitimating him they invalidate an entire people. For example, in *Salon*, David Horowitz states, "The myth Said has so artfully fabricated . . . may play well on liberal guilt strings, but it plays havoc with the historical facts" (n.p.). He moves from an indictment of Said to a dismissal of Palestinian nationalism and resistance movements, claiming that before the establishment of Israel, "the Palestinian elite . . . had no strong sense of national identity, let alone nationalist grievance until . . . after the establishment of the Jewish state. In fact, the Palestine Liberation Organization [PLO] was not created until 1964, 16 years after the birth of Israel" (n.p.). Horowitz's evocation of (a very partial) history insinuates that because Palestinian identity and nationalism are not fixed and unchanging, they, like Said, are suspect. As Horowitz attempts to set the historical record straight, he fails to mention the destruction of Palestinian society in 1948 and the occupation of the West Bank and Gaza, crucial factors in the consolidation of a Palestinian identity and the formation of the PLO. Calling Said's—and by extension Palestinians'—whole story a "political lie," Horowitz moves on to denounce the entire "left," calling its vision "a romance of good and evil, of liberators and oppressors. Is the requirement of sustaining such a Manichaean vision the flattening of a reality that is so much more complex, and the reshaping of its narrative truth?"

The irony here and throughout such responses is that it is Weiner and Horowitz who cannot accommodate the complexity of Said's reality, or see how his class privilege in no way invalidates his political identity or his displacement as a Palestinian. Indeed the complexity of his identity and the privilege he enjoys, accompanied as they are by the historical violations he experiences despite these factors, bring home the material reality of colonial violence all the more powerfully. If someone from an elite class with the right to U.S. citizenship has been subject to displacement and exile, what the memoir leaves unspoken but palpably present is how much greater the loss for those without Said's privilege and mobility. In any number of his other writings Said consciously makes use of his privilege to speak on behalf of—but not in the place of—Palestinians worse off than he.[49] This memoir is yet another way in which he uses his privilege (here, as a public intellectual with the ability to publish his story) on behalf of wider causes as well as more strictly private ones. In *Out of Place*, as Said inventories his past as a way to grapple with his illness, there is no attempt to mask his class privilege or to make his pain representative or his story collective. And yet the attacks on his memoir, as Said himself points out, show the extent to which his story is inseparable from a more collective one. His text is indeed a worldly one in that sense, and one that makes use of a genre of privilege, but not in order to uphold the status quo or to bolster his own "star" status.

This combination—of *Out of Place*'s intense inwardness and of Said's inescapable status as a public intellectual who represents the interest of his people—is a powerful one, particularly in the present era. When Horowitz broadens his attack on Said to issue charges of Manichaean thinking against the entire academic Left, he makes a move that is typical of neoconservative activists out to dismantle, in the name of "academic freedom," oppositional thinking in the academy and, more particularly, Middle Eastern and postcolonial as well as women's and ethnic studies. In the face of such an assault, and given the increasing aporia around Palestine in both the academy and mainstream U.S. culture, Said's traditionally literary memoir is important and timely. If *Out of Place* will not stem the tide of Horowitz's sweeping attack on academe as well as on Palestine, it has a key role to play in reaching those who might be swayed by Horowitz and his allies in what has become the contemporary version of the culture wars. Memoir enables Said, the "Professor of Terror" who embodies the "evils" of both academe and Palestine, to provide a narrative that derails neoconservative caricatures of the Left that involve charges of a reliance on "politically correct" binaries. *Out of Place* powerfully intervenes on two fronts: Palestinian struggles for human rights *and* the humanities' struggles for legitimacy in the mainstream U.S. culture.

In his memoir Said's humanism provides a binding link between public testimony and private memory, individual and collective experience, and literature and politics. As we saw in the culture wars, and in ways that remain true today, humanities scholars who embrace humanism regularly insist on the separation between these spheres and argue for the integrity and inviolability of the literary and the individual. Conversely, many postcolonial and cultural studies theorists depend on critiquing humanism and its basis in Western bourgeois individualism in order to establish the crucial connections between literature and politics and the individual and the collective. In contrast to both of these positions, Said provides a way to rethink humanism so that it joins rather than masks these inter-sections. If Western humanism has been characterized by, among other things, its Orientalism, whereby the humanity of (some of) those from the West has been defined at the expense of those from the East, Said strives for a humanism that is cognizant of power hierarchies, anti-imperialist, and tied to a human-rights agenda. He advocates on behalf of a human-ism that is both particular in its claims to Palestinians' rights to recog-nition and to their homeland and broad-based in its insistence that *all* people are deserving of human rights. In other words, regardless of Said's stated intentions that his memoir is not political, in however fugitive and surreptitious a manner it makes important interventions consonant with those he makes in his explicitly political writings.

In particular, *Out of Place*'s traditionally humanist form, together with Said's representative status, enables a liberal readership to question pro-foundly the Us-Them binaries on which the dehumanization of the Pal-estinian people depends. Indeed, Said's memoir forwards a human-rights agenda by way of, not despite, its intense inwardness and shunning of the overtly political. Moreover, the memoir's inwardness allows it to do this work in a way that reaches a liberal readership without itself replicating weak forms of liberalism or exclusionary forms of humanism.[50] As Said makes use of a genre that finds its basis in a humanist individualism, his memoir resists liberal "why can't we be friends" appeals or assertions that "we're all alike despite our differences." Nor does Said engage in a cel-ebration of differences or refusal of essences. Although the memoir itself resists a depoliticized form of postmodernism or a weak model of liberal-ism, it allows Said to appeal to those invested in such models. In addition the memoir defies neoconservative charges that those on the Left can only deal in polarities, polemics, and binaries. However politically "im-pure" such appeals may be, they are arguably crucial ones, especially in combination with the acute structural analysis that characterizes Said's overtly political writings that take as their subject the escalating crisis in the Middle East.

Said forwards his humanist vision in both an individualized and tradi-tionally literary form of address, and through a collective, on-the-ground human-rights register. A focus on his humanism can make manifest the integral connections between these seemingly opposed forms of address, and the necessity for postcolonial critics to utilize both in order to create a broad base of opposition to U.S. and Israeli state-sponsored forms of terrorism.

Homeland Security, House Resolutions, and a Return to Shangri La

Edward Said's death in 2003 was attended by a huge backlash in the mainstream U.S. press in obituaries that denounced him personally and all that he stood for and embodied.[51] As the controversy over his memoir indicates, this kind of reception was in no way unprecedented; it attended his life as well as his death. Attacks on Said's character have been particularly ferocious at times when the United States has most needed to divert attention from Israel's U.S.-supported human-rights abuses against Palestinians in the Occupied Territories.

To a significant degree Said's tremendous impact, measured in part by the controversy he excites, resulted from his refusal of academic boundedness, his insistence on being a critic in and of the world in its largest senses. Said's life stands as an example of how individuals and larger histories are linked, just as his memoir serves as a reminder of how lives and politics are at once connected and distinct, not reducible to one another. His example speaks to the importance of the work that individuals and their life stories can do for larger causes, and also of the dangers of substituting individual lives for larger political contexts and conditions.

Emerging almost at the same time as Said's death was the International Studies in Higher Education Act of 2003 (House Resolution 3077), a resolution that underwent extensive debate in the U.S. Congress that makes manifest the dangers of a focus on the individual, and—to return to Vicente Rafael's argument—the falseness of opposing the individual academic and the institutional. HR 3077, passed by the House of Representatives in October 2003 before foundering in the Senate, and in 2008 once again before Congress, was drafted to curtail what neoconservatives identify as the politicization of knowledge by area studies and postcolonial studies. As John Carlos Rowe observes, a focus on Said as an individual plays a key role in the federal government's new stage of censorship enacted on behalf of national security. Rowe explains, "named several times as the 'founder of Postcolonial Studies' in Stanley Kurtz's report to the subcommittee, Edward Said and *Orientalism* are central examples of what Kurtz terms the 'anti-Americanism' now taught in U.S. universities" (43). Noting the inaccuracy of identifying Said as the founder of postcolonial studies, Rowe argues that what makes this targeting of Said possible is Said's academic celebrity and his stature as a public intellectual who stands for resolutely "speaking truth to power." In HR 3077 individual history and area studies (the latter conflated with postcolonial studies) converge through the resolution's representation of the figure of Said, providing a cruel twist to Vicente Rafael's speculation that individual academics' histories provide a way to resist the institutionalization of area studies.

House Resolution 3077 not only suggests that academics' lives and institutional histories are intertwined, but it also clearly illustrates, along with the "homeland security" it purportedly serves, that the "private" figures of house and home have public uses that are national and international in scope. As Amy Kaplan notes of the present-day uses of the term "homeland," a "nostalgic notion of the homeland goes hand in hand with a modern security state, for the concept of homeland security emerged in the 1990s to integrate U.S. territory as one unit of command in a global map of military departments. . . . Thus the notion of the homeland draws on comforting images of a deeply rooted past to legitimate modern forms of imperial power" (9–10). In the name of homeland security and the fantasies it cannily conjures and the house resolutions it engenders, people within and outside of U.S. borders find themselves subject to the most intimate, individually registered forms of state regulation and violence.

As a return to Shangri La can help to illustrate, although private homes and "homeland" rulings and rhetoric are interrelated, they cannot be collapsed, nor does the former serve simply as an analogy for the latter. In the *Creating Shangri La* documentary, longtime Shangri La caretaker Jin De Silva tells of joking with Doris Duke when she presented him with his instructions for the day (he was cutting tiles for the floor of her Syrian room) by reminding her, "Rome was not built in a day." De Silva's reference to empire building is indeed an apt one in many if not all regards. In building Shangri La, Duke was engaged in the lengthy process of building from the ocean bottom up a retreat from a world in which her vast fortune afforded her no privacy. At the same time, as she carried on (and, in her ocean excavations, extended) her father's legacy as a "mover of the earth," she was involved in an imperial project. The creation of Shangri La involved Duke in routes of world travel where she used her enormous fortune and influence to extract and amass for herself the labor, raw materials, and artwork she desired in order to realize an Orientalist vision. Moreover, if the individual uses to which she put this fantasy differentiate it in significant ways from more direct forms of empire building (just as Duke's enormous and anonymous contributions in the United

States not only to the arts, but also to children, to domestic-violence victims, to environmental causes, and to education complicate any simple casting of Duke as an imperialist), the setting of Shangri La connects it to an imperialist history quite directly. Bracketing Duke's audacious ownership of ocean ground, the land on which Shangri La sits was, at the time of its purchase, part of U.S. territory—land illegally seized in the 1893 overthrow of the Hawaiian Kingdom. Duke continued to work on Shangri La as Hawai'i became the United States' fiftieth state through a plebiscite that gave voters—who included any U.S. citizen or national who had lived in Hawai'i for a year—one option that decidedly did not include recognition of Native Hawaiian sovereignty and return of never-relinquished lands.[52] Thus, and in a way that Said's *Orientalism* helps us to understand, the history of Shangri La can neither be reduced to an enterprise of empire building nor corded off as a fantasy or retreat from the real world and its imperial practices.

As a reading of Shangri La as, to recall Kazi Ashraf, "kind of an autobiography of Doris Duke" reveals, as do memoirs by Cathy Davidson, David Mura, and Edward Said, homes serve not only as sources of private fantasies and sustenance but also as profoundly worldly places. And if a house can be read as a kind of autobiography, memoir, too, functions as a kind of temporary and semiprivate home, as a constructed, furnished, idiosyncratic space into which readers are invited on intimate terms. Ellen Rooney's remarks about "the semiprivate room" provide a way to think about Shangri La and memoir as spaces that are at once private and public: "The semiprivate room is emphatically not a room of one's own in the home of one's family. The cadre that gathers in the space of the semiprivate is contingent, impermanent, only partially identified with one another, in some respects, wholly antithetical to the permanently bound and legally protected intimates that make up the normative family. Rather than grieve over the exclusions that enable and constrain it, the semiprivate makes active use of its partialities, accidents, and historical limits in order to generate critical exchange—an impersonal intimacy" (145). If Rooney's assertion regarding the privacy of the family home can be qualified, her words nonetheless wonderfully evoke the possibilities that entry into the social space of memoir affords to readers. And memoirs of home and travel, of belonging and displacement, offer particularly rich places for those who enter them to "inventory the traces" that complicate and conjoin individual fantasies and desires with larger hegemonic—and counterhegemonic—histories of nations, worlds, and peoples.

During a time when house resolutions and other measures are threatening to legislate postcolonial studies—and challenges to U.S. imperialism—out of existence, universities remain crucial sites to foster oppositional thinking and to imagine a cosmopolitanism that is not nationalist in nature. In accomplishing this work, memoirs offer academics an important complement to theory. If in today's repressive environment it is critical to maintain a place in the university for a resolutely political postcolonial theory, memoirs suggest the importance of making anticolonial histories available through the particularities of academics' own lives, of imagining worldly alternatives to imperial practices through humanist structures. Perhaps especially when they appear to escape the category of the political, memoirs allow academics to build on, extend the work of, and potentially confront the contradictions within and refashion the work of postcolonial theory during a time when it is under siege, and in a way that provides entry not only to other academics, but to a broader readership as well, allowing access to theories that might otherwise circulate only in academic spaces.

Professor Accused of Sexual Harassment

On November 10, 1999, student leaders at the University of Hawaiʻi were invited to a faculty congress meeting to discuss a proposal to reform the core curriculum. One of the most controversial aspects of the proposal pertained to the language requirement—many faculty members in the sciences vociferously opposed a reduced, but still in place, Hawaiian or second language requirement. The other major controversy concerned a proposed global perspectives requirement. Student leaders and some faculty protested this proposal because it did not ensure a non-Western perspective on non-Western cultures, and because it did not make central a specifically Hawaiian perspective and subject matter. The meeting was heated, with some faculty members even heckling students when they spoke.

Tensions present at the meeting had been building all year. Throughout the fall, Hawaiian activists, who had won seats for every important student office, had been forcefully criticizing the colonial nature of the existing core curriculum and demanding that the new core be more responsive to a Hawaiʻi—and Hawaiian—student body. Student activism, especially Hawaiian-led student activism, was a new phenomenon for many faculty members who were used to a fairly uninvolved student body. Moreover, faculty members were increasingly at odds with one another as they competed for radically shrinking resources in the face of several years of draconian budget cuts that were themselves symptomatic of a demoralizing lack of public respect and governmental support for the university. So at the meeting, when Piʻilani Smith, the president of the Associated Students of the University of Hawaiʻi (ASUH), passionately advocated on behalf of a non-Eurocentric Global Perspectives requirement, she encountered palpable resistance, especially when she called attention to the disparate percentages between the student population, which at the time consisted of 85.5 percent people of color, and the faculty and administration, which were 70 percent white, 73 percent male. She noted that the audience reflected those percentages, stating, "I see a lot of white, and as a Native woman and a person of color, I'm scared." At that point a number of faculty members began booing Smith, who concluded her testimony by stating that this behavior supported her assertion about the diversity problems on campus.[1]

Debates about the language requirements followed, the heat continued to rise, and now we get into the scene that is central to this chapter. My account of what follows draws on the transcript that Mamo Kim shared with me of the press statement that she delivered at a public forum that student leaders organized to protest the events described here.[2] Her account matches the descriptions that other student leaders gave at the forum, at subsequent faculty meetings, and in informal communications to me, and it also conforms with accounts by faculty members who wrote in to the faculty senate Listserv. There was little disagreement about what transpired at the faculty senate meeting and its aftermath (an event I did not witness); rather, the debates about these events concern their significance. When a language professor stated that the university's strategic plan called for diversity and that the study of language provides a way to learn about a culture and its people, one professor we will call B called out, "That's bullshit! That's a myth!" After the meeting, Student Caucus Vice-Chair Lance Collins confronted Professor B. He told him that if he discounted the connection between language and culture, "You need to go the fuck back to college and get a fucking education because you missed it the first time." Collins then left the building, with B following after him, yelling for Collins to stop. Collins refused, demanding to be left alone. B continued his pursuit, accompanied by several other professors. Outside the building Collins told B to "fuck off." B responded to Collins—who has taken public and often flamboyant positions at the university affirming same-sex relationships—by unfastening his belt buckle and moving toward Collins, shouting, "You want to fuck me? I'll fuck you. Let's fuck!" As he kept repeating this threat, Collins began crying and screaming to be left alone. Smith intervened, telling B, "Sir, step back. This is harassment. You are harassing a student. Step back, sir." B persisted, claiming that it was he who was the victim. Smith reminded B that his belt was undone and informed him that he was engaged in sexual harassment. As Smith, aided by an ASUH senator, tried to diffuse the situation *and* to document the illegality of B's behavior by putting a name to it, B shoved the senator aside, again shouting that it was he who was being harassed. The senator had to use his arms to block B from reaching Smith and Collins. Smith, repeatedly identifying herself as a student,

demanded that someone from among the congregated faculty disclose
B's name. B yelled to the other faculty, "Don't tell them! Don't tell them!"
Faculty began to disperse and B claimed, "I didn't do it, look," pointing to
his belt, which he had buckled. Collins again began crying and yelling at
B; two of B's friends advised B to leave. Smith continued to identify herself as a student and to ask for B's name; finally someone told her.[3] When
campus security arrived, B and his cohort quickly left. With their account
corroborated by a student witness, the students involved filed a report.
They also called the Honolulu Police Department. The city officer who
arrived refused to take Collins's statement, saying that he should instead
arrest Collins for harassing a professor.

Student response to the November 10 meeting was swift and decisive.
At a press conference and forum on student rights on November 15,
and in testimony to the Mānoa Faculty Senate at their next meeting, the
Graduate Student Organization (GSO) President Mamo Kim and other
student leaders called for B's immediate removal. Kim requested that the
faculty senate ask the board of regents for a revised and expanded pro-
cedure to handle discrimination complaints to better protect students.[4]
In a formal letter student leaders also notified peers at other universities
about B's actions. Students pursued unofficial responses as well. The day
after the meeting anonymous fliers appeared all over campus featuring a
picture of B, disclosing his home address and phone number and an account of his behavior.

For the most part, faculty responded not by examining B's conduct or
their own but by focusing on the students' behavior. In e-mails on a faculty Arts and Sciences list, what faculty seemed to take most personally
and find most incendiary was Smith's citing of faculty and student de-
mographics, and her admission of fear in the presence of so many white
faces. Faculty members perceived her attention to institutional racism as
itself a racist attack, and denounced her anger but ignored her expression
of vulnerability. Some women of color did address how the events at the
meeting and its aftermath were indicative of a crisis that faculty needed
to take seriously. However, the overwhelming reply was that B and Collins were just two extreme individuals acting badly, and that Collins and
Smith brought on such behavior through their bad manners and disruptive behavior.

After being threatened by B, Collins filed a formal grievance against
him.[5] He charged B with discrimination based on age, sex, ancestry/race
(listed on the grievance form as Filipino, Latvian, Irish, and American

Indian), and sexual orientation in violation of the university's nondiscrimination policy. In addition Collins charged B with violating the university's hostile environment sexual harassment policy. In his grievance Collins asked for the following: (1) that B's employment be terminated; (2) if not fired, that B undergo "psychological evaluation, anger management, chemical castration"; (3) tuition waivers; (4) student housing; and (5) free parking. The university dismissed both the discrimination and the harassment charges. They claimed that because B's comments did not prove that he knew Collins, B therefore was reacting to what Collins said rather than to who he is. In explaining this decision in his letter to Collins and B, the university administrator pointed to the lack of a pattern of discriminatory conduct and said that B's actions neither precluded Collins from speaking nor resulted in the withholding of educational benefits. And although the university labeled B's actions hostile, the administrator noted that Collins's were, too. The university viewed the case as one not of a professor harassing a student, but rather as one involving a mutual failure of civility and respect, and concluded by urging both Collins and B to conduct themselves with a better attitude in the future, and with civility.

This story is suggestive of the complexity of student-teacher relationships. On the one hand it evidences the institutional power that faculty members have over students, and ways that faculty members and administrators can be inattentive to structural differences between students and teachers. What dropped from consideration in faculty discussions of and administrators' responses to the events was Collins's status as a nineteen-year-old student, albeit a flamboyant and disruptive one. On the other hand, as indicated by some of the different forms that students' protests took—and I think here most particularly of the public post of B's picture with his home address and phone number—students do wield real psychological power over faculty, and professors and students can feel emotions toward one another and behave in ways that are influenced but not determined by their institutional standing.

Just as the story involving B and Collins involves students provoking faculty members in ways that are disrespectful, sensationalist, outrageous, and even threatening, so too and more importantly, it includes faculty conduct that cannot be upheld through theory, or put into the service of a tale about "good teaching." Rather, this story speaks as well to abuses of power on the part of faculty toward students. In the ways that it does so, I argue in this chapter, it can be used to expose problems that inhere within a range of progressive pedagogical positions, including those ushered in through feminist and women's studies. The B account can serve, I hope, as a useful way to consider the multiple significances of the stories that we tell about our teaching—even those that occur in academic memoirs by feminists. Stories about teaching often have a certain generic predictability wherein the most egregious errors end up being learning experiences that benefit student and teacher alike. When professors use themselves or their teaching as texts in memoirs, memoir's individual(ist) focus and concern with feelings often preclude rigorous institutional analysis and also, I argue, demonstrate a related lack of empathy or emotional intelligence. I believe that sometimes stories such as the one involving B need to circulate in order to bring us face to face with our naked authority and power. In using the B story in this way, and in my analysis of it in this chapter, my objective is not to level the serious differences between B and the feminist academics whose memoirs I consider, nor is it to dismiss the complex emotional dynamics and forms of agency, and acting out, that structure student-teacher relationships. My intent is rather that we not be seduced by our own and others' interested narratives, and that this story serve as an occasion to think about the institutionally protected authority that professors hold over students, the complications and responsibilities that come with this kind of power, and the self-interest that can fuel theory as well as personal narrative.

The B narrative registers not only issues that attend professorial privilege, but also, and as importantly, academics' anxiety and increasing sense of powerlessness. This crisis in authority, felt perhaps most acutely by white men whose formerly unmarked positions of privilege were challenged in the 1980s and 1990s, can be attributed to conditions that include not only students questioning professors' legitimacy from a politicized standpoint, but also a shrinking budget (cuts in Hawai'i to the university were sufficiently devastating to lead to a two-week strike in 2001), and a lack of support from a public in doubt of the value of a university education.

Academic memoirs, especially those that take pedagogy and the university as their subjects, have become important sites to negotiate this crisis in authority. These memoirs include James Phelan, *Beyond the Tenure Track* (1991); Victor Villanueva, *Bootstraps* (1993); William H. Pritchard, *English Papers: A Teaching Life* (1995); Jane Tompkins, *A Life in School: What the Teacher Learned* (1996); Jane Gallop, *Feminist Accused of Sexual Harassment* (1997); Alvin Kernan, *In Plato's Cave* (1999); Don J. Snyder, *The Cliff Walk: A Memoir of a Job Lost and a Life Found* (1997);

Mark Edmundson, *Teacher: The One Who Made the Difference* (2002); and James M. Lang, *Life on the Tenure Track: Lessons from the First Year* (2005). These memoirs have been published by prestigious academic presses (Yale, Johns Hopkins, and Duke) as well as by top trade presses (Random House and Little, Brown). Some, especially those by white men in retirement or near the end of their academic careers, express nostalgia for an old-fashioned humanism and a love for literature at odds with the contemporary politicization and professionalization of a humanities education as well as its devaluation in the public eye. Writing these memoirs at a time when the star system was at its apex, these authors rely on their cultural capital and assert their authority while simultaneously disavowing it or expressing a sense of having lost their standing with students, and in the profession or with the public at large. Alvin Kernan captures this mix in his opening to *In Plato's Cave*: Yale, he explains, "looks and feels just the same as it did when I first saw it fifty years ago. . . . But I know almost no one there any longer; and it is much the same at Princeton, where (except for a few months when it was stolen) my portrait hangs in Procter Hall in the graduate college among two long rows of graduate deans in bright red, orange, and blue academic gowns, staring defiantly at one another night and day, their names all unknown to the students who gulp down their food on the way to class" (xiii). As Kernan provides a broader history of the academy through his account of his career, he inhabits the authority of his distinguished position while also linking his career's end and his obsolescence to a more general decline in the humanities; he describes the incentives offered for retirement "to get the fossils out of the way so that younger people, women and minorities in particular, could be appointed in our places" (293). Although of a later generation than Kernan, Don Snyder expresses a similar sense of disempowerment in *The Cliff Walk*. He tells of how his wife, a stay-at-home mother, offended "the feminists" at a party before he was denied tenure at Colgate, saying that "when we were alone I cautioned Colleen that someday I might need letters of recommendation from these women in order to grab a better job at a much better school" (14). That Snyder not only is unable to procure that better job, but also that he is fired from the one he has—a condition he attributes to a changing political terrain in the academy that leaves white men in tenuous rather than tenured positions—infuses his account of his former sense of superiority with bitterness as well as irony.[6]

What interests me is how the nostalgia and reactionary elements that accompany these narratives by men at the ends of their academic careers, and the uncertainties that result when their authority is questioned by the entry of "women and minorities," resonate in unexpected ways with memoirs by feminists writing at the pinnacle of their careers, whose scholarship plays a trend-setting role in the humanities. In this chapter I focus on two such memoirs: Jane Gallop's *Feminist Accused of Sexual Harassment* (*FASH*) and Jane Tompkins's *A Life in School*. Whereas Gallop, feeling divested of power when charged with sexual harassment, writes her memoir to shore up her authority in the name of feminism, Tompkins strives through memoir to cast off her institutional authority and a politicized approach to literature. Despite the seeming polarities of these memoirs, as well as their significant differences from memoirs like Kernan's, as *FASH* and *A Life* grapple with issues of power and authority, they partake in Kernan's nostalgia and individualism. I put *FASH* and *A Life* in relation not only to explicitly conservative memoirs, but also in dialogue with black feminist bell hooks's body of work, including her 1994 *Teaching to Transgress* and her memoirs *Bone Black* (1996) and *Wounds of Passion* (1999). Doing so provides a way to gauge the place of feminism and feminist theory in the academy today, and also a sense of how feminists, through narratives about teaching, negotiate both the anxieties that accompany the authority that they have accrued with the institutionalization of feminism and the star system, and also the challenges to this authority brought on by the crisis in the value and meaning of a humanities education. *FASH* and *A Life in School* not only suggest the difficulties of performing institutional critiques of authority through the genre of memoir, but they also dramatize with particular clarity the challenges that feminists face in the academy today. As they do so, these memoirs' emotional failures expose limitations in reigning cultural theories, and also difficulties in accounting for institutional power and privilege.

Taken together, analyses of *FASH*, *A Life*, and hooks's *Teaching to Transgress* provide a way to track the purposes to which stories about teaching are being put in the contemporary academy—feminist academics' accounts of their classroom practices and their relationships to their students yield important insights into conditions that are shaping the humanities in crucial ways: the star system, the professionalization of literary studies, and the institutionalization of feminist and cultural studies. Considered alongside hooks's memoirs and other writings, these three works register the material and psychic impact of these conditions as they exist in relation to the underfunding and devaluation of the humanities.

Vested Interest and Unfeeling Sensations

In 1992 prominent feminist theorist Jane Gallop was charged by two of her women students with sexual harassment. A highly publicized case that her students lost, it perhaps reached its height of notoriety early in 1994, when *Lingua Franca*, then the *People* magazine of the academic world, made it their cover story (Talbot). Shortly after this article appeared, Gallop came to UC Berkeley, where I was a graduate student at the time, to give a talk on Derrida's *Spurs: Nietzsche's Styles*. True to form, Gallop appeared for this talk in full cowgirl regalia—red cowboy hat and frilly red cowboy shirt, red leather boots, and spurs. At the podium before a room packed with humanities faculty and graduate students, Gallop pulled her text from her briefcase and blushed furiously, explaining that she had brought the wrong talk. Instead of the *Spurs* talk she had in hand "The Teacher's Breasts," an essay exploring teacher-student erotics, which she then indeed read. Audience members familiar with Gallop's penchant for the outrageous debated for days after whether or not Gallop had deliberately staged this performance. Was Gallop, using cowboy tactics, flaunting her interest in sexualized pedagogy in defiance of the scandal surrounding her own pedagogy and, at the same time, by pretending to have brought the wrong paper by mistake, staging a situation in which her audience would cut her some slack and not barrage her with questions? Or was her mistake genuine and her embarrassment sincere? Gallop's performance poised her between the roles of outrageous bad girl and naive blunderer, with her outfit's redness—evoking the cover of *Feminist Accused of Sexual Harassment*—signifying either passion and daring, or, alternatively, shame and ignominy.

Whether intentional or not, even for less enthusiastic Freudians than Gallop such as myself, the spectacle of Gallop reading "The Teacher's Breasts" outfitted in red and wearing spurs is ripe for a symptomatic reading, especially at the pinnacle of the academic star system and in the midst of the publicity about her sexual harassment case. This moment, wherein spurs accompany attention to the teacher's breasts, strikes me as a staging of the violence, force, and discipline on which Gallop's "stardom," pedagogy, and sexual experimentation in the classroom are premised. As I argue in this chapter, the spurs aptly register the will to control that characterizes Gallop's assertions of sexuality in the classroom. More generally, Gallop's spurs bespeak the disciplining force that can underlie a professor sexualizing the classroom—calling attention to her breasts in the name of a feminist pedagogy, particularly in an era in which feminism has received institutional recognition, and in one that casts professors as celebrities and performers.

Gallop's performance of "The Teacher's Breasts" at UC Berkeley invites reflection on ways disingenuousness or naïveté can be as much of a performance as—and can work in tandem with—sensationalist and celebrity display or Derridean play. In *Feminist Accused of Sexual Harassment* Gallop both cashes in on her widely known bad-girl reputation and, enabled by the memoir genre, represents herself as a straight-shooting feminist scholar in a way that masks both the performative nature of this sincerity and the desire for power and control that undergird her expressions of sexuality. Nevertheless, in *FASH*, beneath the raciness and bad-girl persona, and the simultaneous assertion of straightforward naïveté, resides a pleasure in power play that is something other than "bad" as in radical and feminist. Exploring this dynamic provides insights into how and why feminists employ stories about teaching to negotiate the changing terrain of the humanities, as these stories also convey lessons about the star system, feminist theory, and the institutionalization of feminism and poststructuralism.

Published in 1997, *Feminist Accused* is Gallop's account of being charged with quid pro quo sexual harassment at the University of Wisconsin–Milwaukee by two graduate students—both lesbian feminists. Despite the promises of complete disclosure intimated by the combination of its tabloid title, its straightforward style, and the memoir genre, and notwithstanding its chatty informality and its brevity (112 pages), *FASH* is a rhetorically sophisticated and complexly organized book in which readers learn details of the case against Gallop piecemeal and never in full. In fact, Gallop's turn to memoir and away from a language full of deconstructive play participates in a wider movement in the academy, one that emerges from a struggle to maintain authority within and beyond the academy, and one that forgoes neither rhetorical sophistication nor participation in academic hierarchy.

FASH's complex structuring both results from and also registers the dissonance between Gallop's perception of her embattled position within the academy as a feminist and the academy's protection of her privilege. Part of *FASH*'s complexity lies in the fact that it is only with the utmost difficulty that readers can assemble the partial details of Gallop's case. The clarity of Gallop's language camouflages the book's patchy presentation of the case, obscuring how, despite Gallop's claims regarding the threat her case posed to feminism, the harassment charge was summarily dismissed by her university. The basic outline of the case as it eventually emerges in *FASH* follows; the page numbers track Gallop's delayed, nonchronological, and erratic presentation. In November 1992 (77) two lesbian feminist graduate students charged Gallop with quid pro quo sexual harassment (32). As Gallop explains, "They both claimed that I had tried to get them to have sex with me and that, when they rejected me, I had retaliated by withdrawing professional support (in one case with negative evaluations of work, in the other with a refusal to write letters of recommendation)" (32). The students filing the charges pinpointed Gallop's harassment as beginning at a 1991 graduate student gay and lesbian conference when Gallop announced that "graduate students are my sexual preference" (81, 86). That night at a lesbian bar Gallop engaged in a public and passionate kiss with one of her advisees, who later charged her with sexual harassment (91). This student and one other filed charges of sexual harassment on a university form headed "Complaint of Discrimination" (77). On their complaint forms, under the section "Resolution Sought," the students listed four demands. They asked that Gallop understand that making the complaint the subject of intellectual inquiry constitutes retaliation, that she be reprimanded, that she be kept out of any decisions regarding their work, and that the department create a mechanism to deal with sexual harassment (77). In April 1993 these students and others formed SASH (Students Against Sexual Harassment) and publicly announced their charges against Gallop (67). The university did not find in favor of the students' charges (33), but did find Gallop in violation of a university policy on consensual amorous relations, a decision for which Gallop's public kiss with one student formed the basis (33, 55, 95). This policy—one never delineated in *FASH*—recommends simply that a teacher engaged in sexual or amorous relations with a student avoid "conflict of interest" or "abuse of power" by reporting these relations to the dean and by arranging for other faculty to evaluate the student's work. Gallop's partial and disjointed presentation of the events in *FASH* obscures how the institution against which Gallop positions herself and feminism in fact supports and protects her, even as *FASH* allows for and signals a disjuncture between Gallop's sense of her own embattled authority and the authority that the institution grants her—a disconnect worth exploring for what it reveals about the place of feminism in the academy today.

The charges against Gallop were highly publicized both locally and nationally. To gain control over headline-making news, in *FASH* Gallop makes herself into dispassionate analyst as well as sensational subject. As Gallop uses the memoir genre to try to *depersonalize* the charges against her, in the process of analyzing them, she strives to gain ownership over the story being circulated about her. Gallop explores the sexual harassment case in relation to a changing historical and political landscape, focusing on the difference between feminism in the 1970s and that of the 1990s, and treating her own experience as a case study by which to understand the evolution of societal views toward sexual harassment. Foregrounding her identity as a feminist, she argues that hers is a "limit case" that demonstrates how sexual harassment is drifting from its feminist framework (7)—a shift that endangers not only feminist teaching and teachers, but also academic freedom. Gallop contends that universities' policies against consensual amorous relations between teachers and students make these relations a version of quid pro quo sexual harassment, a connection that Gallop—a vehement defender of such relations—passionately opposes.

On both surface and deeper levels, Gallop's case differs profoundly from the one involving B detailed at the outset of this chapter. Nevertheless, I analyze their points of convergence to expose problems with Gallop's discourse about "limit cases." As another limit case, B's takes to the other extreme the "excess" in the student-teacher relationship that Gallop valorizes when she analogizes her own "limit case" to others that cast hers in a positive light. Juxtaposing these two limit cases provides a way to account for the significant structural inequities between professors and students that Gallop disregards, and to read this neglect more symptomatically for what it reveals about contemporary academic culture and, in particular, the place of feminism. In order to understand the economy of the academic memoir, the role of feminist theory in the contemporary academy, and the star system, I also include responses to the case against Gallop by Dana Beckelman, one of the students who charged Gallop with sexual harassment, and I compare Beckelman's and Collins's use, as students, of "bad" or outrageous behavior and sensationalist public display that derives from feminist and queer theory. I also relate Gallop's use of sexualized authority and performances of power to B's. Although Gallop's public displays are not homophobic or overtly violent and threatening, as were B's, I find her sexualized behavior toward students to be motivated by a desire for control and power that professors in the 1990s both possess as a result of their institutional position *and* feel to be in jeopardy. This mix, I argue, exacerbates conditions wherein university policies cannot adequately protect students against professorial abuses of power, and exposes limits within feminist theory and its applications. These contradictions also result from ways the academy is at once idealized as a place of knowledge, but is also a workplace. Finally, my use of the B case aims to illuminate problems as well as possibilities that come with reading academics' individual experiences as representative of academic culture.[7]

Gallop's case is, in fact, far from representative. Even as she posits it as one that speaks to historical conditions, Gallop views it in almost complete isolation, neglecting structural analysis of the contemporary state of feminism and sexual harassment in a way that the individual focus of memoir helps to naturalize. Along with a few other limit cases that Gallop presents to bolster her arguments, in *FASH* her case and her other student-teacher sexual relationships stand in for student-teacher sex and the status of feminism from the 1970s to the present. Gallop contrasts the 1970s to the 1990s in order to claim that in the 1990s feminism is wanting and sexual harassment policies are out of control (24, 29). What Gallop's portrayal omits is not only a full analysis of how the institutionalization of feminism complicates feminist professors' relationships to students, but also the bigger picture of sexual harassment in universities. Through a solipsistic and narcissistic rendering that memoir enables, sexual harassment as most commonly practiced (between male professors and female students) simply disappears. Therefore, it bears highlighting, before turning to the specifics of Gallop's narrative, that sexual harassment continues to be a serious problem in universities despite the proliferation of policies against it. A 2005 report issued by the American Association of University Women Educational Foundation finds that two-thirds of college students say they have experienced sexual harassment (C. Hill and Silva), and a study published around the same time as *FASH* finds that 40 percent of women graduate students report experiencing harassment (Alger). Moreover, notwithstanding the presence of feminist critiques of sexual harassment, universities usually protect accused faculty members, and most women who file charges lose their cases.[8]

Despite the worsening of problems of sexual harassment, and in response to how feminist ideas have at once gained purchase *and* failed to solve problems of sexism and sexual harassment, a literature of backlash has emerged in academic as well as mainstream venues. This literature includes works by self-identified feminists who are overly quick to claim feminism's victories, or even its success in opposing men and heterosexual relations. In her review of *FASH*, for example, Daphne Patai criticizes Gallop for not making it clear that "'quid pro quo harassment'—the extortion of sexual favors as a condition of employment or advancement—is now a rarity" (88). Arguing in defense of "ordinary social relations in the workplace and the academy" (90), Patai denounces what she refers to as the "sexual harassment industry" (SHI) for what she takes to be its attack on men. She further argues that the SHI constitutes an "assault on heterosexuality" since she asserts that "the vast majority of people are heterosexual" (95). From a queer studies perspective, Ann Pellegrini and others—Gallop included—also take sexual harassment policies to task for their heterosexism. As they draw on the deconstruction of sex and gender by feminist and queer theory, they frequently fail to address the significance that laws are formulated in response to a society and problems that remain sexist and heterosexist. These studies, which, like Gallop's books and articles, are published by prominent and often progressive presses and journals, deploy queer and feminist theories in often ungrounded ways. Such uses of theory, made possible by the inroads of feminism into the academy, obfuscate the problem of sexual harassment and so partake, however inadvertently, in the antifeminist backlash that is sweeping across the country. Thus, as *FASH* presents Gallop's "liberatory" sexualized relationships to her students as at once representative and as special—a combination engendered by the memoir genre—it suggests how the feminism of the 1990s academy, in failing to address adequately the significance of both its successes and its failures, can participate in the very antifeminism that it decries.

Other academic memoirs also demarcate, through their frequent representations of sexual harassment, an understanding of the place of feminism in the 1990s academy that at once attributes too much power to it, and that reveals its ineffectiveness. Alvin Kernan, for example, nostalgically details the private, quiet, "old way" of handling sexual harassment that causes "less pain" than the current legalistic way, and he assesses how since the 1980s feminists have injected "political and social concerns" into departments (155, 256). In his extended discussion of the Thomas McFarland case at Princeton—in which feminists lobbied to have him fired, McFarland was suspended, then reinstated, then bought out but ruined in reputation—Kernan finds that the outcome "might well have been the same . . . , or maybe the old boys' club would have protected

him, but it certainly would have been managed in a less painful and destructive fashion" (256). In his account, the power that Kernan attributes
to feminist critics exists in tension with the fact that those feminists who
oppose McFarland's sexual practices prove unable to achieve their objectives. As accounts such as Kernan's magnify the power and effectiveness of feminist critique, such representations of sexual harassment both
register anxieties over feminism's successes in transforming the academy
and aim to contain its power.

As Gallop reads the state of feminism in the 1990s through her sexual
harassment case and capitalizes on the controversy that surrounds her,
she illustrates the sensationalism that fuels the memoir boom and the
academic celebrity system. As critics have noted, like the memoir movement to which it is related, the star system feeds on confession and transgression.[9] Kernan caustically remarks on this in his memoir: "Celebrity
became as critical to careers as knowledge of languages once had been.
It didn't much matter whether the publicity was good or bad, scandal
in academe was like blood in the water to reporters and anchors on the
evening news" (262). Gallop not only capitalizes on the promises the
memoir genre holds of self-disclosure, but she also utilizes sensationalist
strategies to turn her case against universities and their sexual harassment policies and less directly—since they are largely absent from her
account—against the students who charged her. If in this way the subject
of her memoir is not herself, Gallop nonetheless harnesses her institutional status and the sensationalism surrounding the charges against her
to further her own career. With expert handling she takes full advantage
of conditions in the academy: her case provides publishing opportunities
with top academic presses and journals, and it garners her invitations to
participate in conferences and other forums.

Gallop's equation of sensationalism and knowledge production puts
her at the forefront of an academic culture that has created prestigious
venues for sensationalist expression by academic stars in the 1990s.
Whereas SASH members must make use of fliers to disseminate their
positions, Gallop has access to Duke University Press—her book appears
as part of its Public Planet series, an affiliation that positions Gallop and
her actions at the cutting edge of academic production, as progressive
and hip. Gallop is arguably able to publish *FASH* with Duke not only or
primarily because of the novelty of her case, but because her name on
a book ensures sales, particularly at a time when memoirs by "academic
stars" circulate as commodities and narratives about public culture are

in vogue. Unlike her students, Gallop is in the position of being able to make her own splashy headlines, as she does in *FASH* as the feminist accused in its sensationalist title, while also serving as the analyst of her own case in the book's more serious contents. Moreover, her version of the case dominates in *Lingua Franca* and its more scholarly but equally starstruck counterpart, the *Chronicle of Higher Education*. Gallop also receives the opportunity to extend her defense of student-teacher sex in the distinguished venue of a 1999 *Critical Inquiry* forum, one that includes only supportive responses to the position she outlines, all by faculty members.[10] Indeed, not until the following year did the journal include negative criticisms of her position, though still none by students. In this way Gallop's case, and her sensationalist account of it, are continuous with, rather than a disruption of, reigning academic hierarchies and knowledge production.

Both in writing *FASH* and in her pedagogy, Gallop fails to calibrate that her sensationalism is sanctioned—even rewarded—by academic institutions. As Gallop herself proclaims with relish, she has built her career on being a bad girl.[11] While her bad-girl activity, which relies on a dramatic thwarting of sexual and professional conventions, has remained consistent over time during her years in the academy—outrageous outfits, frank disclosures, imprudent behavior, and what she calls "shocking informality"—what has changed is her institutional position, and that of the feminism in whose name she performs. Gallop disregards in symptomatic ways the difference between engaging in scandalous acts as a graduate student or assistant professor and doing so under the title of distinguished professor, during an era that has seen the institutionalization of feminist and then queer theory. Sensationalist display—especially of sexuality—if done from a marginalized position is often transgressive. It has been utilized to great effect by such organizations as ACT UP (AIDS Coalition to Unleash Power) and Queer Nation.[12] Done from a position of power, however—and Gallop is someone with heterosexual as well as professional privilege—such display, especially when encoded in a genre also premised on professional status, can translate into either a flaunting or a denial of privilege and can put feminist and queer politics into the service of the status quo.[13] In other words, when Gallop wears that skirt made up of men's neckties, it matters that she now does so as a company girl. And as her example illustrates, when academic stars masquerade as outlaws, feminist politics can be co-opted and queer politics normed.

Establishing correspondences between students' uses of sensationalism in the B and the Gallop cases, and then comparing their sensationalist displays to B's and Gallop's, serve to illustrate not only the importance of institutional position in determining the effects of sensationalist display, but also and more specifically, the extent to which the oppositional energies of feminist and queer theory depend on their eccentric position to the academy. In the B case students, in aggressive acts of disrespect for authority, anonymously posted fliers to render B personally vulnerable in the same institutional space wherein he had taken refuge in anonymity by refusing to give out his name. Beckelman also engaged throughout her graduate school career in sensationalist acts, and in ways energized by her grounding in feminist and queer theory, and she and her peers also used an in-your-face approach in disseminating complaints about Gallop. In FASH Gallop describes how students, including those filing complaints against her, organized SASH (Students Against Sexual Harassment) and picketed a national conference, "Pedagogy: The Question of the Personal," organized by Gallop. This conference convened in 1992 when the sexual harassment charges against Gallop were under investigation. SASH members used this conference to broadcast their charges to a national audience; they distributed bumper stickers that read "Distinguished Professors Do It Pedagogically" and fliers outlining their complaints against Gallop and calling for a boycott of her conference. As in the B case, students' sensationalist tactics were directed against a faculty member with institutional authority; indeed, Gallop's institutional power over these students far outweighed B's over Collins—her departmental standing as a "distinguished professor" and her professional standing gave her tremendous influence over their careers. In both cases students' behavior violated not only academic decorum and codes of civility, but possibly interfered with institutional rules about not discussing an in-process grievance. Their willingness to take recourse in unsanctioned and disruptive forms of expression can be seen to emerge from a lack of faith in the institution and its grievance processes—something Collins also evidenced when he used the grievance form itself as yet another opportunity to act up, with his demands for free parking and chemical castration! Through these various actions students suggest ways queer studies and feminism have politicized students' relationships to their professors and provided them with strategies for protest.

In contrast to the students, whose transgressive behavior suggests queer and feminist theory's possibilities for challenging authority, however problematically, from a position of powerlessness, both Gallop and B engage in sensationalist acts from positions of institutional privilege and protection. When B undid his belt buckle and threatened Collins, he not only displayed his anxiety regarding his institutional privilege but also abused his authority. Moreover, although the university did not condone his behavior, it did not formally condemn it or find B in violation of any university policies. Instead, the administrator's admonishments about civility level the differences between Collins's disrespectful speech ("fuck off") and B's sexual threat (saying "let's fuck" while unbuckling his belt). And finally, when he moves from the realm of the legal to the moral and reprimands both parties equally for their lack of civility, the administrator ends up actually reinforcing B's institutional power and privilege through the failure to acknowledge that B's ethical responsibilities as a faculty member differ from Collins's as a student.

Gallop, too, received institutional support for her sensationalist behavior. However, unlike B's, Gallop's actions—both in writing *FASH* and in the sexualized behavior toward students that led to the writing of it—are not overtly violent or threatening. Also in contrast to B's actions, Gallop's are career enhancing and commensurate with her position as a feminist theorist. Whereas B's behavior resulted from a loss of control and, at least locally, damaged his professional reputation, Gallop deliberately engages in sensationalist displays and professionally profits from them. *FASH* itself is one such display, and in contrast to B's silence regarding his actions, Gallop resolutely—both in *FASH* and in her other writings—argues on behalf of sensationalist and sexualized display that derive from student-teacher erotics:

> When I said that graduate students were my sexual preference, when I kissed my advisee in a bar for all to see, I was making a spectacle of myself. And, at the same time, I was being a teacher.
>
> The performance turned me on and was meant to turn my audience on, literally and figuratively. The spectacle was meant to shock and entertain, and to make people think.
>
> I gave this book a tabloid title because I wanted, again, to make a spectacle of myself. When I told friends of the title, they worried that the book would be mistaken for sensationalism rather than a thoughtful consideration of important issues.
>
> In fact, I'm hoping to produce a sensation. Not the hollow kind where sensation is achieved at the expense of thought. But the best kind, where knowledge and pleasure, sex and thought play off and enhance each other.

When I kissed my student at a conference, I was trying to produce just such a spectacle. But I failed to make myself understood.

By writing this book, I thought I'd give it another shot. (100–101)

Writing a sensationalist book, in other words, becomes the analogue for sexualized behavior toward students—Gallop finds both defensible, even laudable, performances directed toward the making of knowledge.

As Gallop directly links the writing of *FASH* to her sexualized behavior in the classroom and theorizes in support of both kinds of sensationalist display, her narrative reveals how in an academic culture in which teachers become performers playing to a broadly conceived professional audience, students undergo erasure, and in a way that exposes limitations to feminist and queer theory. When Gallop says that her public kiss with her student "turned me on and was meant to turn my audience on. . . . The spectacle was meant to make people think," and then when she acknowledges, "I failed to make myself understood," concluding, "By writing this book, I thought I'd give it another shot," her student is diminished to the status of prop, and any exploration of classroom erotics becomes reduced to a play for power (100–101). Gallop targets as the recipient of the attentions not her advisee, but those witnessing the kiss (and, in *FASH*, those reading about it). Along with—indeed as an integral part of—teaching and writing, sexualized student-teacher displays for Gallop are all about drawing attention to herself, putting herself at the center of the production of knowledge and power.[14] A pedagogy that depends on spectacular display leaves no room for dialogue or community or even agency on the part of students—instead it positions students as passive recipients. Gallop's provocative performances give her a big role in the celebrity circuit that dominates the academy. However, as *FASH* makes evident, this institutionally sanctioned model of pedagogy leaves students with few available roles and even fewer routes of resistance. As *FASH* enacts a spectacular, celebrity-driven pedagogy in the name of feminism, it suggests both the dangers that the star system holds for students, and also feminist and queer theory's shortcomings in addressing the academic hierarchies out of which these theories emerge that complicate their analyses of gender and heteronormativity.

Reasons for inattention to institutional privilege do not reside simply within queer and feminist theories themselves; as Gallop's example indicates, this disregard also results from ways that the academic stars who created these theories can operate in a constellation apart from them:

those very theorists who have forged ways to analyze power dynamics in texts do not necessarily extend this analysis to their own institutional privilege and position, and in fact they can be resistant to doing so. Gallop not only takes her institutional authority for granted, but uses it to try to shut down challenges to her own position. Gallop's unreflective need to control the stage became clear during her performance on *PreText*, during an online "Re/INter/View" about *FASH* moderated by Victor Vitanza.[15] Although Gallop was "the featured author," the e-mail format and Vitanza's irreverent style as host quickly eroded the usual respect given over to a guest. Even as the event itself is symptomatic of the star system, the e-mail format admitted and gave equal weight to a range of questions and opinions, a number of them impertinent. Significantly, Gallop quickly rebelled against challenges to her authority, and withdrew early from this forum. As the forum unraveled, Gallop moved quickly from assumptions that as a "featured author" she automatically deserved respect, to claims to victimhood when she felt inadequately recognized. These shifts demonstrate the extent to which Gallop has naturalized academic hierarchy. So, too, does the way Gallop simultaneously embraces academic hierarchy *and* fails to subject it to analysis when she draws on theories of race and gender to support her place in it. Thus, when asked whether she felt any empathy for her accusers, Gallop refused to answer, stating that for her the list "has become a hostile environment" (Vitanza, part 6). With this charge Gallop invokes a feminist analysis of sexual harassment, but dispenses with attention to the power dynamics that are integral to this analysis. She similarly raises an analysis of race only to overturn it when she likens subscribers to a "lynch mob" (Vitanza, part 6).[16] The inversions Gallop effects—to shore up her authority through claims to victimization—constitute a sensationalist and self-serving appropriation rather than an exposure of problems with race and gender theory. Moreover, the contrast between how Gallop employs sensationalism to inhabit the monological genre of "me-moir" and that of the multivocal and more egalitarian Web-based public writing reveals not only her penchant for control sitting atop a hierarchy of privilege and power, but also suggests memoir's—and the academy's—capacity to sustain this hierarchy.

When Gallop does engage in institutional analysis, her sensationalist approach draws in readers while covering over the self-interest fueling this analysis and the personal damages that result from her approach. Throughout *FASH*, positioning her sensationalist display as a feminist defense of academic freedom, Gallop consistently fails to analyze how it is implicated in supporting—and indeed heightens as it masks—an existing power structure in which professors can act at the expense of their students' welfare. This is all the more remarkable given that Gallop discloses in *FASH* the first and foremost thing sought by the grieving students. As Gallop explains, in the complaint form, under the section "Resolution Sought," one student wrote, "'1. That the respondent understand that making the complaint the subject of intellectual inquiry constitutes retaliation.' The other student went even a little further: '1. That the respondent understand that making this claim any aspect of intellectual inquiry constitutes retaliation'" (78). In writing her own story, then, Gallop defies her students' request. And rather than reflect on why they would make this "extraordinary demand," or on how *FASH* might affect her students, or on what her ethical obligations as a teacher might be to students who feel violated enough to charge her with sexual harassment, Gallop instead focuses on the dangers that granting their request would pose to academic freedom (77). She concludes, "When these complaints define research as retaliation, they put the university under an obligation to prohibit research" (78). Gallop here effects a shift from what the students ask—that *Gallop herself* understand the problems with making the case the subject of intellectual inquiry—to a consideration of what it would mean for the *university* to prohibit Gallop's research activity (something that the students do not in fact request). This shift makes it possible for Gallop to position herself as a faculty member opposed to institutional denials of academic freedom rather than as a professor acting without regard for her students' emotional well-being. Moreover, just as Collins surely never expected the university to chemically castrate B, Beckelman states in *PreText* that never did she or the other complainant expect the university to restrict Gallop's intellectual inquiry (Vitanza, part 9), and Gallop herself provides no evidence that administrators ever considered doing so. Therefore, Gallop's focus not only distracts from but also misrepresents the power dynamic at work here. In representing herself as a "good" bad girl who champions academic freedom in the face of repressive academic institutions, Gallop refuses to calculate—and indeed distorts—how her institutional power not only informs but also makes possible the success of her sensationalist display. She also avoids discussion of what it means to engage in such display when students expressly view it as damaging. Moreover, in this economy of the spectacular, the effects on students who witness but do not achieve bit parts remain the most invisible of all.

As Gallop makes use of sensationalism to protest the university's assault on academic freedom, she partakes in a wider dissatisfaction with the university that is in a complex relationship to the privileges and protections afforded tenured faculty members, especially those who circulate in the star system. Elaine Showalter comments in *Faculty Towers* on this discontent: "To many authors looking at the university around 2000, it seemed that the risks and the joys of the erotics of teaching had succumbed to an increasingly bureaucratic and soulless institutionalization" (99). And yet, as Gallop's case indicates, a disjuncture exists between this perception and the actual limitations universities place on student-teacher relations. Except for the admonition that Gallop receives for not reporting her "consensual amorous relation," Gallop is cushioned by an institution that culturally and legally enables her sexualized display. Moreover, as Gallop's sensationalist approach renders the outcome of her own case invisible, it also obscures the more general difficulty of proving—and winning—sexual harassment cases, particularly those lacking witnesses or clear evidence. In its use of a sensationalism that is expressive of both unperceived privilege and feminist defiance, *FASH* provides insights into how some professors negotiate contradictions that characterize the contemporary academy—that of feminism as an oppositional practice *and* one that has become institutionalized, and that created by a star system that endows professors with an authority that "an increasingly bureaucratic and soulless institutionalization" protects in practice yet threatens in spirit.

Gallop's sensationalism relates to her interest in performance or role-playing in ways that further illuminate professors' complex relationship to both feminism and questions of authority in the 1990s. Throughout *FASH* Gallop emphasizes the performative nature of identity and sexuality in a way that evokes current poststructuralist feminist and queer theory as well as nostalgia for a period wherein feminism was on the cusp of entering the academy and so carried more oppositional energy and less institutional authority and responsibilities. Although Gallop's work is energized and authorized by contemporary feminist and queer formulations of identity as performative, Gallop locates her theorizing about performance in her experiences in the 1970s with the women's movement. Rather than a poststructuralist view that understands the roles each person plays to be multiple, enunciative or language-based, complexly interrelated and not always conscious or volitional, Gallop presents roles as identity-based or derived from the agency of subject position and as singular, but also as exchangeable and consciously chosen. Thus, although Gallop's attention to performance seems to align *FASH* with contemporary theoretical concerns, Gallop attempts a nostalgic return to a bygone moment of feminism. Indeed, Gallop establishes her economy of role-playing through her account of witnessing a student and professor's entry as a couple to an all-women's dance in 1971:

> Although their costuming referred to male/female roles, their performance made us think of the roles they played outside that room: teacher and student. Perhaps, they seemed to be saying, teacher/student, like butch and femme, could be roles we explored for our pleasure and empowerment. It was crucial to this feminist spectacle that the student was the one wearing men's clothing. This seemed a role reversal. Her suit hinted that their connection made it possible for this student to take on power with the teacher. Our institutional roles did not have to limit our relationships, and they also did not have to be ignored in some colorless egalitarian utopia where all women were the same. (14–15)

Here, rather than seeing this couple's institutional and sexual roles as equally present and relevant, Gallop represents them as analogous and exchangeable—when they enter the dance in their butch and femme roles, they have traded these roles for their roles as student and teacher. Gallop's "either/or" logic—which ignores well-established critiques of binary thinking by feminists including Gallop herself—enables her to see the possibility of role reversal for the couple, and not a complex negotiation wherein their sexual roles coexist alongside and work to counterbalance or highlight rather than overturn the inequalities of their institutional roles. Moreover, by anchoring her defense of amorous student-teacher relationships in this prior moment of feminism, when disparities between student and professor were less significant, Gallop takes refuge in nostalgia and avoids the complexities and increased responsibilities that attend feminism's having become ensconced in the academy.

Gallop's use of binary logic wherein people occupy either one role or another not only exists in tension with basic tenets of feminism, but, in its refusal to consider institutional identities, also works to simplify and justify her decisions as a moral agent. Fuelling this approach is Gallop's desire for a return to a renegade feminism, one that allows her to inhabit an outlaw identity. In *FASH* her refusal of her institutional standing enables her to cast her students as her "partners in crime" and then, when they turn against her and file their grievance, to view them as neither her students nor as feminists but simply as her accusers. In *PreText* Gallop makes this separation of roles explicit when list members question her lack of empathy for the students who charged her with sexual harassment. She explains, "'An accuser' is an enemy. I do empathize in general w/ my students. But by accusing me, they had decided they were not my students, & I no longer had responsibility to understand, to help them" (Vitanza, part 10). Here, Gallop's representation of role-playing—that one is either student or enemy-accuser—enables her to ignore the fact that it is precisely *as students* that the two women made their complaints. *FASH* repeatedly enacts this erasure of Gallop's own as well as her students' institutional identities. The book's title sets up this dynamic, singling out Gallop's identity as a feminist, while making no mention of her or her accusers' roles as students and professor. As Gallop systematically erases her and her students' institutional locations and that of feminism itself, she is able to represent sexuality and feminism as the targets in the case, not her own sexualized abuses of power.

FASH's incompletely digested poststructuralist understanding of identity as performative is a conveniently naive or partial one that ignores what have come to be commonplace theoretical insights into ways that roles are multiple, and cannot be adopted, exchanged, or subverted simply at will.[17] What *FASH's* poststructuralist veneer—coupled with its autobiographical narrative form—obscures, especially in its portrayals of student-teacher sex, is a self-serving reliance on binary logic and a willful ignorance about the material realities of roles. As Gallop details her own student-teacher affairs (the only ones considered in *FASH* besides the 1971 model relationship), Gallop uniformly casts these relationships *either* as empowering forms of role-playing for students *or* as pleasurable forays for faculty members. In the world according to *FASH*, student-teacher sex always works to the student's advantage. When Gallop describes seducing two members of her dissertation committee, she states, "seducing them made me feel kind of cocky and that allowed me to presume I had something to say worth saying" (42). As a student, for Gallop, sex with a teacher provides a way to assume a phallic role and disrobe professors of their authority and institutional position, whereas as a teacher, the sex she has with her male and female students is entirely student-initiated and all about fun and companionship and good teaching. Thus although Gallop's attention to role-playing seems to allow for an address of institutional roles, their material effects are diminished, distorted, or cast aside.[18] At stake in *FASH*'s theoretical inconsistencies and incoherencies is Gallop's desire to exercise authority over her students and readers, alongside her refusal to recognize ways this authority comes not only from her theoretical insights but also from her institutional stature.

A complex and often contradictory relationship to authority is not unique to Gallop. Although *FASH* seems to be out of step with current critical thinking in its binary logic and in its selective use of poststructuralist theory, insofar as its theoretical missteps signal a resistance to addressing questions of institutional privilege, it is very much a product of its time. As I have been arguing throughout *Academic Lives*, memoirs expose ways practitioners of identity politics frequently falter when it comes to addressing their own institutional identities. The same holds true for poststructuralist theorists. As Vincent Leitch has observed, poststructuralists evidence a particularly keen suspicion of institutions, given their awareness of how frequently institutions enact a whole range of regulatory and normalizing functions (128–29). For their critiques of the existing social order, most poststructuralists depend on an eccentric location: "As is well known, the preferred vantage point of poststructuralists is in the margin, the place where difference and domination alike characteristically emerge in stark forms" (Leitch 10). Through its self-serving theoretical lapses and through its nostalgia for a prior moment in feminism, *FASH* dramatizes a more general crisis in authority that results when poststructuralist theorists, having come to occupy a position of centrality in academe, hold onto their marginal positioning without acknowledging or accounting for the contradictions and compromises that can accompany their academic arrival.

More particular to *FASH*, but nonetheless symptomatic of how academic memoir can function to assert and elide institutional authority, is how in it Gallop's approach to role-playing and performance enables her to avoid a focus on feelings—her own, and her students'. At the outset of *FASH*, explaining her purpose, Gallop states, "The spectacle taught me a thing or two, and I'd like to try and explain what I've learned" (7). What Gallop's focus on spectacle precludes is analysis, or even acknowledgment, of feelings, or subjectivity. In chapters 2 and 3 I argue that memoir's emphasis on individual feelings can displace or elide the importance of institutional location. Here, however, Gallop's attention to role-playing, or what she calls "impersonation" in her 1995 collection *Pedagogy: The Question of Impersonation*, serves as a dodge for exploring her feelings. In *Pedagogy*, when Gallop explains her use of "impersonation," she conveys her understanding of "the personal as performance" (9). Although *FASH* includes no such overt theorization of the personal, Gallop's focus in *FASH* on role-playing is predicated on the understanding found in *Pedagogy* of the personal "as a result of a process of im-personation, a process of performing the personal for a public" (9). This formulation of the personal relieves Gallop from having to explore or take responsibility for the consequences that her actions have on her students if the effects are "merely" subjective. Combined with the memoir form, which is premised on a belief in the importance of individual subjectivity, Gallop's emphasis on performance or impersonation forms a contradiction that enables her simultaneous assumption and disavowal of the importance of subjectivity, and with it, a position of authority.

Paradoxically, memoir serves Gallop as a vehicle to focus on herself without getting personal.[19] *FASH* evokes but ultimately avoids the personal in its full complexity. Despite—indeed disguised by—her shocking and seemingly frank disclosures about her sex life, Gallop's insistence on role-playing in *FASH* shows how such an emphasis can lead to an impoverished view of the personal, one that also enables a skirting of issues of institutional authority. Her delimiting of the personal serves not as a counter to, but rather as a form of, self-indulgence—one tied to a lack of intellectual rigor. This becomes particularly clear in *FASH*'s treatment of love, especially when contrasted to the place of love in her follow-up article to *FASH*, "Resisting Reasonableness." It is striking that amid all the discussions of sex in *FASH*, love is virtually absent. For example, after Gallop details her various student-teacher affairs, she notes, "they span the usual range of reasons why people make contact: loneliness, sympathy, rebounding from a recently failed relationship, and, of course, admiration. I hope this gallery can give a sense of the diversity and humanity of such relations" (49). Although she explains that in the feminist classroom, "I always try to get us to that place where learning begins to dance. When we get there, my students love me and I'm crazy for them," the students' love is desexualized and, more importantly, not returned in kind (20). Gallop saves her sole reference to her own feelings of love—and the book's only sexualized presentation of love—for her long-time partner. In contrast, in "Resisting Reasonableness" Gallop makes her case for consensual student-teacher amorous relations precisely by focusing on a "limit case" that involves an idealized lesbian love relationship between a dissertation director and her middle-aged advisee. *FASH*'s omission of love and focus on spectacle, performance, and pleasure—especially when viewed alongside the exclusive focus on love in "Resisting Reasonableness"—shows Gallop's unwillingness to explore the complex interrelations of sex, love, pleasure, power, and performance that make student-teacher relationships so vexed. In *FASH*, despite Gallop's tell-all confessional style, as she splits love off from sex, what results is a personal reduced to a realm of appearances, pleasure, and impersonation. *FASH* thus demonstrates how self-reflection in memoir does not guarantee, and even can foreclose, introspection as well as accountability for institutional authority.

Gallop's concentration in *FASH* on impersonation or role-playing diminishes not only attention to her own feelings but also, more damagingly, to those of her students. For this reason her theoretical vantage point fails ethically and politically as well as intellectually. When Gallop discusses her infamous public kiss with her student, she states, "her complaint alleged that she was upset by the kiss but had been too intimidated to tell me." However, Gallop goes on to say, "Whatever her real feelings might have been, those who witnessed the kiss saw her as a willing and even eager participant. And she was well aware of how it looked" (92–93). Gallop's focus on spectacle and appearance renders her students' emotional investments irrelevant. Instead, her reading of her relationships to her students relies solely on how these relationships appear to her. In what sounds like a classic rationale for unwanted sexual advances by an acquaintance, she consistently refuses to consider seriously how the students' viewpoints might differ from her own, or why structural imbalances might make it difficult for students to articulate their perceptions to her. Assuming that her way of seeing is the true or objective one—and that her students and their motives are known to her—depends on assuming a scholarly objectivity that evidences a wholesale disregard for her psychoanalytic and poststructuralist training.[20] This lack of scholarly rigor does not simply result in or derive from a lack of compassion. In Gallop's "success" stories as well as in her account of the sexual harassment charges against her, her disregard for her students as people with complex subjectivities lead to damages that are neither frivolous nor strictly personal, connected as they are to a feminist pedagogy and to an abuse of institutional power. Gallop's take in *FASH* on appearances constitutes a failing that is political, ethical, and intellectual. Her memoir reveals, in a way that theory can mask, the extent to which the professional and theoretical can be fueled by a personal that is self-serving rather than collective in its aims.

Although Gallop consistently positions herself against the university, the university's support for her focus on appearances underlines how her approach supports the status quo. Despite Gallop's worries that universities are moving to outlaw amorous student-teacher relations and concomitantly, she fears, teaching itself (as she knows it), student-teacher dynamics and their effects are difficult not only to theorize but also to legislate, precisely because they are so difficult to witness or to measure. Because what transpires between a teacher and a student is often private as well as subjective, these interactions are difficult for university administrators (and often for the teachers and students, themselves) to assess. A student cannot get a teacher into trouble simply by saying he or she *felt* harassed—it is the student's burden to prove this harassment in material and quantifiable terms. Rather than explore these complexities, Gallop, focusing on appearances, dismisses them. Despite Gallop's claims to the contrary, university administrators share her emphasis; they find no measurable evidence of sexual harassment in the case. Also, they rely on Gallop's public kiss with one of her students to find her guilty of consensual amorous relationships, even though much else that Gallop and her students describe as transpiring privately between them is unquestionably, and, on Gallop's part, admittedly, amorous. So even as Gallop rails against university policies prohibiting consensual amorous relationships, her case and its outcome suggest the difficulty of proving and therefore of legislating against them, especially when administrators rely on what has been materially witnessed. Moreover, again on the basis of appearances, the university is aligned with Gallop in finding her relations to her students consensually amorous rather than, as the students charge, harassing. The central difference is that Gallop celebrates what administrators caution against. The case against Gallop therefore demonstrates the fuzziness of the line between consensual relations and sexual harassment (what Gallop sees as consensual is not so for her students), and the difficulty of moving beyond the realm of measurable evidence or appearances to set and implement policies that can fairly address and assess the psychological complexity of sexualized student-teacher relationships.

Memoir is well suited to move beyond institutional policies' reliance on appearances or material effects. However, Gallop instead uses the genre to reinforce the university's approach even as she positions it as antagonistic to her feminist pedagogy, politics, and principles. As I have argued, the constellation of institutional factors that contribute to such a use of memoir by academics relates to a desire simultaneously to inhabit institutional authority and, especially for those engaged in oppositional critique, to disavow it. What figures into this mix and often renders the memoirs' institutional investments difficult to discern is an avoidance of academic or theoretical discourse that itself, in the 1990s, paradoxically becomes a hallmark of the writings of humanities scholars.

Gallop's delimiting of the personal is masked not only by her use of sensationalism—which lends to *FASH* an air of shocking and complete disclosure—but also by her style of straightforward sincerity. Gallop claims and reflects on her use of sensationalism in provocative ways throughout *FASH*. However, less marked is her use of "plain speak" or clarity as a rhetorical strategy, one that appears to be in tension with, but which works in tandem with, the book's sensationalist tactics, and one with which the genre of memoir, with its promise of truth value, naturalizes.

Gallop's unremarked-on use of clarity in *FASH* is noteworthy from someone who so consistently calls attention to language as performative. Gallop states in *PreText*, "My sense of writing as performance/spectacle is rooted in my understanding of Derrida. That writing is not a vehicle for ideas. That things happen in writing" (Vitanza, part 2). The flip side of Gallop's sensationalism, her use of simple declarative sentences and a chatty style, is performative and strategic. While this style serves to hide Gallop's power, it also bolsters her authority with its claims to sincerity and openness, and supports her need in *FASH* to control meaning.

Gallop's return to "clarity" partakes in a broader movement in the humanities, including the turn in the 1990s to memoir. Gallop's career has been premised on poststructuralist word play, and particularly in her writings on Lacan and Derrida, she has provided compelling critiques of how clear, authoritative language is a phallogocentric tool used to convey hegemonic beliefs as truths.[21] In *FASH*, however, rather than link clarity and straightforwardness to authoritarianism, Gallop instead links it to naïveté. She makes this connection explicit in *PreText* and also historicizes her use of clarity when, reflecting on her style in *FASH*, she states, "It may well be that in our era of comfy post-poststructuralist assumptions clarity may well have the kind of disruptive edge that Irigarayan writing once had." She continues, "By the 90s naïve began to look pretty refreshing, cutting through reigning assumptions" (Vitanza, part 5). As this *PreText* remark suggests, naïveté is not connected to a state of unknowing. Rather, it is a look or a performance, and Gallop casts her use of clarity not as idiosyncratic but as part of a broader historical trend, one that she continues, for example, in her 2002 *Anecdotal Theory*. Gallop's assessment is supported by not only academics' turn to crossover genres including memoir, but also by tracing the career moves of leading theorists such as Judith Butler, Jacques Derrida, Henry Louis Gates, Eve Sedgwick, and Gayatri Spivak, whose language over the course of the 1990s and into the present has become ever more accessible. However, these scholars adopt clarity not as a form of naïveté but rather, as discussed in chapter 1, as a way to make political interventions inside and outside of the academy. By equating clarity with naïveté, Gallop circumvents the authority that it carries and downplays her use of a rhetorical strategy that possesses the capacity to pass itself off as power unaware of itself.

In *FASH*, as Gallop links naïveté to straightforwardness and clarity, she decouples clarity and authority. What results is an effect of innocence that serves as protective cover.[22] *FASH* relies extensively on arguments that, in their naive presentation, belie Gallop's poststructuralist training. These arguments lend to Gallop the kind of authority that she critiques elsewhere, and they enable *FASH* to speak for—and often to ignore the well-being of—her students. In her defense of consensual student-teacher sex, for example, Gallop argues on behalf of the need to "distinguish between socially coerced heterosexuality and women's *actual desires* for men" (37, emphasis added). Coming from a critic with Gallop's training, such clear, straightforward, simple claims to "actual desires" seem disingenuous, ignoring as they do poststructuralist insights into the complexity and socially constructed nature of desire. The naïveté of Gallop's approach to desire makes possible the authoritative ease with which she is able to proclaim on the "real" nature of her own and her students' desires.

Gallop's clarity is accompanied by a chatty style that further obfuscates her desire in *FASH* for authority and control. In *PreText* Gallop links her use of clarity to chattiness as well as to naiveté. She explains, "I'm still completely interested in writing as performance, in experimentation w/ mixed genres, with writing theory in a narrative or a chatty manner. In fact, my move to clarity is a move to this more entertaining or chatty theory (tho I always wanted to be entertaining)" (Vitanza, part 5). This experiment in style is not one she calls attention to in *FASH* itself—rather, she allows her language to do its work without exposing the strategy behind it. Gallop expresses awareness of the effects of her informal style: "'I'm realizing that one of the reasons I can't undercut my authority with students by being shockingly informal is that my authority is based on an authorial persona or a theoretical persona that is itself shockingly informal—that's part of its authority. . . . The sexual innuendo that functioned ten years ago to mark me as one of the girls with my students now marks me as one of the guys'" (quoted in Talbot 30). In *FASH* as Gallop retains her informal style, her style is decidedly unflirtatious. By calling her style "chatty" and dropping the innuendoes that make her "one of the guys," in *FASH* Gallop deploys a feminine naïveté that does not require renouncing, but instead hides, the authority (or phallogocentrism) that attends her institutional position and her informal narrative style. Attention to *FASH*'s use of chatty, informal language that appears to be transparent provides insights into how academic memoirs can carry, even as they appear or strive to abdicate, their authors' institutional position and authority.

If Gallop's lack of flirtatiousness in *FASH* constitutes a rhetorical strategy through which she avoids marking herself as "one of the guys," the absence of sexual innuendo simultaneously works to control meaning. Gallop's flirtatious style has characteristically relied on (sexually) suggestive puns that expand or multiply meaning, and elaborate readings of typos as "tongue slips" that yield layers of unconscious meanings. In contrast, in *FASH* Gallop structures her arguments through analogies that *collapse* or foreclose meaning—that either make disparate things the same or absolute in their differences. Thus analogies function in *FASH* as yet another way to deny or obscure the power that has accompanied Gallop's and feminism's movement into the academy.

Each of *FASH*'s four sections develops and advances its argument by way of one or more central analogies. Despite Gallop's condemnation of "loose analogies" that "impede [the] rampant expansion of the concept of sexual harassment," Gallop's constriction of meaning also often depends on loose analogies that rely on contorted logic and dizzying leaps (8). The sleight of hand by which each analogy operates rests on a linked series of similes, syllogisms, or substitutions that do not quite work despite the perfect confidence with which she presents them.[23] Such formulations frequently depend on the word "like"—*FASH*'s arguments are characterized by a patterned repetition in which disparate things are said to be "like" other things.[24] As Gallop uses analogies to liken actors or events without careful attention to power differentials, these differentials are leveled in ways that at once enable Gallop to claim herself as representative of a feminism under siege *and* as an individual dissociated from a position of institutional authority.

Throughout *FASH* Gallop uses substitutions and analogies to make her case stand in for an era's entire social or political movements. Such self-aggrandizing representation—which the memoir form aids and abets, even naturalizes—functions to render her actions as both representative and politically progressive. In *FASH* it also serves to absolve Gallop from any need to take personal responsibility for the sexual harassment charges against her. At the same time as analogies and substitutions work in *FASH* to depersonalize SASH's attack on Gallop, they paradoxically support Gallop's individual—and individualist—beliefs and desires.

One of *FASH*'s most complex and characteristic uses of analogy and syllogism occurs when Gallop likens her own case to *Disclosure*, a 1993 bestselling novel by Michael Crichton that became a popular Hollywood movie about a female boss (Meredith Johnson) who sexually harasses her male employee. In the first section of *FASH* Gallop uses *Disclosure* to cast the sexual harassment charges against her as evidence of an early 1990s backlash against feminist gains. The discussion is integral to the book's argument that the charges against Gallop involve a "role reversal" and an attack on feminism, and it plays a crucial role in obscuring the significance of Gallop's institutional clout and her students' identities as feminists with lesser institutional standing.

Leading up to the discussion of *Disclosure* is Gallop's explanation of the "complaints of authoritarianism" that she has received from students over the past decade. She explains that "the complaints of sexual harassment are saying the same thing: that I abuse my power, get off on my power at the students' expense, that I am just as bad as the men" (21). Rather than explore these charges Gallop argues that feminists' condemnation of "the woman who is like a man" actually "bears an uncanny resemblance to a larger social prejudice, the vilification of women who are like men" (23). She concludes that in both feminist and mainstream arenas, "what it means for a woman to be 'just like a man' always comes down to two things: sex and power" (23). This series of "likes," which collapses mainstream and feminist vilifications of powerful women, lays the groundwork for Gallop's discussion of *Disclosure* and her analogizing of Meredith Johnson's case to her own. She says of *Disclosure* that "under the guise of despising sexual harassment, we find ourselves once again vilifying women who presume to be sexual and powerful like men are" (26). She presses the connection between Meredith Johnson's situation and her own when she states, "Although feminists have condemned women who are just like men, society at large tends to think of women who are like men as 'feminists.' We might see Meredith Johnson as the fantasy of a feminist sexual harasser" (26). Through Gallop's rapid substitutions of terms ("feminist," "women who are like men," "sexual and powerful women"), what get lost are the differences between these terms and how they are deployed in mainstream and feminist academic culture. These quick substitutions and exchanges enable Gallop to disregard crucial differences between her own case and Crichton's representation of sexual harassment in *Disclosure*.

Gallop's analogy depends on her exclusive focus on the fact that both she and the fictional Meredith Johnson are powerful and sexual women. She emphasizes how *Disclosure*'s "gender-neutral notion of power" turns the feminist issue of sexual harassment against "liberated women" (24, 26). Gallop then likens this limit case, which entails "a role-reversal," to her own: "Both reflect a current trend in thinking about harassment that reduces power to mere institutional position" (26, 25). Gallop's solution seems to be to dismiss institutional position altogether. Thus she links *Disclosure* to her own case (which she also claims involves a "role reversal"): "Crichton's *Disclosure* approaches harassment in just that way: gender doesn't matter, what matters is who is 'behind the desk.' That same year, a university official finds it possible that I could be guilty of sexual harassment without having discriminated against anyone" (28). She concludes the discussion of *Disclosure*—and the first section of *FASH*—with the argument that "Once sexual harassment is detached from its feminist meaning, it becomes possible to imagine feminism itself accused as a form of sexual harassment" (29). Gallop's implication is that this is precisely what has happened in her own case, too.

Gallop's use of *Disclosure* to speak to her own case and to posit it as an instance of the attack on feminism itself (characteristically, Gallop's analogies work to depersonalize and disembody the charges against her) is convoluted and complex. Her analogy ignores that the charges against her are not the creation of Michael Crichton–like antifeminist fantasizing, but are made by lesbian students who initially sought out Gallop because of her well-known feminism. Through her analogy Gallop dismisses the significance that her case is issued from within a feminist framework, whereas, as Gallop rightly argues, *Disclosure* is a mainstream, reactionary representation of sexual harassment that reverses its usual power dynamics. Thus, Gallop's use of the *Disclosure* analogy enables her to represent her case as a clear instance of feminism under attack, one that renders her students' positions as lesbians and feminists immaterial. In concert with her other rhetorical strategies, Gallop's analogies work not to investigate but to cover over her authority and her implication in sexual harassment. They enable her to position herself as the victim of students and as the radical opponent of the university that is in fact her protector as well as her employer.

Ironically, *FASH* can be seen to be guilty of the very charges that Gallop levels at *Disclosure*. With exclusive attention to Gallop's own "limit case" and those that resemble it, *FASH* deflects attention away from—and, in its gender-blind celebration of teacher-student sex, even implicitly defends and trivializes—the most prevalent sexual harassment scenario in academe—that between a male professor and a female student.[25] Moreover, aided by memoir's individual focus, Gallop is able to represent her case as not only the exception that distracts attention from the norm but also as representative of feminism under attack, rather than as a case that either calls into question the actions of one particular feminist or explores the challenges that attend feminism's movement into the academy, or does both. In denying her own institutional power, especially as she claims her case to be representative and historically significant, Gallop also dismisses the changing face of feminism in the academy.[26] Even as she foregrounds her memoir's historical import, feminism is only partially historicized and from a narrowly self-interested perspective that the genre of memoir facilitates. And yet, with its nostalgia and denial, Gallop's memoir—in ways as maddening as they are brilliant—nonetheless marks a broader historical moment, one wherein feminists and other professors negotiate, or refuse to negotiate, what it means to occupy positions in the mainstream of academe. Ultimately, then, what Gallop exposes in *FASH* is memoir's capacity to capture larger historical currents, not so much through the accuracy of Gallop's own analysis, but rather through what this analysis and the forms that it takes reveal about the anxieties, privileges, and self-interest at work in academic memoirs and in the histories that their practitioners generate.

In her lambasting of the "Sexual Harassment Industry," Daphne Patai argues, "not content with freeing women from discrimination in their professional and academic lives, the SHI has, moreover, opened a new avenue for advancement as alleged victims find themselves rewarded with both monetary and professional gains" (89). Patai looks to the example of Susan Hippensteele at the University of Hawai'i to make her case. She implies that Hippensteele created her faculty position as the university's sole sex equity specialist—a position that Patai presumably finds unnecessary as well as opportunistically attained—through inflated, even hystericized, claims to having been "victimized" by sexual harassment (89, 90).

In 2001 Hippensteele was forced to resign from her position as sex equity specialist due to a hostile university administration that, among other things, actively blocked her efforts to attain a law degree so that she could advocate more successfully for students and faculty experiencing sexual harassment.[27] Several months after her resignation, the position of sex equity specialist had yet to be advertised, leaving students such as Lance Collins, as well as those who experience quid pro quo harassment, without a trained adviser or office to go to with their complaints.[28] Meanwhile, Gallop found in her sexual harassment case new avenues for professional gain. From such a vantage point, even as feminists and feminist inquiry have achieved a central place in the humanities, sexual harassment is far from overregulated in the university, and those who experience it far from "rewarded."

And yet, at the same time that an antifeminist backlash is leaving its mark on mainstream and academic culture, definitions of sexual harassment, as both Patai and Gallop argue, have indeed expanded. However, as my analysis of Gallop's case aims to illustrate, this expansion cannot be understood as an attack on men (Patai) or as an assault on feminism (Gallop). Gallop's case instead points to the complexity of sexual harassment, in part because of the institutional power attained by some feminists and the difficulty of addressing less-than-straightforward power dynamics through university policies or other official channels. In contrast, memoir offers the possibility of a site in which the complexities of sexual harassment, the institutionalization of feminism, and its place inside and outside the academy can be addressed and analyzed. It offers a site in which to explore how the personal and political do and should inform university policies as well as feminist and other cultural theories, and a form through which to address ethical questions that cannot be satisfactorily adjudicated by laws and policies. However, as Gallop writes about her case, she not only uses her power to violate her students' expressly stated interests, but she also bolsters support for the very institutions she sets out to critique. And this too is a property of memoir, a genre the possibilities of which are too often tempered in the 1990s academy by its individualism and its capacity to serve as a prop for the privilege of its practitioners. During a period that potently combines the academic star system, mainstream hostility to feminism and to the humanities, and the institutionalization of feminist and poststructuralist theory, memoirs constitute a way to read the resulting, and as yet unresolved, crisis in authority.

Pedagogy of the Privileged

In her highly acclaimed 1996 memoir, *A Life in School: What the Teacher Learned*, Jane Tompkins includes an exuberant description of a student-initiated classroom experiment. During the course of reading Toni Morrison's *Beloved* and discussing its section on the Middle Passage with her students at Duke University, she explains that "[we] squeezed ourselves under the table and talked about what it was like to feel trapped, closed in" (175). She follows up this description with an appeal to the reader, "(Do you see what I mean? Do you see how great it was?)" (175). The assumption that readers—presumably many of them professors—will share Tompkins's enthusiasm for this method of teaching highly privileged students (none of them African American) about slavery is arresting. Tompkins's embrace of such a pedagogy is all the more surprising when considered in relation to her earlier work. Before entering the field of education Tompkins was a distinguished literary critic whose career depended on carefully historicizing structures of feeling from a feminist vantage point. Indeed, in her 1985 book *Sensational Designs*, Tompkins demonstrates the need to attend to historical contexts in order to appreciate nineteenth-century American texts about slavery. With this groundbreaking work Tompkins became one of the key members of the Duke English department's "all-star" faculty, contributing to its reputation for being at the vanguard of change during the "culture wars."

The shift from *Sensational Designs* to *A Life* merits close attention for what it—and the enthusiastic reception of Tompkins's memoir—says about academic culture today. Despite Tompkins's claims to her and her memoir's outsider status, the success that *A Life* has enjoyed suggests it to be moving with rather than against academic currents. In the years following its 1996 publication, *A Life in School* garnered awards and accolades in publications including the *New Yorker* and the *Chronicle of Higher Education*.[29] Tompkins has been sought after on national lecture circuits, serving, for example, as the featured speaker at the 1997 conference for the National Council of Teachers of English. In 1998 Tompkins received an award for *A Life* from the Association of American Colleges and Universities. Despite her lack of any formal training in the field of education, Tompkins was hired in 1999 by the education department at the University of Illinois at Chicago. As of this writing her memoir continues to sell well. What larger structural conditions help account for enthusiastic reception of a memoir that involves students at Duke crouching together under a table as a means to understand slavery and the Middle Passage? How did it become career-enhancing for one of the profession's most respected literary critics to write a book urging students and teachers alike to practice a purely experiential and emotional approach to learning?

In *A Life in School* Tompkins denounces education's devaluation of all but the intellect. As she argues that the academy is emotionally barren, she seeks new forms of teaching that will not deny students their humanity or their "connectedness to ourselves and one another" (xvi). The importance of Tompkins's remarks cannot be underestimated, since all too often Western education focuses exclusively on the development of the intellect and, in today's climate, on professionalizing students. Moreover, as Lisa Ruddick notes, pedagogical reforms attuned to students' emotional lives provide a welcome alternative to Gallop's sexualized form of classroom intimacy. In her 2000 article on professional harassment Ruddick poses bell hooks and Tompkins as counterexamples to Gallop, lauding them for articulating "a similarly impassioned yet not sexualizing view of what teaching is for. These teachers, both of whom see themselves as experimenting with new forms of pedagogical intimacy, express what amounts to a deeply humanizing regard for their students, experienced within the ordinary institutional limits" (607).

On the one hand, Ruddick is right to point to the polarities between Tompkins's and Gallop's pedagogy, especially in terms of Tompkins's "humanizing regard" for students. On the other hand, I argue that *A Life* ultimately does not stand as a counter to Gallop's pedagogical practices. Rather, as Tompkins, like Gallop, struggles with the authority brought on by the star system, the professionalization of literary studies, and the institutionalization of feminism and, in Tompkins's case, a U.S. cultural studies, her memoir, together with Gallop's, suggests the complex and various ways that power operates in the classroom and in stories about teaching. As *A Life* narrates a return in the classroom to a humanist approach to literature in response to these factors, and during a time when the humanities are under fire, it demonstrates how this approach and using memoir to present it can inadvertently reinstall rather than replace academic hierarchies. Moreover, as I argue, a focus on one's own feelings does not guarantee the presence of empathy, and the absence of emotional intelligence can lead to shortcomings that are ethical, political, and theoretical.

In her response to her disappointments with academe, Tompkins tacitly rejects the set of conditions that brought her and the Duke English department to national prominence, and she embraces a humanism that is a mix of traditional and New Age forms. *A Life*'s humanism is crucial to understanding its success and the problems that attend it. Tompkins's ardent belief in an education that respects the full humanity of each of her students depends not only on a return to a "prepolitical" or old-fashioned humanist approach to literature, but also supports a late-twentieth-century humanism that is reflected in popular discourses about reclaiming one's inner child. Tompkins views the individual (here, Tompkins herself) as the unit of measurement and value, and she neglects contemporary as well as historical inequities that divide and differentiate people, and that constitute a major area of critical inquiry for humanities scholars in the 1990s. As Tompkins keeps her focus firmly on her own past, she does not adequately account for the power of institutional structures, particularly those that characterize the present-day academy and that exert a particularly strong presence in the Duke English department—arguably the center of the academic star system during the 1990s owing to hires made under the leadership of Tompkins's husband, Stanley Fish.[30] As a result, Tompkins's classroom practices do not escape but often mask institutional structures and her privilege within them. Such power imbalances operate all the more powerfully when teachers are either unaware or in denial of them. As Tompkins's memoir registers a crisis in the state of the humanities, it, along with the pedagogy it describes, does not escape the confines of "a life in school" or advance a brave new pedagogy, but instead reinstates forms of individualism and humanism that have, in different guises, long characterized institutions of higher learning in the United States.

What concerns me here is not Tompkins's individual refusal to analyze her institutional power and privilege, but rather what the academy's participation in this refusal reveals about academic culture today. As I argue throughout *Academic Lives*, academic memoirs, *A Life* included, are being written—and read—during a time when universities are responding to crises in funding and definition with new surges of racism, sexism, and state nationalism, and with pushes toward "excellence" and "accountability," all of which depend on a bourgeois individualism that memoirs including *A Life* promote. Although old-fashioned humanism can appear progressive in the face of such pressures, *A Life* registers how a retreat into this humanism and away from analysis of difficult social and political conditions can bolster, in the name of refusing, the contemporary status quo.

As I explore such issues in relation to Tompkins's memoir, I am particularly interested in its engagement of sentiment—a cousin to Gallop's sensationalism although it takes a seemingly opposite form. *A Life's* appeal comes in large part from its suggestion that a complex array of societal problems can be managed in the classroom simply through giving expression to one's own emotional landscape.[31] Not only can a focus on feelings contain activist impulses, but feelings themselves require analysis, and Tompkins ignores ways that emotions are "historically contingent, socially specific, and politically situated" (Schnog 8). As Nancy Schnog notes, "If today's therapeutic common sense tells us that the 'psychological' is the deepest part of ourselves," it is important to identify "the vast public resources—institutional, financial, and cultural—that have gone into the making of this distinctively twentieth-century idea" (8). Attention to *A Life* provides insights into how, in the 1990s, the memoir genre can, as a conveyor of "therapeutic common sense," shift attention away from the institutional causes of a crisis in the humanities and effect a return to ideologies of individualism and humanism that contribute to this crisis through their support for a host of institutional hierarchies.[32]

One of the most remarkable qualities of Tompkins's memoir is its exaggerated solipsism, one that bespeaks Tompkins's feelings of alienation from the academy: despite her pleas for a way of learning that builds on the importance of connectedness, through erasing her memoir's scholarly influences, Tompkins creates the illusion that intellectual work is a solitary enterprise. For Tompkins the turn to memoir accompanies the renunciation of scholarly apparatuses and sources, which she poses in direct contrast to the stuff of life and emotions. Reflecting on her lack of references to books on education, she states, "For a long time I was at a loss to explain this myself. . . . Now I realize that this refusal to read about my subject *was* my subject. . . . It was to my own experience that I needed to turn for enlightenment" (*A Life* xii). As Tompkins refuses scholarly references, she denies the collective nature of thinking and learning. Instead, *A Life* is infused by an extreme sense of Tompkins's isolation: it conveys the impression that Tompkins alone is battling questions of the mind/body split, that she alone is struggling to make education more relevant and less hierarchical.

In *A Life* Tompkins draws without acknowledgment on theories of pedagogy and composition in a way that intensifies her lone individualism and aligns these theories with a bourgeois individualism. In the memoir Tompkins cites only four scholarly books on pedagogy—by Paulo Freire, Parker Palmer, Sylvia Ashton-Warner, and Maria Montessori. However, Tompkins mainly credits these books only for inspiring her to look to her own experiences. Nevertheless, their ideas are everywhere evident in the memoir, if often in a depoliticized form. This is particularly true of Tompkins's use of *Pedagogy of the Oppressed*: her focus on validating individual experiences narrows Freire's Marxist commitments as it seems to echo them (see, for example, 139–40 or 175).[33]

Such a use of Freire is not unique to Tompkins: endorsements of his alternative to "the banking model of education" run through the writings of composition and literary theorists of the 1980s and 1990s in a similarly individualizing fashion and suggest how the movement of Marxist thought into the academy can take the teeth out of it. As I argue in chapter 2 in relation to Anzaldúa's borderlands theory, academic memoirs can, with the genre's imbrication in individualism, render more visible how revolutionary social movements become depoliticized and dehistoricized when they become institutionalized in the 1990s academy.[34]

In Tompkins's case, notwithstanding her claims to the solitary nature of her vision, her focus on individual liberation and empowerment both resonates with as well as departs from the scholarship of theorists working in the 1990s in the burgeoning but still marginalized fields of pedagogy and composition studies. Indeed, since the 1970s, feminist educators have been articulating theories that dovetail with Tompkins's.[35] These ideas are often advanced through "personal criticism" that contains a strong autobiographical component. This focus has continued. However, critics note that in the 1990s, this expressivist theory has become less individualistic: as Patricia Sullivan and Suzanne Qually put it, "pedagogies that once aimed at self-actualization now aim at social transformation" (ix). Thus Tompkins's pedagogy is far from unprecedented—a fact that memoir, with its lack of reliance on scholarly citations, can obscure.[36] At the same time *A Life*'s pedagogy, centered as it is on individual empowerment, combined with the individualist underpinnings of memoir, constitutes more of a return to a 1960s expressivism than an attempt to make composition theory more attuned to societal structures and to critiques of the liberated autonomous self.

Although in its return to models of individualism Tompkins's memoir departs from work being done by humanities scholars in the 1990s, it does reinforce already established educational trends in the United States.[37] Indeed, the "new" pedagogy that Tompkins calls for is so well established that since the late 1980s conservative pundits such as George Will were bewailing its impact, linking "educational decline" to a valuing of self-expression and student empowerment that has preempted more scholarly forms of writing (Lowenstein, Chiseri-Strater, Gannett 140). Or, in the *Atlantic Monthly*, Daniel Singal proclaims, "this is a generation whose members may be better equipped to track the progress of their souls in diaries than any group of Americans since the Puritans" (67). Although these commentators certainly overstate their cases, they qualify Tompkins's claims that universities exclude consideration of students' emotions, and they place *A Life* in the mainstream of liberal thinking about education—a fact that helps explain the memoir's popularity.

As Tompkins expresses her feelings of isolation without looking to how her assessments of education articulate with already established ones, she participates in a familiar hierarchy in English departments, one that not only undervalues composition and pedagogy studies but also contributes to the individualism that she laments. The high-profile success of Tompkins's more recent writings on pedagogy, especially given her express determination not to read the experts, testifies to this hierarchy. As she dwells on her feelings without acknowledging the bodies of knowledge that contribute to her ideas, Tompkins is implicated, along with the memoir genre itself, in the very hierarchies she protests.[38] Her memoir exemplifies with particular clarity—and pathos—how the specialization and hierarchization of knowledge combine with the star system to create for professors—even those positioned at the top—systemic conditions of individualism and alienation that become self-perpetuating.

Whereas Tompkins ignores composition and pedagogy studies in ways that are symptomatic and unsurprising, her relationship to feminism is less expected though ultimately no less indicative of currents in academic culture. In marking *A Life* as a departing point for her as an academic and in turning away from feminism in it, Tompkins must ignore how her career as a feminist literary critic has always taken emotions seriously.[39] Her professional success—along with that of the Duke English

Department's—was secured in large part through her intellectually brilliant and passionate valorization of popular literature and its affective powers. In addition, Tompkins's criticisms of binaries come in her memoir without a more general acknowledgment that a central tenet of feminism has been a challenge to the mind/body split. Tompkins proceeds as if French feminists had never seized the imagination of U.S. feminists during the 1980s with their mandates to write the body. Likewise, she ignores the theoretical writings during that same period by feminists of color such as Cherríe Moraga and Gloria Anzaldúa, who insisted on a "theory in the flesh" (*This Bridge* 23).[40] On the one hand, that Tompkins need not mention this scholarship indicates that these feminist insights have become so established that Tompkins has internalized them and views them as the products of common sense. On the other hand, her memoir serves as a reminder of the extent to which these calls remain unmet. Tompkins's disavowal of feminism and her prior engagements with it constitute the flip side of Gallop's nostalgic endorsement of 1970s feminism. Tompkins's rejections and erasures of the contributions of contemporary feminism are necessary to sustain her oppositional relationship to the academy—her memoir at once signals the difficulties that can attend achieving a position of authority while it provides insights into feminism's successes and its failures to achieve full-scale change.

Tompkins's memoir not only dismisses her indebtedness to feminist theory and criticism, but it also renders invisible the personal relationships and the more general institutional contexts that make it part of a more collective movement. The book includes no acknowledgments or dedication. Since Tompkins's informal writing group at Duke was well-publicized, with the group giving interviews about their challenges to academic conventions, this absence is noteworthy. And especially because the other members—Cathy Davidson, Alice Kaplan, and Marianna Torgovnick—wrote memoirs, along with much of the Duke English department in the late 1980s and 1990s (Frank Lentricchia, Reynolds Price, Henry Louis Gates Jr., and Eve Sedgwick), *A Life* stands at the center, not the embattled outskirts, of Tompkins's "life in school." Tompkins instead, however, casts herself as a modern-day Ahab. As do other memoirs in this book, *A Life* dramatizes the disparity that can exist between felt experience and material conditions, and it demonstrates how memoir, which naturalizes a focus on individual experience, can participate in the erasure of institutional structures and conditions. Like Gallop, Tompkins ignores how writing a memoir, even one that positions her in opposition to the academy, both is supported by and extends her place in an academic hierarchy. In addition, as Tompkins proceeds without acknowledgment of the colleagues writing their memoirs alongside her, her representation of her lonely individualism suggests the difficulty of maintaining feminist community in the culture of the 1990s academy.[41]

Instead of addressing her specific institutional contexts, Tompkins insists that her childhood injuries define her adult "life in school." At the outset of her memoir she states, "I am still smarting from wounds sustained long ago" (xii). Revisiting life at her grammar school Tompkins claims, "it was the reality of what had happened at P.S. 98, more than my present one, that had been dictating the terms of my university life, day to day" (7). Tompkins claims childhood, and particularly school, as the major source of trauma with which adults contend (38). To heal her wounds Tompkins seeks to rediscover "the person I had been before I went to school" (xviii). With this rhetoric Tompkins draws on the 1980s discourse of the "inner child."[42] However, rather than explore the influence of this form of therapy, Tompkins presents her search for her preschool self as one that marks an exit from socially constructed forms of knowledge. As she does so she also provides implicit support for a conception of memoir as a vehicle for self-exploration that is unmediated by social structures or ideologies. She thus evades exploration of how the specific conditions of the 1990s academy relate to those of other eras and educational institutions.

"School" appears in Tompkins's memoir not as one of many interconnected institutions but rather as the sole institution through which socialization occurs. In *A Life* school alone instills standards and norms that impinge on people's "true selves." Tompkins views a preschool state as one of prelapsarian happiness and wholeness: she argues on behalf of an education that is "revolutionary" in its recognition "that school, more often than not, has been the place that *causes* stress and anger in people's lives" (xiv). School for Tompkins seems to be narrowly defined by student-teacher classroom interactions, and she includes no recognition of the host of social and economic problems that students carry with them into the classroom. In its refusal of the complexity of all that impacts life in school, Tompkins's memoir can be read as a form of crisis management during a time when higher education is under fire: *A Life* reasserts the importance of educational institutions even in the process of trying to escape them, and places it within the teacher's control to make life better for students.

To maintain *A Life*'s oppositions and the purity with which Tompkins can represent herself as having been a victim to an oppressive educational system, Tompkins must simplify institutional politics in other ways as well. Despite Tompkins's emphasis on the overwhelming importance of school and her insistence that it make a place for the whole person, *A Life* largely avoids discussion of her personal life, although the little that she does include suggests how strongly her personal and professional lives have always been connected. Most particularly, her memoir avoids investigation of how love, ambition, and personal and professional desire are intertwined in her relationship with Stanley Fish, one of the profession's best-known players and a key architect of the academic star system.

A different story that Tompkins could have told, had she written Fish into *A Life*, would have involved an exploration of how the star system contributes to her disillusionment with academe. At least in his public persona Fish stands for all that Tompkins repudiates in *A Life*. Notorious for his brilliant cynicism and showmanship and for his merciless attacks on academics who claim victimization, Fish is described in a 2001 *New Yorker* profile by Larissa MacFarquhar as someone who "likes to humiliate people in public for the fun of it" (62).[43] MacFarquhar also details how Fish helped institute an approach to literature that excludes questions of sensibility and quotes him as saying that "the idea of learning from his students simply never occurs to him" (69, 70). In short, even as Fish is largely absent from *A Life*, he embodies Tompkins's portrayal of academe. The omission of Fish, then, is not merely a cordoning-off of the personal in *A Life* but also a way in which the memoir does not address even as it indirectly indicates the personal and professional costs of the star system and the academic culture of the 1990s.

Throughout *A Life* Tompkins refuses what has come to be the accepted feminist understanding: that the personal is political. Instead, *A Life* details how Tompkins learns to banish the insights that have come with decades of feminist and other standpoint politics, viewing these insights not only as unwelcome guests, but even as vantage points that require reversing—instead, it is privilege in *A Life* that comes to carry the most oppression. At one point admitting, "I know I had all the advantages," she contends, "But that makes it worse, don't you see? . . . That way, all the unhappiness seems to be my responsibility, my fault" (11). The result is not the shedding of theory or of a socially constructed self, but a move deeper into U.S. ideologies of individualism, including "self-help" discourse with its focus on self-esteem. In this way Tompkins works within rather than against memoir's conservative, individualist tenets as she evokes only to refuse actively or at times invert the lessons of feminist politics.

As Tompkins strives to validate and reclaim childhood emotions that she felt were disregarded in school, and to split these feelings off from analysis, she steadfastly refuses the politicization of literature and the cultural theories that transformed the academy in the 1980s and 1990s. The result is an anti-intellectualism and a self-absorption that bolster conservative agendas. The example Tompkins provides to illustrate the tedium of her education illuminates the problems with such an approach. She explains: "For example, there was the little book about how Peter Minuit bought Manhattan Island from the Indians for twenty-four dollars and some glass beads, the only new book our class ever had. We read it over and over, and each time it was presented as if we had never seen it before. What did they think, that we had amnesia?" (21). Tompkins's recovery of her childhood indignation keeps her gaze firmly away from the significant questions that this book's contents might raise for her as a professor of U.S. literary history. For example: What perspective did the book take on this real estate transaction? How did this perspective inform her understanding of America and her place in it? How might it have contributed to Tompkins's forgetting the Indians in her book on westerns, *West of Everything*, an omission that, once realized, as she explains in its preface, brought her to tears?[44]

Because in *A Life* feelings preempt structural analysis, the disparity between Tompkins's feelings of victimization and her institutional authority go unacknowledged, even as her memoir can be read as resulting from a crisis over having achieved a position of authority. In her "Poem Postcard" she proclaims what she believes to be an unspoken, insurmountable truth: that on a daily basis, "To teach is to be battered, / Scrutinized, and drained" (142). Significantly, once Tompkins speaks as a teacher, victim status transfers from student to teacher. This shift generates—and helps explain—the postcard's implicitly expressed desire for, on the one hand, authority to counteract feelings of vulnerability and, on the other hand, a longing to eradicate hierarchies. This tension runs through much feminist pedagogy and is worth exploring. So, too, is the specific pressure that comes with being a professor in a department that draws professionalized graduate students and highly entitled undergraduates. However, because Tompkins instead claims the general identity of "teacher," and because she does not investigate how her institutional position and privilege intensify as well as complicate her feelings of vulnerability and anxiety, her sole focus remains on how to feel more authority and control. She explains that she began taking karate lessons in hopes of achieving "the ability to stand up for myself" (156). As this statement indicates, Tompkins conceives of power as being the product of individual agency rather than deriving from institutional structures. What go unaddressed in *A Life*, in a way that the memoir genre at once masks and attempts to manage, are the very psychic tolls and contradictions of occupying a position of privilege in the star system.

The only time that structural or institutional analysis enters Tompkins's memoir is when Tompkins tells of how she herself experienced gender discrimination. She narrates her discovery of gender politics when Temple University denies her a tenure track position. Tompkins's awakening to gender discrimination leads her to feminist literary criticism. However, once Tompkins achieves full professorship at Duke and realizes that "I could do what I wanted," she disavows feminism, associating it with an unproductive anger (113). She instead addresses her professional dissatisfactions through meditation, psychotherapy and massage (117); takes multiple leaves of absence and spends her time gardening, cooking, reading self-help books and taking karate lessons; and makes plans for partial retirement at age fifty. In a way that bolsters memoir's basis in bourgeois individualism, *A Life* renders feminism as a form of individual empowerment. The memoir thus exposes the limitations of a feminist politics that is fueled by individual rather than collective commitments, and that resides exclusively within one's personal position or experiences.

Tompkins's focus on individual empowerment and her resistance to structural analysis or a collective politics extends to her pedagogy: as she seeks to avoid the pressures of a highly competitive academy and a politicized approach to literature, she ignores the race and class privilege on which her pedagogy is premised. Although she mentions the high price of a Duke education for undergraduates ($100,000 at the time she writes, 216), Tompkins's decision to do away with grades takes for granted students' ability to rely on other markers of value, such as connections or institutional pedigree. Tompkins's account of her course, American Literature Unbound, demonstrates an especially dramatic disregard for the privilege on which her pursuit of community depends. Tompkins explains how students while reading *Beloved* not only conducted their table crouching experiment but also planned a trip to Somerset Plantation, "where we spent time doing work that slaves had done and wrote about it afterward. (I won't forget the gritty-salty taste of the corn bread we fried in fatback or how Erin looked, her blonde hair wrapped in a cotton turban)" (174). Rather than address the inadequacies of such an experiment, Tompkins focuses on how these activities create a community of rebels. Tompkins explains that the course's two texts, *Beloved* and *Moby-Dick*, "played into my ancient sense of victimization at the hands of power. . . . So I loved our rebellion against grades and rules and conventional procedures, and I loved the group ethos. For both novels are also celebrations of communion and spoke to my longing to be rid of loneliness" (175). When students' evaluations are critical of the course, an inconsolable Tompkins realizes, "Criticism was what I'd been trying to avoid all along, criticism of any kind—literary criticism, criticism of myself as a teacher, my having to criticize them. Why else go to the beach, work as slaves, light candles, and put on little plays if not to escape the steel trap of judgment?" (176). With her own feelings and her Duke students as her only reference points, Tompkins cannot consider how these experiences might affect students whose "ancient sense of victimization" might include slavery or other material forms of racial violence. The exclusionary humanism that her pedagogy—and her memoir—depend on carry the assumption that individuals occupy a level playing field and determine their own destiny, and in both, Tompkins divorces teaching—and the forming of community—from what have come to be commonplace considerations of structural inequities and concerns.[45] That Tompkins executes such a pedagogy through having students read *Beloved*, a novel around which a whole critical industry exists by the mid-1990s, indicates how fully she seeks an exit from the emotional and intellectual exhaustions of a highly professionalized academy and a politicized approach to (teaching) literature. Not only in her pedagogy but also in the act of writing about it in memoir, Tompkins opts out of the high stakes of the contemporary academy without forgoing, or acknowledging, the privileges and traditions on which her newly adopted positioning depend. With its accounts of classroom interactions, her memoir therefore serves as a way to index the complex and contradiction-laden economy of the humanities today.

Tompkins's ambivalent relationship to authority, and the costs of the academic star system, are again evidenced in a dehistoricized way in her attempts to escape classroom roles. As Tompkins celebrates students' pursuit of nonacademic avenues and advocates for the return to a preschool state, she emphasizes the need for teachers and students to relinquish socially determined roles. Unlike Gallop, Tompkins wants to escape from rather than into the performative, to shed rather than shore up her authority. For Tompkins the performative is bound up in deadening roles of obedience and control that define students' and teachers' identities. She explains that "to be the one everybody looked at and had to obey, to be standing alone, up in front, performing while other people paid attention was the only thing I knew to aim for" (54). She then narrates her awakening to the "emptiness" (54) and burden that comes with this performance, and the "inexpressible relief" (65) of giving it up. Although Tompkins makes no mention of how performance, in the present tense, is embedded in the star system, her memoir nonetheless suggests its pressures as well as its seductions.

In keeping with her rejection of the present-day academy's professionalism and theoretical approaches, Tompkins opposes the performative nature of teaching to her "real" life and self, which she returns to through her experimental pedagogy. Tompkins claims that her experimental teaching "was about letting chaos in" (132). She describes reaching the point at which to prepare for class, she only brings food and tells students where to meet. Tompkins explains of her classroom practices, "Everything became a roll of the dice. I called it teaching nothing" (122). Tompkins states, "I simultaneously thought of myself as a fraud—someone passing for a teacher who didn't in fact have anything to teach—and as a real person for the first time in my life" (122). Here, as Tompkins opposes being a "real person" to being a teacher, she again registers the weight of authority and professionalism in the 1990s academy. By using the classroom as the primary site to cast off her authority, Tompkins is able to simplify this task and to make it more manageable.

As Tompkins pursues becoming "a real person," she does not aspire to Gallop's intense one-on-one student-teacher relationships, but a classroom community unmarred by power differentials in which she and her students combat isolation and seek a reprieve from the loneliness that she discovers "had long been a feature in my life" (182). In contrast to Gallop, sexual relations have no place in the classroom community she desires to create. Thus, Tompkins's treasured memory of her third-grade teacher telling the class how her son brought her orange juice in the shower "symbolizes something that was missing from education as I knew it: the reality of private life. Taking showers, having a naked body, drinking orange juice, being a member of a family, needing to know that you are loved, needing to tell about it" (xv). Not only domestic intimacy but also "a sense of the classroom as sacramental" (144) characterizes what she is after in her classes. Tompkins's memoir suggests how the classroom serves as a space in which one can escape rather than confront larger institutional pressures and hierarchies.

Tompkins's search to abandon roles and performance and to create classroom communities without power differentials is beset by a number of unreconciled contradictions about the place of the personal in the classroom, and also a refusal to consider how classrooms are situated within larger and various institutional contexts. Whereas in grade school it can be comforting to see your teacher as someone with a body and a private life, in graduate school in the 1990s university, glimpses into a professor's personal life can instead uphold the star system—and the memoir phenomenon—that depends on graduate students and professors valuing each and every peek into an "academic star's" life. Moreover, as Gallop makes evident, self-disclosure and a professional performance are not necessarily incompatible. Tompkins fails to address how, given her particular location, even in the process of trying to escape academic hierarchies, she continues her participation in them.[46]

Tompkins's success not only with her memoir but also in taking it and her pedagogy to the lecture circuit suggests not only that her desires resonate with her peers, but also that she has embraced her new role and her audiences' receptivity to it. For example, writing about a 1998 address, "Toward Wholeness as Teachers, Students, and Institutions," which Tompkins delivered to the Association of American Colleges and Universities after the association had honored *A Life in School*, *Chronicle* reporter Alison Schneider observes how "Professors and administrators squeezed into a conference room, spilling into the hallway to hear her speak. . . . The magic kicked in when Ms. Tompkins grabbed the microphone, strolled into the crowd, and worked the room." Schneider also notes that Tompkins's talks to teachers follow a formula involving bagels and American Indian flute music. Tompkins's success suggests that her return to a liberal humanist pedagogy not only resonates with a more general mood in the humanities but also keeps her in the very economy that she opposes.

What Tompkins does not address in her memoir is just how scripted her pedagogical performances are—how in the guise of shedding the professionalism and sterility that for her characterize educational institutions, she returns to a well-worn form of Arnoldian humanism. The language that Tompkins uses to describe her journey—and the roles that she sees herself playing—shows how strongly this humanism and ideologies of isolated individualism shape her pedagogical experiments. The title to one of her courses, Reading for Yourself, captures the contradiction between Tompkins's attempt to break free of academic strictures and her simultaneous return to conventional forms of learning. On the one hand, the title promises freedom from the fetters of academic expectations and approaches. On the other hand, it bespeaks a return to rugged individualism in the face of a literary profession in which the study of literature has become both professionalized and tied to overtly political concerns. In her memoir Tompkins also registers this return by describing her classroom quest. In moves that are at odds with her search for community, she repeatedly likens herself to quintessentially masculinist heroes who figure prominently in traditionally humanist texts: "I thought of myself, as I taught those courses, as waiting, like the scholar-gypsy in Matthew Arnold's poem, for the spark from heaven to alight, to feel the *atman*, the breath, brushing by my cheek" (123). Describing her lack of preparation for class, she asks, "What would I do next? Not show up at all? I started comparing myself to King Lear" (123). She concludes another chapter by stating, "I feel a little like Prufrock at the end" (131). These references indicate the extent to which Tompkins, as she seems to chart untried directions in the classroom, still is playing roles, and familiar ones at that.

Tompkins's "radical" teaching also finds her both liberally likening herself to masculine heroes of the literary canon (Matthew Arnold's gypsy-scholar, Shakespeare's King Lear, T. S. Eliot's Prufrock), and steeped in literary classics and traditionally humanist approaches to them that she formerly rejected for their sexism and elitism. However, rather than present her embrace of this literature as informed by a life in school, Tompkins describes it as a return to an unmediated appreciation of literature's true greatness. Explaining how she approaches *Moby-Dick* in the classroom, Tompkins states, "I just wanted to glory in it, to revel again, as in the old days, in the genius with which Melville put sentences together" (172). Rather than abandoning already-traveled terrain, Tompkins recovers a traditional humanism, which can be enjoyed unfettered by the concerns of the past thirty years. *A Life in School* thus chronicles a return to the values and to an approach to literature that Tompkins so brilliantly critiqued in *Sensational Designs*. In the nostalgic humanism that results, *A Life* resembles other memoirs, especially those by traditional humanities scholars like Kernan or Pritchard. These memoirs, most of them published by prestigious scholarly presses, evidence the appeal that an old-fashioned humanism holds in the humanities—not only for those nearing or at retirement, but also for those like Tompkins at the peak of their careers who turn to it as an escape from the scrutiny and rigors of a highly professionalized and politicized academy.

These memoirs' nostalgia for a traditional humanism in an era of multiculturalism and feminism partakes in a wider cultural longing. As Tompkins leaves it to students to create their own syllabi and so "allow the student's true self to emerge" (159), the result is a conventionally liberal humanist script that the students draw not only from Tompkins's own cues but from mainstream media as well.[47] For example, students in one class chose to view the hugely popular, Academy Award–winning 1989 film *Dead Poets Society* (the conventionality—and irony—of this choice is suggested by the fact that in 2006 it was the featured text for TermPapersMonthly.com, a Web site that sells term papers). In selecting *Dead Poets*, students followed a script for the unscripted, "free-thinking" classroom. Furthermore, as they made their own syllabus, they chose a movie that stars an unconventional teacher whose approach closely mirrors Tompkins's own—indeed, some scenes from *A Life* and *Dead Poets Society* seem interchangeable. The syllabi students compose reveal the naïveté of Tompkins's desire to return the students and herself to their preschool selves. Moreover, such a pedagogical approach also can play into a consumer model of education.

Far from radical, *Dead Poets Society* teaches the benefits of dominant, patriarchal ideologies of individualism and self-making. Set in 1959 in a New England boys' prep school, the film's exaltation of the literary classics is integrally related to the passing down of membership to "the Dead Poets Society," a world devoid of girls and women. The film, about the apparent rebellion against elitist cold war–era scripts of societal conformity, is in fact deeply traditional. For example, students learn from their spirited teacher (played by Robin Williams) the value of marching to the beat of their own drum as they walk circles in a courtyard. Castigating students for establishing a classroom rhythm, as if the communally created can only signal conformity, their teacher urges them to discover a rhythm unmediated by societal structures or the other marchers, as if this is both possible and the only indicator of integrity and creativity. Even though *Dead Poets Society*, through the literature and values it promotes, critiques the boarding school regime of the 1950s from a contemporary perspective, it endorses a bygone humanist approach to a traditional literary canon and participates in a backlash against the entry of multiculturalism and feminism into the humanities during the era when the film was made. Despite its liberal guise, then, the film supports the views of conservatives of the 1980s (i.e., William Bennett, Harold Bloom, George Will) who were bewailing the passing of dead poets, and their supposed replacement by Alice Walker and comic books.

What both *Dead Poets Society* and *A Life* promote as new and radical can be understood as a return to a humanism that has been challenged on two fronts: first both by multiculturalism and feminism and then also by the increasing corporatization of the university. And although the humanism that these works recruit might be preferable to today's corporatization, they, too, are founded on values of bourgeois individualism and benefit those with class, race, and gender privilege. *Dead Poets Society* and *A Life* participate in a larger, and long-standing, cultural pattern, one premised on entrenched American ideologies of freethinking, antiauthoritarianism, and individualism that are supported by a humanist tradition comprised of great works of Western literature as well as of popular film and memoir.

The recurring mention of *Dead Poets Society* in contemporary academic memoirs about teaching suggest the power and draw of its nostalgic humanism. In *The Cliff Walk*, for example, Don Snyder describes how, after being fired, as he exits his job, he gives a performance designed to leave his students "with the gift of literature. . . . The pure power it conveys when it isn't waterlogged by scholars' literary theories and professors' canned lectures" (29). When a football player applauds, Snyder describes pausing, "a little delirious, I suppose, wondering if he had seen the movie *Dead Poets Society*" (30). Attributing his job loss to his refusal of literary theory, as well as to being a white male, it is the humanist literature and pedagogy of *Dead Poets Society* that serve as Snyder's rebuttal to the contemporary academy. In *Life on the Tenure Track* James Lang also references *Dead Poets Society* as the symbol of good teaching: as a student rushes through an evaluation, Lang resists the temptation to storm after the student and tell him "this is your opportunity to validate me as a teacher, to tell me how great I am, to make me feel that my hellish first semester of teaching was somehow all worthwhile, because I touched your soul in a *Dead Poets Society–Mr. Holland's Opus* kind of way" (145). In contrast to Snyder and Lang, when Mark Edmundson evokes the film in *Teacher: The One Who Made a Difference*, he does so in a way that points critically to the social conservatism that underwrites its iconic classroom vision. Expressing his conviction that "perhaps the great teachers who matter the most" come with a sharp edge, he contrasts these teachers to the "Robin Williams myth," one in which the teacher "loves his students first and last, almost more than he loves himself. . . . If he challenges anything, it is orthodoxies that are already dead in the world at large and have reared their heads in one last corner" (11). Along with the memoirs by Lang and Snyder, in its references to *Dead Poets Society*, *A Life* is symptomatic not only of the pull of a humanist pedagogy and literary tradition (evident in other ways in other memoirs, as well), but also of a turning to the classroom to achieve a submerged desire for control and validation during a time when professors feel, for various reasons and in differing ways, anxiety about their authority in the academy.

Albeit in a less blatant way than Snyder, who so clearly uses his classroom performance to play out, and compensate for, his disappointments in and aggressions toward the profession in which he and his students are situated and in which he feels lacking in authority, Tompkins, feeling by contrast a surplus of authority that she desires to cast off, nonetheless at times reveals the desire for power and control that underwrites her pedagogy. An example of this occurs when the students in her Reading for Yourself course fail to come up with their own assignments. Tompkins enters a yelling match with a student who tells her, "'I hate to read,'" a position for which the course, with all its promised freedoms, does not allow (133). Tompkins storms out of the classroom, telling her students that "it was up to them to come up with a plan for the rest of the semester" (134). When Tompkins returns to her office after the weekend, she finds "a huge pile of Xeroxes outside my door, and taped to the wall was a long complicated list of assignments and responsibilities the students promised to carry out. I was overjoyed and limp with relief. I made a card . . . with 'Hurray!' written all over it again and again. It's still taped to the wall beside my desk, a reminder to me that some experiments, anyway, do turn out" (136–37). What remains underanalyzed here is what finally motivates her students to read for themselves. I would argue that not only does Tompkins's need for authority surface during her outburst, but also that this authority is what the students finally respond to. Rather than an abdication of power (or an aberrant display of it), Tompkins's dramatic exit from class is an outing or intensification of her always-present authority.

Moreover, as the above example suggests, although Tompkins does not wish to reproduce herself in the class as a scholar, she does seek in her students reflections of her own wants and needs. Thus the narcissism about which Gallop and Snyder are so unapologetic and frank resides in a less recognized way in Tompkins. When reflecting on the Reading for Yourself course, Tompkins expresses her pleasure when a student stands on a table and recites "Oh, Captain, my Captain": "My students had reintroduced me to the magic of poetry, and I felt for the first time in a long, long time the enchantment that had originally led me to the study of literature, an enchantment that is summed up for me in the image of Ben standing on the table with his sword of light" (139–40). Since the student is imitating the students in *Dead Poets Society* who leap atop their desks to pay homage to their unconventional teacher, it is difficult not to see Tompkins's pleasure as tied to the link the student's performance creates between herself and the movie's hero. Whereas Gallop unabashedly wants center stage, Tompkins's pedagogic fantasy is standing offstage while her students express their love and loyalty to her, and not as an equal, but as a beloved teacher who makes possible their self-actualization. As Tompkins narrates the experience of decentering herself as a teacher so that her students can reclaim their individuality and creativity, she ultimately recenters herself. In their more blatant staging of such moments in their memoirs, Snyder and Lang unmask the vanity of this position and the *ressentiment* and the need for validation that fuel it. Tompkins's denial of her authority thus proves to be the flip side of Gallop's unabashed assertion of her authority; what enables each is an acute discomfort with and inability to address their own institutional power.[48] Along with other memoirs about teaching, Tompkins's suggests not only the strength—and the allure—of the power dynamics that structure the student-teacher relationship, but also how academics' memoirs about teaching are set up to reinforce rather than restructure the student-teacher relationship, and to reclaim (even if it is anxiously or unconsciously) a more general authority in the profession.

Tompkins ends her memoir with her description of how—having cast aside her desk in her rethinking of her role as professor—she finally finds a writing table at an antique store:

> I was told it was a harvest table. I pictured it in an old-fashioned kitchen, piled with fruit, and felt warm inside. The day I went to pick it up, though, its owner was there, a former professor of education at Duke who had gone

into the antiques business—they phased out his department some years ago. We hit it off right away. He tells me it is not a harvest table; it is a teacher's desk, the kind the teachers at Duke used to stand or sit behind in class. The stains are ink stains.

Of course.

. . . On another day, I went to the lamp store that was going out of business and bought an old student lamp with an oak and brass base and a green glass shade that gives off a kindly light. I feel protected by it. Student lamp, antique chair, and teacher's desk with overtones of harvest table. That should do. (228)

This set of images is indeed an apt way to end *A Life in School*. With these props Tompkins creates for the reader a scene of cozy intimacy, one that blurs the lines between teacher and student, and between school and home, or classroom and kitchen. However, this carefully staged setting masks the reality and effects of institutional roles and structures of power. Moreover, the desk, lamp, and chair references evoke but fail to elucidate how Tompkins's supposed refusal of her professional role results not in an innovative pedagogy but in the return to an old-fashioned (or "phased out") humanism. This humanism—affordable and attractive to, for instance, purveyors of antiques who perhaps participate in a less crass form of consumerism than the contemporary version—depends on no small measure of privilege mixed with nostalgia. If antique hunting bespeaks a more individual and less alienating consumerism than most forms available today, it nevertheless offers no true escape from or alternative to social hierarchies and a consumer economy. In ways that its conclusion encapsulates, *A Life* endorses a humanism that can only be purchased with a certain amount of privilege, and a pedagogy that seems to abdicate even as it reinforces Tompkins's institutional power and position as a professor. Moreover, the ways in which Tompkins inhabits memoir preserve the genre's ties—and strengthen *A Life*'s connections—to contemporary academic hierarchies as well as to traditional humanism.

During an era in which, as Henry Giroux puts it in *University in Chains: Confronting the Military-Industrial-Academic Complex*, the academy is characterized by a corporatization and militarization that involve "for-profit" campuses, "branded" universities, and the clampdown on nonconformity, *A Life* extends to its readers a "kindly light" and an atmosphere reminiscent of better, or less crass, times. However appealing such a vision might be, however, it is not one that offers a true return to a (not so rosy anyway) humanist past, nor does it offer a solution to the problems that face academics struggling with the anxieties and pressures that come externally, and that result as well from having achieved positions of institutional authority and success.

Lessons in World Civilization

This chapter on pedagogy began by discussing the case involving B and Lance Collins. I'd like to return here to the student concerns that triggered this case. For complex reasons that arguably owe in part to Hawaiʻi's geographic isolation, to its large numbers of student commuters saddled with work and family responsibilities, and to its ongoing colonial history, the curricular struggles being played out at the faculty senate meeting were a belated version of the culture wars that spread across many college campuses in the mid-1980s. That the calls for change at UH were far from novel made them no less threatening. Indeed, the increased conservatism in the academy—and the increasingly precarious position of the humanities and of funding for the university—especially when coupled with a Hawaiian sovereignty movement that still was gaining force in the late 1990s, made the students' challenges all the more threatening. As students protested the Eurocentric nature of the university's core curriculum, and called for required courses with both truly global, and Pacific-centered, epistemologies and subject matter, faculty members focused in their e-mails following the meeting on a few student leaders' lack of "civility." However, despite such attempts to make the struggle more manageable and (as B did in an extreme form) to maintain authority at a time when it was under siege from multiple directions, what seems to have threatened faculty most was students' challenges to the racial makeup of the faculty, and to what we teach and how we teach it. Students were demanding changes that required a shift in hiring practices; they were calling for a new curriculum that would "move the center," as student leaders put it in their literature urging other students to action. At a university that only recently has allocated money and too-few faculty positions to a Center for Hawaiian Studies and a School of Hawaiian Knowledge, students' calls for change were not about placing the current faculty alongside students in the classroom, but about removing faculty from some classrooms altogether.[49] In other words, they were demanding changes far more radical than, for example, individual teachers inviting students to design their own syllabi.

As Bill Readings reminds us, "pedagogic pragmatics" cannot be "divorced from attention to institutional forms" (153). To achieve substantive transformation requires far more than "decentering" the classroom through new pedagogical strategies. It requires changing not only what faculty—especially white faculty—teach and how we teach it, but committing as well to diverse hiring practices and admissions policies.

As I argue, it is difficult to remain in the academy without getting co-opted, and surely for tenured faculty members, especially those who occupy "star" status, the difficulties—along with the contradictions and anxieties—increase. And some forms—including the memoir—prove particularly resistant as vehicles for institutional critique and the relinquishing of authority and privilege. It is perhaps especially challenging to employ memoir to tell an oppositional story about teaching with tenure, one that does not justify one's position in ways that are self-validating and thus often ultimately supportive of the educational system. And although personal stories about teaching can be both productive *and* self-serving, too often such stories, however anxiety ridden or oppositional in intent, lose sight of or else end up justifying larger institutional structures or contexts. As Susan Miller argues of personal narratives about pedagogy, "these confessions are neither individual nor even personal" (160). She further contends, "The textual unconscious of our 'personal' narratives about teaching re-establishes authority for the monitorial functions of mass education while suppressing the socialization within institutions that is their logical but unintended outcome" (163). Although I find Miller's argument compelling, I do not think such an outcome is inevitable. However, for personal narratives about teaching truly to challenge an institution and one's own position of authority in it, I believe we must keep a firm grasp on how what happens inside the classroom relates to larger institutional structures and histories, and social hierarchies that involve race, class, gender, nationality, and sexuality as well as student-teacher power differentials. This is perhaps particularly true for personal narratives about teaching that arise as part of the academic star system, and during a period when humanities scholars find themselves on the defensive, in relation to challenges issuing from both inside and outside the academy.

It is not surprising that when such oppositional personal narratives emerged in the 1990s, most often they came from faculty of color who have themselves experienced multiple forms of oppression in the academy (bell hooks, AnaLouise Keating, Haunani-Kay Trask, Victor

Villanueva, Patricia Williams, Janet Zandy). Moreover, this writing often is not "straight" memoir, but rather it disrupts the conservatism of many personal narratives about teaching in part through its genre crossings, often bringing together personal narrative, dialogue, student journal entries, cultural criticism, and institutional history.[50] This chapter considers one such work, bell hooks's 1994 collection of essays, *Teaching to Transgress*, and an exploration of how it relates to hooks's own use of memoir, and to the star system, the institutionalization of feminism, and academic culture today.

Not Spurs, but Hooks

At the outset of my discussion of Tompkins I quoted a passage from Lisa Ruddick in which she favorably contrasts Tompkins's and bell hooks's humanizing pedagogy to Gallop's. There are indeed many correspondences to be drawn between hooks's and Tompkins's pedagogy. Both authors call for an embodied pedagogy that values the whole person. Both draw on Freire. Both have turned to Buddhism and become increasingly interested in writing about healing, spirituality, and love. Both write autobiographically about teaching, after having established their reputations as feminist cultural critics who have politicized structures of feeling. However, hooks realizes through the writing of *Teaching to Transgress* many of the pedagogical objectives that she shares with Tompkins while maintaining a vision that is less based on bourgeois individualism. In her calls for wholeness and spiritual healing, hooks is more attentive to issues of race, gender, and class, more mindful of power dynamics and institutional structures and positions, and more complex and open in her treatment of eroticism in the classroom. Transgressing boundaries of genre better enables hooks to fulfill the goals that she shares with Tompkins, whose reliance on memoir provides no resistance either to the individualism inherent in the pedagogy she promotes, or to the institutional structures that she wishes to challenge. At the same time, despite her political commitments and sophisticated deployment of identity politics and feminist theory, hooks, like Tompkins—and also like Gallop—ultimately is unable to account for her institutional power. Thus, this final section further develops this chapter's explorations of the insights that memoirs provide into the star system and its relationship to shortcomings in feminist and other cultural theories that have become institutionalized in the contemporary academy.

An enormously influential and prolific cultural critic, by the time she writes *Teaching to Transgress*, hooks had become one of the premiere public intellectuals in the United States. As the author of more than two dozen books that attract academic and nonacademic audiences, hooks argues on behalf of wide-ranging social changes, especially those that will better the lives of black people. With her interest in self-transformation and healing as crucial psychic components to addressing racism, sexism, classism, and other social ills, hooks's work is characterized by the effectiveness with which she has mixed autobiography and theory in order to demonstrate—and utilize—connections between the personal and the political. "Radicalizing consciousness," she argues, cannot be achieved through personal narrative alone. Indeed, in her essay "On Self Recovery," hooks criticizes the contemporary feminist movement for too exclusively relying on women telling their own stories: "In most cases, naming one's personal pain was not sufficiently linked to overall education for critical consciousness of collective political resistance" (*Talking Back*, 32). This insistence on placing the personal in relation to structures of domination sounds a keynote in hooks's work through the 1980s and 1990s, and is what has helped to make her work so important and influential.

Teaching to Transgress occurs close to a turning point in hooks's career, one in which she moves away from genre-crossing works that combine theory and autobiography, and toward increasingly accessible books that fit more neatly into the genres of memoir or self-help. In groundbreaking books including *Feminist Theory: From Margin to Center* (1984), *Talking Back: Thinking Feminist, Thinking Black* (1989), *Yearning: Race, Gender, and Cultural Politics* (1989), *Black Looks: Race and Representation* (1991), and *Teaching to Transgress: Education as the Practice of Freedom* (1994), hooks explores multiple and interlocking forms of oppression through analyses of her own experiences and cultural texts. hooks has continued this work in books including *Where We Stand: Class Matters* (2000), *Feminism Is for Everybody: Passionate Politics* (2000), and *Teaching Community: A Pedagogy of Hope* (2003). She also has started writing children's books (*Homemade Love*, 2002) as a way of "making feminist thought available to everyone" (*Feminism* 113). At the same time, however, in recent publications including *Bone Black: Memories of Girlhood* (1996), *Wounds of Passion: A Writing Life* (1997), *Remembered Rapture: The Writer at Work* (1999), *All about Love: New Visions* (2000), *Communion: The Female Search for Love* (2002), and her poetry collection *When Angels Speak of Love* (2007), hooks's inward drama has become more absorbing to her. These books, which forego the critical rigor that characterizes her earlier works, are more accessible to a wider readership and thus contribute to her ongoing commitment to democratizing feminist and antiracist ideas. They also partake in the trend in the humanities to adopt nontheoretical language aimed at a "cross-over" readership. However, what often drops out of these books, which were being published at the rate of up to three per year, are the historical contexts, materialist analyses, and genre crossings that have given her work its transgressive possibilities. hooks's rapid publication rate and her fame and popularity arguably contribute to her greater reliance on personal memories, and her less specific engagements with historical and political contexts.[51] What results in these later works that utilize the memoir and self-help genres is a less suggestive and supple play between the personal and the political and the private and the institutional. In the conclusion to this chapter I trace the trajectory of hooks's career in order to continue my exploration of what it means for cultural critics writing to effect social change to enter into the academic star circuit and to participate in the related phenomenon of academic memoirs. hooks's memoirs illuminate how such an entry can engender a humanism that, as it exposes the limits or forgets the lessons of feminist and other critical theory, reveals the difficulty of theorizing privilege, and also the problems of a politics that does not value ethos and emotional intelligence.

Through the 1980s and 1990s, along with other feminists of color, hooks was at the forefront of the movement in the humanities to combine personal experience and theory. In *Teaching to Transgress*, in her sophisticated practice of identity politics, hooks grounds her experiences of educational institutions in analyses of larger societal structures of domination and oppression (those having to do with race, class, and gender). In contrast to Tompkins, for hooks theory can illuminate the ills of education. Rather than generalize from her negative experiences of graduate school, in *Teaching to Transgress* hooks subjects them to a racial analysis and contrasts them to her early days in all-black schools (4). Highly critical of those who display anti-intellectualism, hooks argues that to split theory and practice is to "deny the power of liberatory education for critical consciousness, thereby perpetuating conditions that reinforce our collective exploitation and repression" (69); hooks instead insists on the connection between theory and practice (10). In accounting for how schools alienate students, hooks addresses oppressed peoples' dispossession from language (175). She also ties students' inability to come to voice in the classroom to the bourgeois values, racism, and sexism that make classrooms unsafe spaces (180, 186). In making these arguments hooks deftly builds on identity politics and on other feminist and cultural theories that by the 1990s had assumed a prominent place in the academy.

hooks's commitment to putting "critical thinking" at the heart of her pedagogy (202) does not exist in tension with her concerted desire to reach students on a spiritual and emotional level; for hooks, spiritual well-being, although often neglected in academe, *requires* rather than exists at odds with critical thinking. Approaching teaching from a spiritual, even religious, vantage point, hooks views the classroom "always as a communal place" (8), perceives of teaching as a "sacred" vocation (13), and believes that teachers must "teach in a manner that respects and cares for the souls of our students" (13). hooks expresses indebtedness to Vietnamese Buddhist monk Thich Nhat Hanh for "a way of thinking about pedagogy which emphasized wholeness, a union of mind, body, and spirit" (14). Each of these quotations could come from Tompkins's *A Life* (and indeed, the authors share an interest in Buddhism, though it takes a more individualized and muted form in *A Life*). However, hooks differs from Tompkins in that she perceives the intellect and theory to be integral to the pursuit for spiritual well-being. Whereas for Tompkins all forms of criticism are socially imposed ones that deny individuals access to their true selves, for hooks, informed as she is by feminist, Marxist, and Buddhist thought, critical consciousness is necessary in order to achieve liberation from societal forms of oppression.

In *Teaching to Transgress* hooks departs from Tompkins not only in her valuing of theory to account for structures of domination and oppression that characterize educational institutions and impoverish students, but also in her focus, which is collective as well as individual. Unlike Tompkins, hooks foregrounds a collective politics over personal exploration. "My commitment to engaged pedagogy," hooks explains, "is an expression of political activism" (203). For hooks, as for Tompkins, Paolo Freire serves as a model for how to combat an alienating curriculum and an authoritarian pedagogy. However, hooks finds in Freire's work not only inspiration for individual empowerment, but also "a way to place the politics of racism in the United States in a global context wherein I could see my fate linked with that of colonized people everywhere struggling to decolonize, to transform society" (53). With this vantage point hooks positions her pedagogy as counterhegemonic, and directed at turning individual empowerment into a collective social movement.

As is indicated by her citation of other educators and intellectuals, hooks does not represent herself as acting alone, nor does she reject constructed forms of knowledge in exchange for some inner and wholly individual truth that exists apart from the rest of the academy. *Teaching to Transgress* acknowledges the importance of other teachers as well as theories of pedagogy; it includes, for example, a dialogue about the pursuit for a liberatory pedagogy with her friend, the philosopher Ron Scapp. hooks is especially affirming of the contributions made by feminist scholars, particularly their promotion of passionate and embodied ways of knowing. In a remark that echoes those made by Gallop in *FASH*, hooks explains, "In the heady early days of Women's Studies classes at Stanford University, I learned by the example of daring, courageous woman professors (particularly Diane Middlebrook) that there was a place for passion in the classroom, that eros and the erotic did not need to be denied for learning to take place" (193). hooks chronicles the influence of the early days of women's studies not, as Gallop does, in order to lament their passing, but rather to mark them as both an origin and a departure point for her own feminist praxis.

Just as hooks acknowledges the feminist foundation on which she builds her liberatory pedagogy, she makes conscious use of the authority of her institutional position, even as she expresses awareness of how professors can exercise their power in oppressive ways. Like Tompkins, hooks writes of learning that education is about "obedience to authority" (*Teaching to Transgress* 4) and she witnesses her teachers in graduate school using the classroom "to enact rituals of control that were about domination and the unjust exercise of power" (5). However, in contrast to Tompkins, liberation for hooks does not translate as escape from a position of power. Rather, she realizes she must create ways to use her "professional power constructively" (188). As hooks states, "commitment to engaged pedagogy carries with it the willingness to be responsible, not to pretend that professors do not have the power to change the direction of our students' lives" (206). For hooks using power responsibly means influencing students to be socially conscious. For example, she tells of how, after taking her class, a student decided against a career in corporate law (206)—a success story for hooks that contrasts sharply with Tompkins's more individualist hopes that she and her students will recapture their childhood dreams to become sailors or bareback circus riders. In *Teaching to Transgress* hooks embraces rather than anxiously struggles with a professorial authority, using it to further her political and pedagogical aims.

Academic feminism in particular carries an authority that hooks at once claims and critically engages for its complicity in institutionalizing racism and classism. In particular, from a distinctly black feminist perspective hooks takes issue with the idea of the classroom as a safe space that, by the 1990s, had become pervasive among feminists. With a clear understanding of how such a concept can support the status quo, and especially dominant racial and sexual identities, hooks's vision of community instead allows for discomfort and discord—being liked and creating a classroom community that provides the comfort of home are not her goals. She explains, "Students do not always enjoy studying with me. Often they find my courses challenge them in ways that are deeply unsettling. This was particularly disturbing to me at the beginning of my teaching career because I wanted to be like[d] and admired. It took time and experience for me to understand that the rewards of engaged pedagogy might not emerge during a course" (206). hooks's pedagogy stands in contrast to Tompkins's desire to banish conflict from the classroom, and to find in her students a panacea for her own loneliness that depends on wishing away structural differences.[52] At the same time, although comfortable with her authority hooks does not capitalize on her students as a captive audience as Gallop does; instead, in *Teaching to Transgress* she expresses her conviction that teachers' "work is not meant to be a spectacle" (11). Thus, hooks neither espouses a pedagogy that claims spectacle—and the carefully cultivated narcissism that attends it—as a teaching tool, nor does she seek forms of nonhierarchical companionship that make her classroom an escape from "a life in school."

At the same time, over the course of her career, as black feminism—if not black feminists—has become ensconced in the academy, hooks has come to inhabit her authority in a way that at times slides into narcissism and lacks critical awareness. Critics including Michele Wallace have taken hooks to task for "'eating the other,'" or for failing to acknowledge adequately the work of other scholars in her habitual lack of footnotes and documentation, refuting hooks's reasoning that these are absent so as to empower nonacademic readers (8). Paradoxically, it is perhaps hooks's dialogic essays that most clearly demonstrate her uncritical displays of authority. Throughout her career, hooks has regularly staged dialogues with herself—or rather between her writing and nonwriting selves, bell hooks and Gloria Watkins—as a way to counter individualism or isolation. Whereas hooks's use of a writing name arguably functions in earlier works including *Ain't I a Woman* so that, as she notes in *Wounds of*

Passion, "her ego cannot be identified with this book," once she is well-known and publishes dialogues between her two selves, the effect can instead be self-aggrandizing (227). For example, a chapter on Freire in *Teaching to Transgress* consists of a dialogue between hooks and Watkins that, as hooks explains, allows for "an intimacy—a familiarity—I do not find it possible to achieve in the essay. And here I have found a way to share the sweetness, the solidarity I talk about" (45). hooks's claims here to solidarity and intimacy refer both to that shared between herself and Freire (Watkins remarks on hooks's similarities to Freire) and between her two selves. Such moves position hooks as her own best interlocutor and also demonstrate her narcissism more convincingly than her capacities for solidarity and intimacy. Other claims to the dialogic in *Teaching to Transgress* seem similarly narcissistic, and uncharacteristically naive in their positing of distinct voices split off from hooks's ego. For example, hooks includes glowing excerpts from student journals or evaluations that testify to the power of her teaching, with explanations such as the following: "I have quoted [my student's] writing at length because it is testimony affirming engaged pedagogy. It means that my voice is not the only account of what happens in the classroom" (20). Selectively including testimony that consists of students expressing their love and gratitude to hooks can seem more a way for hooks to affirm herself than an engaged pedagogy. hooks's turn to memoir, a genre that encourages individualized, socially dislocated, and self-absorbed forms of writing, follows from, and extends, this development in her work.[53]

As hooks, and her feminist praxis, accrue institutional authority, her writings fail to address the significance of this shift. And although she continues to utilize an identity politics, this politics does not require that she take stock of her institutional identity and the specific conditions—including the star system—that have come to characterize the contemporary academy. Whereas in her earlier work, relying on the categories of race, class, and gender to analyze her social location seems sufficient, they become less adequate as her privilege grows and as she and her work achieve an increasingly established place in the academy. *Teaching to Transgress* marks a pivotal moment in this regard, especially in its discussion of the place of eros in the classroom. On the one hand, in her analysis of her relationships to her students, hooks addresses her authority and larger social structures that impact these relationships in complex ways. On the other hand, her inattention to the specific stature she holds in the present-day academy limits her analysis in ways that are symptomatic of academic culture and of feminist theory as it has become institutionalized in the 1990s academy.

In *Teaching to Transgress* hooks directly confronts the difficulties as well as the transformative possibilities that attend the presence of eros in the classroom. Love is at the center of hooks's relationships—intellectual, personal, and political—to her students. hooks posits an eros that encompasses sexuality and love—of others and of self—as a way for teachers to challenge the mind-body split as well as distinctions between the public and private, and the academic and nonacademic worlds. To restore eros and passion to the classroom, hooks contends, makes it "a dynamic place where transformations in social relations are concretely actualized and the false dichotomy between the world outside and the inside world of the academy disappears" (195). If this assertion is overly idealistic, unlike Gallop, hooks expresses awareness of how, given her authority, her desires can affect students' well-being. Analyzing one such personal experience, hooks explains that once she learned how repressing sexual attraction to students can "lead to the 'wounding' of students, I was determined to face whatever passions were aroused in the classroom setting and deal with them" (192–93). Also, in distinction to both Gallop and Tompkins, she admits in *Teaching to Transgress* to complaints that students made in their journals "about the perceived special bonding between myself and particular students" (198). For hooks, students' responses become an opportunity to teach about "the notion of privatized passion" (198): "I asked students once: '. . . . Why do you think there is not enough love or care to go around?' To answer these questions they had to think deeply about the society we live in, how we are taught to compete with one another. They had to think about capitalism and how it informs the way we think about love and care, the way we live in our bodies, the way we try to separate mind from body" (198–99). As hooks asks students to engage their feelings at a level that is both analytical and political, she does not dismiss the personal significance students' feelings hold. At the same time hooks herself does not here address how the privatized passion that she asks her students to critique might, in fact, be at work in her special ties to particular students, and she positions herself as above the ideologies that she works to overturn through her pedagogy, rather than investigating how she, too, might be implicated in them, and how a critique of any given ideology does not ensure liberation from it. Furthermore, hooks's analysis of love includes no discussion of the significance of her own position as not simply a teacher, but as an internationally renowned public intellectual.

Although she does not include a historicized analysis of her position in the academy, hooks's accounts of her classroom experiences introduce the presence of personal investments that exceed her analyses of eros in productive ways that invite critical consideration. And with her embrace of eros, hooks deftly steers a course between those offered by Tompkins and Gallop: as she productively resists splitting apart love and sexuality, she provides effective counterpoints to Gallop's focus on sex without love and to Tompkins's search for a love uncomplicated by sexuality. This is particularly evident in the passionate relationship that hooks details between herself and O'Neal LaRon Clark, the student to whom she dedicates *Teaching to Transgress*. In the excerpts that hooks includes from students' journal entries about her, she includes one from LaRon in which he expresses "that he will 'love me now and always'" (197). hooks says of LaRon, "We had a passionate teacher/student relationship" and she describes how, exercising their mutual love for dancing, they created passion in the classroom and "danced our way into the future as comrades and friends bound by all we had learned in class together. . . . He died unexpectedly last year—still dancing, still loving me now and always" (197–98). Unlike hooks's other accounts of classroom eros, this moment moves hooks's essay in a direction that is intensely personal in ways that are only partially analyzed. hooks does not divulge whether or not this relationship became sexual, and she neither warns against nor celebrates student-teacher sexual relations in *Teaching to Transgress*. Although her account does not address the complexities of how love and sex operate in the classroom, it does create a space for her readers to think about how they relate to the book's overall call for an engaged and liberatory pedagogy. hooks's personal experience thus anchors the reader and provides a place to theorize from, without this experience serving (even implicitly) as representative or exemplary, as happens so frequently in memoir.

When hooks turns to memoir and to meditations on love that fit into the "self-help" genre, although her concerns with love, self-recovery, healing, and transformation remain constant, the rich interplay between personal experience and theoretical inquiry diminishes. Moreover, although—in contrast to Tompkins—when hooks writes memoir she avoids casting herself or her experiences as representative, her memoirs nevertheless do not escape the problems of individualism, which she so rigorously critiques in earlier work. Indeed, her insistence on the uniqueness of her suffering and her exaltation of art and artists result in an intense and familiar form of humanist individualism that is a hallmark of memoir, and that signals a turning away from a collective politics and structural modes of analysis of race, class, and gender. This shift is not revelatory in regard to genre so much as it conveys lessons about contemporary academic culture and the seductions of the star system, both of which unmask not only theorists' self-directed interests but also the self-centeredness that can drive some of the theories themselves.

The beginning and midpoint of hooks's career correspond to the entry and then the rise of feminist theory in the academy, and it is in the intervening period that I find her work most transgressive and best able to realize a politics based on personal experience. Her first published book, *Ain't I a Woman?*, a work key to the institutionalization of black and feminist studies, usefully complicates the divides between personal and scholarly writing. Although this book depends least of all of her writings on personal narrative, she later declares about it, "'It is the book of my heart, . . I will not write such a book again.' I say this now. Then it was experienced, and felt, as a private joy—then I had no language to speak this joy in political terms" (*Talking Back* 30). Even as *Ain't I a Woman?*, which served as hooks's ticket into academe, to date is the most straightforwardly academic of her books, it evidences how the personal is not coterminous with the autobiographical, any more than the theoretical need be opposed to the emotional. Following *Ain't I a Woman?*, the books that hooks wrote from the mid-1980s to the mid-1990s provide an arresting mix of personal narrative, cultural critique, and theory. They successfully bring personal narrative and theory into a dialectical relationship and demonstrate how personal experience can be used in collective and profoundly political ways. For example, in *yearning* hooks addresses how women in her family have struggled to make a homeplace (40). She then connects her family history to a broader one: "Historically, African-American people believed that the construction of a homeplace, however fragile and tenuous (the slave hut, the wooden shack), had a radical political dimension. Despite the brutal reality of racial apartheid, of domination, one's homeplace was the one site where one could freely confront the issue of humanization, where one could resist" (42). At the forefront of establishing a methodology that proved key not only to the establishment of African American and women's studies, but also to new directions in the humanities more generally, in her writings hooks skillfully connects the domestic and political spheres, and her individual, personal history to a collective one.

Since the late 1990s the genres in which hooks has chosen to write, and the increasing individualism of her concerns, not only reflect the inroads of the academic star system but also suggest the limits of premising a politics too strictly on the personal, especially when one has risen to a position of privilege not accounted for by identity politics' usual categories. These arguments are evidenced by hooks's most recent writings about home. What have dropped out of these autobiographical accounts are the historical and political contexts that both broaden *and* deepen her stories. In her memoir *Wounds of Passion*, her chronicling of her obsessive search for the perfect house is unaccompanied by any historical contextualizing. As a result, her obsession seems to exist in contradiction to her repeated assertions that "she was not into possession," especially when combined with hooks's close attention to cars and clothes, and her proclamation that, "My motto is 'I die for style'" (175, 195). By *All about Love* (2000), her descriptions of her city apartment and her country house take for granted her ability to own two homes, and they lack her earlier attention to how being a property owner historically signifies differently for black people than for white people: "My flat in the city has the theme 'love's meeting place.' As a small-town person moving to a big city I found that I needed my environment to truly feel like a sanctuary. . . . My country place has a desert theme. I call it 'soledad hermosa,' beautiful solitude. I go there to be quiet and still and to experience the divine, to be renewed" (66). Because hooks's class ascent is not one that is broadly shared by black women, the absence of discussion of this, or of the contemporary conditions in the academy and the broader culture that have made possible her economic privilege, demonstrate her shift away from collective feminist, antiracist politics. Along with the memoir movement itself, this shift does not belie the understanding that the "personal is political" but rather reveals the problems with not thinking beyond the self, and the need as well to consider categories of identity that extend beyond those of race, class, gender, and sexuality.

With hooks's turn to memoir comes a near-exclusive focus on her own emotional landscape as an extraordinarily sensitive individual and as a lone writer. *Bone Black* is an exploration of loneliness, but unlike Tompkins, hooks seeks answers not in the classroom but rather through writing. Although neither writer positions her loneliness in relation to present-day conditions in academe, whereas Tompkins generalizes her loneliness and finds her isolation representative of every person's experiences of "school," hooks instead associates her loneliness with her unique and artistic sensitivity, and depicts her pain as part of what makes her extraordinary and different. Although in the preface hooks presents her story as a marginalized one of black girlhood, what prevails is the narrative of hooks as individual and tortured writer. Even though the title *Bone Black* evokes hooks's racial identity, blackness over the course of the memoir becomes marked more as a deeply internal and individualized state, one from which hooks's art emerges: "My soul is dark like the inner world of the cave—bone black. I have been drowning in that blackness. Like quicksand it sucks me in and keeps me there in the space of all my pain. I never say out loud that I could die in this space of loneliness, of outsiderness" (181). This black cave becomes a source of creativity as well as suffering and loneliness. hooks concludes her memoir with an account in which she escapes the loneliness of her home by taking refuge in a "bone black" cave of words: "At night when everyone is silent and everything is still, I lie in the darkness of my windowless room, the place where they [hooks's family] exile me from the community of their heart, and search the unmoving blackness to see if I can find my way home. I tell myself stories, write poems, record my dreams. In my journal I write—I belong in this place of words. This is my home. This dark, bone black inner cave where I am making a world for myself" (183). As these lines suggest, blackness becomes dissociated from—indeed defined in opposition to—any collective or relational sense of home or identity. On the one hand, hooks's refusal to homogenize African American communities constitutes a brave political intervention. On the other hand, too often this refusal only spotlights hooks's specialness as a writer. Throughout her memoir, as hooks insists on her difference, she represents her pain, past and present (her use of the present tense renders her childhood pain still palpably present), as extraordinary and isolating rather than as part of a shared experience. Her brother and sisters remain nameless for the most part, and as hooks represents herself and her family from an omniscient viewpoint, she defines herself and feels defined by her difference from them in an absolute way: "To her younger sisters, she is the one who is different. They cannot sleep at night because she is always crying" (110). When, due to her grief and need for solitude, her parents give her a room of her own, she represents this move as exile, noting of her sisters, "they are glad to see her go. . . . Like in church, they excommunicate her" (111). Highly individualistic and solipsistic, hooks's memoir upholds the ideology of the lonely and tortured artist who is distinguished by her suffering. Moreover, as hooks goes public with private childhood pain that still clearly impacts her (and, in her ability to do so, complicates, as do other memoirists, her representation of her outcast status), she not only sets herself apart from her family and her wider African American community, but she also leaves unexplored how present-day conditions contribute to her pain—a move that might provide insights into what it means to be a black feminist in the academy today.[54]

As does Tompkins in *A Life*, in *Bone Black* hooks slips in and out of a child's point of view, and in part the self-absorption of *Bone Black* can be explained by hooks's attempts in it to capture such a point of view. Reclaiming her childhood perspective magnifies but also justifies hooks's egocentrism. Thus, hooks describes her piano teacher's voice as "cutting across her back like the whip on the flesh of slaves picking cotton. Hitting a wrong note she thought about their aching backs, their dry throats, the hot sun" (36). What differentiates hooks's claim to an experience akin to slavery from Tompkins's in *A Life* is that hooks is herself African American, that the point of view she purports to express here is a child's, and that she is representing the connection as one individually and spontaneously experienced.

Even as memoir serves hooks as a place to explore private pain in a way that other genres do not, it also can make evident the problems of making claims to art and humanity that leave behind structural forms of analysis. *Wounds of Passion* highlights some of these problems. In this memoir hooks's claims to a unique narrative of victimization and suffering continue and exist as markers not of a history of racial violence, nor as a register of the loneliness that can accompany her present-day success, but rather as evidence of her particular artistic sensitivity. In *Wounds* she repeats an account from *Bone Black* of the childhood trauma of seeing her father violently threaten her mother. In one of the memoir's many shifts into third person, hooks states, *"And as with all things she seemed to take it harder than everybody else"* (9, original emphasis). Such an assertion, coming from an adult perspective—one further legitimated by being rendered in third rather than first person as it is in *Bone Black*—seems presumptuous about what her family members, who also lived through this violence, experienced. Such claims to the uniqueness of hooks's suffering not only exist in tension with but also can potentially trivialize moments that suggest, as hooks does in *Bone Black*, how the history of slavery can inform the perspective of an African American child. In *Wounds of Passion*, as hooks portrays her suffering as exceptional, she links it to art in ways that lift both above the concerns with the structures of power that characterize her earlier work. So, too, in both memoirs are poets themselves portrayed as transcendent over matters of race, class, and gender through statements such as, "White folks we meet in the world of poetry always seem to be beyond whiteness" (*Wounds* 126). In distinction to the complex analysis to which she subjects artists and cultural texts in her earlier body of work, hooks's memoirs set poetry apart from cultural critique. As these memoirs do so, they register a return in the humanities to an old-fashioned humanism and they suggest the liabilities of failing to account for the privileges and historical conditions that underwrite this return.

In the books that follow *Bone Black* and *Wounds of Passion*, hooks does call attention to the limits of dwelling on one's own grief and suffering, although she stops short of reflecting on how her memoirs romanticize ideologies of the lone and suffering individual artist and recuperate a form of humanism that her earlier works counter. In *All about Love*, in her reflections on self-recovery, she observes, "it is far too easy to stay stuck in simply describing, telling one's story over and over again, which can be a way of holding on to grief about the past or holding on to a narrative that places blame on others" (55). Her aims in her trilogy on love—*All about Love, Salvation: Black People and Love* (2001), and *Communion: The Female Search for Love*—are more collective. As hooks states at the outset of *All about Love*, "I feel our nation's turning away from love as intensely as I felt love's abandonment in my girlhood. . . . I write of love to bear witness both to the danger in this movement, and to call for a return to love" (x–xi). Each of these books on love are directed toward individual healing as a means toward a larger recovery—for the nation, for black people, for women.

These books on love, especially *All about Love*, read a lot like self-help books. *All about Love*, which draws on the work of self-help gurus such as M. Scott Peck, shares that genre's and her memoirs' neglect of the kind of rigorous analysis of how class, race, and gender work together that characterizes her earlier work.[55] Indeed, some of hook's later books instead tend to focus on a single aspect or form of identity—gender, race, or class. Others, such as *All about Love*, address people as a whole across any differences. A striking example of the limitations of such an approach occurs in *All about Love*, when hooks asserts that then–President Clinton's affair with Monica Lewinsky "no doubt mirrors moments of childhood shaming when some authority figure in his life made him feel he was worthless" (61). From his affair hooks concludes, "Anyone who suffers from low self-esteem can learn by his example" (61). Working within the self-help genre, hooks's focus here is strictly on how individuals, whoever they are, must learn self-esteem. Such a passage stands in dramatic contrast to hooks's earlier work, where it would be unimaginable for Clinton's actions to be reduced to a lesson in individual self-esteem. Even as *Salvation* and *Communion* return hooks—momentarily, if not consistently—to foregrounding issues of racism and sexism, and although these two works are more collective insofar as they address black people and women as groups, they share *All about Love*'s individual, psychological focus. For example, in *Communion* hooks proclaims of her generation of "women who love," "Loving that girl within has healed the woundedness that often led us to search for love in all the wrong places" (xix). This language of cliché mixed in with "inner-child" rhetoric combines to suggest that social transformation depends simply on individuals deciding to improve their self-esteem.

By placing this chapter's initial reading of *Teaching to Transgress* within this broader context of hooks's career, and tracing hooks's decreasing attention to structural and institutional forms of analysis, and her less successful mixes of autobiography and analysis, I aim to complicate the points of difference this chapter establishes between hooks and Tompkins.[36] Attention to hooks's career span paradoxically provides a way to shift my focus *away* from her and Tompkins as individuals, in order to arrive at more general structural arguments about the place of memoir and contemporary academic culture. hooks's movement in her earlier work between personal narrative and theory allows, as straightforward memoir does not, for a play between theory and practice. Her mixing of genres combines in potent ways with her marginalized position. At their most successful in *Teaching to Transgress*, hooks's genre crossings allow for an account of pedagogy that is at once personal as well as situated in relation to a larger institutional history and a broader set of societal conditions. In such an interplay, elements of narcissism and self-absorption, and unanalyzed personal moments, can in fact be productive for readers, as they provide a window into, rather than theorize away, the often vexed relationship between the personal and the political, the private and the institutional.

When we view hooks's earlier writings in relation to her more recent ones, these writings reveal insights into academic institutions and what various genres, and cultural theories, enable and foreclose at different historical junctures. Along with Gallop and Tompkins, hooks's career trajectory is suggestive of the difficulties that accompany the institution-alization of feminism, and also of the seductions and traps of academic stardom. Such difficulties challenge not only those who achieve such suc-cess and must negotiate the problems and possibilities that accompany a position of authority, but also all of us in the academy who are complicit in this system and in its shift from a culture of ideas to one of personal-ity. Such a shift—which the explosion of academic memoirs both results from and supports—paradoxically can be emotionally as well as intellec-tually limiting, even with its promise of attention to the "whole person" or the "purely" personal. "Star status" usually results from a breakthrough in theory or some other form of intellectual brilliance. Memoirs by academic stars, as they display the person behind the theory, often involve the at-tempt to strip away the academic or the theoretical and readmit forms of individualism and humanism that forget anew how emotions are neither "natural" nor beyond the need for critical analysis. In ways that mem-oirs that include accounts of pedagogy perhaps make especially clear, as memoirs leave behind poststructuralist analysis and identity politics, what often results is an uncritical return to a traditional, and exclusionary, humanism, one that rests on unacknowledged forms of privilege.

As critics negotiate issues of authority that have come with the star sys-tem and the institutionalization of feminist and cultural studies in their memoirs, they also often expose limitations in theory that are not other-wise readily apparent and that, as do returns to exclusionary humanism, pertain to failures in emotional intelligence. By emotional intelligence I mean an intelligence that is empathic, one that attends to the importance of structures of feeling which—be they others' or one's own—are not beyond the need for critical analysis or individual and social responsibil-ity. Emotional intelligence is not an essential human quality. Emotions are, of course, profoundly social, shaped in relation to one's historical, political, and cultural locations, and therefore they are as important to analyze as intellectual ideas are. Sensitivity to structures of feeling there-fore constitutes a form of intelligence—an emotional intelligence—that is not simply a "leftover" from reason. Nor can emotional intelligence be equated with being nice or caring or psychologically insightful; rather, it involves understanding, taking seriously, and ethically assessing with-out exclusively attending to, others' and one's own feelings when making analyses or taking actions. Memoirs by Gallop, Tompkins, and hooks all demonstrate—in ways that the authors' groundbreaking books of the-ory and criticism often obscure—oversights when it comes to emotional intelligence, especially when it involves negotiating their authority and representing the emotional terrains of the other people who populate their memoirs. Whereas Gallop's takes on sensationalism and performance evidence a flagrant disregard for her students, Tompkins's exclusive focus on her own feelings, which she then generalizes to understand her students', blinds her to the social structures that differentiate her feelings and needs from those of others. In hooks's case, her concentration on the unique nature of her emotional landscape leaves her insensitive to how her familiars may be feeling. In each of these cases, these failures are not simply emotional, and reading these writers' scholarly work back through the memoirs illuminates political, ethical, and intellectual shortcomings in the theory, too.

In the 1990s, then, academic memoirs by feminist educators in positions of prominence register the anxieties and challenges that come with the star system, the institutionalization of feminism, and challenges to a humanities education. As they do so they provide insights into ways reigning theories can be fuelled by personal investments and how failures in emotional intelligence can be linked to an inability to acknowledge and account for institutional privilege.

Whereas this chapter enables speculation about the significance of emotional intelligence through marking its failings in the memoirs under consideration, the next chapter argues for the importance memoirs about disability hold for the humanities at large, as they demonstrate the incisive role that emotional intelligence has to play not only in interpersonal relationships, but also in institutional analysis.

CHAPTER 5 Disability Studies and Institutional Interventions

Previous chapters of this book critique memoirs for basing their politics on the claim to feelings in a way that precludes attention to institutional analysis and to an author's institutional privilege. We've already explored how, in the context of the 1990s academy, and especially for those who occupy positions of privilege within it, academic memoirs reveal that too exclusive a focus on feelings, or a politics based wholly on identification and empathy, can lead to an upholding of institutional hierarchies (chapter 2). As we've seen, given the contexts of the academic star system, the focus on "the whole person"—especially as evidenced through the memoir phenomenon—can, paradoxically enough, be impoverishing emotionally as well as intellectually (chapter 4). Because the memoirs in chapter 4 demonstrate emotional blind spots that impair their intellectual contributions, they suggest the need for what I identify at the end of that chapter as emotional, or empathic, intelligence.

In this chapter, as I analyze memoirs that intersect with disability studies, I argue for the importance of empathy, though not as an endpoint and not as something defined in opposition to rationality, but rather as a structure of feeling that can play a crucial role in institutional analysis. I further contend that memoirs about disability often can demonstrate the power of the connections between emotional or empathic intelligence and institutional analysis, two ways of knowing that usually are not considered together: as they conjoin institutional critique and emotional intelligence, memoirs demonstrate disability studies' possibilities for transforming relations between individuals and universities as institutions. My position here is that empathy need not replace—but rather can constitute an integral part of—an analysis of institutional forms of power. Thus this chapter revisits, from a different angle, concerns articulated at the outset of the book about the role that memoirs—and structures of empathy and identification—can play in rethinking exclusionary forms of individualism and bourgeois humanism, in challenging the status quo, and in effecting institutional change.

In the contemporary academy, memoirs about disability can serve as especially apt vehicles for conjoining empathic engagement and institutional analysis. Memoir's spotlighting in the 1990s of the individual critic—whether it be as feminist, traveler, teacher, or racialized or ethnic subject—can often work, however inadvertently, to uphold bourgeois individualism and an exclusionary humanism, especially if the critic has "star status." However, the consequences can be more complex—and arguably more transgressive—in memoirs that accentuate the individuality and complex humanity of persons with disabilities, even including "academic stars" who have either visible or invisible disabilities. Indeed, academic memoirs about disability can make particularly powerful interventions, as they often represent accounts by those who have "lived the life of the mind" and placed a premium on intellectual production confronting their own or others' bodies and mental and emotional states in ways that require them to transform their understandings of themselves and of what intelligence is and how it matters. Although academic culture regularly questions norms, it leaves in place bodily norms while it celebrates norms that relate to intelligence. Focusing on memoirs that challenge these norms suggests how stories that intersect with disability studies can work to transform rather than reinforce exclusionary forms of individualism and humanism.

Disability studies offers possible answers to questions humanities scholars are asking with some urgency today about how to bring together the humanities and human rights struggles. Although relegated to the sidelines in the academy, disability studies has the potential to reconfigure the definition of the subject as such and also can bring authors—and readers—up against the limitations of conventional definitions of a whole host of categories that define the bourgeois individual against the disabled subject. Memoirs about disability offer ways to rethink the value and meaning of independence and dependence, intelligence and retardation, mind and body, health and illness, and ability and disability, all of which have been key to defining who is human and whose life is worth living. Particularly during a time in the academy when traditional humanisms are returning in new guises, these memoirs embody the possibility of an expansive, inclusive humanism—one that can reinvigorate cultural theories and make a case in the wider culture for the humanities' value as a carrier of human rights.

"Getting Real": Identifying Disability

While I was writing this chapter my work was punctuated—and at times brought to a standstill—by a series of crises involving illness and disability. Several family members, friends, and colleagues experienced severe depressions and other critical illnesses. In addition, I spent many telephone hours with friends on leaves of absence to care for terminally ill parents. Entering an illness or a disability—one's own or a loved one's— is, as any number of disability studies critics have attested, to enter an alternate often isolated world, at the same time as such an experience is absolutely ordinary, and to be expected as people age. As Lennard Davis notes: "Even without the baby boomers, currently 15 to 20 percent of people in the United States have disabilities. Add to this caregivers and family members, and about half the population is dealing with disability" (*Bending over Backwards* 4). He further explains: "the category of disability is permeable—anyone can become disabled, and in fact, most people will develop impairments with age" (36). Despite their frequency and importance, experiences with illness and disability receive little serious consideration in the academy, if they are admitted at all. As Davis concludes in his 1995 *Enforcing Normalcy*, "the concept of disability has been relegated to a sideshow, a freak show at that, far away from the academic midway of progressive ideas and concerns" (158).

I have been thinking about Davis's words in relation to my own experiences with disability, particularly as they apply to my participation in March 2003 on a roundtable titled "Getting Real: The Place of Identity Politics Today." This roundtable involved a colleague and me conversing with Satya Mohanty about his insights as a postpositivist realist that experience is theoretical and mediated, and considering his contention that critics evaluate identity claims with the understanding that not all are equal, that some are truer than others. I asked Professor Mohanty about the faith he places in the ability of the critic or a community of critics to read and to discern among various identity claims. How, I wondered, do you get around the critic's privilege and vested knowledge? Who is doing the assessing of different identity claims and how do you assess the assessor? How, when making such evaluations, do you avoid reinscribing the "view from nowhere" or the idea of a perfect or disinterested reader? I brought up examples from Jane Tompkins's and a few other memoirs in noting ways critics are deeply invested in, but often do not address or even articulate, their institutional privilege in discussions of identity politics and while making their own identity claims.

My participation on this roundtable occurred on a Monday afternoon. The previous Friday, my husband at the time had been released from a weeklong stay in the hospital after a suicide attempt that followed an especially terrifying bout of depression, a heartbreaking consequence of his ongoing struggle with bipolar disorder.[1] So for me this discussion of identity politics was shadowed by extreme anxiety about leaving him alone for two hours, and was cut short by the need to make a dash to the airport to pick up his sister, who was arriving to help care for him. My insistence during the roundtable that critics foreground their institutional privilege and location in their analyses of their feelings and experiences was underwritten by my sense at that moment of the utter unimportance of my own academic position, and by a sudden and foreboding sense that I had seriously underestimated the importance of the feelings expressed by those academics I was subjecting to critique. In short, I felt keenly how my own experiences challenged the arguments I was making. At the same time, I still believed in these arguments. Moreover, I felt that even if it would not be irrelevant, it would most certainly be too personally revealing and traumatic to address how my own experiences at that moment were informing (or working to unform) my thinking about academics' engagements with and positions regarding identity politics. It is also the case that my professional identity and roundtable performance offered an almost-absorbing distraction from an overwhelming personal crisis. Staying focused on questions of institutional power and privilege—and making use of my own institutional position—at the "Getting Real" roundtable was as much my own escape from the personal during a time of trauma as it was a calling of other critics to accountability for ignoring the significance of their institutional locations.

In any event, it was an unsettling experience for me to appear on this panel. I felt no small share of ambivalence about my performance, not only because of the arguments I was making but also in terms of even participating on a "Getting Real" panel during such a time, at all.

Whereas the above account addresses an extreme instance, invisible acts of on-the-job juggling that involve a suppression of struggles with one's own or family members' illnesses or disabilities occur every day, and over the course of time often take a far greater toll than do occasional moments of crisis. These everyday acts affect any number of academics—

and indeed all others who work for money—perhaps especially women, who do a disproportionate amount of "private" caretaking in addition to other, paid work. As Susan Wendell notes, disability is regularly that which is relegated to the private realm, forced underground (266). This arguably creates particular tensions for women and people of color dealing with "private" forms of disability who, on the one hand, endorse the idea that the personal is political and, on the other, often must work harder than white male counterparts to maintain their professionalism so their competence is not questioned. The need to maintain privacy and separate spheres can be particularly pressing when the disability involves a form of mental illness. With that in mind, I must acknowledge that even having obtained the consent of those my story involves and even though my former husband writes and speaks quite openly about his experiences with bipolar disorder, I still would be much less likely to insert it into this discussion if I did not have tenure. Academics also might hold their silence out of the belief that addressing such personal matters is best done in the presence of a therapist, or friends and family, both because it is not always clear that public disclosures will contribute to the production of knowledge and also because it can be too painful to reveal personal struggles in a professional context, especially when dealing with highly stigmatized forms of illness or disability.

This autobiographical moment appears here for three reasons. First, along with Wendell and other disability studies scholars, I think that experiences with disability should not remain confined to the private sphere, because they raise pressing political issues that need to be addressed institutionally and collectively. Second, my personal experiences with disabilities account for a shift in perspective on arguments that I make in this book. Although I continue to believe that academics need to foreground questions of institutional privilege and position, such experiences have brought home to me what my arguments diminish—as they also have underlined the importance of empathy, and the fact that to a certain extent empathy is situation-specific and learned. Namely, I realized how my arguments tended to overlook the pain that can accompany privilege and make it seem irrelevant. In addition, my experience caring for a family member with a life-threatening illness has informed my understandings of narratives about disability. Therefore, it seems important to mark this position, just as I have marked my whiteness in discussions involving race, which is not to say that these subject positions are equivalent, since in many ways they operate quite differently.

Including discussion of my own experience with disability is in keeping with the theoretical positions of disability studies scholars. In the face of the silences that surround disability, stories and theories about disability started to emerge from the academy in the 1990s in two important but often nonintersecting ways. First, disability studies has developed as a burgeoning interdisciplinary field pioneered by academics and activists including Michael Bérubé, Brenda Jo Brueggemann, G. Thomas Couser, Lennard Davis, Simi Linton, David Mitchell, Susan Schweik, Tobin Siebers, Sharon Snyder, Rosemarie Garland Thomson, Susan Wendell, and others, many of whom live with disabilities. Disability studies emerged in the 1970s and 1980s, with a second wave of writing appearing in the 1990s, after the passage of and backlash against the Americans with Disabilities Act (ADA) of 1990. Second, there has been a recent proliferation of memoirs that provide accounts of illness and other forms of disability. As Nancy Mairs has remarked, illness narratives have emerged as "a distinct subgenre of autobiographical writing" (xi). Thomas Couser, too, finds that although book-length accounts of illness were uncommon before 1950, they are now flourishing as a new form of life writing that is "gaining momentum in the era of civil rights and other liberation movements," with breast cancer and AIDS having literatures of their own (*Recovering Bodies* 5). Some of these memoirs, which Couser has named "autopathographies," are written by disability studies scholars (Lennard Davis, *My Sense of Silence*; memoirs by Nancy Mairs) or others with specific interest in or experience with disability (Jane Bernstein, *Loving Rachel*; Marion Deutsche Cohen, *Dirty Details*; Eva Feder Kittay, *Love's Labor*; Jim Lang, *Learning Sickness*; Lata Mani, *Interleaves*; and Sharon O'Brien, *The Family Silver*).[2] Other personal narratives by academics provide accounts that, although not situated in relation to disability studies, can be usefully analyzed through the lens of disability studies. These include memoirs discussed earlier in this book, especially Edward Said's *Out of Place* (1999), which is occasioned by Said's battle with leukemia, and *Bone Black* and *Wounds of Passion*, memoirs that address bell hooks's struggles with depression. Revisiting these memoirs in this chapter, I suggest how resisting a focus on disability can be individually empowering and can support group identities and modes of analysis other than those based on disability, even as the memoirs open up possibilities for productive connections between theories of disability and other forms of analysis. I also argue that these memoirs can leave in place dominant understandings—particularly of intelligence and of individualism—that a direct engagement with disability studies would productively challenge.

After reconsidering memoirs by Said and hooks, this chapter includes readings of Eve Sedgwick's *A Dialogue on Love* (1999) and Michael Bérubé's *Life as We Know It* (1996), memoirs that, as they more directly address issues of disability, profoundly question conceptions of intelligence. Sedgwick's *A Dialogue* also anticipates important intersections between queer theory and disability studies, and suggests the potency of this combination in challenging institutional ways of knowing, even as her insistence on the uniqueness of her position as a therapy patient limits the memoir's institutional analyses. Of the memoirs considered in this chapter, *Life as We Know It*—an account of Bérubé's love and advocacy for his son with Down syndrome—is most squarely situated within the field of disability studies. Writing as a caretaker analyzing what he has learned from caring for his son, Bérubé tells what the other memoirs show, providing a structural context in which to situate them. As exploration of this memoir along with the others considered here indicates, disability studies has the potential to define the human through a principle of inclusivity, and to route institutional analysis and critique through empathic understanding in ways that reconfigure relations between individuals and institutions.

The texts addressed in this chapter cover a range, not only in terms of degree of engagement with disability studies, but also in terms both of the nature of the disability addressed (cancer, depression, Down syndrome) and also whether the writer is experiencing the disability or illness directly, or is in a caretaking role. These disparities suggest but by no means represent just how large disability is as a category. Differences within this umbrella category matter enormously—for example, some disabilities require and can at times be alleviated or cured by medical treatment, whereas others only incur suffering because they do not conform to—indeed are defined in opposition to—established societal norms.[3] Throughout this chapter, however, I am less interested in engaging these significant differences than I am in thinking through a question more particular to *Academic Lives* as a whole. Namely, I am concerned with what academic memoirs that intersect with disability studies have to say about an academic culture that regularly questions all norms save those having to do with intelligence and able-bodiedness. Focusing on memoirs that question these norms suggests how stories that intersect with disability studies can work to transform exclusionary forms of individualism and humanism. While maintaining a specific focus on issues particular to disability, these memoirs show the potential for distinguishing between individualism and self-determination, and for conjoining emotional intelligence and institutional critique.

As disability studies scholars have pointed out, disability—socially constructed from biological reality—is an identity that supports a vast network of inequitable social, political, and economic structures on which bourgeois individualism rests.[4] Homogenized, pathologized, and catastrophized, over the course of the past few centuries, "disability" has developed as an identity category that not only shapes the generic and the normal, but also the human subject as such, and the very structures on which societies and nations rest.[5]

According to disability studies scholars, dependence has been characterized in the West as a form of disability against which the normative, "independent" subject has been defined from the Enlightenment to the present. Rosemarie Garland Thomson traces the development of the Cartesian subject as a separate, autonomous, efficient machine whose goal was self-mastery. From Foucault, Garland Thomson extrapolates "that the modern social identity of 'disabled' . . . arose in tandem with its opposite: the abstract, self-possessed, autonomous individual" (*Extraordinary Bodies* 40). Humanist and Enlightenment thinking depend on understanding the subject as capable, self-making, and independent and, as Deborah Marks points out, we equate dependency with having a life not worth living (38). Postmodernist formulations of the subject, in these regards, can be seen as continuous with Enlightenment humanist models. Paying particular attention to postmodernism's definitions of the normal and to its focus on "independence," Davis contends "that postmodernism is still based on a humanistic model. Politics have been directed toward making all identities equal under a model of the rights of the dominant, often white, male, 'normal' subject"; he concludes that "the by now outdated postmodern subject is a ruse to disguise the hegemony of normalcy" (*Bending* 30).

As Davis's analysis implies, the history of disability cannot be understood independently of the histories of racism, sexism, classism, and other forms of oppression. From the Enlightenment forward, faith in science and "progress" has led to the medicalization, institutionalization, and categorization of all sorts of "species." The development of eugenics has played a key and often murderous role in scientifically pathologizing and dehumanizing people by categories of "disability" that include not only physical and mental impairments, but also those of race, class, gender, and sexuality. As the Nazi regime makes so starkly evident, eugenics has provided a scientific rationale for the enforced sterilization and even mass extermination of various peoples classified as "diseased" who fit under the broad category of disability. Ruth Hubbard establishes connections between Nazi practices of eugenics and legislative programs in the United States that pertain to immigration and involuntary sterilization. Garland Thomson, too, sees the dangers of the modern eugenics movement—particularly reproductive technologies—as an ongoing part of U.S. history, and one that depends on ideologies of individualism: "Eliminating disabled people [through these means] as discordant social elements is the logical extension of an ideology that esteems national and individual progress toward self-reliance, self-management, and self-sufficiency" (*Extraordinary Bodies* 35). And as Douglas Baynton illustrates, in the United States "the exclusion of disabled people was central to the laws and the work of the immigration service" (565). In *Crip Theory* Robert McRuer establishes how complexly intertwined are disability, sexuality, class, race, gender, and age. As these critics indicate, the history of disability—along with other histories of oppression—is intimately connected to the development from the nineteenth century onward of national identities, racial and other identity categories, and ideologies of individualism.

The past few decades have seen the rise of disability studies and a wide range of activism directed at tracing and exposing the history of disability and challenging present-day forms of discrimination against people with disabilities. In the United States, activist work culminated in the passage in 1990 of the ADA. An expansive law affording protection to U.S. citizens who either identify or are identified as disabled, the ADA has been under serious attack since it was passed. Davis observes that "Ten years later, it has been estimated that 95 percent of the cases brought before the court under the provisions of that act have been lost by people with disabilities." Foreseeing the possible dismantling of the ADA, Davis cautions, "The Supreme Court has been steadily hacking away at the provisions of the ADA, and the Court will hear cases whose outcomes could completely end the effectiveness of that legislation" (*Bending* 2).

In part this backlash against hard-gained and recent disability rights depends on individuals' failure to identify with people with disabilities or to see them as fully human. As Sharon L. Snyder, Rosemarie Garland-Thomson, and Brenda Jo Brueggemann note, "in our present collective cultural consciousness, the disabled body is imagined not as the universal consequence of living an embodied life but rather as an alien condition" (2).[6] Davis attributes this response to fear: "what people fear is that disability is the identity one may become part of but didn't want" (*Bending* 4). Emphasizing the material consequences of judges' and juries' refusal to identify with disabled people, Davis observes, "Since the Supreme Court advises us to consider trial participants not as 'members of a faceless, undifferentiated mass,' but as 'uniquely individual human beings,' we have an obligation to imagine and bring to life these individual states of mind" (*Bending* 121). Representations of individuals with disabilities, then, constitute a necessary form of activism, one that, though enacted through nonjuridical channels, impacts the workings of the law.

Given the importance of resisting the sometimes deadly ways that people with disabilities are dehumanized, the humanities has served as an important site through which to analyze and revise representations of disability, though how best to represent disability remains a matter of debate. At the same time as disability activists and scholars argue the need to provide representations attesting to the humanity of those with disabilities, they also insist on the need to spotlight the social contexts that are so instrumental in defining disability. As Davis contends, "One of the major struggles of the disability rights movement has been to create public awareness that the problem of disability is not solely located in the individual using a wheelchair or in the Deaf person, but rather that the problem resides in the society that does not mandate curb cuts or allow American Sign Language to satisfy foreign language requirements in high schools and colleges" (*Bending* 125).[7] Perhaps it is for this reason that Davis elsewhere argues *against* the need for empathic understanding, and instead urges the importance of staking out disability studies as a scholarly discipline. He argues that writing that aims to let "normals" know what it is like to have a disability ends up being writing that is *for* "normals," and that this maintains existing inequalities.[8] So, too, David Mitchell and Sharon Snyder urge on behalf of the need not to arouse pity and sympathy but rather to educate the public about the social and political meanings of disability ("Introduction" 11). As these arguments make clear, representing and analyzing disability constitute not merely an academic enterprise, but a site of activism.

In addition, with these various analyses, scholars suggest both the possible pitfalls of autobiographies about disability, and also how they can provide a way for people with disabilities to resist dehumanization within the dominant culture and within educational, medical and legal institutions. As Couser notes, "in recent decades the flourishing of narratives of illness or disability poses a significant challenge to the stigmatization of illness and disability and to the general valorization of mind over body in Western culture, the tendency to deny the body's mediation in intellectual and spiritual life" (*Recovering Bodies* 4). Commenting on the crucial role that representation plays, Garland Thomson contends, "The aim of much disability studies is to reimagine disability, to reveal how the storied quality of disability invents and reinvents the world we share" ("Disability and Representation" 523).

Autobiographies about disability also can serve to challenge dominant ideologies of individualism and, as Eva Feder Kittay describes it, "the Kantian position that autonomy is that feature of human existence that gives us our dignity" (9).[9] For example, Mairian Corker and Sally French use personal narrative to fight the individualization of disability; they set out to challenge "ways of conflating disability and impairment that insist that both the 'problem' and the 'solution' are always our individual responsibility" ("Reclaiming Discourse in Disability Studies" 10). Thus, personal narrative need not fall solely into a plea for empathy that curtails a consideration of the need for collective, structural change. Narratives of disability can refuse individualist representations of the subject as autonomous and independent without, as I discuss in this chapter, dismissing the importance of or equating individualism with possessing a sense of agency and self-determination.

By representing a subject who is dependent, and by normalizing—and revaluing—dependency, memoirs of disability can unmask "the inevitable dependencies and asymmetries that form part of the human condition" (Kittay 14). Working within the context of literary criticism, Garland Thomson contends, "the disabled figures operate in varying degrees as challenges to the cultural status quo, introducing issues and perspectives with the potential to refigure the social order" (*Extraordinary Bodies* 38). In particular, personal narratives about disability can critique rather than reinscribe liberal individualism, and challenge still-operative models of the universal subject formulated under exclusionary humanism and the Enlightenment by advancing models of reciprocity rather than independence.

In contrast to the narratives that disability scholars uphold for their counterhegemonic possibilities, many of the memoirs considered thus far in *Academic Lives* explore feelings and experiences of marginality and vulnerability that can accompany privileged forms of identity (i.e., that of professor, that of white person) in ways that ultimately uphold the status quo. When academics explore forms of disability—either their own, often hidden, disabilities or those of loved ones—their insistence on their individual particularity and on their humanity can instead transform rather than bolster exclusionary definitions of "the human." As I contend in this chapter, whether memoirs that feature disability do this work depends in large part on the extent to which they engage—and thus partake in—the work being done in disability studies, a field of study that is transforming the humanities and the university as an institution.

Politics and Poetics of Stigmata

In her memoirs bell hooks details extensive experiences with lifelong depression and other illnesses as they simultaneously resist a disability studies framework, instead representing these conditions as part of hooks's artistic genius and thereby reproducing the cliché that links disability and artistic genius. In both *Bone Black* and *Wounds of Passion*, hooks's "wounds of passion" become distinguishing marks of an exceptional grief that that provides the conditions from which her identity as an artist emerges. As hooks describes often debilitating and ongoing experiences with depression and other illnesses, she resists language that would cast her suffering as a form of disability; she refuses medicalized terms that could pathologize her. Although individually empowering in ways that are especially important given how black women are continuously denied individual agency and self-definition, such an approach can ultimately obfuscate and support rather than illuminate and critique social norms. Therefore, as hooks's desire to assert her independence as a black woman writer trumps a choice to foreground issues of dependency that a disability studies framework would introduce, her memoirs suggest the difficulty, but also the importance, of maintaining intersectional identities and of simultaneously fighting different but interconnected fronts of oppression.

Because African American women have been systematically pathologized and robbed of their individuality, hooks's memoirs do important work in asserting her independence and agency as a black woman and as a successful writer, even as they leave a number of established norms in place. To a certain extent, hooks's autobiography supports Garland Thomson's argument in *Extraordinary Bodies* that many African American women writers of the past several decades, partaking in a broader cultural shift that characterizes the post–civil rights era, have celebrated disability not as deviance but rather as variation, not as something to compensate for, but rather as something to accommodate or celebrate (106) as they "simultaneously repudiate such cultural master narratives as normalcy, wholeness, and the feminine ideal" (105). However, although hooks clearly claims and values her "deviance," her aim in her memoirs is not to critique master narratives of wholeness and normalcy. Instead, her energies are more fully directed at establishing her own uniqueness, a move that requires leaving established norms in place, even if these norms are reversed in value in relation to hooks's extraordinary difference. hooks's positioning registers not only the pressures black feminist critics face in the academy, and in the wider culture, to fight oppression by asserting agency and independence, but it also suggests the ghettoization of disability studies in the academy and, as argued in chapter 4, the seductions and pitfalls of the star system.

As also discussed in that chapter, hooks's memoirs mark a shift from her earlier work, in which she places discussions of self-healing in communal and political contexts. Her writings of the late 1980s regularly politicize issues of mental health, which she posits as "a central revolutionary frontier for black folks" (*Yearning* 218). In *Yearning*, resisting an individualistic understanding of "self-recovery," hooks draws on the work of Buddhist monk Thich Nhat Hahn to argue that self-recovery be understood "in relation to ways people who are oppressed, dominated, or otherwise politically victimized recover themselves" (217). Although her memoirs demonstrate her continued interest in self-healing and recovery, they neither retain a sense of larger political contexts and stakes nor do they engage the discourse of disability studies that is circulating in the humanities in the late 1990s.

In hooks's memoirs, depression and the other illnesses that she experiences (including an acute menstrual disorder, see *Wounds* 135–37, and an eating disorder) are manifestations of her unique sensitivity as an artist; these experiences do not connect her to others with similar medical histories, nor does she highlight and probe their societal causes. For example, at various points hooks describes her prolonged inability or refusal to eat, making clear its psychological component: "I say no to food and no to punishment" (*Wounds* 19). In *Bone Black* when her parents tell her she "must sit and eat even if it takes all night," instead of eating, "sitting in the cold kitchen, staring out the window, she thinks about

Wordsworth and Shelley, about Dickinson, Whitman and Frost" (168). Through such descriptions, hooks represents her refusal of food not as a form of anorexia but rather as romanticized resistance inseparable from her identity as a poet.

Depression appears in her memoirs as a condition that hooks courts as a source of art, and also fights. Despite the severe, at times life-threatening, nature of her depression, hooks resists a medical vocabulary or solution; instead, she regularly uses the word "sadness" to describe her condition. hooks describes her feelings of pain and suffering as a condition that serves her as a writer. hooks does assert in her preface that, "against a cultural backdrop where black females have been reluctant to explore in autobiography work the full range of our emotional universe, writing *Wounds of Passion: A Writing Life* was both daring and difficult." However, as hooks continues, the sentences that follow shift the focus from this cultural context to a more general one that pertains to hooks's status a writer: "It is never an easy decision or task to write about one's emotional landscape. Yet I wanted to document the context that prepared me to become a prolific writer" (xxi). When she describes suicidal longings in response to overwhelming sadness, she dismisses these thoughts as less important than her fierce desire to be a writer: "I'm not afraid of dying, I'm afraid of not becoming the writer I want to be" (255).[10] A fear of madness runs through both memoirs, with poetry serving hooks as an anchor against it; she describes her feelings of pain and fear that *"threatened to overwhelm her—to lead her away from herself into madness. Poetry always brought her back home"* (*Wounds* 26, original emphasis). hooks represents her suffering as that which is not only alleviated by, but also makes possible, her art, and she expresses her conviction that "Women sacrifice for words. They suffer and they die" (212). This romanticization of depression, as it supports clichéd connections between artistic greatness and madness, precludes exploration of depression as an often decidedly unromantic illness, one with connections to the forms of oppression that hooks experiences.

hooks's representation of depression places *Bone Black* and *Wounds* in a tenuous relationship to a disability studies framework. Nevertheless, the cover of *Wounds of Passion*, with its depiction of stigmata, and the book's representations of hooks's suffering as wounds of passion, or stigmata, evoke a disability studies context. Erving Goffman's 1963 foundational book *Stigma: Notes on the Management of Spoiled Identity* provides a crucial vocabulary and theoretical framework to contemporary scholars of disability for understanding how disability constitutes a form of stigma, and for socially and historically contextualizing disability. As Goffman explains, the Greeks "originated the term *stigma* to refer to bodily signs designed to expose something unusual and bad about the moral status of the signifier. The signs were cut or burnt into the body and advertised that the bearer was a slave, a criminal, or a traitor—a blemished person, ritually polluted, to be avoided, especially in public places. Later, in Christian times, two layers of metaphor were added to the term: the first referred to bodily signs of holy grace that took the form of eruptive blossoms on the skin; the second, a medical allusion to this religious allusion, referred to bodily signs of physical disorder. Today the term is widely used in something like the original literal sense, but is applied more to the disgrace itself than to the bodily evidence of it" (203). Goffman's work, so central to disability studies, provides a suggestive way into hooks's *Wounds*.[11]

hooks's use of stigmata in *Wounds of Passion* sets her apart, in her spiritual quest, from her colleagues in academe: her stigmata resonate neither with contemporary meanings that attach to stigma, nor with disability scholars' critical engagement with these meanings, but rather with the Christian perspective that Goffman describes. hooks does not represent her "wounds of passion" as signs of disgrace, even though they result from and cause her tremendous suffering and set her apart from others, and she does not attempt to socially critique understandings of stigma. Instead, and in defiance of academic trends, she portrays stigmata as, to quote Goffman, "bodily signs of holy grace." At the start of *Wounds* hooks depicts herself as a Christ figure. After witnessing her father's violence toward her mother, she expresses her conviction that "we should lay our all on the altar of sacrifice and let her [hooks's mother] know that in the loneliness of this summer night, . . . at least she will know love" (11). Later that night she has a dream that again casts her as a Christ figure undergoing crucifixion. She dreams of reaching inside her body and touching her shattered heart, and "when I pulled out my hand all the tiny cuts were bleeding. All I could do was watch my body bleed to death" (12). Although painful, these wounds of passion or stigmata are inextricable from religious exaltation, and from hooks's identity as an artist whose deep feelings cause the suffering from which her art emerges. At one point hooks describes her fascination with John the Baptist. Naming him as "the writer, the bringer of the word, the word that will be made flesh," she states, "Religion offers me a way to understand the meaning of passion. The marks on his hands are a sign of love's suffering" (151). As is the case for John the Baptist, hooks's passionate suffering materializes as wounds that set her apart as a writer and that at times even cast her as a religious saint.

hooks's representation of wounds brings together these two roles (artist, saint) with that of renegade outlaw. In the conclusion to *Wounds*, where hooks most fully engages the cover's image of stigmata, she asserts, "it is suffering that brings us closer to the gods" (257). Then, in a bizarre concluding passage—and a truly unexpected one given hooks's usual racial politics—hooks celebrates Clint Eastwood as a renegade cowboy who leaves dead bodies "behind like stigmata" in his search for freedom (258). hooks establishes her intense identification with Eastwood as a cowboy-hero who is "never compelled by dreams of conquest. He is a man of heart who follows the call of all wild murmurings—the wildest of which is sorrow. My sorrow is so great it breaks me" (159). Having seamlessly shifted from Eastwood to herself, she follows this description of the "renegade cowboy" with an account of her own drive toward the desert where she enters

> a landscape of wounds. When I was a child I heard again and again how our savior went into the desert to find his life again. Into the desert he fled with his heartache and his unrequited love. When he reappeared from his longest journey, to the desert only he had seen, the wasteland of the cross and death hanging there, he was recognized, known only by the wounds of passion imprinted on his hands. My favorite saint, Teresa of Avila, wanted to share his wounds, for him to give her what she called *a taste of this love*, so he pierced her with a golden dart. Stigmata were her witness and her testimony (259–60, original emphasis).

Wounds concludes, "The story was written so that it could stand alone, two hands raised to glory, that the spirit may descend among us, one hand raised to glory, that the spirit has come—touched me and left my body whole" (260). In this fantastic array of linked images, hooks is at once renegade cowboy, religious saint, and a conduit for art. Connecting these images is the story of how hooks comes to exalt her wounds as blessings. Her embrace constitutes a form of healing and self-love, an overcoming of shame and fear, and an assertion of spiritual and artistic greatness. Thus hooks's celebration of her wounds echoes with how saints' stigmata were interpreted in the early days of Christianity as distinguishing marks of power and prestige; they are not simply modernity's causes for or evidence of a subordinated identity.

hooks's spiritual quest is symptomatic of a dissatisfaction in the humanities with the spiritual shortcomings of cultural criticism; and, in its individualism, it partakes in the wider academic culture but differentiates her from other feminist critics who share her religious or spiritual commitments. Black feminist scholars have been particularly interested in incorporating spirituality into their work, sometimes through memoir. In Karla Holloway's memoir *BookMarks*, for example, religious faith coexists alongside the author's analyses of race. It also sustains her after the death of her son, and plays an important role in the black community that she represents. Other feminists, too, claim spirituality as a source of solace and as a companion to cultural critique. In *Interleaves: Ruminations on Illness and Spiritual Life*, Lata Mani provides an account of "the social construction of illness" as she also explores her discovery that "the personal is not merely social, but also deeply spiritual" (73, 74). When Mani is hit by a truck and sustains a serious brain injury, it "skewered her out of the chaos" and a depression that her immersion in cultural theory did not address, and allows her to discover "the Divine Mother in all Her forms" (3–4). As is Holloway's, Mani's memoir is at once individual spiritual quest (though Hindu, rather than Christian, in context), social commentary, and expression of collectivity. (It is worth noting here, though, that Mani's investments in cultural critique are quite limited, and that she has left academe by the time she self-publishes *Interleaves*). Although hooks shares these critics' explorations of religious faith, her journey is an individualistic one that also removes her memoirs from analyses of race, gender, or disability.

hooks also departs from both black feminist and disability frameworks in her use of and fascination with psychoanalysis, which instead reflects dominant U.S. attitudes toward therapy as an individualistic form of self-help. Even as she seeks out therapy, hooks evidences a belief that only she can help herself, and her analyses of race occur in sporadic and problematic ways. For example, at one point, after her lover Mack hits her and she insists on couples therapy, when the white counselor they see tells hooks and her lover, "you two are poison for each other," she rejects this therapist's analysis as racist (190). However, here, as throughout, hooks's critique is not a systemic one of psychoanalysis's racial biases, but rather of the therapists she engages. Despite her assertion that she has a "thing" for shrinks, she manifests throughout *Wounds* an aversion to the therapists she encounters, and she represents her depression as a condition that can best be addressed through self-therapy (197). Indeed, hooks consistently positions herself not as a patient but rather as her own and others' analyst: as hooks explains, "I always really wanted to be a psychoanalyst" (185). As hooks puts her healing into her own hands, she not only claims an individuality that transcends race, but she also need not depict her depression or other illnesses as sources of dependency or weakness.

Although hooks's self-positioning enables her to resist pathologizing her depression or relying uncritically on the medical establishment, the way she does so implicitly supports liberal ideologies of autonomy and independence that disability scholars challenge. As Garland Thomson explains, when feminists uphold these ideologies as a means to female empowerment, this practice "often leaves no space for the needs and accommodations that disabled women's bodies require" (*Extraordinary Bodies* 26). By so individualizing—and romanticizing—her discussion of depression and anorexia, hooks foregoes offering support to others who experience these widespread and sometimes life-threatening illnesses, except insofar as she provides a model for establishing one's own uniqueness and for valorizing suffering through acts of imaginative identification with sacred figures. However, because such acts of identification are so tied to hooks's status as exceptional writer, possibilities for identification are limited; instead, hooks's memoirs encourage readers to view her condition with reverence, to see it as a thing set apart from everyday people and social structures.

hooks's memoirs provide neither emotional nor intellectual impetus to connect forms of suffering or stigma to social structures that are in need of transformation: her approach forecloses not only identification, but also investigation of the connections that exist among social formations of disability, gender, class, and race, and it rules out the revaluing of disability. Connections between gender and disability have been perhaps particularly well established by feminist disability theorists because, as Garland Thomson points out, a meaningful boundary cannot be established between disabled and nondisabled women. She notes, "Not only has the female body been labeled deviant, but historically the practices of femininity have configured female bodies similarly to disability" (*Extraordinary Bodies* 27); she further observes that "such conditions as anorexia, hysteria, and agoraphobia are in a sense standard feminine roles enlarged to disabling conditions, blurring the line between 'normal' feminine behavior and pathology" (*Extraordinary Bodies* 27). As hooks's memoirs represent her depression and her refusal to eat as forms of artistic genius, they preclude interrogation of how illness is in significant part social in its causes, structures, and reception.

Although individually empowering for her, hooks's memoirs contribute only obliquely to disability studies, which politicizes and critically analyzes experiences of illness and disability and suggests how to understand them in relation to other forms of oppression. Attention to Goffman's theorization of stigma creates bridges among different forms of oppression as his work leads to an understanding of how few individuals conform to the category of the normal; as Garland Thomson notes, "Goffman reveals the illusory, ideological nature of the normate subject position" ("Theorizing Disability" 32). In contrast to this, with their individualist framework, hooks's memoirs uphold her difference not only from "normates" but also from others stigmatized in the ways that she is—by gender, by race, by class background, by lifelong bouts with depression and illness. Although hooks successfully rejects perceptions of herself as inferior, she accomplishes this not by redefining normality but rather by embracing her wounds of passion, figured as stigmata, as ennobling marks of suffering. hooks's memoirs therefore do not challenge the social environment so much as they celebrate the extraordinary depth of her passions. Thus they suggest how disability can be at once front and center and yet in the service of narratives about individual triumph and genius.

By failing to consider "stigma" in the context in which it is best known in the 1990s academy—as a socially constructed identity against which the category of "the normal" is established—and by refusing use of medical terminology to describe her suffering, hooks is able to emphasize her individual agency. To establish such autonomy given her multiple forms of marginalization is no small matter, and it can be politically as well as personally important for black women to write such accounts. hooks's memoirs also give her a way to express an emotional pain for which the analyses of race, class, and gender on which she has built her career have proved inadequate. However, the drawback, especially when written by those who already have achieved status as "exceptional," is that such narratives can reassert a traditional liberalism that leaves formulations of the individual and "the normal" in place as they simultaneously romanticize illness. Moreover, given hooks's prominence in the academy, this self-representation implicitly upholds the tokenism of the academic star system and the academy's exclusion of black women. Disability studies offers a challenge to hooks's positioning through its critiques of independence and self-sufficiency as debilitating myths. And although it clearly is not hooks's aim to work within a disability studies framework in her memoirs, an analysis of them suggests the possibilities and importance of such an approach as a way to account for experiences of pain and suffering that theories of race, class, and gender cannot encompass. So, too, hooks's memoirs suggest the need for humanities scholars to probe the significant intersections among these different theories and identities that too often, despite the interdisciplinarity of each, remain competing and distinct.

Illness, Exile, and Empire

Like hooks's memoirs, Edward Said's *Out of Place: A Memoir* exists in a tenuous relationship to disability studies. And as is the case for hooks's memoirs, reading of *Out of Place* in relation to theories of disability illuminates both possibilities and limitations that can attend a disability studies framework, as well as memoir's possibilities as a vehicle for disability studies. As does hooks, Said casts his illness as an enabling condition for his writing rather than as a condition to engage from a disability studies framework. hooks's representation of depression offers few connections between herself and those who are not aspiring writers, or between disability and forms of oppression. Said also resists the kind of universalism that invites readers' identification and that at times gives expression to an individualist autonomy the memoir genre reinforces. However, in contrast to hooks's memoirs, *Out of Place* shows how memoir and its particular representations of and challenges to bodily norms can enable readers to understand interrelations among various forms of bodily displacement and regulation—and counterhegemonic assertions, in the face of these conditions, of self-determination—in ways that indicate productive points of intersection between disability studies and postcolonial studies.

Out of Place is a memoir occasioned by Said being diagnosed with and treated for chronic lymphocytic leukemia. Although the memoir is not about his illness, Said represents its writing as an important way to battle the ravages of cancer and chemotherapy:

> the time of this book is intimately tied to the time, phases, ups and downs, variations on my illness. As I grew weaker, the number of infections and bouts of side effects increased, the more this book was my way

of constructing something in prose while in my physical and emotional life I grappled with anxieties and pains of degeneration. Both tasks resolved themselves into details: to write is to get from word to word, to suffer illness is to go through the infinitesimal steps that take you through from one state to another. . . . Curiously, the writing of this memoir and the phases of my illness share exactly the same time, although most traces of the latter have been effaced in this story of my early life. This record of a life and ongoing course of a disease (from which I have known from the beginning no cure exists) are one and the same, it could be said, the same but deliberately different. (217)

As this reflection suggests, the writing of the memoir is at once a way to chronicle the movements of his leukemia and a refusal to be defined by it; it offers solace and escape from an illness that itself gives the book its structure without also defining who Said is. Thus, in writing his memoir, Said's intent is not to make connections with others with cancer or even to write about the cancer itself, nor is the memoir a political project in the sense that many of his books are; he describes it as "a project about as far from my professional and political life as it was possible for me to go" (*Out of Place* 217). His illness is not to be described so much as transcended, and as with hooks, writing serves Said as a survival strategy. However, whereas hooks documents her extreme vulnerability in the past and present, Said alludes to his present and the pain and any fear it carries only rarely. Writing his memoir becomes an individual assertion of dignity, an exercise for his mind, and a way to survive waves of illness and treatments. The passage quoted above is one of the few direct descriptions of his illness; in the rest of *Out of Place* there are only fleeting and largely undefined references to the host of symptoms that must have come with four years of chemotherapy. This lack of detail exists in striking opposition to the luxurious detail that characterizes Said's descriptions of his childhood. His dwelling on his past provides him with a constructive refuge from his illness as it also provides a way for him to explore (and displace) the losses it carries. His illness and sense of impending loss trigger memories of and grief for other losses—of his parents and the places of his boyhood—that become the focus of his writing, in a way that serves him both emotionally and intellectually. In his memoir Said lays claim to a self-determination that can be differentiated from individualism, and that allows him to live with dignity within the confines of an illness whose outcome is known.

Said's other late writings make more overtly political uses of his ill-ness. In the wake of September 11, 2001, Said published a number of impassioned articles in response to the escalating crisis in the Middle East. In each it is the extreme dehumanization of Palestinians that Said hammers home as the condition that George W. Bush and Ariel Sharon depend on in amassing support for their violent agendas in the Pales-tinian Occupied Territories. Excoriating the Bush administration for its role in Israel's "inhuman punitive policies" in an August 2002 *Al Ahram Weekly* article, Said explains Sharon's plan "entails nothing less than the obliteration of an entire people by slow, systematic methods of suffoca-tion, outright murder, and the stifling of everyday life" ("Punishment by Detail" n.p.). Said goes on to describe how "Gaza is surrounded by an electrified wire fence on three sides; imprisoned like animals, Gazans are unable to move, unable to work, unable to sell their vegetables or fruit, unable to go to school. They are exposed from the air to Israeli planes and helicopters and are gunned down like turkeys on the ground by tanks and machine guns. Impoverished and starved, Gaza is a human night-mare." Here, as elsewhere, Said's protest is fueled by a delineation of the everyday but extraordinary effects of dehumanization. Said begins this article by stating that it is his illness that enables his heightened aware-ness of the devastating nature of these daily forms of dehumanization in Gaza. He explains that "in addition to the physical discomforts and the terrible feeling of hopelessness" caused by his leukemia, it has also brought "intermittent passages of lucidity and reflection that sometimes give the mind a perspective on daily life that allows it to see things . . . from a different perspective." Illness, in other words, provides Said with heightened political insight into the pain, senselessness and injustice of a suffering that is both everyday and inhuman, and his experiences with it provide occasion for engagement with rather than retreat from these political exigencies.

In chapter 3 I address the seeming dissonance between Said's memoir and his overly politicized body of work, and argue that the memoir in sig-nificant ways advances the work that he has done as a public intellectual and as an activist for the Palestinian cause. In this chapter, with a focus on a disability framework, I argue that Said's representation of his ill-ness in *Out of Place* similarly works to inform his understandings of—and strategies for surviving and at times challenging—forms of bodily dis-placement. As he narrates his physical experiences of dislocation both as a healthy boy and as a cancer patient, and also as a stateless Palestinian, and his embodied affirmation, within these contexts, of his dignity, integrity, and self-determination, his memoir counters hegemonic formulations of citizenship. Moreover, the distinctions his memoir poses at times between self-determination and individualism nuance, extend, and connect the insights of postcolonial and disability studies in embodied ways that offer scholars possibilities for supporting the humanities *and* human rights agendas.

As Said refuses to dwell on his illness or to live fully within a body that is so ill, he also, in doing the hard work of memory, refuses to idealize his past health or relationship to his body. Rather, his memories of his former health and vigor (Said recalls being a fine athlete) are complicated by early memories of how his body—never quite right according to his parents—always needed correction. *Out of Place* includes descriptions of his parents' concerted efforts to "fix" his body; his mother gives her critical attention to fixing his hands, and his father buys him a harness and insists that he do exercises for his posture (67–68, 62). Although Said says that he retains no anger about this, he also states of his father, "What I cannot completely forgive, though, is that the contest over my body, and his administering of reforms and physical punishment, instilled a deep sense of generalized fear in me, which I have spent most of my life trying to overcome" (66). In *Recovering Bodies* Thomas Couser explains, "Bodily dysfunction is perhaps the most common threat to the appealing belief that one controls one's destiny. Perhaps, then, narratives of disability and illness serve to expose and dramatize what we would prefer to ignore most of the time, to arouse and (ideally) assuage our anxiety about our somatic selves" (9). Although *Out of Place* focuses not on the ill body, through troubling assumptions about the well body, Said marks precisely the anxieties that attend regulation of the body and the imposition of norms as a form of asserting control over that which is always escaping control. His memoir bears out Robert McRuer's contention that able-bodied identity "is simultaneously the ground on which all identities supposedly rest and an impressive achievement that is always deferred and thus never really guaranteed" (9). As Said refuses an illness/wellness binary, he disrupts the divide between the abnormal and the normal body and illuminates the extent to which norms are aggressively constructed, imposed, and maintained. His memoir thus makes use of what David T. Mitchell calls "the materiality of metaphor": Said's representations of his body give his narrative, as Mitchell puts it, "the one thing it cannot possess—an anchor in materiality" ("Narrative Prosthesis and the Materiality of Metaphor"

28). As *Out of Place* exposes the often violent constructedness of bodily and other related norms, it materializes, in a way that theory cannot, the efforts of disability studies scholars to effect "a shift from the ideology of normalcy, from the rule and hegemony of normates, to a vision of the body as changeable, unperfectable, unruly, and untidy" (Davis, *Bending over Backwards* 39).

The memoir establishes striking continuities between being out of place in one's own body, in one's family, in one's social world, and in one's country. Said links his experiences with leukemia to the experience of exile. Describing his emotional state in the spring of 1952, just months after his father sent him off to boarding school in the United States, he explains, "I had suspended my feelings of paralyzed solitude . . . and allowed another less sentimental, less incapacitated self to take over. Forty years later a similar process occurred, when I had been diagnosed with leukemia and discovered myself for a while almost completely gripped by the grimmest thoughts of imminent suffering and death" (*Out of Place* 244). Although Said explains how he overcame this paralysis, he discloses how "it has become possible—as with my early exile—to regard all the day's hours and activities (including my obsession with my illness) as altogether provisional" (244). Here experiences of illness and exile inform, without being collapsed into, one another. Said's dis-ease with his body and his worries about impending death are at once specific to his leukemia as they also speak to his experiences of displacement. He states, "To me, nothing more painful and paradoxically sought after characterizes my life than the many displacements from countries, cities, abodes, languages, environments that have kept me in motion all these years," and then he explains that his fear of and desire for departure has "intensified dramatically during the period I've been ill" (217). By the conclusion to the memoir, illness is but one of the many ways in which Said experiences being "out of place," and these various experiences lead him to conclude, "With so many dissonances in my life I have learned actually to prefer being not quite right and out of place" (295). In his memoir Said establishes connections among without collapsing various forms of displacement—familial, social, national, bodily. His illness and bodily discomfort become both conduits for understanding and related, but not equivalent to, national forms of displacement. The ravages and uncertainties of his cancer—his sense that his body has become a site of impermanence, disease, and pain—resonate for Said without being indistinguishable from his exile from Palestine, or from his multiple experiences of loss and displacement. Said harnesses these various feelings of unrest and experiences of displacement, paradoxically using them as the grounds on which to base his sense of himself as a moral and political agent. As Said makes a moral imperative from being out of place, his memoir supports disability studies scholars' challenges to the self as whole and contained.

Through Said's representations of his parents' disciplinary efforts, coupled with those of his U.S. and British schoolteachers (see chapter 3), his memoir illustrates both the coerciveness and putative nature of norms and of disciplining the body in the name of improvement, and also the connections between imposing bodily norms and constructing a body politic.[12] Said's former student Lennard Davis is one of the few disability scholars to bring a postcolonial perspective to bear on disability studies. Theorizing the connection between Enlightenment thought and modernization, both crucial components of the development of the nation-state, Davis asserts "that for the formation of the modern nation-state not simply language but bodies and bodily practices also had to be standardized, homogenized, and normalized" (*Bending* 106). Said reflects the connection between the disciplining of his body and coercive westernization as he recreates in his memoirs his experiences being disciplined and "normalized" by the colonialist British and American educational institutions that he attended and by an American father intent on establishing his son's American identity. Garland Thomson, in her discussion of how the regulation of the body is integral to the creation and regulation of the body politic, contends that U.S. liberal individualism relies on four interrelated ideological principles: "self-government, self-determination, autonomy, and progress. Such a self-image parallels the national ideal in an individualist egalitarian democracy that each citizen is a microcosm of the nation as a whole. A well-regulated self thus contributes to a well-regulated nation. However, these four principles depend upon a body that is a stable, neutral instrument of the individual will. It is this fantasy that the disabled figure troubles" ("Theorizing Disability" 42).[13] These four principles describe well Said's father's goals for his son who continually resists or fails his father's regulatory pressures and insistence on Americanizing him, in part due to the conflicting national and cultural contexts in which the young Said finds himself (see *Out of Place* 5 and my discussion in chapter 3). As *Out of Place* "normalizes" being out of place in one's body and connects forms of bodily displacement and discomfort to forms of social regulation and cultural and national displacement, it offers a critique of liberal individualism and the colonialist politics that accompany it. Said's memoir shows the psychic and bodily damages wrought and the imperialist politics that are imbricated in a Cartesian understanding of the subject as a separate, autonomous, efficient machine whose goal is self-mastery. Thus, his memoir points the way, in narrative form, for developing connections between the usually distinct fields of postcolonial and disability studies.

Although Said troubles the illness/wellness divide and the norms that govern the body and links these norms to forms of social and national regulation and control, he breaks with a disability studies framework as he in significant ways leaves in place a dominant understanding and valorization of the subject as individual, autonomous, and independent. As fiercely independent and individualist as are his other writings, *Out of Place* does not support disability scholars' and activists' urgings that the cultural obsession with independence be replaced with a model of reciprocity.[14] At the very heart of Said's identity as an intellectual is his fervent belief in independent thinking, and his memoir represents a related belief in establishing his independence and individualism. As discussed earlier, at times his self-assertion poses a challenge to hegemonic norms. However, this is not the case when he represents himself as battling his illness on his own. Although he thanks his wife Mariam Said and his physician Dr. Kanti Rai in the memoir's acknowledgments and conclusion for their support, they and his children scarcely enter the body of his memoir, despite his claim in an interview that his memoir is for "his children's generation" (Said, "Interview" 420). The memoir itself is largely one about loneliness and solitude, about the experience of living in one's mind. Indeed, Said's strategy for surviving his illness is to retreat into his memories, an activity that while peopled with figures from his past, is also intensely private and removed from his bodily realities. As Said asserts, "So many returns, attempts to go back to bits of life, or people who were no longer there: these constituted a steady response to the increasing rigors of my illness" (*Out of Place* 215). As Said's meditation on the losses that will attend his death leads him to dwell on that which he has already lost and on the relationships that he already misses, he represents himself as isolated and alone, distanced from his wife and children. Thus, at the same time that his memoir challenges assumptions that those with disabilities or illness lack the independence and autonomy that characterize "normal" people, and while providing glimpses into the loneliness that accompanies a serious illness, it also maintains the ideal of the abstract, self-possessed, autonomous individual.

In particular, as Said renders his aloneness, both in the face of his illness and in his experiences of boyhood, he excludes from the body of
his memoir his wife and the roles of other caretakers in decidedly masculinist ways. In the conclusion he does extend a particular thanks to his
doctor, and in his acknowledgments he explains, "From the beginning of
my illness, he and Mariam Said cooperated benignly, and literally kept
me from sinking. I gratefully dedicate this book to Mariam for her loving support and to Kanti for his humane skill and friendship" (x). Yet
it is precisely this life-sustaining support that does not find its way into
the body of Said's memoir. Although this could in part be a preservation
of the privacy of his family members who are still alive, it nonetheless
upholds conventional forms of masculine individualism and autonomy
and erases the crucial work that women in particular do as caregivers. In
her study *Love's Labor*, Kittay finds that "equality will continue to elude
us until we take seriously the fact of human dependence and the role of
women in tending to dependent persons" (4). Kittay further contends:
"The encounter with dependency is, I believe, rarely welcome to those
fed an ideological diet of freedom, self-sufficiency, *and* equality. It was,
after all, as a rejection of dependency on the feudal lord that Rousseau
(echoing the sentiment of his day) declared the equality of men (*sic*). But
the deeper dependencies of infancy and early childhood, frail old age,
disease and disability, do not vanish in a revolution. We have no lords
to fight for this independence. So we have built fictions" (5). As Said's
memoir partakes in these masculine fictions of independence, this aspect
of the memoir limits, along particularly gendered lines, the challenges it
poses to the liberal humanist subject.

These moments of individualism, the shortcomings of which feminist
and disability studies make evident, coexist in *Out of Place* alongside what
I have earlier described as assertions of self-determination that, from a
postcolonial as well as a disability studies perspective, resist rather than
support oppressive norms and hegemonic social structures. *Out of Place*
thus suggests the need to contextualize and, using different theoretical
perspectives, to connect or differentiate related concepts of autonomy,
independence, individualism, sovereignty, and self-determination—concepts that are often conflated if working exclusively within the paradigms
of disability studies.

Especially as it connects bodily discomfort to imperial practices,
Said's memoir also provides an implicit but important challenge to the
universalizing discourse that is becoming increasingly common among

proponents of disability studies. Lennard Davis, for example, forwards disability as a form of identity that escapes the exclusions and other problems of identity politics and allows for a universalism that is nonexclusionary and unifying of people across their differences. Quoting Paul Gilroy to support his belief that disability studies "should become a universalizing discourse," Davis claims, "'The reoccurrence of pain, disease, humiliation, grief, and care for those one loves can all contribute to an abstract sense of human similarity powerful enough to make solidarities based on cultural particularity appear suddenly trivial'" (*Bending* 32). In *Out of Place* Said's illness and pain do precisely the opposite of trivializing such solidarities, nor can a postcolonial perspective be contained within a disability studies one. Instead, the pain caused by Said's illness sharpens the particular pain of exile that he experiences and his illness intensifies his commitments to his homeland. Moreover, when Said recounts how his mother, dying of cancer, is refused medical care in the United States because her visa has expired, he suggests that questions of national belonging do not dissolve, but indeed can be heightened in the face of loved ones' experiences with illness. Said's memoir complicates Davis's assertion in *Bending over Backwards* that "disability may turn out to be the identity that links other identities" and his conviction that disability potentially offers a solution to the "dead end" of identity politics (13–14, 29).[15] The particularities that Said develops in his memoir (a genre well-suited to this) proffer an important challenge to the kind of universalism that Davis and other disability scholars advocate.

Within disability studies, cautions about universalism take a different direction. Michael Bérubé, for example, points to how, in making universalist claims, scholars must guard against making disability studies "a goodwill ambassador to the normal humanities," or a field of study that "will be understood not to enable but to humanize the rest of the humanities" ("Afterword" 339). Bérubé's concerns are important, but mine are different: my focus is on how making disability the umbrella, or overarching, identity will at times elide specific issues and concerns that other identities' theoretical approaches foreground. What I am advocating, then, enabled by the insights Said's memoir affords, is that different theoretical perspectives need to exist in dialogue, with the understanding that sometimes they will converge or complement one another, and at other times one approach or identity must be strategically chosen ahead of the other.

In its resistance to universalizing discourses, Said's memoir not only offers an angle into disability studies discourse on universalism but also, in combination with the intensely inward and oblique nature of Said's account of his illness, gives readers access to Said's particular experiences of displacement as it refuses easy routes of empathy or glibly arrived at forms of identification. In chapter 3 I argue that Said's memoir advances a human-rights agenda by way of, not despite, its inwardness and seemingly apolitical stance. The memoir's traditionally humanist form, together with Said's representative status, enables a liberal readership to rethink the Us-Them binaries so necessary to the dehumanization of Palestinians. Although the memoir itself resists a depoliticized, postmodernist celebration of difference or a weak model of liberalism that asserts "we're all alike despite our differences," it does allow Said to reach those who believe in such models. I want to make a similar argument in this chapter through the lens of disability studies. In his memoir Said neither uses his pain and illness to exalt himself as an individual or as a writer and an intellectual, nor does he make his experiences representative for others with leukemia or other kinds of cancer or illness. In this way Said keeps his memoir from establishing easy liberalisms that invite forms of identification that collapse different ways of being out of place. At the same time, *Out of Place* permits readers entry into the particularity of Said's life and his meditations on it, in a way that complicates illness-health divides and shows interconnections among various forms of bodily displacement and regulation. In addition, the processes through which he goes to establish a sense of self when the ground is literally shifting under him, and when his body itself proves unreliable, offer readers located inside and outside the academy a model for self-determination that is emotionally grounding and that does not depend on an individualism that is as fictional as it is oppressive.

The Erotics of Illness and Institutional Intimacies

Eve Kosofsky Sedgwick, literary critic and author of foundational books in queer theory (*Between Men* in 1985 and *Epistemology of the Closet* in 1990), has also written books and articles that, as they continue her investigations into queer theory, make forays into disability studies as well. Her essays in *Tendencies* (1993); her poetry book *Fat Art, Thin Art* (1994); *Gary in Your Pocket* (1996), her edited collection of the writings of Gary Fisher, a young, gay, black man who died of AIDS complications; and her therapy memoir, *A Dialogue on Love* (1999); are works that suggest rich correspondences between queer studies and disability studies. These books engage Sedgwick in celebrations of fatness as queerness; in musings on what it means to one's gender identity to lose a breast and hair; in explorations of the interrelationships among illness, sexuality, gender, and race; and in considerations of a host of other topics that further unsettle bodily norms and, with them, conventional understandings of gender and sexuality.

Like hooks's and Said's memoirs, *A Dialogue on Love* does not explicitly situate itself within the field of disability studies, even as it productively can be explored from that vantage point. A book that documents Sedgwick's experience in therapy with her doctor, Shannon Van Wey, it is comprised of Van Wey's therapy notes (which appear in all capitals) and her own account of her therapy with "Shannon" interspersed with haiku, in a combination that resembles the Japanese form of *haibun*. As with Said, a cancer diagnosis occasions but is not the main subject of Sedgwick's memoir. Sedgwick enters into psychotherapy at age forty, having entered a depression eighteen months after learning she has breast cancer and undergoing chemotherapy and a mastectomy. While in therapy, and six years after her initial cancer diagnosis, Sedgwick learns that the cancer has metastasized in her spine. However, as Nancy Miller notes in "Reviewing Eve," her review of *Dialogue*, the cancer "isn't so much the subject of her new book as its pretext" (217). As Miller observes, "*A Dialogue on Love* is above all the remarkable account of a psychotherapy" (217). Sedgwick's approach dramatically differs from Said's in its adherence to the present tense, and from hooks's in its relationship to suffering. Unlike hooks, Sedgwick views her depression as existing at odds with the pleasure and success that attend her writing, and she provides complex—and decidedly queer—accounts of how her cancer, her depression, her sexuality, and her gender identity interact in relation to institutional contexts. And whereas both hooks and Said uphold valorizations of independence and autonomy and are deeply invested in how their intellects can carry them through even the most difficult of illnesses or adverse circumstances, Sedgwick comes to question the importance of intellectual brilliance and self-reliance. Thus, as Sedgwick narrates the course of her psychotherapy and her relationship to her therapist, the narcissism that characterizes this memoir allows for connections with others, for complexly structured moments of empathy and identification. However, even as Sedgwick insists on how her relationship to her therapist transcends or escapes its institutional contexts—and his appearance in her book as the character Shannon is but one marker of this—her memoir stops short of a full exploration of how institutions and individuals interact. As *Dialogue* evidences the long-standing tension between performing institutional analysis and asserting individual agency, it suggests the particular challenges and possibilities of bringing together queer studies and disability studies.

Dialogue attests to Sedgwick's experiences not only with cancer but also with an ongoing and often serious depression, although she resists treating this depression as an illness. Sedgwick explains of her decision to enter therapy, "on record, the triggering event was a breast diagnosis eighteen months ago" (3), but she also enters therapy to address a depression that is an ongoing "ontological problem" (15). Sedgwick repeatedly expresses how she experiences sadness as a "groundtone"; how she obsessively desires death, viewing it as a relief or rescue, and even mentally writing her own obituary, an exercise that allows her to take narcissistic pleasure in her morbidity (62, 39, 132, 17, 23). Perhaps because, as her therapist observes, her depression comes at "an unexpected angle" to her articulateness about it and to her interpersonal competence and empathy, Sedgwick resists his diagnosis of depression (38, 2). As Shannon notes, Sedgwick "WORRIES, IS SHE BADLY OFF ENOUGH TO MERIT HELP" (37). Viewing her depression as peculiarly at odds with a life filled with love, friendship, a satisfying career, and freedom from money worries, Sedgwick, weeping "tears of privilege," expresses to Shannon and her readers the fright that accompanies feeling "so little attachment to a life that's so full of the things other people long for—rightly long for, I think" (15). Although Sedgwick mentions in passing her decision to take antidepressants and their effectiveness, these references to medication, and more generally to depression as an illness, are fleeting.

Thus Sedgwick neither romanticizes depression nor does she address it as an illness or form of disability to be reckoned with as cancer is. This might be because Sedgwick's own depression is not life threatening—as her cancer is—nor are its treatments as debilitating. Indeed, psychotherapy is for her a source of deep pleasure, and Sedgwick is highly functional even in the midst of depression. Perhaps for this reason, although Sedgwick breaks silences around mental illness in making public her experiences with depression, her memoir might in fact reinforce a wider ignorance about how serious an illness depression can be, and it fails to disrupt disability scholars' relative inattention to it. This neglect may result from the way that depression is on the one hand linked to creativity and even genius (c.f., hooks) and, on the other hand, is more difficult to view as a positive or socially constructed "difference" than are physical impairments that can be accommodated by altering the social landscape. (That said, depression has recently been on the map in cultural studies, if not in the context of disability studies: Ann Cvetkovich argues for the political possibilities of depression as part of her work for the collective, interdisciplinary cultural studies project titled Public Feelings. Also, in the late 1990s Prozac became a topic at conferences, including the MLA.) Although *Dialogue* takes up depression even as many disability scholars neglect it, it nevertheless does not address depression as a disability that is widespread, stigmatized, often debilitating and at times fatal.

With cancer then the catalyst for the therapy relationship that is *Dialogue's* focal point, and with depression an important component of the memoir but not one that is given weight as an illness, *A Dialogue on Love* doesn't slot easily into a disability studies framework. However, in *Dialogue*, as with Sedgwick's other post-1990 work, queerness comes to be connected to illness and disability in nuanced and multiple ways that illuminate both fields of study and help establish and extend connections between them. Sedgwick's work in queer theory has invited such connections since its inception. Throughout her body of work, Sedgwick—a self-proclaimed "fat woman" who claims her identity as a "gay man"—has valued deviance of all kinds and any destabilizing of norms, especially those pertaining to sexuality and gender.[16] Her embrace of "queerness" is a welcoming of "the open mesh of possibilities, gaps, overlaps, dissonances and resonances, lapses and excesses of meaning when the constituent elements of anyone's gender, of anyone's sexuality aren't made (or *can't* be made) to signify monolithically" (*Tendencies* 8). The important work that Sedgwick has done both in exploring shame and in reclaiming a queer identity despite ways it invariably remains stigmatized resonates deeply with work done in disability studies, particularly by feminists such as Garland Thomson. Sedgwick has remarked about the meaning of "queer" that "there's no way that any amount of affirmative reclamation is going to succeed in detaching the word from its associations with shame and with the terrifying powerlessness of gender-dissonant or otherwise stigmatized childhood."[17] Richly suggestive for disability studies scholars, Sedgwick's work in queer theory anticipates work done in disability studies.[18] It also has been directly useful to disability studies scholars and queer theorists who are just beginning to think about how the two fields interrelate.[19]

Especially since being diagnosed with cancer and losing loved ones to AIDS, Sedgwick has started bringing her theorizing in queer studies to bear on an exploration of illness and disability. *Tendencies*, for example, brings together Sedgwick's claiming of a queer identity with her experience undergoing treatment for cancer, both of which destabilize presumed connections among sex, gender, and sexuality. Sedgwick's accounts of losing a breast and, during chemotherapy, her hair, further her long-stated aims to disarticulate the linkages among sex, gender, and sexuality. She announces:

> Just getting dressed in the morning means deciding how many breasts I will be able to recognize myself if I am wearing (a voice in me keeps whispering, *three*); the apparition of my only slightly fuzzy head, facing me in the mirror after my shower like my own handsome and bald father, demands that I decide if I would feel least alienated or most adventurous or comforted today as Gloria Swanson or Jambi, as a head-covered Hasidic housewife, as an Afro wannabe. . . . Indeed, every aspect of a self comes up for grabs under the pressure of modern medicine. ("White Glasses," *Tendencies* 263)

Sedgwick elaborates on this unfixing of identity that her illness brings on in "Gosh, Boy George, You Must Be Awfully Secure in Your Masculinity!" In addition to theory that crosses into both queer and disability studies, Sedgwick has involved herself in more directly activist ways to politicize breast cancer. She is an advice columnist for the mass-market magazine *MAMM: Women, Cancer, Community* and has written other articles on breast cancer for publications such as the *Lesbian and Gay Studies Newsletter*, in which she advocates on behalf of women with breast cancer. Sedgwick also has become engaged in making fiber and textile art focused on her experiences with cancer that feature medical X-ray and CT scan images of her spine and other parts of her body.[20] These later projects signify how the experience of illness leads Sedgwick not only to cross boundaries between disciplinary fields, but also to discover limits to and move beyond academic ways of knowing and the confines of the academy.

Dialogue, itself a genre-crossing work, reflects these crossings and convergences, with explorations of Sedgwick's cancer coming together with her claim to a queer identity, each reinforcing the other's destabilization of norms of sex, sexuality, and gender. Sedgwick explains the

disappearance of her autoerotic life after her cancer diagnosis, dependent as this life is on fantasies in which the person featured is both herself
and not herself: "Because as my body got weirder with the treatment,
I kept feeling that I had to choose, and couldn't. Either the girl in the
fantasy would have one breast, or she would have two. Either she would
have hair, or she would be bald. Apparently it couldn't be both ways.
But if she was me, a bald woman with one breast, that ruined the fantasy—and if she wasn't me, wasn't marked in those ways, then that ruined
the fantasy, too" (47). As her body ceases to conform to the characteris-
tics that define "woman" generically (hair, two breasts), Sedgwick's delineation of her difficulty fantasizing throws into crisis assumptions about
what constitutes a woman. So too, her disclosure that she finds losing her
hair more traumatic than losing a breast challenges how women define
themselves, their gender, and their sexuality (64). Complicating this further is Sedgwick's claim to a queer identity. Sedgwick's identification as
a gay man is enacted almost entirely in the realm of fantasy and intellect
(sexuality doesn't connect for her genitally, she asserts in *Dialogue*), so
that "even when // I had the two breasts / I kept forgetting them. They
/ weren't there for me" (78). In *Dialogue* her account of losing a breast
makes material an already-claimed but unmarked queer absence. As we
see later, the fantasies that Sedgwick develops after her diagnosis further
bring together her queerness and her illness.[21] As Sedgwick narrates experiences that are grounded in her body, *Dialogue* suggests the artificial-
ity of distinguishing between queer and disability theory, and also the
limits of theory itself, *and* the possibilities of narrative. Thus her memoir
supports Sharon Snyder and David Mitchell's contention that disability
theory has lacked "a sensual and sensory language to theorize the body
itself. The theoretical diagnosis had been limited to an archaeology of
institutional power that sought artificially to stabilize meanings of the
body," and it illustrates their point that "to narrate a phenomenology of
the body requires an approach that can capture its defining elasticity—
not as an established fact, but rather as a mutable, temporal, 'first-person'
organism. Such is the domain of literature and art" ("Re-engaging the
Body" 381–82).

Up until the time she begins her therapy, Sedgwick has pleasurably
and productively exploited the incongruities and discontinuities among
mind, body, and emotions in a way that has privileged her desires and
intellect over her body. She has made a life for herself in which, as she
tells Shannon, "'work and love are impossible to tell apart. Most of my

academic work is about gay men, so it might seem strange to you that I would say that—not being a man, not even, I don't think, being gay'" (23). It is precisely by exploiting the gap between her assigned and chosen sexual and gender identities, and between her sexual fantasies and her bodily realities, that Sedgwick has made her career. For example, in *Dialogue* Sedgwick confesses to a "vanilla" sex life—missionary position, once a week, with her husband of many years—that she juxtaposes with her queer persona and her fantasies and desires that involve gay men, S&M, and perverse (often institutional) settings. Her experience with cancer, however, puts her up against the reality of her body and its limitations even as it and her account of it in *Dialogue* put the queer identity she has claimed more fully and visibly into play.

An unspoken pathos in *Dialogue* is that no amount of intellectual brilliance, no paradigm-shifting claims to queer subjectivity, will allow Sedgwick to theorize away her cancer and its potentially lethal effects. Indeed, one of the lessons that Sedgwick learns in *Dialogue* is that cancer is not a condition that is necessarily best addressed through an intelligence that pays no heed to the body and to the realm of feelings. As *Dialogue* delves into what an emphasis on theory and the intellect makes possible and leaves out, her narrative provides a challenge to disability studies' insistent focus on the social construction of disability or, as Eli Clare puts it, to disability activists who are "so busy defining disability as an external social condition that they neglect the daily realities of our bodies" (364). So, too, Sedgwick's account interrogates the relationship between intelligence and emotions and implicitly challenges the value system on which Sedgwick's academic career is based.

The Sedgwick who enters therapy is very much in step with academic culture in her obsession with intelligence as a primary measure of her own and others' value. Sedgwick reveals how fully she finds self-definition and meaning in her intellect and in her academic success when she expresses her sense that the timing for her possible death sentence is good since she has just published *Epistemology of the Closet* to much praise. She tells Shannon, "'when the diagnosis came I was feeling—as an intellectual—loved, used, appreciated. I would have been very, very content to quit while I was ahead" (*Dialogue* 4). Her chief worry in beginning therapy with Shannon is that he is stupid (11). Repeatedly evidencing her anxiety that Shannon will not prove intellectually up to par, Sedgwick puts him under rigorous scrutiny. Reflecting on her first visit to him, she writes, "First encounter: my / therapist's gift for guyish / banalization"

(5). She describes holding back her impatience with Shannon when he appears slow to catch her point: "Deconstruction 101, I do *not* say impatiently" (31). Later she expresses embarrassment regarding Shannon's "stupidity" about race in a way that shows how entwined good politics, theoretical acumen, and intelligence are for her (119). Foundational to her self-definition is both her sense of herself as an intellectually gifted critic and her contempt for those who are not (133). With such descriptions of her "pre-therapy" self, Sedgwick indicates how despite being a critic who has made a career out of challenging norms, the academy's dominant values—powers of analysis, fluency with theory, depth and complexity of ideas, intellectual capaciousness, critical abilities, originality and independence of thought—have escaped her otherwise relentlessly deconstructive intelligence as ultimate goods.

Dialogue discloses how, with Shannon's guidance, Sedgwick learns to put pressure on academic forms of intelligence and to claim ways of knowing that are more embodied and keyed to emotions. Shannon steadily and gently resists Sedgwick's emphasis on brilliance. At one point Shannon questions her fear of talking to someone "dumb" (121), and at another point Sedgwick complains, "I try and try but never succeed in getting Shannon interested in genius—or even in 'brilliance.' It's an area of possibility and pathos that leaves him cold. The furthest he'll go, in his blandness, is describing someone as 'really bright'" (72). Shannon instead focuses on what Sedgwick perceives as her lack of feelings. At the outset of the therapy Sedgwick tells Shannon, "Now as far as I can tell, I don't even have what are normally called feelings!" (6). Disclosing that she doesn't really miss her sister, from whom the family is estranged, Sedgwick explains, "that kind of thing is why I say I don't quite have emotions" (21). Sedgwick's earlier work assumes bodily sensations to be constructed, and "part of the discursive apparatus that performs the work of what Foucault has described as the disciplining of the body."[22] Cancer and menopause (triggered by chemotherapy) disrupt Sedgwick's faith in contemporary cultural theories that assume that emotions are discursive in origin, that they derive from and are controlled by the intellect. As Shannon notes, "RE MENOPAUSE, TALKS ABOUT HOT FLASHES HAVING BROUGHT HER INTO THERAPY IN THE FIRST PLACE—DRAMATIZING SHAME, HEAT, AFFECTIVE AURA OF FEELING AWFUL AND 'BAD'—'MADE ME ABLE TO THINK ABOUT AFFECT AS A TOPIC'—HAVING SEEN HERSELF AS SOMEONE WITHOUT EMOTIONS OR WITHOUT ACCESS TO THEM—WAS ABLE TO QUESTION THIS WHEN AFFECTS AND BODILY SENSATIONS CAME

TO HER AS IF FROM OUTSIDE, AS A SYMPTOM, IN THE FORM OF HOT FLASHES" (83). As Sedgwick's experiences of menopause and cancer challenge her perceptions regarding feelings, they precipitate a rethinking of the primacy of the intellect, along with what constitutes intelligence and how and why it is valued. Memoir, then, becomes a vehicle through which Sedgwick can assess and counter the limits of a scholarly brilliance that goes largely unquestioned in the academy.

In her immersion into psychotherapy, as Sedgwick learns to set aside her obsession with intelligence, she works to reconfigure the interconnections between mind, body, spirit, emotions, and sexuality. She tells Shannon, "So I think I may have made a near-conscious decision a year ago, after the chemo was over, when my hair was growing back. If I can fit the pieces of this self back together at all, I don't want them to be the same way they were. Not because I thought I could be better defended, either: what I wanted was to be realer" (7). Disclosing to Shannon that other therapy has not worked because she always has been charged with intellectualizing (6), she moves toward this "realer" space in *Dialogue*—one that is not encompassed by academe and the life of the mind. In part, this involves a return to poetry, and, "returning with it, and with Shannon's escort, is some of the long-ago life of the girl whose first passion it was" (136). As is true for hooks, for Sedgwick, poetry remains something apart from her academic writing, something that cannot be accounted for simply through the intellect. The form of *Dialogue*, the *haibun*, as it ranges between poetry and prose, reflects a deliberate crossing of ontological thresholds. As the work moves between criticism, narrative, notes, and haiku poetry, it integrates intellectual and analytical activity with an exploration of emotions and affect. Thus the space of therapy, and then the writing about it in *Dialogue*, are simultaneously intellectual adventures and a way for Sedgwick to get "real," to live more fully in her body. This journey is continuous with her foray into Buddhism and her immersion in textile projects and fiber art installations that explore what Sedgwick, in an artist's statement, calls "the bardo of dying," or "the space between contracting a terminal illness and death itself," a space which "is electric with spiritual possibility."[23] In these various enterprises Sedgwick troubles academic norms and claims a queerness that is not just discursive as she moves into embodied ways of knowing that connect spirituality, emotions, and intellect.[24]

One of the crucial lessons Sedgwick learns in therapy is that her own and others' valuing of her brilliance has exacted a toll on her—that she herself and others have viewed her precocity as a form of invulnerability, as a form of superiority that places her above the need or even the ability to be supported or nurtured by those less intellectually gifted than she. *Dialogue* narrates Sedgwick's increasing willingness to be dependent, and her realization that she can receive support from Shannon despite his supposed intellectual inadequacies. Shannon notes the hard work she has done on herself—"the person I know is someone who's been torturously polished, rubbed" (32)—and going through therapy and then writing *Dialogue* involve acknowledging the exhaustion and costs of this difficult and solitary work. Shannon notes how when Sedgwick feels anomalously smart, she also feels abandoned with her intellect as her only way out (54). Sedgwick, weeping, reflects in therapy on "precocity, its queerness, its sinister ramifications" and on how her own precocity led to her mother's fear of her, which in turn made Sedgwick feel that her childhood was "like being an adult in bad drag as a child, and being a child in bad drag as an adult" (30). Sedgwick, viewing her parents through Shannon's eyes, writes, "Shannon makes it sound as though they were apt to treat me as a kind of independent contractor living in the house—or ambassador of a neighboring principality, maybe" (153). Sedgwick gains from her experience with Shannon both an ability to view this deference to her extraordinary intelligence as a deprivation, and a willingness to put aside her worries about Shannon's intelligence and to surrender to his care. When Shannon is "stupid" about race, Sedgwick takes pleasure in "being able to say all my meanest things to him," but more importantly she takes comfort in "the sense that he'll be able to weather this storm of devaluation—that stays rock solid" (120, 121). *Dialogue* not only describes the process through which Sedgwick comes to place her trust in Shannon, but it also evidences this trust through the inclusion of Shannon's notes: "E NOTES THAT SHE IS FEELING MORE RELAXED SOMEHOW ABOUT THERAPY, ABOUT WRITING DOWN OUR SESSIONS; THE FEELING THAT SHE DOES NOT HAVE TO DO ALL THE WORK OR KEEP TRACK OF JUST WHERE WE ARE OR WHAT WE ARE PURSUING. THAT SHE CAN LEAVE SOME OF THAT TO ME" (160). Sedgwick's shift from viewing Shannon as a passive listener to an active participant is what allows the psychotherapy to become a "dialogue" in which Sedgwick can surrender her independence and autonomy, and can put herself in Shannon's hands. *Dialogue* charts how Sedgwick comes to place her trust in Shannon, a process that involves both relinquishing the high value she puts on a certain kind of intelligence, and coming to understand dependency as a form of love, and empathy as a form of emotional intelligence. In adopting this position Sedgwick's memoir supports disability studies' critique of independence. It also endorses a form of empathic listening over and against intelligence as defined in academic culture as *the* marker of distinction and way to navigate problems.

Sedgwick's willingness to depend on Shannon is linked to her decision to claim the identity of "patient," and the way that she inhabits this identity with agency complicates the passivity with which disability scholars associate this positioning. Having long resisted the role of "patient"—"My history as a patient is like my history as a smoker: I tried it a lot of times years ago, but never learned to inhale"—once Sedgwick takes on this role, she turns it into one of possibilities (5). Sedgwick opens her memoir with the assertion that, "apparently it's as a patient that I want to emerge" (1). For Sedgwick this identification affords opportunities not only for an emotional intimacy and nurture, but also for a queerly constructed eroticism. In some respects it is precisely the institutional nature of this role that Sedgwick highlights, perversely turning these qualities into a source of sexual pleasure, even in relation to her cancer. As she tells Shannon, "the cancer treatment did answer to my fantasies in a 'warm' way, not in that horrifying, vengeful way. Because it's important, for some reason, that the fantasies always have an institutional pretext—almost a bureaucratic one" (46–47). These sexualized fantasies involve, for example, a nurse drawing Sedgwick's blood and demanding that she spread her legs (49). If Sedgwick's desire is ignited by turning a clinical site of pain, illness, and sterility into one rife with erotic possibilities, so too does she positively charge the space of therapy with adventure, warmth, and pleasure. These qualities emerge out of and not despite the therapy being part of a larger medicalized institutional structure. Shannon observes how the structure of their doctor-patient relationship is one that Sedgwick finds enabling rather than limiting: "THINKING ABOUT CONDITIONAL AND UNCONDITIONAL LOVE CONTINUUM. . . . FROM ME IT IS UNCONDITIONAL BUT ALSO IS NOT QUITE LOVE. SHE FINDS SOMETHING USEFUL IN LEAVING IT UNDEFINED OR NOT QUITE DEFINED AS LOVE" (139–40). In demonstrating that love can flourish in institutional, professional contexts, *Dialogue* profoundly challenges and illuminates preconceptions about love as something that distinguishes the personal from the impersonal, the private from the public or professional. In this way she challenges, from a queer studies perspective, assumptions in disability studies that an institutional identity is a disempowering one.

At the same time, it is precisely the boundaries between the personal and the impersonal that *Dialogue* crosses and undoes in provocative ways. In her memoir Sedgwick establishes therapy as something that is at once a private relationship of love, deep caring, and intimacy, at the same time as it is a professional relationship, an impersonal form of health care, a job for which the therapist must be licensed and credentialized by the state. By crossing these boundaries Sedgwick offers up formulations of love and intimacy the power and consoling nature of which come from their impersonal and institutional contexts.[25]

And yet, the crossings that Sedgwick effects often depend on her asserting her own specialness and the exceptional nature of her relationship to her therapist. Indeed, a significant part of the pleasure that Sedgwick takes in the therapy is that it both exists within *and* exceeds its professional contexts, with its excesses serving as proof of Sedgwick's exceptionality. As revealed in *Dialogue*, throughout her therapy, Sedgwick shows an investment in Shannon seeing her as unique, and she includes in the memoir his sense of how his stakes in their relationship differ from his usual ones with his patients. A high point for Sedgwick is when Shannon tells her, "'I'm feeling something I rarely do about my patients: that being really seen by you is something that matters to me. Not that I just get narcissistically recirculated back to myself through your eyes, which happens all the time—but that I'm changed to myself in some way as I see that you see me'" (163). Although Shannon raises this point for the possible insight it gives him into Sedgwick's relationship with her father, what Sedgwick holds most meaningful is Shannon's disclosure of how she matters to him. Sedgwick arguably values her exchanges with Shannon so much precisely because they exist in excess of the terms of the therapeutic relationship: although this relationship requires that the therapist treat—or *care for*—a patient, it does not require the therapist to love the patient or to have a stake in "being really seen" by him or her.

Most importantly, when Shannon agrees to give over his therapy notes to Sedgwick for her to use in her book, their relationship shifts from the usual doctor-patient one into one that is more collaborative, with Sedgwick positioned as both author/authority *and* patient. In *Recovering Bodies* Thomas Couser focuses on how, with the establishment of modern medical practices and institutions, patients are dehumanized and denied forms of agency; he explores the widening gap between doctors' diagnoses, which occur in the absence of the patients themselves, and the patients' testimonies (22). In contrast to how other doctor-patient relationships are structured in other medical fields, in psychotherapy the patient is not silenced; indeed, the relationship is structured as one in which the patient's psyche and self-narrative take center stage. Therefore, therapy provides an effective counter to Sedgwick's experience as a cancer patient. At the same time, of course, in the therapeutic relationship a hierarchy exists, with the therapist holding the powers of diagnosis and authority over treatment plans and medications. Couser's contention that doctor and patient engage in "a sort of narrative collaboration" that produces "a new 'life text'" in which doctors interpret their patients' lives in a process that "is collaborative but one sided" holds largely true for the therapist-patient relationship as well as other medicalized relationships (10). In turning her therapy experience into a book containing Shannon's notes, Sedgwick subverts this hierarchy. Couser further argues, "just as patients wish to vanquish the illness that alters their lives, they may also wish to regain control of their life narratives, which they have yielded up to 'objective' medical authority" (10). By obsessively documenting her meetings with Shannon (115), making use of Shannon's notes, and turning both into a book at the same time as Van Wey the psychotherapist becomes the character Shannon, Sedgwick quite literally obtains control over her narrative. Using her skills as a literary critic to analyze Shannon and to read her relationship to him (skills critics and therapists hold in common), Sedgwick claims and furthers her own institutional identity as she shifts power and authority from Shannon to herself. By publishing an account of her therapy Sedgwick takes ownership over it, and turns the role of patient and the experience of therapy into that which is the academic's premier commodity fetish and material marker of achievement: the book.

By writing *Dialogue*, Sedgwick not only subverts and invests the role of "patient" with agency, but she also extends the time and space of therapy and, through the process of narrative, gives the love she experiences from Shannon a form of permanence. Shannon's notes, written from Sedgwick's point of view, show her wondering if it is time to end her therapy, even as she expresses her attachment to it: "WHEN WE ARE MESHING I'M HAPPY, A WHILE SINCE I'VE FELT LIKE THAT. A RECURRENCE WOULD HAVE GIVEN AN UNDERLYING NARRATIVE CONSISTENCY, FOCUS, RATIONALE FOR OUR TASK. ASKS IF I THINK IT'S TIME TO TURN AND WALK AWAY OR DOES IT CLEAR A SPACE FOR US TO WORK? (NOT A, B) . . . OK, BUT I SEEM TO NOT HAVE GOTTEN OVER THE SENSE THAT ONE HAS TO BE VERY SICK TO DESERVE THIS KIND OF ATTENTION. I'M NOT PHYSICALLY

SICK AND DON'T FEEL EMOTIONALLY SICK NOWADAYS. ALSO, IT'S AWFUL TO THINK OF GIVING UP THE NARRATIVE SPACE OF THERAPY" (91). Here, as throughout, not only are Shannon's and Sedgwick's words difficult to disentangle, but also as Shannon subordinates recording his own thoughts to capturing Sedgwick's, his notes provide Sedgwick with a material record of his attentive listening and empathic care. The contents of the notes reveal how important and interconnected for Sedgwick are narrative consistency, "meshing" with Shannon, and feeling held emotionally, all of which the notes give to her in their very structure. Sedgwick makes explicit her desire to capture and extend the therapy session and its holding relations when she expresses to Shannon her desire that he "carry me like that / around in your pocket for / a couple of weeks" (57).

This haiku poem resonates with the title that Sedgwick gives to a collection she was editing during her therapy, *Gary in Your Pocket*. In this book, Sedgwick gathers together writings by Gary Fisher, a beloved former student of hers who died of AIDS-related complications at a young age. Through the title *Gary in Your Pocket*, Sedgwick conveys how for her, books provide a way to hold—and perhaps even own, or appropriate—people or relationships once they are gone. Both *Gary in Your Pocket* and *Dialogue* also make public relationships that would otherwise remain private. Sedgwick illuminates the importance of this form of exhibitionism when she says of her obsessive documenting of her sessions with Shannon, "One thing it does do is let me indulge that desire, identified by Proust, to *show oneself to be loved*. (A shy glance at Shannon. Yes! He is nodding. As if he agrees that an account of our interactions will *show me to be loved*)" (116). Thus, for Sedgwick *Dialogue* serves as a way to transform her role as patient into one that, as author, gives her agency, control, and ownership both over her own story and over her doctor as well. It also serves as means to overcome and even extend and preserve the restrictive limits of the fifty-minute therapy session, creating an object and performance of love. Whereas Sedgwick details in *Dialogue* how, at the outset of her therapy, her publication of *Epistemology of the Closet* makes her feel valued as an intellectual, what she wants to assert in the writing of *Dialogue* is her worthiness as someone who is loved. In other words, *Dialogue* matters not as the highest marker of intellectual achievement, but rather because it evidences and makes permanent a relationship of love. *Dialogue* therefore registers a shift in Sedgwick's values as it provides an implicit critique of the emotional shortcomings of those that characterize the contemporary academy.

At the same time, that Sedgwick's "dialogue on love" takes place between herself and her therapist means that it is in many ways a narcissistic one. Therapy is one of the few forms of exchange in which adults are *supposed* to focus on themselves, in which there is emotional intimacy without the expectation of mutuality, and in which the intimate other acts out of bounds by turning the exchange toward her or himself. Sedgwick muses on this aspect of therapy when she states, "the space of Shannon is both myself and not," then shifting to haiku, "The place where talking / to someone else is also / talking to myself" (115). This circuit of exchange resonates with the pleasure and sense of self that Sedgwick derived as a child from masturbating. When she observes to Shannon, "'it's awfully striking how much the thread of a self, for me, seems to have been tied up with all this masturbating,'" Shannon notes that masturbating made her feel safe and held (75, 76). In *Dialogue* it is precisely Shannon's attention to Sedgwick, and the way in which he circulates her back to herself, that seems to be for her what makes this relationship so satisfying, and what makes this *Dialogue* on love in many ways a profoundly masturbatory, narcissistic one. The inclusion of Shannon's notes deepens rather than disrupts this quality, as the notes consist almost entirely of Sedgwick's words and perceptions or Shannon's thoughts about Sedgwick. Although the use of capitals seem to keep Shannon's voice distinct from Sedgwick's in *Dialogue*, their voices merge, an effect that is heightened by Shannon's shifts between the pronouns "I" and "you" so that they sometimes refer to himself, and sometimes to Sedgwick. The result is a book that is almost entirely "all about Eve," insofar as Shannon is present only to reflect Sedgwick back to herself and to give her the sense of being "safe and held," and also loved. In her review of *Dialogue*, Nancy Miller finds that as it progresses, "the psychic wiring behind the theoretical endeavor is finally laid bare; that the therapy memoir becomes intellectual autobiography" (219). What Miller ignores with this keen insight is the significance of conveying intellectual autobiography as therapy memoir given the therapeutic relationship's institutional constraints on reciprocity, and what it means for a dialogue on love to be so fundamentally, foundationally, one-sided.

Nevertheless, Sedgwick's narcissism is very different from Gallop's, Tompkins's, or hooks's in that her self-reflection makes room for and invites others to engage in similar acts. Sedgwick's narcissism has the rare quality of not eclipsing but rather of allowing others to insert themselves into her narrative. Critics remark on this quality in the anthology

Regarding Sedgwick; in an interview with Sedgwick, for example, editors Stephen Barber and David Clark observe how "part of your own queer performativity lies in or is generated by a notion you've described more than once: 'being available to be identified with'" (Sedgwick, "This Piercing Bouquet" 250).[26] *Dialogue* is entirely narcissistic and unashamedly self-absorbed in a way that at once invites readers to identify and to disidentify with Sedgwick.

Sedgwick repeatedly affirms the importance and power of identification as a mode of learning and as an incitement to activism, particularly when it comes to addressing issues of illness and disability. In "White Glasses," written for her beloved friend Michael Lynch as he is dying of complications from AIDS, Sedgwick writes that she has learned from him "the injunction—not the opposite of 'Out, out' but somehow a part of it—'Include, include': to entrust as many people as one possibly can with one's actual body and its needs, one's stories about its fate, one's dreams and one's sources of information or hypothesis about disease, cure, consolation, denial, and the state or institutional violence that are also invested in one's illness. It's as though there were transformative political work to be done just by being available to be identified with in the very grain of one's illness" (*Tendencies* 261). Sedgwick's commitment to making intellectual, emotional, and bodily experiences of illness available to others can be seen to inform *Dialogue*, which, like her textiles and other work, explores the "bardo of dying," or "the space between diagnosis and physical death." Sedgwick explains of this state, "I think just the recognition of it as a distinct place that many people spend a fair amount of time in, out of which they can speak directly to others as well as to themselves—I think that recognition affords its own opportunities, its own tasks and also anxieties. I do think it was one of the big discoveries that potentiated AIDS activism. It is full of potential for activism as well as reflection around other slow-acting diseases" ("This Piercing Bouquet" 256). Thus for Sedgwick the identification or recognition afforded by first-person narratives of illness not only can offer individuals points of connection and knowledge, but also can serve as the basis for more directly political and collectivist forms of action. As she endorses the injunction to "include, include" that also informs her approach to queer identity, Sedgwick offers an alternative position to that of disability theorists who caution against the depoliticizing qualities of narratives that invite empathy or identification, and she paves the way for a nonexclusionary humanism—one that invites participation in political struggles that extend beyond one's self.

As *Dialogue* speaks to others in the "bardo of dying," and as Sedgwick offers forth her own range of experiences "without trying to appear as attractive or exemplary as possible" ("This Piercing Bouquet" 251), what it leaves undeveloped is her insight in "White Glasses" that "under the present regime of systemic exclusion from health care in at least the United States, *every* experience of illness is, among other things, a subjection to state violence, and where possible to be resisted at that" (261–62). Indeed, if there is one area that *Dialogue* leaves wholly untapped, it is the economics of illness, the ways in which the state determines how illness is defined, regulated, and attended to—or not attended to—and who can afford what.

Even as the "space of therapy" is the subject of *Dialogue*, as Sedgwick brings a queer-studies perspective to bear on it, there is no mention that her intimacy with Shannon constitutes a economic relationship, presumably one that is paid for in fifty-minute increments. Sedgwick ignores therapy's costs and availability, and how economics structure the relationship between therapist and patient and the love that can emerge from this relationship. In *Epistemology of the Closet* Sedgwick theorizes ignorance as a willed "not knowing," and her neglect of the economic nature of the therapeutic relationship seems to fall into this category, and dovetails with her failure to explore limits to the reciprocity of her relationship with Shannon. Instead, its institutional contexts exist solely as a source of erotic, and decidedly queer, pleasure or as one that can be subverted or overcome. *Dialogue* also makes no mention of the fact that even the most generous health plan would be unlikely to cover so much intensive therapy in any given year. Attention to this fact would raise questions about whether the therapy that Sedgwick undergoes, given her ability to function so well, is a bourgeois "luxury" or care that should be available to everyone. Although Sedgwick does voice doubts about whether attending therapy constitutes a self-indulgence, at no point does she factor money into her reflections, nor does she acknowledge that it is a privilege even to pose such questions given the current state of health care in the United States and its inadequate attention to mental health.

In part this owes to how Sedgwick defines illness; in her other writings on illness she does not include depression, but rather focuses on cancer and AIDS. Without consideration of depression as illness (or as a common result of a cancer or HIV diagnosis), therapy can more readily be made into a queer space of adventure and love without it also being interrogated as a space of medical intervention or treatment. *Dialogue* affords readers points of identification and access into the terrain of cancer (and other topics, too, including what it means to claim a queer identity), thus making the narcissism of *Dialogue* not merely an inward-looking loop but an affective structure that can extend outward to others. However, because the memoir, with its emphasis on a queer erotics, lacks an angle of institutional analysis in regard to therapy, it less clearly fulfills Sedgwick's injunction that people understand—and resist—how every experience of illness entails, among other things, subjection to state violence.

In other work, such as in her advice column for the cancer magazine *MAMM*, Sedgwick, working more strictly from a disability studies framework, focuses precisely on politicizing illness, breast cancer in particular, which, as Sedgwick notes in "Breast Cancer: Issues and Resources," "an unconscionable one-in-eight" women will contract (10). Addressing the difficulties of agitating for serious cancer prevention in that same article in the *Lesbian and Gay Studies Newsletter*, she exposes the "interlocking relationships between industry, pharmaceutical companies and the medical establishment" (14). At the end of the article Sedgwick describes getting a phone call from the medical editor of a local daily newspaper who is writing an article on the abnormally high incidence of breast cancer in Durham County, North Carolina. Sedgwick explains, "he wants to 'humanize it' by interviewing someone who has actually had the disease. He's heard from somewhere that I'm willing to be public about my experience. And I am." He asks what advice Sedgwick has not for women with cancer, but "for the average woman, for our readers"; how, he wonders, "can they avoid getting breast cancer?" Sedgwick's responds, "I'm afraid I have no idea. The best strategy would probably be not growing up five blocks from a major toxic incinerator" as she herself did, noting that this incinerator "was on the grounds of the National Institutes of Health in Montgomery County, Maryland." Sedgwick concludes the interview,

> The smoke it spewed was from the medical waste of the countless research experiments of the 1950s and 60s. Under community pressure, the NIH closed down the incinerator.
>
> Now I'm sick, and lots of other Montgomery County women are sick: it's one of the hottest breast cancer hot-spots in the whole country.
>
> But the same experiments, *they're* still going on. (15)

Here the advice and analysis that Sedgwick offers are insistently structural and at the macro level. Refusing the editor's desire that she "humanize" the issue (and subtly challenging his characterization of women
without cancer as "average"), Sedgwick also refuses to make cancer into
a "human interest" or purely personal story. Sedgwick does important
work in publications such as this one to raise awareness of cancer as a
political condition, both in its inception and in the lack of options for
treating it. Individuals, particularly those who suffer from particularly
stigmatized forms of cancer such as melanoma and lung cancer, often are
treated as if they have incurred cancer through bad habits. Sedgwick's
cancer writings contribute to disability studies as they address what goes
too often unmentioned: the link between individual cases of cancer and
the systematic destruction of the environment that accompanies the U.S.
government's and corporations' reckless squandering of resources.[27]

Although *Dialogue* certainly "humanizes" the issue of breast cancer,
with its focus on her personal experience of therapy, it does not do the
explicitly political work that Sedgwick does and calls for in some of her
other writings that concentrate on the social causes of illness and disability. In *Dialogue* the high incidence of breast cancer in the United States
goes unmentioned, as do the implications of—to use a shorthand—capital in this epidemic. So, too, does the medical establishment's complicity
in the spread of breast cancer go unnoted, along with the institutionalized and everyday forms of state violence, such as systemic exclusion
from health care, that women with cancer experience. As Thomas Couser
observes, in the medical establishment individuals' health problems are
regularly detached from their social contexts (*Recovering Bodies* 20).
Couser argues medical institutions preserve the status quo "by minimiz-
ing or ignoring social and cultural factors contributing to illness" (33).
Thus, medical institutions not only dehumanize and take agency from
those experiencing illnesses or impairments, but they also decontextual-
ize disability. Although Sedgwick's memoir counters problems of dehumanization, it does little to politicize or contextualize cancer. Even less
present in *Dialogue* is any discussion of depression as an illness, let alone
one that subjects those who experience it to state violence.

If *Dialogue* does not address forms of state violence, it does make other
important contributions. The memoir precipitates a rethinking of what
constitutes intelligence and how and why it is valued, at the same time
as it suggests the value of other ways of knowing, including those that

centrally involve love, nurture, and empathy. As *Dialogue* demonstrates the connection between mind and body, it also shows how maintaining such a split can be enabling: although suffering a bodily illness may trigger a depression, the life of the intellect and the emotions can provide solace from if not transcendence over this illness. (By the same logic, physical health can provide its consolations when grappling with a depression, even as a depression can and does impact physical health.) In narrating a therapeutic relationship, *Dialogue* also shows how narrative can become part of this therapy even as it subverts the power dynamic between patient and doctor, giving to the patient a form of agency and control. Sedgwick's memoir extends to readers a form of impersonal intimacy, one that allows for forms of identification that make useful the narcissistic impulse of the therapy and one that provides provocative crossings between the private and the public, the personal and the political, the intimate and the public, and in ways that anticipate—and demonstrate the possibilities of—bringing together queer and disability studies.

Bringing Public Policy Home

Life as We Know It: A Father, a Family, and an Exceptional Child (1996) marks Michael Bérubé's entry into the field of disability studies. A prolific American studies scholar and cultural critic with an interest in transforming the academy in progressive ways, he is also the author of *Marginal Forces/Cultural Centers: Tolson, Pynchon, and the Politics of the Canon* (1992), *Public Access: Literary Theory and American Cultural Politics* (1994), *The Employment of English: Theory, Jobs, and the Future of Literary Studies* (1997), *What's Liberal about the Liberal Arts? Classroom Politics and Bias in Higher Education* (2006), and *Rhetorical Occasions: Essays on Humans and the Humanities* (2006), and he has edited (with Cary Nelson) *Higher Education under Fire: Politics, Economics, and the Crisis of the Humanities* (1995) and *The Aesthetics of Cultural Studies* (2005). His body of work, which reflects his ongoing interest in reaching academic and nonacademic readers, also includes over 150 essays that appear in academic journals and more popular venues such as *Harper's*, the *Village Voice*, the *Nation*, and the *New York Times Magazine*; interviews; podcasts; and an award-winning blog. Quick witted, verbose, and precocious, Bérubé has based his career on being a master of different media, genres, discourses and disciplines. With the publication of *Life as We Know It*, his account of bringing up a son with Down syndrome,

Bérubé became known not only as a prolific and wide-ranging critic of American culture and contemporary politics, but also as a leading figure in disability studies. His memoir received immediate critical acclaim in mainstream venues—it was a New York Times Notable Book of the Year for 1996 and was chosen as one of the seven best books of the year by Maureen Corrigan of National Public Radio. Bérubé's reception by disability studies scholars has been similarly enthusiastic, as indicated by the frequency with which he is chosen to write forewords and afterwords to key anthologies in the field (to name a few, *Enforcing Normalcy*, *Disability Studies: Enabling the Humanities*, and *Crip Theory*).

What is so moving about *Life* is that it entails Bérubé embracing a whole other kind of intelligence and values other than those on which he has built his academic career. Along with its incisive criticisms of medical discourses and social institutions, what radiates from this memoir is Bérubé's love for his child Jamie and an appreciation for Jamie's kindness and brightness of spirit. As *Life* rethinks intelligence, it also rigorously engages how individuals and institutions interact. From his perspective as caretaker, Bérubé questions a social order that values intelligence (as defined in the academy and then in the broader culture that takes its cues from the academy) over kindness and empathy, and independence over interdependency. Through his narrative that centers on his child, Bérubé assesses—and critiques—societal institutions for how they shape and respond to Jamie's experiences, and he argues for the importance of formulating a broadly inclusive concept of citizenship, one that accommodates rather than excludes his son.

Whereas *Dialogue* is driven in large part by Sedgwick's desire to show herself to be loved, *Life*, dedicated to Jamie with love and admiration, articulates the knowledge that Bérubé has gained from his love for Jamie. Indeed, love is in many ways the unannounced subject of *Life*: the political project of *Life* is an extension of Bérubé's love for his child. As a labor of love, Bérubé's memoir is readable for its empathy and its turning from the family outward—it proffers a love and humanity that bring its social critiques and institutional analyses to life. Love serves as the catalyst for Bérubé's critiques, and animates them for a readership whose investments in issues of disability are not emotional (or even nonexistent). The memoir stands as an expression of Bérubé's love for his son, as it also seeks to make a political intervention, to educate and persuade readers about public policy in a way that the other memoirs discussed in this chapter do not. Thus *Life*, as it mediates between the inside and outside of the academy, demonstrates the potential of the academic discipline of disability studies to effect social change. It also evidences memoir's possibilities for combining empathy and institutional analysis in order to develop the work of disability studies and to carry its insights and calls for change to a broad readership.

In large part it is Bérubé's perspective as caretaker and advocate rather than subject struggling with a disability that sets his memoir apart from the others in this chapter and that gives it its particular political charge. Whereas memoirs by those with disabilities must negotiate the stigma that attends dependency, Bérubé, as his son's caretaker and advocate, is better positioned to focus on the social structures that produce definitions of dependency and independency, and to formulate more collective, less individually based definitions of autonomy. Rather than thinking about self-care, his structurally ennobling role requires considering what he and his family need to thrive given each member's various forms of interdependency. Disability involves both patients and caretakers, and viewed alongside this chapter's other memoirs, *Life* suggests different ways to carve out agency from these distinct subject positions.

Although collective in its analysis, *Life* makes its arguments through a focus on Jamie's value as a particularized individual. *Life* thus demonstrates how the individual focus of memoir can be politically enabling as it simultaneously humanizes *and* individualizes people living with a disability that is regularly used to dehumanize them—and often to institutionalize them and make them disappear. Similar to how Said's memoir effectively works against dehumanization of Palestinians, Bérubé's works against dehumanization of a highly stigmatized group: people with Down syndrome. Early in *Life* Bérubé tells of obstetricians informing parents that their child had been born with Down syndrome "by explaining that human children had forty-six chromosomes, whereas their child would have forty-seven" (38). Bérubé's protests against dehumanizing discourses about Down syndrome and their attendant public policies derive from his understanding of Jamie's value as a beloved child with his own idiosyncrasies, and on his insistence that his child be accorded the same rights and respect as any other human being. His claims, in other words, are both particularized—Jamie is an individual or, as Bérubé puts it, "entirely sui generis" (xi)—and universal—like any individual, Jamie is a human being. There is no contradiction here. Indeed, Bérubé remarks in *Life* on the necessity to assert individuality as a means of achieving a more generalized recognition of humanity.[28] He explains, "For some reason we don't yet understand, we seem incapable of empathizing with other humans in the abstract, and we need to have them *represented* to us before we can imagine what it might be like to share their feelings and their dreams" (255). When wondering in his afterword to *Disability Studies* what universalism would look like, Bérubé reflects on "the staggering complexity of the subject, adequate to the ancient imperative of the humanist to perceive nothing human as alien" (343). In *Life* he illustrates this humanist imperative as he invites readers to identify with and to recognize his son's humanity, because of, not despite, his particularities.

Although empathy is key to the political protest that the book makes, it is not an endpoint, nor is identification with Jamie, or with Bérubé, the goal. Rather, in *Life* Bérubé sets forth the capacity to imagine others—or to possess empathy or emotional intelligence—as an ethical imperative, as a social responsibility that leads to better public policies and more inclusive models of citizenship and human community. As Bérubé announces in the preface, "it is part of my purpose . . . to represent Jamie as best I can—just as it is part of my purpose, in representing Jamie, to ask about our obligations to each other, individually and socially, and about our capacity to imagine other people" (xix). Through the memoir genre, Bérubé effectively counters ways in which people with disabilities appear lacking in both individuality and humanity to those without disabilities—Bérubé resists this dominant form of seeing (or, drawing on Wittgenstein, not seeing, or "seeing-as"). The opening words of his memoir, "My little Jamie loves lists," claim loving connection to his son and set the terms in which Jamie is to emerge as his own person, replete with his own opinions and tastes (ix). Through his representation of Jamie, Bérubé extends readers' capacities to imagine other people; he provides readers with new ways both to perceive those with disabilities and to rethink commonly understood norms. For Bérubé such acts of empathy and imagination are not extraneous but rather are absolutely integral to affecting political change. By viewing culture and society from a perspective that centers Jamie, Bérubé demands that readers consider questions of public access and social justice in accordance with a new set of norms, with an understanding of "human" that begins with rather than excludes those defined as dependent or disabled. In this way his memoir suggests the crucial role that disability studies has to play in answering the urgent question in the humanities today about how to formulate a nonexclusionary humanism.

One of *Life*'s most significant interventions from a humanities stand-point is its radical rethinking of intelligence. Whereas *Dialogue* puts pressure on intelligence as a primary marker of value, *Life* carries this project even further (something the subject of Down syndrome makes more necessary).[29] Intelligence is prized in our culture; indeed, IQ tests have been linked to the development of eugenics and to decisions about who has a life worth living.[30] If this is true for the culture at large, it holds especially true for academics, and for Bérubé in particular. A prolific writer whose prose is characterized by his enormous vocabulary, his quick wit, and his dizzying command of factoids, his experience fathering Jamie causes him to question seriously his valorization of intellectual brilliance, and *Life* narrates this process. When he and his wife, Janet Lyon, learn about Jamie's Down syndrome soon after his birth, they pore over literature and, in a medical chart that Lyon peeks at, they discover the nurse's notation that the "parents seem to be intellectualizing" (14, 24). Throughout *Life* Bérubé fully engages in intellectualizing as a means of addressing the challenges his son's Down syndrome presents for him. Employing his skills as a literary critic and his ability to assimilate facts, Bérubé achieves quick command over medical terminology, and the philosophical questions that Jamie's condition raise for him are central to his memoir. This "intellectualizing," however, does not substitute for emotional engagement with Jamie, and one of the lessons that Bérubé learns from his son is to revalue—or devalue—the ability to intellectualize if this activity is not accompanied by empathic engagement with others and a sense of social responsibility. Bérubé's eldest son, Nick, whose intelligence registers remarkably high on standardized tests, is most appreciated in *Life* for his generosity of spirit (9). By valuing Nick's kindness over and above his intelligence, Bérubé offers a challenge to the standards by which worth is measured. Early on in *Life*, Bérubé tells about being at an amusement park with his children; he witnesses Jamie's unending fascination as he watches, but refuses to ride, a train as it circles repetitively round a track (xiv). Bérubé's stultifying boredom and depression over his son's limitations turn at dinner that night as he watches Jamie serving imaginary meals to imaginary customers. Seeing Jamie anew, Bérubé finds, "the ability to imagine what other people might like, what other people might need—that seems to me a more crucial, more *essential* ability for human beings to cultivate than the ability to ride trains" (xvii). Bérubé learns from Jamie to value empathic imagination and to question the importance of the skills that normally measure maturity and growth, or "ability." In a reversal of the usual parent-child dynamic, Jamie serves as his father's teacher. Through Jamie's teachings, Bérubé comes to redefine ability and to revalue intelligence, and to claim that imagination (or emotional intelligence, though this is not a term that Bérubé uses) should be a prerequisite for citizenship rather than an extraneous or "bonus" form of intelligence or, in a more negative casting, a source of weakness or vulnerability.

Life includes a thorough questioning of development, and particularly of its expected telos, independence, a quality associated in dominant U.S. culture with being an individual and with having social value, even with being fully human. In this way the memoir partakes in a wider movement in disability studies. In *Love's Labor*, a book that similarly reevaluates questions of intelligence and independence from a caretaking perspective, Eva Feder Kittay writes of her own daughter Sesha, born with severe cognitive disabilities, "I fear that the stress on independence reinstates Sesha as less than fully human. With every embrace, I know her humanity. And it has no more to do with independence than it has to do with being able to read Spinoza" (173). In *Bending over Backwards* Davis looks toward an era in which "dependence, not individual independence, is the rule" (27). Under Davis's model, "Dependence is the reality, and independence grandiose thinking. Barrier-free access is the goal, and the right to pursue happiness the false consciousness that obscures it" (31). In *Life*, although his parents encourage Jamie's independence, Jamie's full humanity is asserted and prized through the descriptions of his dependency. For example, as Bérubé and his wife learn to insert tubes into Jamie's nose so they can feed him without surgical intervention, it is this model of "dependency and interdependence," or the ways that family members support and sustain one another, that become the norm, that become "life as we know it." As Bérubé provides this more collective model from which to view understandings of dependence and independence, he accomplishes in his memoir some of the imaginative rethinking that Carol Breckenridge and Candace Vogler call for when they state, "we need to ask what justice would look like if we assumed that everybody who is here belongs here and that any reasonable image of collective flourishing will take this into account" (356). At the same time as he recontextualizes dependence, Bérubé does not, as do some disability theorists, glibly idealize or romanticize Jamie's dependency any more than he casts it simply as a socially constructed marker of difference; instead he looks forward to the day when Jamie can tell his own story.[31] Indeed, he concludes his memoir by saying, "My job, for now, is to represent my son, to set his place at our collective table. But I know I am merely trying my best to prepare for the day he sets his own place. For I have no sweeter dream than to imagine—aesthetically and ethically and parentally—that Jamie will someday be his own advocate, his own author, his own best representative" (264).

Life provides nuanced critiques not only of the language of dependency but also of medical discourse. Bérubé's memoir rigorously demonstrates Couser's arguments about how medical discourse exerts tremendous societal power, and in ways that can obstruct empathy and alienate doctors from patients and patients from their bodies and bodily experiences (*Recovering Bodies* 19). Bérubé resists medicalizing Jamie even as his own acquisition and use of medical discourse shows its power. Introducing Jamie to his readers, he presents Jamie's diagnosis, wryly remarking, "that's a lot of text to wade through to get to your kid" (7). Also speaking as a parent, Donna Avery analyzes ways medical language can devalue the lives of children with disabilities (123). Avery contends, "The 'tragedy' of disability . . . is not only in our language, or in the way we story the body; it is embedded in our reification of the medical field" (124). With his baby thoroughly medicalized from birth, after Jamie has been in the intensive care unit for two weeks with his parents immersed in a world of doctors and insurance claims, Bérubé laments, "Jamie was beginning to seem less like a baby to me than a policy" (40). And yet, in a memoir saturated with medical discourse, Bérubé appropriates the power of this discourse for himself even as he exposes its dehumanizing powers. Rather than simply excising this language from his memoir, Bérubé both challenges its discursive power through analyses of it, and also suggests that for parents to appropriate rather than simply reject this language can be enabling—it can be a way to command respect from medical practitioners. His own quick study of medical terminology is fueled by his experience getting his terms wrong and witnessing "the doctors exchange significant glances with each other, thinking, *We don't have to listen to this guy, he can't tell his duodenum from his jejunum*" (36, original emphasis). As Bérubé moves back and forth between personal narrative and a medicalized narrative, he interjects both with analysis of the importance of approaching medical discourse critically. Bérubé reflects on how other parents have redefined Down syndrome, including their success in "uplifting the [human] race" by shifting the medical term "mongoloid idiot" to "person with Down syndrome" (26). He emphasizes that progress often results from such a change in language and perspective rather than from medical advances (127). Bérubé counteracts his use of medical discourse and its alienating tendencies as he insists on Jamie's status, first and foremost, as a beloved child. Thus, the overall impetus of *Life* is to resist stories that situate children with disabilities as "patients" rather than as individuals. Bérubé's use of medical discourse serves to shift the images and narrative structures through which we see people with Down syndrome, in order to alter the very experiences of those lives.[32] As he does so, his memoir implicitly helps to realize poststructuralist understandings of the political power of language in a way that grants agency not only to poststructuralist theorists such as himself, but also to those acting from the position of parents.

As Bérubé's memoir takes positions on specific public policy issues such as reproductive rights, prenatal testing, health care, family leave, health insurance, and other crucial public policy issues, it puts into practice arguments that Bérubé makes in *Public Access* and *Higher Education under Fire* about the need for cultural critics to engage the "inevitable entanglement" between cultural politics or textual analysis and public policy without conflating the difference between them.[33] As he claims in the epilogue to *Public Access*, the "textual" and the "discursive" constitute "a crucial site of social contestation for our 'private' identities and the legal/social apparatus in which we take up, claim or transform those identities" (264).[34]

At the same time that Bérubé challenges and crosses the public versus private divide, he keeps these categories in place. On the one hand, he shows the crossing of the public and private, how they together constitute "the terms under which we assume our semiprivate 'identities' as citizens and subjects" (Bérubé and Lyon xiii). Throughout *Life* he argues the need to understand and analyze how "private" identities are socially constructed, and that discourse and texts play important roles in setting the terms of being a citizen and a subject.[35] However, while showing how the "private" is publicly regulated and constructed, and how the public is being privatized, Bérubé also resists collapsing these spheres. Indeed, in *Life* he argues the need for "a public and legal concept of 'privacy,'" one that allows no right to access for certain areas of life (87, 79). Although he details and subjects to analysis the staggering financial costs, both out-of-pocket and state covered, that accrue when bringing up a child with Down syndrome, he simultaneously and resolutely refuses to consider Jamie in terms of cost-benefit analysis, utilitarianism, or productivity in economic terms (52). At the same time that Bérubé uses the experience of parenting Jamie to try to make public policy interventions, he refuses to make Jamie representative or to reduce him to a type or an object lesson. Rather, he argues the need for "a social and legal consensus that there are some areas of human life in which individuals should be free to apply the rules of social and legal consensus as they see fit" (87). By investing his reader in Jamie and their relationship, Bérubé uses memoir to demonstrate this need in a way that is intellectually as well as more emotionally compelling than theory or analysis alone could be. As his memoir works the intersections of the personal and the public spheres, it maintains the need to maintain distinctions between private choices and public policies, and embodies insights of disability theorists in the emotionally engaging form of personal narrative.

As Bérubé's memoir centers Jamie and the rest of his family, it quite literally brings home the importance of disability issues, and the need for institutional analysis and change. In his preface to Davis's *Bending over Backwards*, Bérubé looks forward to the day when "everyone who works at the intersection of culture and society will know that disability is a pivotal concept for any comprehensive account of culture and society" (xii). In the preface to his own memoir, Bérubé places Jamie's story precisely at the center of this intersection: "Jamie has no idea what a busy intersection he's landed in: statutes, allocations, genetics, reproduction, representation—all meeting at the crossroads of individual idiosyncrasy and sociopolitical construction" (xix). The importance of these larger contexts to the memoir is reflected in the chapter titles (for example, "Genetic Destiny," or "Sapping the Strength of the State"), which are issue-based rather than a chronological account of Jamie's life. The memoir then, is at once a loving tribute to his son and a blueprint for forms of change that would benefit not only Jamie and other people living with disabilities, but society at large.

In *Life* Bérubé strives to realize the argument he makes in *Public Access* that intellectuals should attempt "to open a public access channel" (x). Although he acknowledges the difficulties of accomplishing this, he urges, "the political, cultural, and social context of academic 'theoretical' debates needs to be broadened and 'popularized'" (37).[36] He describes *Life*, an excerpt of which appeared in *Harper's* magazine, as his first "crossover" work (*Higher Education* 219). Humor plays an important role in making his memoir accessible. In *Public Access* he tells a story about his aunt asking him if his book is funny. He explains coming to realize "that it was a fairly important question to consider if I ever wanted to write for people other than my dissertation committee and their colleagues" (xi). In *Life*, humor functions both as a form of social critique and as what Bérubé might call an "open access channel" through biting remarks such as, "Humans, it would appear, have an innate 'right to life'—but only until they're born. After that, it's their job to become self-sufficient" (51). This humor serves to temper his memoir's difficult language and academic citational practices (Wittgenstein figures prominently in the opening pages along with Faulkner). So too does Bérubé's focus on his two children: he animates theoretical explorations of genetics, language, and reproductive rights by embedding them in narratives about Jamie and Nick. Moreover, Bérubé challenges assumptions about access when he insists that readers' experiences with disability render his theoretical points clear to them regardless of their academic training. As he explores the intimate relations between language and social attitudes and practices, he asserts, "you don't have to be a poststructuralist or a postmodernist or a post-*anything* to get this; all you have to do is meet a parent of a child with Down syndrome" (32). As a "crossover" work, *Life* does not shun contemporary theory but rather assumes its relevance and readability for a broader reading public who can arrive through their own experiences at its insights.

Academics' exhaustion with the language of theory, and their interest in the 1990s in writing "crossing-over" works in more accessible language and genres has not been accompanied by a higher tolerance for liberals. As Bérubé takes a leading role in reaching a nonacademic readership, he not only maintains a belief in theoretical discourse, but he also counters left academics' dismissal of liberals. In *Public Access* he argues that "radicals" must work to legitimate the center in order to combat the right, since "the moderates seem to have engaged in a kind of intellectual fire sale, unburdening themselves of 'controversial' ideas and positions with which they can no longer afford to be associated" (11). A pragmatist, Bérubé argues in *Public Access* the need for coalitions that bring together progressives, traditional liberals, and "fairminded fencesitters." Instead, according to Bérubé, "some wings of the academic left, armed with intricate critiques of What Is Insufficiently Oppositional, haven't seen an antagonist further right than Al Gore in a long, long time" (30). He further contends, "the very fact that the right is trying to divide progressive academics from their potential nonacademic political constituencies is our best indication that we cannot give up on the hope that cultural criticism can do some work in the world" (34). While acknowledging the validity of leftist critiques of liberalism, Bérubé also argues that "liberal constituencies are among the most likely to be persuaded that egalitarian conditions for the exercise of power do not yet exist and must be brought into being" (35). Bérubé uses *Life* to push liberalism to progressive limits on the issues he addresses, using humor and personal narrative without forgoing poststructuralist critique and without giving into it when it allows no room for human agency. For example, Bérubé exposes the exorbitant costs of medical care, especially for those without health insurance, and he critiques a system that spends so much time identifying Down syndrome in utero and so little time researching how to treat it symptomatically ex utero (43, 76, 78). At the same time, he proffers optimism about the medical benefits and social services available to his child in a way that offers hope to parents and others addressing disabilities, and encouragement that it is possible to exercise agency and make resourceful use of the system. This attention to what the state and its workers are doing well is part of a pragmatic politics. As Bérubé acknowledges early on in *Life*, for him to engage in relentless critique would be a luxury since both of his sons would have died in infancy without advanced medical care (11). By refusing a wholesale denouncement of the state while subjecting its institutions to rigorous critique, Bérubé works to appeal to, rather than alienate, liberals and other readers for whom disability issues are not merely theoretical.

Academics who write their memoirs instead of more scholarly works are often accused by other academics of "selling out," especially if their work successfully reaches a mainstream readership. In *Higher Education under Fire* Bérubé addresses the dual meaning of "selling out" (217). Arguing that "having a full house" need not entail "abandoning one's principles," Bérubé details his response to a colleague who accuses him of selling out because not only has he written a memoir, but he also has published its conclusion in *Harper's* (and received honorable mention for it in *Best American Essays* for 1994). In this excerpt Bérubé plays off the platitude "do unto others," reinvigorating it as he adapts it to highlight Deaf culture and, more generally, disability issues, with the claim that we should "sign unto others as we would have them sign unto us." His colleague takes this conclusion as evidence that Bérubé is pandering to a popular readership. Bérubé explains: "I told my colleague that matters were even worse than he thought: I actually *believe* my conclusion . . . . That's no sellout, I said, that's just me" (220). At the same time Bérubé recognizes "that our task in selling out is not to capitulate to the terms our historical moment has offered us, but rather to find the terms with which we can best *contest* those terms, and in so doing redescribe and redefine both our cultural politics and our social policies" (240). This is precisely what Bérubé accomplishes in his memoir. Some of the other memoirs in *Academic Lives*, in reaching out, "sell out," as the seductions of the genre combine with the authors' own success so that they do not push against the memoir form or productively occupy its contradictions. In contrast, along with Edward Said's *Out of Place*, *Life* suggests how the dictates of the genre do not demand a "selling out" that plays into the problems of liberalism. As Bérubé works within a popular literary form to represent Jamie to his readers, he not only contests and redescribes specific public policy issues that pertain to reproductive rights, prenatal testing, health care, family leave, and health insurance, but he also redefines life as we (should) know it.

Almost ten years later, Bérubé picked up Jamie's story—and his commentary on disability issues—in his blog—a forum that, unlike the book form of memoir, allows for immediacy, updates, and dialogue involving a wide range of readers. Unlike memoir, blogs enable academics to intermix personal stories about and images from daily life, analysis of unfolding political events, and responses from and about particular institutional locations. Blogs allow writers to respond to events with an immediacy that memoir and its processes of publication foreclose, making it possible for writers to try out ideas in provisional ways. Moreover, as Bérubé contends in *Rhetorical Occasions*, blogs not only can chronicle daily life, but they also serve "as a legitimate vehicle for cultural criticism, occasional essays, extended book reviews, and political satire" (290). Their generic indeterminacy allows bloggers to move effortlessly between these different registers, much as people do in their daily lives. With their mix of daily thoughts, family pictures, and off-the-cuff political analysis, they offer unrefereed, relatively free spaces that, given their human interest attractions and, sometimes, the blogger's stature, draw wide readerships.

Bérubé's blog—which he started in 2004 and ended in 2007 and then resumed again in 2008, and which receives up to nine thousand hits a day, and anywhere from a few to a few hundred responses to each entry—suggests possibilities for how academics can build on their public persona and use personal narrative to create online discursive communities that are democratic in nature.[37] Bérubé introduces the last section to his book *Rhetorical Occasions*, a selection of excerpts from his blog, by relaying husband-and-wife blogging team Patrick and Teresa Nielsen Hayden's conviction that "blogs have managed to re-create the zine fandoms and readerships of the 1980s" (290). At the same time he notes, "blogs attempt to create a virtual public sphere in which claims can be advanced irrespective of the identity of the claimant" (290). In other words, although blogs build on the star system, they are more democratic and communal in structure (and, for better and for worse, can circumvent identity politics). As Bérubé observes, the best blogs "are renowned not only for the quality of their writing but for the quality of writing they stimulate in response" (289). In distinction to memoir, then, blogs constitute interactive sites that invite dialogue between blogger and reader, and provide viewers access to a variety of other sites, including other blogs, that can be accessed with a keystroke. They also offer academics a way to disseminate ideas that does not depend on an ever-shrinking academic book publishing industry. The lack of any review process or need to generate sales also means that blogs serve as sites in which academics can exercise their thoughts and ideas with relative freedom, and tell many different stories.

For Bérubé his blog in part extends the work of *Life as We Know It* in new directions. He notes that the most popular of his many blog topics is Jamie, and the blog features photos of him, and anecdotes, sometimes accompanied by analysis, of things Jamie has done and said. Bérubé also occasionally corrects his claims in *Life*: in the blog entry, "Was I Ever Wrong [13 April 2005]" (published as the conclusion to *Rhetorical Occasions*), he apologizes to Jamie for implying "that a child with Down syndrome will never have the intellectual capacity to understand the Beatles' oeuvre" (328). After describing Jamie's command of the Beatles, he writes, "And so, Jamie, I admit it. Even when I was trying to represent you to the best of my ability ten years ago, I underestimated you. I was wrong, and I apologize. And [echoing one of Jamie's Beatles references] through thick and thin, I will always be your friend" (330). As Bérubé continues Jamie's story in his blog (and then encodes his blog in book form, using one form to support the other), he demonstrates new possibilities for a kind of "memoir-on-the-go" that disrupts the hierarchies of the star system and that invites intellectual connections and community. As he places Jamie's story alongside other entries that range in subject from disability studies conferences, to electoral politics, to ice hockey, to liberalism, to family vacations, to Republican vice-presidential nominee

Sarah Palin, he once again puts Jamie at the center of a busy intersection, one full of possibilities for readers as well as Bérubé himself to forge unpredictable but productive connections among the wide range of subjects that together constitute life as Bérubé and his readers know it.

Memoir and Institutional Responsibility

Marking forms of disability through stories and analyzing them matters, and also is one way to begin thinking about how the general category of "disability" is one of problems as well as of possibilities. If the intersections at which we all stand are busy ones, it is far from a simple matter to map the various ways in which our paths meet, and it is easy to overlook ways in which these paths brutally diverge. In terms of how this translates to disability studies, counter to the claims of some critics, sensitivity to one type of disability does not necessarily engender awareness of or an emotionally intelligent response to other types, let alone to forms of oppression that fall outside the category of disability.

An opportunity to think through these issues presented itself to me when I attended the international Pacific Rim Conference on Disabilities in spring 2004 at the Sheraton Waikiki in Honolulu. The keynote speaker opened the conference with a joke in acknowledgment of his lei: "I always wanted to get lei-ed in Hawai'i." On the one hand, the joke, though tasteless, seemed too trivial to dwell on. On the other, what made the speaker's cultural ignorance possible, and a structural part of the conference itself, was how conference organizers with the UH Center on Disability Studies promoted Hawai'i as a vacation destination. In order to draw participants able to pay the conference's registration fees, organizers touted Hawai'i's location, and also Hawaiian cultural markers, without any perceptible attention during the conference to Hawai'i's ongoing colonial history. Colonialism remains a present-day condition in Hawai'i, one supported by continuing U.S. control over and military occupation of land that legally belongs to Native Hawaiians.[38] As a number of Native Hawaiian scholars and activists have contended, it is sustained as well by the tourist industry's commodification of Native Hawaiians, including the proliferation of transnationally owned Waikīkī hotels that, especially for Hawaiians, have environmentally, economically, culturally, and politically devastating effects.[39] Some of these effects connect directly to disability studies: cancer, diabetes, obesity, mental illness, and other chronic health conditions suffered by disproportionate numbers of Native Hawaiians arguably have their roots in the processes of colonization.[40] These conditions are at once collective and individually experienced, personally felt ones. If those working in disability studies are to contribute to realizing its goals of social and political justice for all, we must mark forms of disability that remain invisible. We also must take on the challenging work of analyzing the connections between disability and forms of oppression based on other identity categories, exposing and working to transform the institutional structures and histories that create and perpetuate them. So, for example, to hold a conference in Waikīkī—a crossroads of the Pacific—offers an opportunity to consider ways in which issues of disability articulate with the forms of sexism and colonialism that the speaker's joke evidenced. As the books considered in this chapter suggest, memoirs that engage disability studies are particularly well suited to explore these intersections, not least because they can bring home to a potentially wide readership the personal effects—and thus the stakes of transforming—forms of oppression that otherwise too often remain abstractions or isolated and underanalyzed experiences. In ways *Academic Lives* begins, I hope, to suggest, creating such an inclusive but also critical form of humanism is work that is as insistently personal as it is pressing.

At the start of the new millennium, as memoir's currency continues, it is accompanied by a new, post–September 11 phenomenon: a McCarthy-like assault by the media and politicians on academics' freedom to express views critical of U.S. foreign policy.[1] This clampdown frequently takes place in the name of championing the very principles of free expression that it undermines. Moreover, as early-twenty-first-century high-profile cases against academics such as Ward Churchill, Joseph Massad, and Norman Finkelstein illustrate, what is striking is that many of these attacks on free speech are mounted against individual academics in ways that conflate engaging in Left political analysis with rude or dishonest behavior.[2] Thus, the practice of progressive politics becomes a form of unprofessional conduct, and "uncivil" behavior or "bad citizenship" becomes, interchangeably, anti-Americanism *and* rudeness.[3] This post–September 11 tactic on the part of neoconservatives is not new but resonates, for example, with how objections to proposed changes in hiring practices in the UH English Department were dismissed as uncollegial (chapter 2) or with how political protest by student activists at UH was disregarded as "a lack of civility" (chapter 4). Thus we currently have an academy in which the personal and the political appear to be sharply bifurcated. At the same time that professors are rewarded for publishing accounts of their individual experiences and intimate thoughts, they are experiencing mounting pressures not to present oppositional political views in classrooms, in faculty governance, or even in their scholarship.[4]

In a culture in which personal feelings, political positions and platforms, human-interest narratives, and institutional histories so complexly support and undermine one another, humanist narratives have a role to play. In this conclusion I briefly consider the possibilities memoir holds for forwarding a far-reaching humanism that can help counter the crackdown on critical dissent. I speculate about ways that academics can harness the power of personal narrative, which is neither inherently conservative nor progressive, to maintain a place in and beyond the academy for an oppositional politics that is premised on a humanism that opposes exclusions and false universalisms.

In contrast to the climate in the 1980s academy, humanist discourses in the early twenty-first century can be effectively employed for counter-hegemonic purposes. During the culture wars, progressives' battle for new curricula and the abolishment of entrenched canons depended on challenging an exclusionary humanism. Conservatives made their arguments in the name of a humanism that they defended from professors and students purportedly out to replace the great works of Western culture with comic books and political tracts. In the post–September 11 era, humanism—especially a humanism that opposes false universalisms and "West vs. the rest" binaries—has a more progressive role to play. Those on the Left arguably must rely on humanist discourses to counter the attempt to outlaw critical thinking and to replace a liberal arts education with one that follows a corporate or consumerist model. As the mainstream media give students and other taxpayers a vocabulary and license to curtail not only cultural and ethnic and women's studies but also critical thought, appeals to humanism can be marshaled to disarm this attack.

As I seek in *Academic Lives* to understand memoir's currency in the 1990s academy, I consider how memoirs by academics uphold as well as disrupt and positively reconfigure the return of exclusionary forms of humanism. In pointing to the conservative role they play in the academy today, I argue that memoirs can reinforce individualism; that they at times naturalize and perpetuate the star system and class, race, and other hierarchized structures of privilege; and that they can participate in the academy's co-optation of identity politics, feminist politics, and other oppositional politics and practices. I also insist that attention to memoirs by academics can expose unexamined forms of privilege or self-interest that undergird cultural theories themselves—including, for example, theories of identity politics, cosmopolitanism, and diaspora. And throughout, I demonstrate how memoirs make manifest the need to take on the challenging work of considering disparate fields of study as intersecting rather than as distinct. At the same time, I look to the more progressive possibilities of academic memoirs and the cultural theories that they embody and disseminate within and beyond the humanities. Contemporary academic memoirs that engage cultural theory can, I argue, make interventions in academic and wider cultural spheres that carry on the work of third world, feminist, disability, and cultural studies scholars and activists; counter Us-Them ways of dividing the world; and bring together the humanities, humanism, and human-rights agendas. I claim that memoir's ties to liberalism and its traditionally humanist form create bridges between humanism and human-rights struggles, and between cultural studies critics and nonacademic audiences.

Creating such bridges is particularly important in the present day, and in the remainder of this conclusion, I consider how the currency and crossover capacities of memoir, and its popular reception as a de-politicized, personal, and unthreatening literary form, make it a vehicle through which academics might employ a humanist discourse to disseminate positions that oppose violence-inducing binaries. In a culture in which individual personalities stand in so readily for political positions, it is worth considering whether memoirs afford academics one way to circumvent and creatively resist, if not overturn, attempts on the part of mainstream media and legislators to eradicate the expression of political dissent in the academy and beyond.

Such a practice of memoir cannot, of course, be prescribed. This is especially true when some academics seem to be turning to memoir precisely because it offers a vehicle for more purely interior explorations, and a rejection of institutional engagements and structural analysis that can be emotionally exhausting and spiritually sapping. And yet, as I hope that the heterogeneity of the memoirs considered in *Academic Lives* begins to suggest, the turn to memoir cannot be generalized, and it affords possibilities for reimagining a humanism that refuses repressive ways of dividing the world. Many academics, in fact, take up the genre because they wish to communicate a political agenda or an institutional critique in a way that will appeal to a cross-over audience.

This urge is particularly strong in the post–September 11 era, which has seen both the decline (if not the disappearance) of the academic star system and threats to academic freedom that, combined with renewed acts of U.S. imperialism and attacks on the most basic of human rights as well as on civil liberties, have resulted in a new soberness in the humanities. From today's perspective an academic culture of celebrity and gossip looks tawdry; the stakes for conjoining humanism, the humanities, and human rights are high; and academic memoirs can appear decadent. Nonetheless, academic memoirs continue to be published in this first decade of the twenty-first century, and in steady numbers. And although some attempt to ignore the current critical crossroads (i.e., Lang, *Life on the Tenure Track*; Perloff, *The Vienna Paradox*), others are sites of negotiation.

A cursory comparison of Marianna Torgovnick's *The War Complex: World War II in Our Time* (2005) with her *Crossing Ocean Parkway* (1994) provides one register of changes brought on by the post–September 11 climate. Like *Crossing*, *The War Complex* is part memoir, part history, part literary criticism. However, it departs from *Crossing* in its urgent focus on an international landscape. September 11, Torgovnick contends in the prologue to *War Complex*, offers "a point of entry into the war complex but, as I hope to show, [it] can also be a point of exit" (xiv). In the epilogue she circles back to this idea: "For our culture to exit from the war complex, we've got to start from our reality, project a future—even if it is, at first, only imagined—and build from there to an ethic large enough to include others as though they were our families or ourselves" (144). In other words, for Torgovnick, personal stories have a role to play in formulating an ethic that encompasses others and that allows confirmation of their and one's own humanity without making them the same. This ethic marks a departure from the one discussed in chapter 2, in *Crossing*, where Torgovnick extended empathy to her father, at the expense of the young black men in her neighborhood whom she did not know, and with whom she makes no attempt to identify. And yet, as Torgovnick presses in *The War Complex* on the need to identify beyond one's self and one's family, she does not fall into glib universalisms. In a chapter titled "Eichmann's Ghost," Torgovnick claims, "The cliché 'Eichmann is in all of us' sounds like an immersion in the gray zone, an acceptance of the complexities and ambiguities of identification—but it's not. In fact, it evades the ethical process of identification and empathy I have described, which requires not blanket identification with anyone and anything at all, but parsing the possibilities of empathy and identification situation by situation" (69). If such a statement does not align Torgovnick with Ward Churchill when, in the wake of September 11, he likened some of the workers killed in the World Trade Center to "little Eichmanns," neither, in combination with her statements urging an ethic of identification with the other, does she endorse a universalizing form of humanism.[5] Such a humanism would encompass a kind of empathy and identification that can be used to defend the most inhuman of acts, whether they be those of suicide bombings or of open-ended acts of war and aggression on the part of the United States against those living within its borders or in other parts of the world.

In its opening and closing moments, what *The War Complex* suggests are the possibilities for using family stories to shape larger histories:

personal stories become a means of struggling with questions of ethics and identification, without losing sight of the larger structures in which we are situated. As responses to the life and death of Edward Said made clear (see chapter 3), neoconservatives are all too adept at telling tales about individuals to divide people and to perpetuate histories of colonialism and imperialism. And yet, personal stories—and a return to humanism—also can serve in the post–September 11 era as the basis for connecting with others without ignoring the institutions and histories that differently structure people's lives and worlds. Given the current crisis in the academy and in the wider culture, interventions on both academic and broader playing fields seem not only important but also necessary. In a period characterized by decreasing opportunities for academics (and others) to give voice to counterhegemonic narratives, the memoir movement and the cultural obsession with individual stories can provide academics with a means, albeit a modest one, for harnessing the power of personal stories to shape collective histories.

NOTES

Chapter 1. The Academic Memoir Movement

1. In addition to those referenced in this book, a partial list of humanities scholars in the United States who have published memoirs from the late 1980s to the present includes Michael Awkward, Sharon Cameron, Joy Castro, Mary Ann Caws, Henry Louis Gates, June Jordan, Annette Kuhn, Toni McNaron, Josie Mendez-Negrete, Nancy Miller, Reynolds Price, and Robert Stepto. The majority are literary critics, located in English or literature departments, sometimes with affiliations in women's studies or African American studies.

2. One of the few studies to discuss memoirs by academics extensively is Nancy Miller's 2002 *But Enough about Me*. However, Miller's focus is primarily on women's experiences of aging, friendship, and parent-child relationships. Moreover, as a writer of memoir herself, Miller defends the genre against charges of narcissism by using "personal criticism" and stressing memoir's capacity to establish textually based moments of recognition and identification for women. My approach includes a critique of the limitations of reading for identification, as I instead foreground structural issues of power in relation to memoirists' institutional location (see, especially, chapter 2). Aside from Miller's book, Aram Veeser's *Confessions of the Critics* (1996), Diane Freedman, Olivia Frey, and Francis Murphy Zauhar's *The Intimate Critique* (1993), and Freedman and Frey's *Autobiographical Writing Across the Disciplines* (2003) are widely read collections that have served more to evidence academic autobiographical writing than to reflect on and theorize critics' autobiographical turns.

Recent calls for papers (including those for an interdisciplinary conference titled "Academic Autobiography, Intellectual History, and Cultural Memory in the 20th Century" to be held at the University of Navarra in Pamplona, Spain, in March 2009) on academic memoir suggest the critical tide may be turning.

3. This reception articulates with the polarized reception that memoir has received in nonacademic venues, where responses range from Patrick Smith's denouncement in the *Nation* of memoir's focus on the "purely personal" or William Gass's satirical attack in *Harper's* on "Autobiography in an Age of Narcissism" to *New York Times Magazine*'s applause for "The Age of the Literary Memoir" as the success of a form of writing that is democratic and accessible.

4. My own entry into this project is perhaps symptomatic of this. I finished my first academic book with my tenure secured, with the luxury of a teaching-free

summer stretching before me. Too well interpellated into academe to spend the summer reading novels and hiking, and not yet ready to engage in the research needed to develop a new project, I picked up a few academic memoirs. These, it seemed to me, occupied an in-between territory, a way to catch without becoming immersed within academic currents. I approached the memoirs with my critic's radar turned low and with a combination of curiosity, idleness, and exhaustion not deep enough to warrant a turning away from the academy and its concerns altogether.

5. For analyses of the conditions in the present-day academy, see Aronowitz's *The Knowledge Factory*, Brennan's *Wars of Position*, Miyoshi's "Ivory Tower in Escrow," Readings's *The University in Ruins*, S. Slaughter and Leslie's *Academic Capitalism*, or Washburn's *University, Inc.*

6. See, for example, Anzaldúa's *Borderlands/La frontera* or Moraga's *Loving in the War Years*.

7. The same holds true for memoir's role in dominant U.S. culture, wherein the obsession with individual stories and entertaining media personalities arguably substitutes for, and fatally distracts from, analysis of larger stories that need telling. A recent example of this can be found in the 2006 controversy surrounding James Frey's memoir, *A Million Little Pieces*. When the investigative Web site the Smoking Gun (www.TheSmokingGun.com) exposed its lies, the resulting media storm stood in striking contrast to the relative silence over the release of the Downing Street Memo, exposing how the Bush administration had marshaled made-up intelligence to justify the invasion of Iraq.

8. In *Reading Autobiography*, Sidonie Smith and Julia Watson also provide a useful account of critics who have remarked on the use of the personal in the academy. Critics whose work they address include Smith in *Moving Lives* and Rita Felski, Suzanne Fleischman, and Herman Rapaport.

9. Perusal of Amazon.com sales figures supports my point that memoirs do not ensure crossover appeal. On July 7, 2005, whereas Edward Said's *Orientalism* ranked 8,977 in sales, his memoir *Out of Place* stood at 45,069, and Eve Sedgwick's *Between Men* ranked at 98,092 in comparison to her memoir *A Dialogue on Love*'s standing at 433,048. By contrast, Jane Tompkins's memoir *A Life in School* ranked 42,490 and *Sensationalist Designs* ranked 413,407. Even allowing for a large margin of error, these figures indicate striking discrepancies.

10. It is worth noting that Begley makes this assertion in *Lingua Franca* during the heyday of the star system, after Stanley Fish had recruited and made "stars" of renowned literary critics and catapulted the Duke University English department to fame. However, this period was followed by one of mass exodus from the department (though not from the profession itself) when the university went into receivership in the late 1990s. In his analysis of this history in *The Knowledge Factory*, Aronowitz notes that the fate of the Duke English department—and indeed, the disappearance of *Lingua Franca*—evidence the perils of

the star system. Thus, if the risks of writing memoir are more felt than materially realized ones, as I discuss later in this book, the instabilities of the star system are real.

11. For a particularly influential poststructuralist evacuation of human agency, see Michel Foucault's statement in *The Order of Things*: "As the archeology of our thought easily shows, man is an invention of recent date. And one perhaps nearing its end" (388).

12. As Bill Readings notes, with the publication of landmark cultural studies anthologies, 1990 marks the achievement of cultural studies' professional disciplinarity (97).

13. Important books that historicize emotions include Joel Pfister and Nancy Schnog's *Inventing the Psychological*, Helena Flam and Debra King's *Emotions and Social Movements*, and Jeff Goodwin, James Jasper, and Francesca Polletta's *Passionate Politics*.

14. In *Giving an Account of Oneself*, Judith Butler also provides insight into how one's life's story is importantly shaped by conventions of genre when she notes, "If I try to give an account of myself, if I try to make myself recognizable and understandable, then I might begin with a narrative account of my life. But this narrative will be disoriented by what is not mine, or not mine alone. And I will, to some degree, have to make myself substitutable in order to make myself recognizable. The narrative authority of the 'I' must give way to the perspective and temporality of a set of norms that contest the singularity of my story" (37). See also Ellen Rooney, who in "A Semiprivate Room" observes how "any typology of the social spaces of critical exchange must confront the question of form" (138).

15. For example, in "Policing Truth," Leigh Gilmore historicizes autobiography "as a literary discourse that develops in line with the emergent political discourses of individualism" (72).

16. Claims such as Miller's have been contested, as Simpson does in *The Academic Postmodern*. In *Postmodernism, or, The Cultural Logic of Late Capitalism*, Fredric Jameson also provides an implicit challenge through his understanding that postmodernism is characterized by not only the disappearance of the subject, but also by a "liberation" from every kind of feeling (15) and from his contention that "our daily life, our psychic experience, our cultural languages, are today dominated by categories of space rather than by categories of time" (16). Read in relation to Jameson's definition of postmodernism, memoir, with its assertion of the self, emphasis on affect, and attention to time, can be read as a reaction *against* the tenets of postmodern theory and culture.

17. As defined in the online MIA: Encyclopedia of Marxism, "Individualism," a word "first used in a translation of de Tocqueville's *Democracy in America* in 1835," is "the ethos which emphasises the autonomy of the individual as against the community or social group." The Web site further explains that "the growth

of individualism in the 18th century played a crucial role in further bolstering the development of bourgeois society upon which it had been founded"; historically, the Web site details how "in Tribal Society, individual consciousness is absent, and only begins to develop on the basis of a social division of labour and in particular, the emergence of private property." <http://www.marxists.org/glossary/terms/i/n.htm>, accessed July 11, 2008.

18. Paul Gilroy, for one, remarks in *Against Race* on how "enlightenment pretensions toward universality were punctured from the moment of their conception in the womb of colonial space" (65).

19. For a history of humanism's role in education, see Torrance, 64.

20. For an overview of these and other humanist discourses, see Tony Davies' *Humanism*.

21. At the 2003 ASA Conference, at a session titled Premature Death, Ruth Wilson Gilmore brilliantly addressed how the rapidly moving line between the human and the inhuman, guilt and innocence, and violence and nonviolence plays a key role in keeping in place systems of oppression. See too Judith Butler's *Precarious Life* for analysis of the shifting and contextual nature of what constitutes the human, and the political stakes that attach to definitions of the human.

22. On the dismantling of the human subject, see Said's account in *Beginnings* of how for French new critics, "Man is occasionally *a* measure of things, but by no means is he *the* measure" (374).

23. In 2001 Robert M. Torrance finds that up until three or four decades ago, "Books and essays with 'humanism' in their titles crowded the library shelves. In contract, the term has recently seemed a dead letter, if not a term of opprobrium. . . . Humanism is now threatened by the worst fates of all, disdain, neglect, and irrelevance" (166).

24. In her president's column, "Human Rights and the Humanities," in the *MLA Newsletter*, as she reports on this conference, Stanton predicts that we are about to "witness the emergence of a new interdisciplinary field, one that conjoins the critical and interpretive practices of the humanities with the ethical activism of the international human rights political movement."

25. See Said, "An Interview with Edward W. Said (1999)," 433. See also *Humanism and Democratic Criticism*, where Said attributes the lack of public support for universities to a failed humanism, one he urges humanities scholars to revive.

26. Theorists including Butler (*Precarious Life*), JanMohamed and Lloyd, Satya Mohanty, Minh T. Nguyen, Martha Nussbaum, Ellen Rooney, Naomi Schor, and S. Shankar also have mounted recent arguments on behalf of a reformulated humanism.

27. Although I do not analyze memoirs that unequivocally endorse an old-fashioned humanism with the assumption that they have less to say about the current cultural milieu than those considered in *Academic Lives*, such projects

exist. For example, William Pritchard's *English Papers* and Alvin Kernan's *In Plato's Cave* nostalgically embrace a humanism eroded by a "p.c." politics. Don Snyder's *The Cliff Walk* and Marjorie Perloff's *The Vienna Paradox* likewise support outdated humanist values, albeit from strikingly different vantage points.

28. This is true as well for other academics not addressed in detail in this book. Mark Edmundson, for example, follows his memoir *Teacher* with lectures with titles such as "Humanism and Faith," "What's a Liberal Arts Education For?," and "What Is Humanism?"

29. In *Memory Speaks*, as Jill Ker Conway observes, given the "outpouring" of memoirs about parents, "what Rousseau introduced as a first chapter in his *Confessions* now occupies an entire volume" (152).

30. A few examples of U.S. scholars from other disciplines writing memoirs include psychologist Roger Brown; historians Peter Carroll, Martin Duberman, Jo Freeman, and Alice Wexler; anthropologist Michael Dorris; economist Deirdre McCloskey; and law professor Patricia Williams.

Chapter 2. Whiteness Studies and Institutional Autobiography

1. This Gloria Anzaldúa passage comes from the essay "*Tlilli, Tlapalli*, the Path of the Red and Black Ink," which I have located in two Norton anthologies— *Postmodern American Fiction* (1998) and *The Norton Anthology of Literature by Women* (1996). *The Heath Anthology of American Literature* also includes work from *Borderlands*, as do many composition textbooks and anthologies on multiculturalism.

2. In "Speaking in Tongues" Anzaldúa urges women of color, "Write on the bus or the welfareline. . . . While you wash the floor or clothes listen to the words chanting in your body" (171).

3. The politics of collegiality has begun to receive attention, although mostly in regard to pressures untenured faculty members experience. See the "Collegiality" section in the MLA publication *Profession 2006*.

4. As exemplified by memoirs such as Rob Nixon's *Dreambirds* and Dalton Conley's *Honky*, white men as well as white women use memoir to do antiracist work.

5. Whereas in the U.S. studies of ethnicity used to focus on white ethnic groups, racial minorities have been the focus since the inception of ethnic studies programs in the late 1960s until the advent of whiteness studies in the 1990s. Who is considered "ethnic" depends largely on the political climate.

6. See, for example, Carby's *Reconstructing Womanhood*; hooks's *Yearning*; and Morrison's *Playing in the Dark*.

7. Important studies with an antiracist focus include, for example, Noel Ignatiev's *How the Irish Became White*; the journal *Race Traitor*; David R. Roediger's

Towards the Abolition of Whiteness; and *Displacing Whiteness*, edited by Ruth Frankenberg.

8. The January 1998 *PMLA*, a special issue on ethnicity coordinated by Sander Gilman, includes six articles, three of which concern Jewish identity, plus an introduction by Gilman and a forum. Despite the excellence of these essays, as a collective statement about the academy's position toward ethnicity, I find the issue disturbing for its inattention to present-day material conditions and racial inequities.

9. For thoughtful considerations of such problems see, for example, Mike Hill's introduction to the *Minnesota Review*'s 1996 "white issue" and, in this same issue, Peter Chvany's "What We Talk about When We Talk about Whiteness."

10. Although these narratives mark Hirsch's displacement without re-marking her white privilege, by including the photos and insisting on the subjective nature of reading them, Hirsch enables resistant readings such as my own.

11. I owe this insight to Laura Lyons.

12. My critiques of *Family Frames* are ones that benefit from the body of postcolonial feminist theory that exists at the time of my writing; "Pictures" might have been written quite differently a decade later. Indeed, when I encountered Hirsch at Australian National University, at "Testimony and Witness: From the Local to the Transnational," a 2006 symposium for which she was a keynote speaker, in her two lectures and during discussions, Hirsch's many comments addressing issues of identification and difference suggested to me that our approaches to Anzaldúa in 2006 probably would be much more aligned ones. At the same time, as I discuss near the end of this chapter, the problems of how to theorize white ethnicity and how to maintain oppositional practices of identity politics in the academy have not become obsolete with the passing of the 1990s, and with gains in theories of race and gender. Moreover, while problems attend white feminists' attempts to build on theories of identity politics that women of color have introduced into the academy, ignoring these theories presents no solution, either. An instructive counterpoint exists between Hirsch's use of identity politics in her memoir, and Marjorie Perloff's in *The Vienna Paradox*. Whereas Hirsch implicitly builds on and supports the identity politics of women of color, Perloff defies such a politics, even as her memoir explores her ethnic identity and registers identity politics' impact. In her memoir she consistently refuses the moves that those versed in an identity politics would expect: she states that although she left Vienna as a refugee from the Nazis in 1938 when she was six, she "had no horrific tale to tell" (xiv). She dismisses the one experience of anti-Semitism that she experienced in school in New York as an aberration (145). She celebrates adopting the "golden Manhattan name [Marjorie] rather than the 'foreign' Gabrielle" (169). In a moment that stands in direct counterpoint to that in "Pictures" when Hirsch gives her school speech, in the epilogue to *The Vienna Paradox* Perloff includes a chapter she wrote as "a child patriot" titled

"The Statue of Liberty," in which she details going afterward to a café where "the *Sachertorte* tasted sweet." (257). At every turn Perloff refuses what critics of identity politics would call a "victim" narrative, instead telling a celebratory story of assimilation that is strikingly at odds with the critical currents in the U.S. academy. On the one hand, Perloff's insistence on looking to her own and others' forms of privilege is refreshing and important. On the other hand, her refusal to consider how systemic forms of oppression can and do operate in the United States limits her analysis of U.S. life and culture.

13. In "Slasher Stories" (*Crossing Ocean Parkway*) Torgovnick more successfully interweaves personal narrative and social analysis. As she brilliantly intertwines an analysis of slasher stories with the painful and moving account of the death of her son, she complicates the gendered analysis she forms in her reading of the slasher stories.

14. As I discuss in the conclusion to *Academic Lives*, over ten years later, in *The War Complex* Torgovnick forwards a more compelling and far-reaching account of the importance of empathy and identification; see, for example, 145.

15. Such a use of memoir is not a given. In *Honky*, for example, Dalton Conley, a sociologist at New York University, posits his memoir, an account of growing up as a white child in an inner-city housing project, as capturing truths that his statistical surveys cannot convey (206).

16. In some ways, Lim's memoir, which asserts her commitment to feminist community—and which expresses Lim's indebtedness to Miller herself, and describes her experience in Miller's National Endowment for the Humanities seminar—invites Miller's reading. For example, Lim states, "Although some feminist theorists have bracketed the concept of 'sisterhood' as an anachronistic embarrassment, it is the only term I can find to suggest not only the necessity for coalition and the work of solidarity but also the sensibility of support that grows when social gender is recognized as a shared experience" (156–57). Even here, however, Lim's attention to coalition and solidarity, and the passages that surround this remark, which underline Lim's differences from the white, middle-class feminists that she meets in graduate school, differentiate her position from Miller's.

17. Whereas Lazarre moves toward overriding the importance of race, African American memoirists exploring racial identity tend to hold such a position in tension with one maintaining the importance of race. For example, the title of James McBride's memoir, *The Color of Water: A Black Man's Tribute to His White Mother*, maintains both positions. Or, in *BookMarks: Reading in Black and White: A Memoir*, even as Karla FC Holloway concludes her memoir with a color scheme for shelving her books that defies race schemes and instead asserts "a certain quiet and calm and an order of my own" (193), race's centrality remains the subject of her memoir.

18. These criticisms applied to some memoirs by academics of color, too. However, given the scarcity of academics of color, my graduate class discussed how

these memoirs—including some that do not foreground issues of institutional racism—can serve antiracist functions in universities. Memoirs we found to be particularly effective in this way included Lim's *Among the White Moon Faces*, Deborah McDowell's *Leaving Pipeshop*, and Victor Villanueva Jr.'s *Bootstraps: From an American Academic of Color*.

19. For an account of the difficult process of cutting down the manuscript, see Anzaldúa's preface to *This Bridge We Call Home*, 4. The second volume envisioned by the editors has yet to be published.

20. Relevant to this situation are identity politics in Hawai'i that include divisions among people of color who identify as "local" and those not from Hawai'i. For insights into this dynamic, see Candace Fujikane and Jonathan Okamura's special issue of *Amerasia*, *Whose Vision? Asian Settler Colonialism in Hawai'i*.

Chapter 3. Postcolonial Studies and Memoirs of Travel, Diaspora, and Exile

1. Amazon.com's customer reviewers register Mura's immersion in academe when they take his memoir to task for its academic jargon (accessed July 8, 2008).

2. The resurgence of interest in cosmopolitanism is registered by the many journals and books that feature "cosmopolitanism" in their title. In addition to those cited in this chapter see, for example, Amanda Anderson, *The Powers of Distance*; Seyla Benhabib, *Another Cosmopolitanism*; Carol Breckenridge et al., eds., *Cosmopolitanism*; Pheng Cheah, *Inhuman Conditions*; Jacques Derrida, *On Cosmopolitanism and Forgiveness*; Camilla Fojas, *Cosmopolitanism in the Americas*; Steven Vertovec and Robin Cohen, eds., *Conceiving Cosmopolitanism*; and Kok-Chor Tan, *Justice without Borders: Cosmopolitanism, Nationalism, and Patriotism*.

3. Mixed-genre works constitute another important form through which diaspora is being theorized. In *Mirror Talk*, Susanna Egan, who claims that "explorers of diasporic identity are surely the quintessential autobiographers of the late twentieth century," focuses on those autobiographers who "move among genres with an imaginative ease that suggests all borders are permeable" (122). Scholars who do this boundary-crossing work (albeit with greater complexity than Eagan's description allows for) include anthropologists such as Ruth Behar, James Clifford, Dorinne Kondo, and Ty Tengan, all of whom incorporate autobiographical narrative into their theory and fieldwork as a way to reposition themselves in a field under fire for assuming the objectivity of its predominantly white, Western, male, middle-class practitioners.

4. For a discussion of early Asian American writers' ambassadorlike roles, see Elaine Kim, *Asian American Literature*.

5. For an overview of the history Davidson is working within, see H. D. Harootunian, "America's Japan/Japan's America."

6. As Masao Miyoshi notes in *Off Center*, during this period Japan had a higher per capita income than the United States; eight of the ten largest banks were Japanese; the Japanese corporation Nippon Telegraph and Telephone was worth more than IBM, AT&T, General Motors, General Electric, and Exxon combined; Japanese investors shouldered nearly one-third of the United States budget deficit; and the total real estate value of Japan was double that of the United States (64).

7. In her interview by Jeffrey Williams, Davidson asserts that her memoir is "informed by a constellation of my own personal politics, antiracist politics, multicultural politics, feminist politics, and there's an economic agenda" (172).

8. For a discussion of this tradition, see Inderpal Grewal, *Home and Harem*, esp. 50 and 84. See also Pratt, *Imperial Eyes*, esp. 171.

9. For a fascinating historical account (1870–1940) of white U.S. women's relationship to Orientalism, see Mari Yoshihara, *Embracing the East*.

10. For various perspectives on Japan's increasingly complex relationship to the West, see Joseph Tobin, ed., *Re-made in Japan*; Kondo, *About Face*; Miyoshi, *Off Center*; and Miyoshi and Harootunian, *Postmodernism and Japan*.

11. See Lisa Yoneyama, "Traveling Memories, Contagious Justice"; and Gwyn Kirk and Margo Okazawa-rey, "Women Opposing U.S. Militarism in East Asia."

12. This view of cosmopolitanism characterizes not only theory but also other memoirs of the 1990s. See, for example, Diawara, *In Search of Africa*.

13. In *Invisible Privilege*, Paula Rothenberg suggests the difficulty of using a deathbed scene to analyze race and class. The memoir ends with Rothenberg's encounter with her mother's caretaker, a woman of color who, as she was leaving her mother's tiny apartment, asks for a few of her mother's cheap belongings. Rothenberg imagines her mother berating her, "'Couldn't you wait until I was dead to pick over the remains?' Of course, she will be right. But then, so was I. What my mother had, even at the end, still looked like so very much—who could blame the aide for wanting to carry a piece of it away with her, and who would begrudge it to her? Some would say she had earned it" (229). This passage suggests the agonizing difficulty of subjecting the most painful of losses to structural analysis, especially when that analysis and one's emotional response do not line up.

An exceptionally powerful example of a memoir that brings together personal and structural analysis occurs in Karla FC Holloway, *BookMarks*. In oblique but movingly rendered moments, Holloway links her son's tragic life and death to that of Malcolm X's, without suggesting that the historical contexts of racism can wholly account for her son's story.

14. Here it is worth citing a point that Davidson herself makes in her 2004 introduction to *Revolution and the World*. Drawing on Lora Romero's work, she

contends, "we do not have to praise or condemn a given writer or genre that isn't oppositional ('subversive') enough. Opposition is part of, contiguous with, and a contributor to 'culture.' Opposition cannot be outside of culture, nor can writers (or anyone else). For Romero, it is not the job of the critic to find instances of subversion or complicity since power relations themselves are always mobile. This formulation frees us from what Paul Ricoeur calls a 'hermeneutics of suspicion' by which every action gets parsed out for its presumed political impurities" (26).

15. In *Turning Japanese*, Mura also works to counter the negative views of Japan that characterize Nisei memoir and fiction (e.g., John Okada, *No-No Boy*; Daniel Okimoto, *American in Disguise*; Monica Sone, *Nisei Daughter*; Yoshiko Uchida, *Desert Exile*).

16. Although outside the parameters of this study, it would be interesting to explore *Turning Japanese* in relationship to texts such as Michael Crichton, *The Rising Sun*; Miyamoto Musashi, *The Book of Five Rings*; or William Ouchi, *Theory Z*.

17. The song carries additional meanings when considered in broader relation to Mura's autobiographical writing. In *Where the Body Meets Memory*, he describes obsessively masturbating to images of white women, linking this activity to the history of racism against Japanese Americans. So, too, the song's expressions of boredom resonate with Mura's.

18. Investigations of diaspora and transnationalism within Asian contexts continue; more recent scholars doing this work include Kandice Chuh, Monisha Das Gupta, Gayatri Gopinath, Laura Kang, and Sheng-mei Ma.

19. It is interesting to note how often references to urination are used to insert the body into writing—the most widely known example occurs in Jane Tompkins, "Me and My Shadow."

20. Mura also shows how postmodernism can prop up patriarchal narratives: while a "straight" reading of Mishima gives Mura a model for a heroic authentically Japanese masculinity, a postmodernist one supports Mura's interest in performative notions of identity and sexuality, and his investments in maintaining a sense of irony and a gendered sense of "cool." See Alan Wolfe, "Suicide and the Japanese Postmodern," for a postmodernist reading of Mishima.

21. See Miyoshi, "Against the Native Grain," esp. 147.

22. For a work by a Japanese American that highlights rather than erases differences of gender, region, and class, see Kondo, *Crafting Selves*, esp. 63–71.

23. Given Mura's attraction to Japanese traditions with cultural capital in Europe, it seems fitting that Kenzo lives in France and displays his work in Paris.

24. In "Turning Japanese/Returning to America" I frame the discussion of Mura presented here in relation to his support for Lois-Ann Yamanaka's receipt of an AAAS literary award for her novel *Blu's Hanging*. I argue that in his position in this controversy as in his memoir, Mura's focus on his individual experience enables him to neglect his own privilege in relation to other Asian

Americans—Filipinos in particular—and other U.S. racial minorities. Mura's position is symptomatic not only of fractures within Asian American studies and a pan-ethnic Asian American identity, but also of the problems that adhere within many contemporary memoirs that, despite their authors' poststructuralist sensibility, do not radically challenge the genre's basis in romanticized individualism. For an account of the *Blu's Hanging* controversy, see Candace Fujikane, "Sweeping Racism under the Rug of 'Censorship.'"

25. Nussbaum provides one example of this in *For Love of Country?* when she observes that Us-Them thinking can slide into "a general call for American supremacy" (x). In the volume's conclusion she contends, "the challenge of world citizenship . . . is to work toward a state of things in which all of the differences will be nonhierarchically understood" ("Reply" 138).

26. For example, Jorge Fernandes demonstrates how Nussbaum's model borrows from an earlier colonial cosmopolitanism that assumes European superiority (123).

27. The coexistence of Mura's cosmopolitanism and his investments in his American identity are not anomalous. As Cheah points out in *Cosmopolitics*, the perception that cosmopolitanism and nationalism are opposed is historically inaccurate (22).

28. In Mura's other work he writes extensively about how his addiction to pornography and sex relate to the history of Japanese American incarceration and to sexually demeaning stereotypes of Asian men. See *Where the Body Meets Memory* and *A Male Grief: Notes on Pornography and Addiction*.

29. Recent studies such as those by Gopinath and Martin Manalansan (*Global Divas*) in fact do this.

30. See, for example, his *The Argumentative Indian*.

31. In "The Currency of Feminist Theory," Jane Elliott comments on this phenomenon of dismissing lines of thought because they have become predictable: "Yet when we assume that familiar approaches can no longer serve as tools to dislodge the present, we demonstrate a continued affinity for the modern logic that equates the new, the interesting, and the valuable. In so doing, we sidestep the difficult realization that while intellectual work should be exciting, political work may be dull, that things may stay true longer than they stay interesting. Perhaps more significantly, we miss the opportunity to see what our boredom might have to tell us" (1701).

32. It is similarly both serendipitous and yet within the logic of institutions and their organization of knowledge that, while waiting at the Honolulu Academy of Arts to board the bus for the Shangri La tour, I wandered into a room displaying four prints from the 1848 *Thirty-six Views of Mount Fuji* series—two by Katsushika Hokusai, and two by Utagawa Hiroshigi. The museum headnotes focused on their influential importance to Impressionist artists including Monet and Van Gogh, each of whom owned one of the prints on display. Correspondingly

noteworthy: the Hokusai prints were gifts to the museum from James Michener, a contemporary of Doris Duke's who shared her attractions to Hawai'i and "the Orient."

33. For a fuller biography of Said, see Bayoumi and Rubin, introduction to *The Edward Said Reader*.

34. This documentary's May 1998 release was timed to commemorate the fiftieth anniversary of the *nakbah* (catastrophe).

35. As Said documents his obsessive relationship to time along with his exploration of space, or "place," his memoir complicates Susanna Eagan's claim in *Mirror Talk* that that "autobiographers of diaspora privilege space over time in order to retain all their possibilities. Space, as realized in these narratives, enables plural identities to coexist simultaneously despite their being contradictory" (158). In *Out of Place*, Said asserts plural simultaneously existing identities through his intensive investigation of time as well as space.

36. Said draws again on this quotation in *Zionism from the Standpoint of Its Victims*, in arguing for the need to understand what Zionism's victims endured in the framework provided by imperialism (130–31).

37. Given the Abu Ghraib prison scandal in spring 2004 and the debates surrounding whether the treatment of Iraqi prisoners qualifies as torture, Said's stance and his assertion that "torture is torture" ("Interview with Edward W. Said" 433) are ever more relevant. Indeed, in a 2004 *New Yorker* article, Seymour Hersh cites *The Arab Mind* for providing "the intellectual backdrop for the torture and sexual abuse that took place at Abu Ghraib," and an article by Emram Qureshi, "Misreading 'The Arab Mind,'" documents how the book is used to brief military teams being deployed to the Middle East. Said denounced *The Arab Mind*, originally published in 1973, in his chapter on contemporary Orientalists in *Orientalism*.

38. In the aftermath of September 11, 2001, if there is one thing that has become clear it is the extent to which binary thinking, and the division of the world into humans and those who do not meet this standard, continues to be key to an imperial politics. Indeed, if under President Clinton we had an affect of ambivalence, we might dub George W. Bush's presidency "the age of brutal binaries."

39. In this way, the memoir is consonant with his belief that theory gets impoverished and rarefied if not exposed to the complex enfolding of the social world. See Said, *Traveling Theory*, 211.

40. Said here can be seen to complicate his concept of "the affiliation order" as that which he argues in *The World, the Text and the Critic* "surreptitiously duplicates the closed and tightly knit family structure that secures generational hierarchical relationships to one another. Affiliation then becomes in effect a literal form of *re-presentation*, by which what is ours is good, and therefore deserves incorporation and inclusion in our programs of humanistic study, and what is not ours in this ultimately provincial sense is simply left out" (21–22). In this moment

in *Out of Place*, the affiliative does not duplicate the filiative but rather works in its service to secure the relationship between Said and his mother.

41. For Said's critique of the Western canon, see *The World, the Text and the Critic*, esp. 21 and 175.

42. The "family album" the memoir includes provides a way to trace Said's complex formulation of identity. On the one hand, the photographs show Said's British, American, and Arabic selves to be performative identities. For example, one page juxtaposes a studio picture of Edward and his sister Rosy "in traditional Palestinian dress," as the caption reads, with a picture of the siblings posed in Western-style prep school uniforms; both their British and their Palestinian identities appear equally staged. On the other hand, Said's family album, like his narrative, shows these identities to be no less real for being constructed: another picture of the children in their school uniforms captures them in an unposed moment at home. The family album forecloses readings that either would celebrate a hybrid and constructed identity, or that would use this hybridity to discredit Palestinian identity.

43. See Ashcroft and Ahluwalia for a discussion of Said's hostility to poststructuralism (7). See Parry for a discussion of the relationship between Said's poststructuralism and his humanism.

44. See Ammiel Alcalay's review "Stop Time in the Levant" for an insightful discussion of the fluidity and cultural crossings that characterized Said's childhood, before the consolidation of nation-states.

45. See Wicke and Sprinker, "Interview," for Said's discussion of Cairo as a metropolitan center that presents an alternative to Western and Levantine metropolitan sites (223).

46. See also Ahmed, *A Border Passage*, which includes a chapter addressing Arab nationalism from a strongly critical perspective.

47. For discussion of how cosmopolitanism is tied to consumerism, see Brennan, *Wars of Position*, esp. 206.

48. The last two articles, dated September 11, 1999, are discussed in Maya Jaggi, "The Guardian Profile: Edward Said." One of them also compares Said to Rigoberta Menchú. Also, FrontPageMagazine.com published an article by Jeff Jacoby that expresses dismay that Columbia University did nothing to punish Said for his "concocted tale of exile and dispossession," whereas a nineteen-year-old student who lied in order to get more time on an assignment was suspended for two years.

49. Said explains in "Defamation, Zionist Style" his response to Weiner: "I have been moved to defend the refugees' plight precisely because I did not suffer and therefore feel obligated to relieve the sufferings of my people, less fortunate than myself."

50. In "Places of Mind," Brennan argues that Said's reach outside the academy derives from his humanism (92).

51. For one account of the attacks on Said's character following his death and their implications, see Robert Fisk, "When Did 'Arab' Become a Dirty Word?"

52. On March 12, 1959, the U.S. Congress made Hawai'i a state, and then three months later conducted a plebiscite that gave voters only one voting option. The single question on the ballot was, "Shall Hawaii immediately be admitted into the Union as a State?" Those eligible to vote were any U.S. citizens or nationals who had lived in Hawai'i for at least a year. Out of a population of over 630,000 (with Hawaiians making up about 17 percent), the voting turnout was approximately 16 percent, with 132,773 people voting for statehood and 7,971 against. Thus Hawai'i became a state with only 15 percent of the population's approval, most of them settlers.

Chapter 4. Feminist Studies and the Academic Star System

1. My account of this meeting and its aftermath draws on written statements by Mamo Kim and Pi'ilani Smith that they delivered at the Nov. 15, 1999, public forum, and on e-mails sent to the faculty senate Listserv. These accounts were fairly consistent. Thanks to Mamo Kim for sharing her statement with me (Mamo Kim, "Statement to the Press on the Matter of Student Safety at UH-Mānoa," Nov. 15, 1999).

2. Kim, "Statement to the Press."

3. In withholding B's name I may be complicit in faculty members' protection of B. However, because my goal is to provide a more far-reaching critique of academic culture, I hope that this decision helps focus attention on, rather than perpetuates, the hierarchies of power that I analyze. I have honored the wishes of the students that their names appear in this account.

4. Testimony to the Mānoa Faculty Senate, Nov. 17, 1999.

5. Collins filed his grievance Nov. 12, 1999, and then amended it Nov. 19, 1999. The formal response came from the university on Jan. 13, 2000. Thanks to Lance Collins for sharing the contents of the university's letter with me that details Collins's grievance and also gives the university's formal response to it. The information in this paragraph all comes from Collins's account to me of the grievance process and from the letter.

6. Kernan's sense of being replaced by "women and minorities" runs through the pedagogy memoirs. One register of the mix of anxiety, hostility, and feelings of victimization that white male academics experience in this regard can be tracked through their identifications as "Indians." Sometimes, these moments are tied to a refusal of "politically correct" thinking. Kernan, for example, fondly reminisces about how he and his classmates used to drink and "paw" girls in cars and dark corners, resembling, in their "tribal rituals" "a bunch of young Indians in an Iroquois longhouse" (29). A particularly dramatic disregard for reigning cultural theories comes from Don Snyder in *The Cliff Walk*, as he identifies

with "Indians" in order to express his feelings of dispossession due to his status as a white man. Unemployed and embittered from having lost his job—a loss he attributes in part to not being a minority—he begins taking his son to a private golf course where, spying, they observe white male golfers cheating to win. They also encounter a stone marker that reads, "Here on June 24, 1713, Josiah Hunniwell, the great Indian fighter, and eighteen men were killed by Indians in a surprise attack." Snyder explains how he and his son made "good arrows in honor of the Indians who had been killed on the golf course, rather than the white men whose death was commemorated on the headstone. From then on, Jack and I were Indian warriors returning to reclaim the land that white men had taken from us. All golfers riding in carts were the cavalry . . . . It was us against them. Jack and me against the people in charge of things in this country, the inheritors of power and privilege, the people who were dedicated to keeping everything the way it always had been" (182). Snyder and his son spend "a long Indian summer" (183) on the golf course, hollering "Indian war cries" (183) and shooting arrows at the green (186). After Snyder is hired to work at the golf course, he learns that the manager was aware of but benevolently overlooked his and his son's activities. The ironies, reversals, and blindness to the racial privilege he has enjoyed while "playing Indian" go entirely unremarked in these passages.

If white men, in working through their relationship to authority, identify as Indians, we see women identifying as cowboys. As discussed later in this chapter, Jane Gallop has no qualms about occupying the position of cowboy. More surprisingly, as discussed in the next chapter, bell hooks takes up this role as well.

7. Although my interest lies the institutional analyses that a psychoanalytic focus can obscure, in my use of B, as well as in this and other symptomatic readings in this chapter, I am indebted to Gallop herself, who provides brilliant models for such a methodology in *The Daughter's Seduction*, *Reading Lacan*, and *Around 1981*.

8. See, for example, Sanger, "The Erotics of Torts," 1876.

9. For example, Benjamin Kunke makes note of this hallmark of contemporary memoirs in "Misery Loves a Memoir."

10. Particularly irresponsible is the contribution by Gallop's friend, James Kincaid. Violently rewriting Beckelman's representation of her kiss with Gallop, he ends his essay, "Away with power and bring on your mashing mouth and your sweet tongue. I wish I had been that student" (616). The positive spin he puts on "mashing"—the word Beckelman used to highlight the unpleasantness of the kiss—is especially distasteful.

11. See, for example, Gallop, *Around 1981*, iii, 238.

12. For accounts of ACT UP and Queer Nation, see Lauren Berlant, *The Queen of America Goes to Washington City*; or *Fear of a Queer Planet*, edited by Michael Warner.

13. For a discussion of how cross-dressing is transgressive only if the position of the transgressor is marginalized, see Anne McClintock, *Imperial Leather*. As someone with a child and in a monogamous heterosexual relationship, Gallop enjoys the benefits that come with a socially sanctioned lifestyle. At the same time, her endorsement of a queer or lesbian politics gains her cultural capital without carrying the costs that lesbian identity entails. For example, Gallop exited from PreText to deliver an invited talk at the "Anxious Pleasures: A Symposium on the Erotics of Pedagogy" conference held at the Center for Lesbian and Gay Studies at CUNY Graduate Center. In that talk, "Resisting Reasonableness" (later published in *Critical Inquiry*), Gallop argues for an understanding of student-teacher sex as "queer." Such a claim is to me symptomatic of how, in coming to describe any and all "differences" and desires, "queer" can become emptied of oppositional energy.

14. Gallop's actions bear out Cvetkovich's speculations in *Mixed Feelings* about how sensationalism serves to naturalize ideology: "Sensationalism thus produces the *embodiment*, in both the literal and figurative senses, of social structures. It not only renders them concrete, by embodying them in a single and powerful representation, but the responses it produces are bodily or physical experiences that seem immediate and natural" (24–25).

15. Permission to quote from the archives from this "Re/INter/VIEW" was granted to me by Vitanza, Gallop, and Beckelman. The conversation is archived in twelve parts; in the body of the text, I note which part of PreText citations are drawn from.

16. This forum's impertinence contrasts with that of the lecture format's; at the UC Berkeley talk, despite all the buzz about the sexual harassment case before and after Gallop's talk, the subject was studiously avoided during the Q&A.

17. That this view of performance as game playing is less carefully theorized in *FASH* than it is in Gallop's *Pedagogy: The Question of Impersonation* suggests, as I discuss later, that this naïveté is itself performative.

18. Gallop also disregards the fact that for some of her students lesbianism is not a role. Although Gallop's casualness about the gender of her sexual partners is in many ways progressive—her stance emphasizes the fluidity of sexual roles and presents lesbianism as hip, happening, and feminist—she ignores the responsibilities she might have to a vulnerable student population.

19. Another example of this occurs in *Anecdotal Theory* (2002). In the chapter "Castration Anxiety and the Unemployed Ph.D.," Gallop explores why a woman on the academic job market is surprised to learn that Gallop, too, once was an unemployed doctorate. Rather than analyze her institutional location, Gallop uses the setting for this encounter—the locker room—as the occasion to get "nakedly psychoanalytic" (131). The resulting analysis is decidedly less revealing (a fact that its "risque-ness" obscures) than a consideration of Gallop's institutional standing would be. Indeed, Gallop reduces her analysis to the understanding

that the woman "had presumed that I was phallic and she was castrated" (131). This essay's effectiveness depends on Gallop's representation of the locker room as both setting for the anecdote and as theoretical key. However, as the locker room's symbolic freight naturalizes Gallop's focus on "castration anxiety," it invites a crude form of psychoanalysis that distracts from a more searching analysis of Gallop's institutional location. The context for which Gallop wrote this essay—an MLA panel on job seeking—makes her approach even more inadequate. She posits her focus on castration as a way "to connect our scholarship with our professional situation" (134). However, Gallop here—and throughout *Anecdotal Theory*—sidesteps her professional situation in the name of scholarship. Moreover, her use of autobiography enables this dodge even as she claims for it (or "anecdote") an ability to allow for a fully embodied encounter between the personal, the professional, and the theoretical.

20. *FASH* displays an interesting (symptomatic) separation of psychoanalysis and institutional analysis and of the personal and the political from a scholar trained to explore their interrelations. Likewise, in "Talking Across," Gallop again resists a consideration of how the personal, political, and professional intermix in her relationships with her students. Included in *Generations*, a collection on relationships among different generations of feminists, "Talking Across" is a conversation between Gallop and Elizabeth Francis, a graduate student in American civilization at Brown. Francis is married to Chris Amirault, the dissertation advisee included in Gallop's dedication to *FASH*. Gallop opens "Talking Across" by saying to Francis, "I thought maybe we could talk about things more freely because we don't have any literal institutional relation to each other. . . . But also because we know each other" (104). Gallop's assertion seems disingenuous. Whereas Gallop might feel free in the presence of Francis, the reverse seems far from true given Gallop's institutional weight in Francis's life as her husband's dissertation director. Inequities between the two are visible in the interview itself. Whereas Gallop feels free to speculate that Francis's voice is cracking due to anxiety, Francis presumably does not feel free to raise the subject of the sexual harassment case, despite its relevance to a consideration of generations, and despite Gallop's references to the "terroristic" feminists in her classes. Since Gallop was writing *FASH* at the time of this conversation, and since Francis would have had intimate knowledge of the case, the absence of the topic in the conversation can only be the result of concerted effort on both their parts, and on Gallop's setting the terms of a separation between the personal and the professional. In this interview Gallop ignores her institutional power over Francis even as she takes advantage of it—and her personal relationship to Francis—in a way that denies the complex intersections of the personal and institutional among generations of feminists.

21. See, for example, Gallop, *Reading Lacan*, esp. 20–21.

22. See Sedgwick, *Epistemology of the Closet*, for a brilliant analysis of ignorance as an active unknowing (4).

23. In "Critical Response II," Lisa Ruddick provides insight into how the rhetoric Gallop uses in both *FASH* and "Resisting Reasonableness" effects boundary violations and "trance logic" (602).

24. Indeed, Gallop's use of "like" rather than "as" instances a pervasive grammatical error that her arguments in *FASH* depend on leaving intact. Thanks to Susan Schweik for pointing out Gallop's use of "like" to me; indeed, her observations about its function inspired this section on Gallop.

25. Both Tania Modleski and Ruddick make this point forcefully in their critiques of "Resisting Reasonableness." See Modleski, 596, and Ruddick, 601.

26. Historicizing feminism keenly interests Gallop: it is the impetus behind *Around 1981* and "Talking Across." Reading these works back through *FASH* as analyzed here, it becomes clear that for all their insights into feminism they do not satisfactorily confront issues of institutional power.

27. See Suzanne Tswei.

28. Although the position eventually was advertised and filled, the university avoided investing it with the powers to take legal action that Hippensteele was seeking.

29. In a feature story on Tompkins in the *Chronicle*, Alison Schneider notes her reception both as "another New Age, crystal-carrying, touchy-feely crank" and, from another viewpoint that has of late "gained steam," as "a 'revolutionary,' a 'pathbreaker,' a 'standard-bearer for honesty.' She is 'the teaching conscience of academe.'" In the follow-up forum inviting responses to Tompkins's pedagogy, nearly fifty faculty and students wrote in, most strongly supportive.

30. In *Life on the Tenure Track* James Lang testifies to Fish's influence when he divulges that his fantasy in 1996 involves "being chauffeured around Raleigh-Durham in Stanley Fish's Jaguar as he courted me to become the newest divinity in the pantheon of Duke University's English department" (5).

31. Although in *A Life* Tompkins seems to repudiate her earlier scholarship, her belief in the revolutionary potential of engaging and changing readers' emotional landscapes aligns her memoir with Stowe's *Uncle Tom's Cabin*, a work she champions in *Sensational Designs* for successfully fighting slavery by changing people's hearts.

32. Another example of this would be Mark Edmundson's account of an influential high school teacher in *Teacher*, which shifts attention away from the conditions in the present-day academy that hover beneath the story he tells.

33. Freire's concerns are with how a "banking approach" to education not only alienates individuals, but also enables dominant elites in Third World countries to continue exploiting the masses.

34. So, too, Tompkins's take on Freire resonates with contemporary "self-help" or new-age appropriations of revolutionary social movements. A similar critique might be made of Tompkins's turn to Buddhism, another system of thought that has been taken up widely in the United States in ways that ignore its collective

and revolutionary origins and history. For illumination regarding these origins, see *The Essential Writings of B. R. Ambedkar*, especially the chapter "Buddha or Karl Marx."

35. For a very partial sampling of this theory, see Jane Martin, *The Schoolhome*; Nell Noddings, *Caring* and *The Challenge to Care in Schools*; and June Crawford et al., *Emotion and Gender*.

36. Expressivists included Peter Elbow (*Writing without Teachers*), Ken Macrorie (*Telling Writing*), and Donald Murray, all of whom exhorted students to reclaim their voices, to recover and value "the language within" (Macrorie), and to assert their individuality. For a contemporary critique of these theorists' emphasis on voice, see Otte, "In-Voicing."

Expressivism has its roots in older theories, including those of John Dewey. See Michael Kiskis, "Adult Learners, Autobiography, and Educational Planning," 39. See also the introduction to *Empowering Education*, where Ira Shor details decades of work developing student-centered classrooms and "dialogic pedagogy," noting work by theorists including Dewey and Piaget (12).

37. See, for example, the 1984 and 1985 reports cited in Shor's *Empowering Education*, 21 and 22.

38. Moreover, Tompkins does not consider how "educating the whole person" can dovetail not with a humanist tradition but rather with the corporatizing of the university, which involves focusing on "student services" at the expense of academics, in order to "sell" education to students-consumers. For discussions of the corporatization of higher education, see Aronowitz, Giroux, Readings, and S. Slaughter and Leslie.

39. Consider, for example, Tompkins's assertion in *West of Everything* that to comprehend Westerns "in an intellectual or conceptual way, one must begin with their impact on the body and emotions" (6). However, whereas in that book Tompkins is interested in mind-body connections, in *A Life*, her focus shifts entirely to her emotions, reinstalling a binary that her earlier work refuses.

40. Despite Tompkins's insistence on the importance of the body, and her protests of its exclusion from academe, the body is largely absent from her memoir. Even the seemingly intimate bodily details that Tompkins provides—for example that in grade school she "lived in terror of wetting my pants in front of the whole class" (14)—refer to generic experiences, and ones that interest her more for their symbolic value. This lack of embodiment is perhaps disguised by the fact that it is considered inappropriate to write about having to go to the bathroom in an academic book. And although such a mention, as does her disclosure about having to learn to get a drink of water (118), reminds readers that academics have bodily needs, such writing does not significantly illuminate understanding of the relationship between the intellect and the body.

41. This difficulty is not new to the 1990s. For example, in *Faculty Towers*, Elaine Showalter remarks of *Death in a Tenured Position* (1981) by Carolyn

Heilbrun, "But this novel nevertheless struck a personal chord with me; in it Heilbrun begins to talk about problems plaguing women who had made it in academia and to caution those who had not. . . . Its themes of loneliness, alienation, and self-punishment can be seen as precursors of her own suicide in the fall of 2003" (68).

42. For an example of a popular take on the "inner child" see Alice Miller. As I discuss in the next chapter, bell hooks's memoirs also rely, more explicitly, on theories of the inner child.

43. Fish's unapologetic and well-known appetite for consumerism and his relish for being an operator are widely known through David Lodge's Morris Zap, a thinly fictionalized version of Fish who appears in novels including *Small World*.

44. As Tompkins explains in this preface, "I never cried at anything I saw in a Western, but I cried when I realized this: that after the Indians had been decimated by disease, removal and conquest, and after they had been caricatured and degraded in Western movies, I had ignored them too" (10). However well-intentioned, this response sets the problems with an exclusive focus on feelings in sharp relief. After all, tears do not rectify the omission.

Although in her memoir Tompkins pays no mind to the questions I pose here, she does take them up obliquely, but with insight and intelligence, in "'Indians,' Textualism, Morality, and the Problem of History." Because that article revisits the same memory she represents in *A Life*, it is all the more noteworthy that Tompkins discards the value of such intellectual inquiry in *A Life*.

45. For example, Susan Wall indirectly addresses this problem when she advocates that teachers ask themselves questions including: "Do we recognize that what *we* define as adaptive or empowering may not be so regarded by students who do not share our histories, who may indeed want to resist the cultural identities we define for them?" (181, original emphasis).

46. By contrast, Tompkins's colleague and writing group member Alice Kaplan addresses these issues in *French Lessons*. Reflecting on the fact that she never spoke while at Yale to de Man, who "covered his work with the clean veil of disinterestedness," she thinks in regard to her own doctoral students, "I don't want to fail them the way that de Man failed me." She wonders, "What do students need to know about their teachers?", with her memoir serving as her implicit answer to this question (174).

47. For insightful commentary on how teaching film can lead students to uncritical celebrations of experience and of media apparatuses, see Paul Smith, "Pedagogy and the Popular-Cultural-Commodity-Text," esp. 42–43.

48. In saying this I do not mean to argue on behalf of traditional student-teacher power relations or to view them as fixed and unchanging. Rather, I wish to underline the need to consider, as pedagogy experts including Bourdieu, Passeron, and Brodkey so insightfully have, that these relations are more structural

than Tompkins credits them with being. See, for example, Brodkey, "On the Subjects of Class and Gender in 'The Literary Letters,'" or Amirault, "The Good Teacher, the Good Student." See also Bourdieu and Passeron, *Reproduction in Education, Society, and Culture*, for discussion of the difficulties of eradicating institutional hierarchies.

49. Although the University of Hawai'i has a long way to go in making changes students were calling for, under the UH president who followed President Mortimer, Evan Dobelle, and his administration, especially the chancellor of the UH-Mānoa campus, Peter Englert, funding for the Kamakakūokalani Center for Hawaiian Studies improved dramatically, as did acknowledgment of the university's responsibility to attend to the politics, history, and peoples of Hawai'i. By the time of this writing both Dobelle and Englert, for reasons that are far from transparent, had been fired; it remains to be seen the direction the new administration will take, though in May 2007 the board of regents approved establishment of Hawai'inuiākea School of Hawaiian Knowledge.

50. See, for example, Janet Zandy, *Hands*, where, as she explains, "Through a sequence of essays and intersecting collages, I construct a form that seeks a dialogue between the tactile world of work and the textured world of the academy. I combine literary analysis, pedagogy, memoir, and cultural critique to probe the myriad ways class circumstances affect the making and reception of culture" (2).

51. In *Remembered Rapture*, hooks includes an essay titled "Women Who Write Too Much." This essay does not consider any of the limitations that can result from writing so rapidly, or the privilege on which such a rate of publication depends. hooks instead assumes—reductively if not altogether wrongly—that any criticism of how much she writes is a sexist and racist attack.

52. For yet another, interesting, exploration of how teaching ideally should create discomfort, even crisis, that contrasts to those presented in this chapter, see Shoshana Felman, "Education and Crisis."

53. This problem intensifies in hooks's memoirs, especially sections in *Wounds of Passion* that purport to give her lover's point of view. For example, after explaining that upon their first meeting, "I forgot about Mack," she shifts into third person to give Mack's perspective: "He does not forget about her. . . . She walks so slow as though eternity is before her so she can take her time, never noticing anyone watching" (28). Bracketing the possible ironies that attend hooks recounting her lover watching her as she professes herself to be unmindful of his gaze, this passage, and the others from Mack's point of view, arguably appropriate, rather than give voice to, Mack's perspective. Such a move can be seen as a fitting way to disempower an abusive ex, only hooks's complete lack of self-consciousness makes the passages instead seem narcissistic.

54. This individualism is not endemic to those writing their memoirs or to the genre itself. See, for example, Karla Holloway, *BookMarks*. This memoir puts

Holloway's pain over the loss of her son, Bem, into a more collective context, one that speaks to a grief that is shared among black people experiencing an ongoing history of violence, criminalization, and dispossession.

55. At the same time, in *Communion*, hooks defines her work against self-help books, *Women Who Love Too Much* and *Men Are from Mars, Women Are from Venus* in particular, because they fail to critique sexism. Although hooks frequently addresses male domination in *Communion* and *All about Love*, her solutions are nevertheless individual ones. In addition, these works partake in the neglect of class and race that characterize the best-selling self-help books, and, even as they include discussion of homosexual relationships, do so to find them characterized by the same dynamics that shape heterosexual ones.

56. This section perhaps too neatly correlates achieving academic stardom, turning to popular genres, and forgoing a feminist and antiracist politics: hooks's most recent books, although also directed at a nonacademic audience, do not all share the individualist focus that characterizes her engagements with the memoir and self-help genres. *Feminism Is for Everybody* (2000), a "short handbook" (ix) on feminism published by the progressive South End Press, echoes (sometimes literally) the political objectives of her earlier books, at the same time that it less successfully achieves them. Attention to *Where We Stand: Class Matters* (2000) also suggests that it is not simply a shift in genre that accounts for hooks's less transgressive politics. In this book hooks makes use of a mixed-genre format and continues her commitment to theorizing and resisting intersecting forms of oppression, but in ways that ultimately circumvent what it means to do so from a position of prominence and class privilege. Indeed, as do the memoirs analyzed in this chapter, in its use of autobiography *Where We Stand* demonstrates the difficulties of theorizing about and from a position of institutional privilege and authority in a way that maintains an oppositional politics and a sensitivity to collective forms of oppression and suffering.

Chapter 5. Disability Studies and Institutional Interventions

1. For his own writings on the subject and for access to his blog, which includes discussion of living with bipolar disorder, send an e-mail to murdockmoo1@hawaii.rr.com.

2. For a discussion of what Peter Kramer calls "the era of autopathography" (7), see G. Thomas Couser's introduction to *Recovering Bodies*. According to Couser, autopathographies "characterize personal narratives about illness or disability that contest cultural discourses stigmatizing the writer as abnormal, aberrant, or in some sense pathological. . . . It critiques social constructions of the disabled body and incorporates a counternarrative of survival and empowerment that reclaims the individual's or a loved one's body from the social stigmatization

and impersonalization of medical discourse" (quoted in S. Smith and Watson, *Reading Autobiography* 187–88).

3. For discussions of the difficulties of distinguishing disability and illness, and scholars' failures to explore their interrelations, see Hearndl, "Disease versus Disability."

4. Disability studies scholars are in general agreement that an impairment is a physical or mental condition that imposes limits; that a disability is a socially constructed condition; and that the lines between the two can be blurry. See, for example, Wendell, 263. For delineation of how the World Health Organization (WHO) distinguishes among impairment, disability, and handicap, see Sander Gilman, "Defining Disability"; see also Simi Linton's insightful discussion of problems with the terms "impairment" and "disability" in "What Is Disability Studies?"

5. For an analysis of how disability is homogenized and catastrophized, see Ruth Hubbard, "Abortion and Disability." For discussion of how and why it is pathologized, see Rosemarie Garland Thomson, *Extraordinary Bodies*, 20, 38. See also Carol A. Breckenridge and Candace Vogler, "The Critical Limits of Embodiment."

6. Lata Mani comments on this phenomenon and its psychic effects on the person experiencing the disability in *Interleaves*: "The incomprehension of those who are well, the continual search for language on the part of those who are ill, the shame of one's condition, the sense of worthlessness and the repeated experiences of feeling demeaned, all point to the social dimensions of illness. For in a society driven by an obsession for happiness and bent on refusing to recognize suffering as an inescapable aspect of humanhood, there is no legitimate function or place for the chronically ill person" (56–57).

7. For a similar argument, see Wendell, 270.

8. Given L. Davis's position here, it is interesting that he has written a memoir about being a CODA (child of a deaf adult); see *My Sense of Silence*. Catherine J. Kudlick makes an argument related to Davis's when she urges the need to "stop individualizing and sentimentalizing disability through people like [Helen] Keller" (558).

9. Thanks to Vrinda Dalmiya for referring me to Kittay, *Love's Labor*, and for extremely helpful discussions of the relationship between it and Michael Bérubé, *Life as We Know It*.

10. In *All about Love* hooks more directly discusses her suicidal impulses; after quoting from *Bone Black*, she details how "Suicidal longings dominated my waking thoughts and my nightmares" (235).

11. Critics who draw on Goffman include Lerita Coleman, Davis, Susan Schweik, and Garland Thomson. See, for example, Coleman, "Stigma: An Enigma Demystified."

12. See *Extraordinary Bodies*, 40, for a discussion of this process.

13. Breckenridge and Vogler make a similar argument in "Critical Limits of Embodiment"; see esp. 350.

14. Said consistently refused adherence to party lines; indeed his formulation of the intellectual is premised on the valorization of independent thought (hence Said's well-known pronunciation, "criticism before solidarity"). Regarding the model of reciprocity, see, for example, Wendell, 273.

15. Such arguments are becoming increasingly common. For example, in an analysis that resonates with Davis's, David Mitchell and Sharon Snyder describe disability as "the master trope of human disqualification" that enables an understanding of power itself (*Narrative Prosthesis* 3). The editors of *Disability Studies: Enabling the Humanities* also make claims to disability studies' universalism in their introduction (S. Snyder, Garland-Thomson, and Brueggemann).

16. On Sedgwick's self-publishing as queer, see, for example, *Tendencies*, 256.

17. Quoted in Barber and Clark, 30.

18. Similarly, as Barber and Clark comment in their introduction to *Regarding Sedgwick*, although Sedgwick does not have the vocabulary of queer theory at her disposal in *Between Men*, which she writes from a feminist studies framework, this book anticipates and creates a foundation for it (16).

19. For example, Garland Thomson quotes from *Epistemology of the Closet* to argue that "disability studies should become a universalizing discourse in the way that Sedgwick imagines gay studies and feminism to be" (*Extraordinary Bodies* 22).

For examples of how queer studies and disability studies are beginning to come together, see for example, Robert McRuer, *Crip Theory*, in which he theorizes the "construction of able-bodiedness and heterosexuality, as well as the connections between them" (2). See also Eli Clare, "Stolen Bodies, Reclaimed Bodies," and Breckenridge and Vogler's announcement that "There are also signs that the time has come to examine the relation between disability studies and queer theory" (351).

20. For a discussion of Sedgwick's use of these images, see Melissa Solomon, 216.

21. Sedgwick's interest in shame as an affective ground for the psyche— and her conviction that witnessing another's shame productively opens one to shame—could be usefully analyzed here. For a discussion of Sedgwick's relation to shame, see Sedgwick and Adam Frank, "Shame in the Cybernetic Fold." See also Barber and Clark, esp. 26–27.

22. This passage in which Sedgwick quotes from Ann Cvetkovich, *Mixed Feeling*, appears on 15–16 of Sedgwick and Frank.

23. Sedgwick's statement for her fiber installation, "Floating Columns/In the Bardo" is cited in Solomon, 212, fn. 3. Another commentary that Sedgwick

distributed called "In the Bardo" that brings together experiences of Buddhism, the bardo, and cancer is included in Nancy K. Miller, "Reviewing Eve"; see 222.

24. For a view of *Dialogue* as embodying Sedgwick's notion, building on Melanie Klein, "of a nonparanoid, reparative work," or of "non- or at least other-than-theorizable labor," see Sedgwick, Barber, and Clark, 258.

25. From a very different angle, Karla Holloway explores how seemingly impersonal forms can be conveyors of great intimacy. In her memoir *BookMarks*, she explains, "I am left without my son, whose terrible death maintains its grip on my spirit. I do have left the sense that books and our memories of them and their spaces have a potential for both marking and mourning a far greater intimacy than we might at first imagine could come from our touch of its pages" (53). See also Holloway's insights into how "a recitation of books is intimately attached to the bodies of black folk" (184–85).

26. For other commentary in *Regarding Sedgwick* on how Sedgwick's work elicits self-reflection that invites identification as well as dis-identification, see N. Miller, "Reviewing Eve," 224, and Deborah P. Britzman, esp. 137.

27. For further insights into the role that corporations, government agencies, and organizations play in the problem of cancer, go to the Breast Cancer Action Web site, <http://bcaction.org/index.php?page=politics-faq>, accessed Oct. 10, 2008.

28. Bérubé's approach directly contradicts Michael Dorris's in *The Broken Cord*. In his memoir, Dorris's love for his son and his representation of his son as an individual exist in direct and painful contradiction to the book's overall argument that children should not be born with fetal alcohol syndrome. Whereas *Life* begins with a diagnosis and fully humanized Jamie, in *The Broken Cord* Adam's FAS diagnosis is not revealed until midway through the book, and it is at this point that Adam becomes rendered as a type with the narrative unfolding at odds to his very existence. See G. Thomas Couser's insightful critique of this dynamic in "Raising Adam."

29. For a parental memoir that does a similar kind of work, see Kittay, *Love's Labor*.

30. See Hubbard, 189. See, too, Jacqueline Bhabha, "The Child—What Sort of Human?" where the author explores the problems that follow from the fact that the "human rights field has not satisfactorily resolved the challenge posed in article 1 of the UDHR [Universal Declaration of Human Rights], to uncouple the treatment of human beings from their physical and intellectual ability" (1534).

31. In spring 2004 I attended the international Pacific Rim Conference on Disabilities in Honolulu, at which one keynote speaker addressed the future possibility of surgery capable of intercepting and repairing chromosomal irregularities in a developing fetus. At lunch my tablemates denounced the speaker for assuming Down syndrome needed fixing and for working within dominant understandings of intelligence and independence. Bérubé's *Life* staunchly refuses

such moralizing and theorizing away of impairments that makes life difficult for those who live with them.

32. Dona Avery advocates the need for both these things in "Talking 'Tragedy'"; see 118.

33. See, for example, Bérubé's epilogue in Bérubé and Nelson, *Higher Education under Fire*, 229 and 234.

34. See also ibid. On the one hand, Bérubé there takes the academic left to task for failing to work to impact public policy (219). On the other hand, he contends, cultural studies critics too readily conflate cultural and "practical politics" (236).

35. For Bérubé's discussion of the importance of this work, see the epilogue to *Public Access*, esp. 264.

36. One of the impediments to public access that Bérubé critiques in *Public Access* is that there is "no professional 'reward'" for reaching a "hybrid readership" (30); therefore he proposes that evaluations of merit and promotion consider "humanities professors' 'public' work as well" (30).

37. Le Blogue Bérubé, <http://www.michaelberube.com/index.php/weblog>, accessed July 18, 2008. Bérubé's retirement from his blog proved to be relatively short. He resumed it at the same address under its new name, American Airspace, on Sept. 30, 2008, to protest the government's response to the financial crisis that broke on Wall Street—and to comment on the presidential debates between Barack Obama and John McCain. Accessed Oct. 12, 2008.

38. For an account of the militarization of Hawai'i, see Kathy E. Ferguson and Phyllis Turnbull, *Oh, Say, Can You See?: The Semiotics of the Military in Hawai'i*.

39. For accounts by Native Hawaiian scholars that situate present-day Hawai'i in relation to a long history of colonialism, see, for example, Lilikalā Kame'eleihiwa, *Native Land, Foreign Desires*; J. Kēhaulani Kauanui, *Hawaiian Blood*; Jonathan Osorio, *Dismembering Lāhui*; Noenoe Silva, *Aloha Betrayed*; and Haunani-Kay Trask, *From a Native Daughter*. See also Keala Kelly's documentary, *Noho Hewa*, and essays in Candace Fujikane's anthology *Asian Settler Colonialism*.

Other insightful accounts of tourism and its connections to colonialism in Hawai'i include Laura E. Lyons's "Dole, Hawai'i, and the Question of Land under Globalization"; Paul Lyons's *American Pacificism*; Gaye Chan and Andrea Feeser's innovative Historic Waikīkī Web site; and John Zuern's beautiful and arresting "Ask Me for the Moon: Working Nights in Waikīkī."

40. For an excellent and wide-ranging list of articles on Native Hawaiian health issues that analyze their connections to political and cultural conditions, see Moku Indigenous People at the Native Hawaiian Healthcare Web site, <http://www.nativehawaiianhealth.net/moku/IndigenousPeople.cfm>, accessed July 23,

2008. See also David Stannard, "The Hawaiians"; and Richard Kekuni Blaisdell, "Update on Kanaka Maoli (Indigenous Hawaiian) Health."

Conclusion. Memoir and the Post–September 11 Academy

1. See *Academic Freedom after September 11*, edited by Beshara Doumani.

2. For an account of the Churchill controversy, see the "Ward Churchill 9/11 essay controversy" entry on Wikipedia, <http://en.wikipedia.org/wiki/Ward_Churchill_9/11_essay_controversy>, accessed July 20, 2008. For background on the Massad and Finkelstein cases, see the Wikipedia entries on Massad (<http://en.wikipedia.org/wiki/Joseph_Massad>, accessed July 23, 2008) and Finkelstein (<http://en.wikipedia.org/wiki/Norman_Finkelstein>, accessed July 23, 2008). I chose these Wikipedia pages rather than other Web sites because they seemed to provide more balanced narratives as well as links to a number of other articles from various viewpoints.

That pro-Palestinian academics are perceived in the United States to be particularly dangerous is, of course, no coincidence. See Joel Benin, "The New American McCarthyism: Policing Thought about the Middle East." Benin was attacked by David Horowitz's Center for the Study of Popular Culture (Horowitz is also the publisher of FrontPageMag.com) and responded creatively by filing suit against the center for copyright infringement for the center's use of the photograph of him that appeared in its pamphlet *Campus Support for Terrorism*.

3. The inverse holds true as well: repeatedly, support in summer 2005 for John Roberts's nomination as chief justice of the U.S. Supreme Court was made on grounds of how well-mannered he was. Attention to his good manners replaced discussion about and distracted from the fact that Roberts, who assumed the bench in September 2005, was on record as defending torture. In short, in the mainstream media, and for the Bush administration, a civil demeanor apparently trumps supporting human-rights violations. See Molly Ivins's commentary on this in "Manners and Morons."

4. Indeed, the chilling curtailment of academics' political freedom is keeping pace with the increase in freedom—and career incentives—for academics to tell all about their childhood or their personal lives in memoirs, Web sites, blogs, and even television shows. See Stephanie Rosenbloom, "The Professor as Open Book," which comments on this trend as it focuses on the new cult-hit cable television series, *Professors Strike Back*.

5. Churchill made this comment in "Some People Push Back—On the Justice of Roosting Chickens." An expanded version of this essay, "The Ghosts of 9-1-1," appears in his 2003 book, *On the Justice of Roosting Chickens: Reflections on the Consequences of U.S. Imperial Arrogance and Criminality*.

BIBLIOGRAPHY

Aciman, André. *Out of Egypt: A Memoir*. New York: Farrar, Straus & Giroux, 1994.

Ahmed, Leila. *A Border Passage: From Cairo to America—A Woman's Journey*. New York: Farrar, Straus & Giroux, 1999.

Alcalay, Ammiel. "Stop-Time in the Levant." *Nation* (Dec. 20, 1999). <http://www.thenation.com/doc/19991220/alcalay/2>, accessed July 21, 2008.

Alcoff, Linda Martín. "Who's Afraid of Identity Politics?" Moya and Hames-García 312–344.

Alexander, Meena. *Fault Lines: A Memoir*. New York: Feminist P, 1993.

Alger, Jonathan R. "Love, Lust, and the Law: Sexual Harassment in the Academy." *Academe* (Sept./Oct. 1998). <http://findarticles.com/p/articles/mi_qa3860/is_199809/ai_n8814787>, accessed July 18, 2008.

Amirault, Chris. "The Good Teacher, the Good Student: Identifications of a Student-Teacher." *Pedagogy*. Gallop 64–78.

Anderson, Amanda. *The Powers of Distance: Cosmopolitanism and the Cultivation of Detachment*. Princeton NJ: Princeton UP, 2001.

Anzaldúa, Gloria. *Borderlands/La Frontera: The New Mestiza*. San Francisco: Spinsters/Aunt Lute, 1987.

———, ed. *Making Face, Making Soul/Haciendo Caras: Creative and Critical Perspectives by Feminists of Color*. San Francisco: Aunt Lute, 1990.

———. "Now Let Us Shift . . . the Path of Conocimiento . . . Inner Work, Public Acts." Anzaldúa and Keating 540–78.

———. "Preface: (Un)natural Bridges, (Un)safe Spaces." Anzaldúa and Keating 1–5.

———. "Speaking in Tongues: A Letter to 3rd World Women Writers." Moraga and Anzaldúa 165–73.

———. "Tlilli, Tlapalli, the Path of the Red and Black Ink." *The Norton Anthology of Literature by Women: The Traditions in English*. Ed. Sandra Gilbert and Susan Gubar. 2nd ed. New York: W. W. Norton, 1996. 2272–79.

———. "Tlilli, Tlapalli, the Path of the Red and Black Ink." *Postmodern American Fiction*. Ed. Paula Geyh, Fred G. Leebron, and Andrew Levy. New York: W. W. Norton, 1998.

Anzaldúa, Gloria, and AnaLouise Keating, eds. *This Bridge We Call Home: Radical Visions for Transformation*. New York: Routledge, 2002.

Appiah, Anthony. *Cosmopolitanism: Ethics in a World of Strangers*. New York: W. W. Norton, 2006.

———. "Cosmopolitan Patriots." J. Cohen 21–29.

Aronowitz, Stanley. *The Knowledge Factory: Dismantling the Corporate University and Creating True Higher Learning*. Boston: Beacon P, 2001.

Arreglo, Carlo. *Alibata*. Self-published 'zine (spring 1999), Honolulu, Hawai'i.

Ashcroft, Bill, and Pal Ahluwalia. *Edward Said*. London: Routledge, 1999, 2001.

Asian Women United of California, eds. *Making Waves: An Anthology of Writing by and about Asian American Women*. Boston: Beacon P, 1989.

Atlas, James. "Confessing for Voyeurs: The Age of the Literary Memoir Is Now." *New York Times Magazine* (May 12, 1996). 25–27.

Avakian, Arlene. *Lion Woman's Legacy: An Armenian-American Memoir*. New York: Feminist P, 1992.

Avery, Donna. "Talking 'Tragedy': Identity Issues in the Parental Story of Disability." *Disability Discourse*. Corker and French 116–26.

Awkward, Michael. *Scenes of Instruction: A Memoir*. Durham NC: Duke UP, 1999.

Barber, Stephen M., and David L. Clark, eds. *Regarding Sedgwick: Essays on Queer Culture and Critical Theory*. New York: Routledge, 2002.

Baynton, Douglas. "Slaves, Immigrants, and Suffragists: The Uses of Disability in Citizenship Debates." *PMLA* 120.2 (March 2005): 562–67.

Bayoumi, Moustafa, and Andrew Rubin. Introduction. *Edward Said Reader*. Said xi–xxxiv.

Beck, Evelyn Torton, ed. *Nice Jewish Girls: A Lesbian Anthology*. Rev ed. Boston: Beacon P, 1989.

Begley, Adam. "The I's Have It: Duke's 'Moi' Critics Expose Themselves." *Lingua Franca* (March/April 1994): 54–59.

Behar, Ruth. *Translated Woman: Crossing the Border with Esperanza's Story*. Boston: Beacon P, 1993.

Benhabib, Seyla. *Another Cosmopolitanism: Hospitality, Sovereignty, and Democratic Iterations*. Ed. Robert Post. Oxford and New York: Oxford UP, 2006.

Benin, Joel. "The New American McCarthyism: Policing Thought about the Middle East." *Race and Class* 46.1 (2004): 101–15.

Berlant, Lauren. *The Queen of America Goes to Washington City*. Durham NC: Duke UP, 1997.

Bernstein, Jane. *Loving Rachel: A Family's Journey from Grief*. Urbana: U of Illinois P, 2007.

Bérubé, Michael. "Afterword: If I Should Live So Long." *Disability Studies*. S. Snyder, Garland-Thomson, and Brueggemann 337–34.

———. *Life as We Know It: A Father, a Family, and an Exceptional Child*. New York: Vintage Books, 1996.

———. *Marginal Forces/Cultural Centers: Tolson, Pynchon, and the Politics of the Canon*. Ithaca NY: Cornell UP, 1992.

———. "Preface." *Bending over Backwards*. L. Davis vii–xii.

———. *Public Access: Literary Theory and American Cultural Politics*. London: Verso, 1994.

———. *Rhetorical Occasions: Essays on Humans and the Humanities*. Chapel Hill: U of North Carolina P, 2006.

———, ed. *The Aesthetics of Cultural Studies*. Oxford and New York: Oxford UP, 2005.

———. *The Employment of English: Theory, Jobs, and the Future of Literary Studies*. New York: New York UP, 1997.

———. *What's Liberal About the Liberal Arts?: Classroom Politics and 'Bias' in Higher Education*. New York: W. W. Norton, 2006.

Bérubé, Michael, and Janet Lyon. "Preface: When Good Things Happen to Bad Subjects." *Bad Subjects: Political Education for Everyday Life*. Ed. The Bad Subjects Production Team. New York: New York UP, 1998. xi–xviii.

Bérubé, Michael, and Cary Nelson, eds. *Higher Education under Fire: Politics, Economics, and the Crisis of the Humanities*. New York: Routledge, 1995.

Bhabha, Jacqueline. "The Child—What Sort of Human?" *PMLA* 121.5 (Oct. 2006): 1526–35.

Blaisdell, Richard Kekuni, M.D. "Update on Kanaka Maoli (Indigenous Hawaiian) Health." *Motion Magazine* (Nov. 16, 1997). <http://www.inmotion magazine.com/kekuni3.html>, accessed July 23, 2008.

Bourdieu, Pierre, and Jean-Claude Passeron. *Reproduction in Education, Society, and Culture*. Trans. Richard Nice. London: Sage, 1970.

Bourne, Jenny. "Homelands of the Mind: Jewish Feminism and Identity Politics." *Race and Class: A Journal for Black and Third World Liberation* 29.1 (summer 1987): 1–24.

Bové, Paul A. *In the Wake of Theory*. Middleton CT: Wesleyan UP, 1992.

Brah, Avtar. *Cartographies of Diaspora: Contesting Identities*. London: Routledge, 1996.

Bramberger, Bill, and Cathy N. Davidson, *Closing: The Life and Death of an American Factory*. New York: W. W. Norton, 1997.

Braziel, Jana Evans, and Anita Mannur. "Nation, Migration, Globalization: Points of Contention in Diaspora Studies." *Theorizing Diaspora: A Reader*. Ed. Jana Evans Braziel and Anita Mannur. Malden MA: Blackwell, 2003, rpt. 2005. 1–22.

Breckenridge, Carol A., Sheldon Pollock, Homi K. Bhabha, and Dipesh Chakrabarty, eds. *Cosmopolitanism*. Durham NC: Duke UP, 2002.

Breckenridge, Carol A., and Candace Vogler. "The Critical Limits of Embodiment: Disability's Criticism." *Public Culture* 13.3 (2001): 349–57.

Brennan, Timothy. *At Home in the World: Cosmopolitanism Now*. Cambridge MA: Harvard UP, 1997.

———. "Places of Mind, Occupied Lands: Edward Said and Philology." Sprinker 74–95.

———. *Wars of Position: The Cultural Politics of Left and Right*. New York: Columbia UP, 2006.

Britzman, Deborah P. "Theory Kindergarten." Barber and Clark 121–42.

Brodkey, Linda. "On the Subjects of Class and Gender in 'The Literary Letters.'" *College English* 51.2 (1989): 125–41.

Brown, Roger. *Against My Better Judgment: An Intimate Memoir of an Eminent Psychologist*. Binghamton NY: Haworth P, 1996.

Brownstein, Rachel M. "Interrupted Reading: Personal Criticism in the Present Time." Veeser 29–39.

Butler, Judith. *Giving an Account of Oneself*. New York: Fordham UP, 2005.

———. *Precarious Life: The Powers of Mourning and Violence*. London: Verso, 2004.

Cameron, Sharon. *Beautiful Work: A Meditation on Pain*. Durham NC: Duke UP, 2000.

Carby, Hazel. *Reconstructing Womanhood: The Emergence of the Afro-American Woman Novelist*. Oxford: Oxford UP, 1987.

Carroll, Peter. *Keeping Time: Memory, Nostalgia, and the Art of History*. Athens: U of Georgia P, 1990.

Castro, Joy. *The Truth Book: Escaping a Childhood of Abuse Among Jehovah's Witnesses*. New York: Arcade Publishing, 2005.

Caws, Mary Ann. *To the Boathouse: A Memoir*. Tuscaloosa: U of Alabama P, 2008.

Chan, Gaye, and Andrea Feeser. "Historic Waikīkī" Web site. <http://www.down windproductions.com/>, accessed July 23, 2008.

Cheah, Pheng. "Humanity in the Field of Instrumentality." *PMLA* 121.5 (Oct. 2006): 1552–57.

———. *Inhuman Conditions: On Cosmopolitanism and Human Rights*. Cambridge MA: Harvard UP, 2007.

———. "Introduction Part 2: The Cosmopolitical—Today." Cheah and Robbins 20–43.

Cheah, Pheng, and Bruce Robbins, eds. *Cosmopolitics: Thinking and Feeling Beyond the Nation*. Minneapolis: U of Minnesota P, 1998.

Christian, Barbara. "The Race for Theory." *Making Face*. Anzaldúa 335–45.

Chu, Kandice. *Imagine Otherwise: On Asian Americanist Critique*. Durham NC: Duke UP, 2003.

Churchill, Ward. "The Ghosts of 9-1-1." *On the Justice of Roosting Chickens: Reflections on the Consequences of U.S. Imperial Arrogance and Criminality*. Oakland, Calif.: AK Press, 2003. 5–38.

———. "Some People Push Back—On the Justice of Roosting Chickens." Dark Night P (Sept. 11, 2001). <http://www.kersplebedeb.com/mystuff/s11/churchill.html>, accessed July 23, 2008.

Chvany, Peter A. "What We Talk about When We Talk about Whiteness." *The White Issue*. Mike Hill, ed. *Minnesota Review* 47 (1996): 49–55.

Clare, Eli. "Stolen Bodies, Reclaimed Bodies: Disability and Queerness." *Public Culture* 13.3 (2001): 359–65.

Clifford, James. *Routes: Travel and Translation in the Late Twentieth Century*. Cambridge MA: Harvard UP, 1997.

Cohen, Joshua, ed. *For Love of Country?* By Martha C. Nussbaum. Boston: Beacon P, 1996, rpt. 2002.

Cohen, Marion Deutsche. *Dirty Details: The Days and Nights of a Well Spouse*. Philadelphia: Temple UP, 1996.

Coleman, Lerita. "Stigma: An Enigma Demystified." *Disability Studies Reader*. L. Davis 216–31.

"Collegiality." Section in *Profession 2006*. Introduced by Heather Dubrow. 48–118.

Conley, Dalton. *Honky*. New York: Vintage Books, 2001.

Conway, Jill Ker. *When Memory Speaks*. New York: Vintage, 1998, rpt. 1999.

Corker, Mairian, and Sally French. "Reclaiming Discourse in Disability Studies." Corker and French 1–12.

———, eds. *Disability Discourse*. Buckingham UK: Open UP, 1999.

Couser, G. Thomas. "Raising Adam: Ethnicity, Disability, and the Ethics of Life Writing in Michael Dorris's *The Broken Cord*." *Biography* 21.4 (fall 1998): 421–44.

———. *Recovering Bodies: Illness, Disability, and Life-Writing*. Madison: U of Wisconsin P, 1997.

Crawford, June, Susan Kippax, Jenny Onyx, Una Gault, and Pam Benton. *Emotion and Gender: Constructing Meaning from Memory*. Newbury Park CA: Sage, 1992.

Crichton, Michael. *The Rising Sun*. New York: Ballantine, 1992.

Cvetkovich, Ann. *Mixed Feelings: Feminism, Mass Culture, and Victorian Sensationalism*. New Brunswick NJ: Rutgers UP, 1992.

Das Gupta, Monisha. *Unruly Immigrants: Rights, Activism, and Transnational South Asian Politics in the United States*. Durham NC: Duke UP, 2006.

Davidson, Cathy N. *Revolution and the Word: The Rise of the Novel in America*, expanded ed. New York: Oxford UP, 2004 (1986).

———. *Thirty-six Views of Mount Fuji: On Finding Myself in Japan*. New York: Plume, 1993.

———. New afterword to *Thirty-six Views of Mount Fuji: On Finding Myself in Japan*. Durham NC: Duke UP, 2006.

Davies, Tony. *Humanism*. London: Routledge, 1997.

Davis, Angela Y. *Angela Davis: An Autobiography*. New York: International Publishers 1974, rpt. 1988.

Davis, Lennard J. *Bending over Backwards: Disability, Dismodernism and Other Difficult Positions*. New York: New York UP, 2002.

———, ed. *The Disability Studies Reader*. New York: Routledge, 1997.

———. *Enforcing Normalcy: Disability, Deafness, and the Body*. London: Verso, 1995.

———. *My Sense of Silence: Memoirs of a Childhood with Deafness*. Urbana: U of Illinois P, 1999.

The Dead Poets Society, dir. Peter Weir, perf. Robin Williams, 1989.

Derrida, Jacques. *On Cosmopolitanism and Forgiveness*. London: Routledge, 2004.

———. *Spurs: Nietzsche's Styles*. Chicago: U of Chicago P, 1978.

Diawara, Manthia. *In Search of Africa*. Cambridge MA: Harvard UP, 2000.

Dorris, Michael. *The Broken Cord: A Family's Ongoing Struggle With Fetal Alcohol Syndrome*. New York: HarperCollins, 1989.

Doumani, Beshara, ed. *Academic Freedom after September 11*. Cambridge MA: Zone Books, 2006.

Duberman, Martin. *Cures: A Gay Man's Odyssey*. New York: Dutton, 1991.

Eagleton, Terry. *After Theory*. New York: Basic Books, 2003.

———. *The Gatekeeper*. New York: St. Martin's P, 2001.

———. *Ideology: An Introduction*. Minneapolis: U of Minnesota P, 1991.

Edmundson, Mark. "Humanism and Faith." Lecture. Georgeton U. March 18, 2005.

———. *Teacher: The One Who Made the Difference*. New York: Random House, 2002.

———. "What's a Liberal Arts Education For?" David G. Osborne Lecture. Ohio Wesleyan U. April 6, 2006.

———. "What Is Humanism?" Dana College. President's Inaugural Lecture. April 27, 2006.

Edward Said: A Very Personal View of Palestine. BBC documentary. May 1998. Broadcast in the United States by the Public Broadcasting System as *In Search of Palestine*.

Egan, Susanna. *Mirror Talk: Genres of Crisis in Contemporary Autobiography*. Chapel Hill: U of North Carolina P, 1999.

Elbow, Peter. *Writing without Teachers*. New York: Oxford UP, 1973.

Elliott, Jane. "The Currency of Feminist Theory." *PMLA* 121.5 (Oct. 2006): 1697–703.

Felman, Shoshana. "Education and Crisis, Or the Vicissitudes of Teaching." Ed. Felman and Dori Laub. *Testimony: Crises of Witnessing in Literature, Psychoanalysis, and History*. New York: Routledge, 1992. 1–56.

Felski, Rita. "On Confession." *Beyond Feminist Aesthetics: Feminist Literature and Social Change*. Cambridge MA: Harvard UP, 1989.

Ferguson, Kathy E., and Phyllis Turnbull. *Oh, Say, Can You See?: The Semiotics of the Military in Hawai'i*. Minneapolis: U of Minnesota P, 1999.

Fernandes, Jorges. "Return of the Native." Diss. U of Hawai'i, 2002.

Fine, Michelle, Lois Weis, Linda Powell Pruitt, and April Burns, eds. *Off White: Readings on Power, Privilege, and Resistance*. New York: Routledge, 2004.

Fisher, Gary. *Gary in Your Pocket; Stories and Notebooks of Gary Fisher*. Ed. Eve Kosofsky Sedgwick. Durham NC: Duke UP, 1996.

Fisk, Robert. "When Did 'Arab' Become a Dirty Word? Smearing Said and Hanan Ashrawi." *CounterPunch* (Nov. 4, 2003). <http://www.counterpunch.org/fisk11042003.html>, accessed July 17, 2008.

Flam, Helena, and Debra King, eds. *Emotions and Social Movements*. London: Routledge, 2005.

Fleischman, Suzanne. "Gender, the Personal and the Voice of Scholarship: A Viewpoint." *Signs* 24.4 (summer 1998): 975–1016.

Fojas, Camilla. *Cosmopolitanism in the Americas*. West Lafayette IN: Purdue UP, 2005.

Foucault, Michel. *The Order of Things: An Archeology of Human Sciences*. New York: Vintage, 1970, rpt. 1994.

Frankenberg, Ruth, ed. *Displacing Whiteness: Essays in Social and Cultural Criticism*. Durham NC: Duke UP, 1997.

Franklin, Cynthia G. "Turning Japanese/Returning to America: Gender, Class and Nation in David Mura's Use of Memoir." *LIT (Literature, Interpretation, Theory)* 13 (2001): 235–65.

———. *Writing Women's Communities: The Politics and Poetics of Contemporary Multi-Genre Anthologies*. Madison: U of Wisconsin P, 1997.

Freedman, Diane, and Olivia Frey, eds. *Autobiographical Writing across the Disciplines: A Reader*. Durham NC: Duke UP, 2003.

Freedman, Diane, and Francis Murphy Zauhar, eds. *The Intimate Critique: Autobiographical Literary Criticism*. Durham NC: Duke UP, 1993.

Freeman, Jo. *At Berkeley in the 60s: The Education of an Activist: 1961–1965*. Bloomington: Indiana UP, 2004.

Freire, Paulo. *Pedagogy of the Oppressed*. New York: Seabury P, 1970.

Frey, James. *A Million Little Pieces*. London: John Murray Publishers, 2003.

Fujikane, Candace, ed. *Asian Settler Colonialism: From Local Governance to the Habits of Everyday Life in Hawai'i*. Honolulu: U of Hawai'i P, 2008.

———. "Sweeping Racism Under the Rug of 'Censorship': The Controversy Over Lois-Ann Yamanaka's *Blu's Hanging*." *Amerasia Journal* 26. 2 (summer 2000): 158–94.

Fujikane, Candace, and Jonathan Y. Okamura, eds. *Whose Vision? Asian Settler Colonialism in Hawaii*. Special issue. *Amerasia* 26.2 (2000).

Gallop, Jane. *Anecdotal Theory*. Durham NC: Duke UP, 2002.

————. *Around 1981: Academic Feminist Literary Theory*. New York: Routledge, 1991.

————. *The Daughter's Seduction: Feminism and Psychoanalysis*. Ithaca NY: Cornell UP, 1982.

————. *Feminist Accused of Sexual Harassment*. Durham NC: Duke UP, 1997.

————, ed. *Pedagogy: The Question of Impersonation*. Bloomington: Indiana UP, 1995.

————. *Reading Lacan*. Ithaca NY: Cornell UP, 1985.

————. "Resisting Reasonableness." *Critical Inquiry* 25.3 (spring 1999): 599–609.

Gallop, Jane, and Elizabeth Francis. "Talking Across," *Generations: Academic Feminists in Dialogue*. Ed. Devoney Looser and E. Ann Kaplan. Minneapolis: U of Minnesota P, 1997. 103–31.

Gass, William H. "The Art of Self: Autobiography in an Age of Narcissism." *Harper's* (May 1, 1994): 43–52.

Gates, Henry Louis, Jr. *Colored People: A Memoir*. New York: Alfred A. Knopf, 1994.

Gilligan, Carol. *In a Different Voice*. Cambridge MA: Harvard UP, 1982.

Gilman, Sander L. "Defining Disability: The Case of Obesity." *PMLA* 120.2 (March 2005): 514–17.

————, ed. *Ethnicity-Ethnicities-Literature-Literatures*. Special issue. *PMLA* 113.1 (Jan. 1998).

Gilmore, Leigh. "Policing Truth: Confession, Gender, and Autobiographical Authority." *Autobiography and Postmodernism*. Ed. Kathleen Ashley, Leigh Gilmore, and Gerald Peters. Amherst: U of Massachusetts P, 1994. 54–78.

Gilmore, Ruth Wilson. "Premature Death: A Roundtable on Racism." American Studies Association Conference. Hartford CT. Oct. 17, 2003.

Gilroy, Paul. *Against Race: Imagining Political Culture Beyond the Color Line*. Cambridge MA: Belknap P, Harvard UP, 2000.

Giroux, Henry A. *University in Chains: Confronting the Military-Industrial-Academic Complex*. Boulder CO: Paradigm Publishers, 2007.

Goffman, Erving. "Selections from *Stigma*." *Disability Studies Reader*. L. Davis 203–15.

Goodwin, Jeff, James M. Jasper, and Francesca Polletta. *Passionate Politics: Emotions and Social Movements*. Chicago: U of Chicago P, 2001.

Gopinath, Gayatri. *Impossible Desires: Queer Diasporas and South Asian Public Cultures*. Durham NC: Duke UP, 2005.

Grewal, Inderpal. *Home and Harem: Nation, Gender, Empire, and the Cultures of Travel*. Durham NC: Duke UP, 1996.

Haraway, Donna J. *Simians, Cyborgs and Women: The Re-invention of Nature*. London: Free Association, 1991.

Harlow, Barbara. "The Palestinian Intellectual and the Liberation of the Academy." Sprinker 173–93.

Harootunian, H. D. "America's Japan/Japan's America." *Japan in the World*. Miyoshi and Harootunian 196–221.

Hearndl, Diane Price. "Disease versus Disability: The Medical Humanities and Disability Studies." *PMLA* 120.2 (March 2005): 593–98.

The Heath Anthology of American Literature. Vol. E, *Contemporary Period (1945 to the Present)*. 5th ed. Ed. Paul Lauter. Boston: Houghton Mifflin, 2005.

Hersh, Seymour M. "The Gray Zone." *New Yorker* (May 24, 2004). <http://www.newyorker.com/archive/2004/05/24/040524fa_fact>, accessed July 21, 2008.

Hill, Catherine, and Elena Silva. *Drawing the Line: Sexual Harassment on Campus*. Washington DC: American Association of University Women Educational Foundation, 2005. <http://www.aauw.org/research/dtl.cfm>, accessed 22 July 2008.

Hill, Mike. "Introduction: Through the Ethnographic Looking Glass." *The White Issue*. Mike Hill, ed. *Minnesota Review* 47 (1996): 5–8.

———, ed. *Whiteness: A Critical Reader*. New York: New York UP, 1997.

Hirsch, Marianne. *Family Frames: Photography, Narrative, and Postmemory*. Cambridge MA: Harvard UP, 1997.

———. *The Mother/Daughter Plot: Narrative, Psychoanalysis, Feminism*. Bloomington: Indiana UP, 1989.

———. "Pictures of a Displaced Girlhood." *Displacements: Cultural Identities in Question*. Ed. Angelika Bammer. Bloomington: Indiana UP, 1994. 71–89

———. "Pictures of a Displaced Girlhood." Veeser 121–140.

Hirsch, Marianne, Elizabeth Abel, and Elizabeth Langland, eds. *The Voyage In: Fictions of Female Development*. Hanover NH: UP of New England, 1983.

Hirsch, Marianne, and Evelyn Fox Keller, eds. *Conflicts in Feminism*. New York: Routledge, 1990.

Hitchens, Christopher. "Commentary's Scurrilous Attack on Edward Said." *Salon.com* (Sept. 7, 1999). <http://www.salon.com/news/feature/1999/09/07/said/>, accessed July 17, 2008.

Hoffman, Eva. *Lost in Translation: A Life in a New Language*. New York: Penguin Books, 1989.

Holloway, Karla F. C. *BookMarks: Reading in Black and White: A Memoir*. New Brunswick NJ: Rutgers UP, 2006.

hooks, bell. *Ain't I a Woman? Black Women and Feminism*. Boston: South End P, 1981.

———. *All about Love: New Visions*. New York: Perennial, 2000.

———. *Black Looks: Race and Representation*. Boston: South End P, 1991.

———. *Bone Black: Memories of Girlhood*. New York: Henry Holt, 1996.

————. *Communion: The Female Search for Love*. New York: William Morrow, 2002.

————. *Feminism Is for Everyone: Passionate Politics*. Boston: South End P, 2000.

————. *Feminist Theory: From Margin to Center*. Boston: South End P, 1984.

————. *Homemade Love*. With pictures by Shane W. Evans. New York: Hyperion Books for Children, 2002.

————. *Remembered Rapture: The Writer at Work*. New York: Henry Holt, 1999.

————. *Salvation: Black People and Love*. New York: Perennial, 2001.

————. *Talking Back: Thinking Feminist, Thinking Black*. Boston: South End P, 1988.

————. *Teaching Community: A Pedagogy of Hope*. New York: Routledge, 2003.

————. *Teaching to Transgress: Education as the Practice of Freedom*. New York: Routledge, 1994.

————. *When Angels Speak of Love: Poems*. New York: Atria, 2007.

————. *Where We Stand: Class Matters*. New York: Routledge, 2000.

————. *Wounds of Passion: A Writing Life*. New York: Henry Holt, 1997.

————. *Yearning: Race, Gender, and Cultural Politics*. Boston: South End P, 1989.

Horowitz, David. "The Myth Weavers," Salon.com (Sept. 27, 1999). <http://www.salon.com/news/col/horo/1999/09/27/said/print.html>, accessed July 17, 2008.

Hubbard, Ruth. "Abortion and Disability: Who Should and Who Should Not Inhabit the World?" *Disability Studies Reader*. L. Davis 187–202.

Ignatiev, Noel. *How the Irish Became White*. New York: Routledge, 1995.

Ivins, Molly. "Manners and Morons." Alternet (July 29, 2005). <http://www.alternet.org/columnists/story/23784/?comments=view&cID=19700&pID=19484>, accessed July 23, 2008.

Jacoby, Jeff. "The Lies of Edward Said." FrontPageMagazine.com (Oct. 2, 2000). <http://www.frontpagemag.com/guestcolumnists/jacoby/>, accessed Dec. 10, 2000.

Jaggi, Maya. "The Guardian Profile: Edward Said. Out of the Shadows." *Guardian* (Sept. 11, 1999). <http://www.guardian.co.uk/saturday_review/story/0,,268488,00.html>, accessed July 17, 2008.

Jameson, Fredric. *Postmodernism, or, The Cultural Logic of Late Capitalism*. Durham NC: Duke UP, 1991.

JanMohamed, Abdul R. "Worldliness-without-World, Homelessness-as-Home: Toward a Definition of the Specular Border Intellectual." Sprinker 96–120.

JanMohamed, Abdul R., and David Lloyd. "Introduction: Minority Discourse— What Is to Be Done?" *Cultural Critique* 7 (fall 1987): 5–17.

Johnson, James Weldon. *The Autobiography of an Ex-Coloured Man*. Garden City NY: Garden City Pub., 1927.

Jordan, June. *Soldier: A Poet's Childhood*. New York: Basic Books, 2000.

Kameʻeleihiwa, Lilikalā. *Native Land, Foreign Desires: Pehea Lā e Pono Ai? How Shall We Live in Harmony?* Honolulu: Bishop Museum P, 1992.

Kang, Laura. *Compositional Subjects: Enfiguring Asian/American Women*. Durham NC: Duke UP, 2002.

Kaplan, Alice. *French Lessons: A Memoir*. Chicago: U of Chicago P, 1993.

Kaplan, Amy. "Violent Belongings and the Question of Empire Today: Presidential Address to the American Studies Association, Oct. 17, 2003." *American Quarterly* 56.1 (March 2004): 1–18.

Kaplan, Caren. *Questions of Travel: Postmodern Discourses of Displacement*. Durham NC: Duke UP, 1996.

Kauanui, J. Kēhaulani. *Hawaiian Blood: Colonialism and the Politics of Indigeneity and Sovereignty*. Durham NC: Duke UP, 2008.

Kauffman, Linda S. "The Long Goodbye: Against Personal Testimony or, an Infant Grifter Grows Up." *Changing Subjects: The Making of Feminist Literary Criticism*. Ed. Gayle Greene and Coppélia Kahn. London: Routledge, 1993. 129–46.

Keating, AnaLouise. "Charting Pathways, Marking Thresholds . . . A Warning, an Introduction." Anzaldúa and Keating 6–20.

———. "Interrogating 'Whiteness,' (De)Constructing 'Race.'" *College English* 57.8 (Dec. 1995): 901–18.

Kelly, Anne Keala, dir. *Noho Hewa: The Wrongful Occupation of Hawaiʻi*. Documentary. 2008.

Kernan, Alvin. *In Plato's Cave*. New Haven CT: Yale UP, 1999.

Kim, Elaine. *Asian American Literature: An Introduction to the Writings and Their Social Context*. Philadelphia PA: Temple UP, 1984.

Kincaid, Jamaica. *Lucy*. New York: Farrar, Straus & Giroux, 1990.

Kincaid, James R. "Critical Response 1: *Pouvoir, felicite, Jane, et moi* (Power, Bliss, Jane, and Me)." *Critical Inquiry* 25 (spring 1999): 610–16.

Kirk, Gwyn, and Margo Okazawa-rey. "Women Opposing U.S. Militarism in East Asia." *Peace Review* 16.1 (March 2004): 59–64.

Kiskis, Michael. "Adult Learners, Autobiography, and Educational Planning: Reflections on Pedagogy, Andragogy, and Power." Sullivan and Qualley 56–72.

Kittay, Eva Feder. *Love's Labor: Essays on Women, Equality, and Dependency*. New York: Routledge, 1999.

Kondo, Dorinne K. *About Face: Performing Race in Fashion and Theater*. New York: Routledge, 1997.

———. *Crafting Selves: Power, Gender, and Discourses of Identity in a Japanese Workplace*. Chicago: U of Chicago P, 1990.

Kudlick, Catherine J. "Disability History, Power, and Rethinking the Idea of 'the Other.'" *PMLA* 120.2 (March 2005): 557–61.

Kuhn, Annette. *Family Secrets: Acts of Memory and Imagination*. London: Verso, 1995.

Kumar, Amitava. *Passport Photos*. Berkeley: U of California P, 2000.

Kunke, Benjamin. "Misery Loves a Memoir." *New York Times Book Review* (July 16, 2006): 27.

Kwasny, Andrijka. "Ethnic Occupations." *Minnesota Review* 48–49 (1997; pub. date 1998): 227–34.

Lang, James M. *Learning Sickness: A Year with Crohn's Disease*. Herndon VA: Capital Books, 2004.

———. *Life on the Tenure Track: Lessons from the First Year*. Baltimore: Johns Hopkins UP, 2005.

Layoun, Mary. *Travels of a Genre: The Modern Novel and Ideology*. Princeton NJ: Princeton UP, 1990.

Lazarre, Jane. *Beyond the Whiteness of Whiteness: Memoir of a White Mother of Black Sons*. Durham NC: Duke UP, 1996.

———. *The Mother Knot*. Durham NC: Duke UP, 1997 (1976).

Leitch, Vincent B. *Cultural Criticism, Literary Theory, Poststructuralism*. New York: Columbia UP, 1992.

Lentricchia, Frank. *The Edge of Night: A Confession*. New York: Random House, 1994.

———. "Last Confessions of a Literary Critic." *Lingua Franca* (Sept./Oct. 1996): 59–67.

Levinas, Emmanuel. *Humanism of the Other*. Trans. Nidra Poller. Urbana: U of Illinois P, 2006.

Lezra, Jacques. "Unrelated Passions." *Differences: A Journal of Feminist Cultural Studies* 14.1 (2003): 74–87.

Lim, Shirley Geok-lin. *Among the White Moon Faces: An Asian American Memoir of Homelands*. New York: Feminist P, 1996.

Linton, Simi. "What Is Disability Studies?" *PMLA* 120.2 (March 2005): 518–22.

Lodge, David. *Small World*. New York: Penguin Books, 1995 (1984).

Lorde, Audre. *Sister Outsider*. Berkeley CA: Crossing P, 1984.

Lowenstein, Sharyn, Elizabeth Chiseri-Strater, and Cinthia Gannett. "Re-envisioning the Journal: Writing the Self into Community." Sullivan and Qualley 139–52.

Lutz, Catherine A. "Emotion, Thought, and Estrangement: Western Discourses on Feeling." *Unnatural Emotions: Everyday Sentiments on a Micronesian Atoll and Their Challenge to Western Theory*. Chicago: U of Chicago P, 1988. 53–80.

Lyons, Laura E. "Dole, Hawai'i, and the Question of Land under Globalization." *Cultural History and the Global Corporation*. Ed. Purnima Bose and Laura E. Lyons. Bloomington: U of Indiana P, forthcoming.

Lyons, Paul. *American Pacificism: Oceania in the U.S. Imagination*. New York: Routledge 2005.

Ma, Sheng-mei. *Immigrant Subjectivities in Asian American and Asian Diasporic Literatures*. Albany: SUNY P, 1998.

MacFarquhar, Larissa. "The Dean's List: The Enfant Terrible of English Lit Grows Up." *New Yorker* (June 11, 2001): 62–71.

Macrorie, Ken. *Telling Writing*. Portsmouth NH: Boynton/Cook Publishers, 1985.

Mairs, Nancy. Foreword. *Recovering Bodies: Illness, Disability, and Lifewriting*. By G. Thomas Couser. Madison: U of Wisconsin P, 1997. ix–xiv.

Manalansan, Martin F., IV. *Global Divas: Filipino Gay Men in the Diaspora*. Durham NC: Duke UP, 2003.

Mani, Lata. *Interleaves: Ruminations on Illness and Spiritual Life*. Bangalore, India, and Oakland CA: Lata Mani, 2001.

Mansfield, Nick. *Subjectivity: Theories of the Self from Freud to Haraway*. New York: New York UP, 2000.

Marks, Deborah. *Disability; Controversial Debates and Psychosocial Perspectives*. London: Routledge, 1999.

Martin, Jane R. *The Schoolhome: Rethinking Schools for Changing Families*. Cambridge MA: Harvard UP, 1992.

McBride, James. *The Color of Water: A Black Man's Tribute to His White Mother*. New York: Riverhead Books, 1996.

McClintock, Anne. *Imperial Leather: Race, Gender, and Sexuality in the Colonial Context*. New York: Routledge, 1995.

McCloskey, Deirdre N. *Crossing: A Memoir*. Chicago: U of Chicago P, 1999.

McDowell, Deborah. *Leaving Pipeshop: Memories of Kin*. New York: W. W. Norton, 1996.

McNaron, Toni. *I Dwell in Possibility: A Memoir*. New York: Feminist P, 1992.

McRuer, Robert. *Crip Theory: Cultural Signs of Queerness and Disability*. New York: New York UP, 2006.

Méndez-Negrete, Josie. *Las hijas de Juan: Daughters Betrayed*. Durham NC: Duke UP, 2006 (rev. ed.).

Miller, Alice. *The Drama of the Gifted Child: The Search for the True Self*. New York: Basic Books, 1996.

Miller, Nancy K. *Bequest and Betrayal: Memoirs of a Parent's Death*. New York: Oxford UP, 1996.

———. "'But Enough about Me, What Do You Think of My Memoir?'" *Yale Journal of Criticism* 13.2 (2000): 421–36.

———. *But Enough about Me: Why We Read Other People's Lives*. New York: Columbia UP, 2002.

———. "The Entangled Self: Genre Bondage in the Age of the Memoir." *PMLA* 122.2 (March 2007): 537–48.

———. "Public Statements, Private Lives: Academic Memoirs for the Nineties." *Signs* 22.4 (1997): 981–1015.

———. "Reviewing Eve." Barber and Clark 217–28.

Miller, Susan. "*In Loco Parentis*: Addressing (the) Class." *Pedagogy*. Gallop 155–64.

Mitchell, David T. "Narrative Prosthesis and the Materiality of Metaphor." S. Snyder, Garland-Thomson, and Brueggemann 15–30.

Mitchell, David T., and Sharon Snyder. *Narrative Prosthesis: Disability and the Dependencies of Discourse*. Ann Arbor: U of Michigan P, 2000.

———. "Introduction: Disability Studies and the Double Bind of Representation." *The Body and Physical Difference: Discourses of Disability*. Ed. Mitchell and Sharon Snyder. Ann Arbor: U of Michigan P, 1997. 1–34.

Miyoshi, Masao. "Against the Native Grain: The Japanese Novel and the 'Post-mostmodern' West." *Postmodernism and Japan*. Miyoshi and Harootunian 143–68.

———. "Ivory Tower in Escrow." *boundary* 2 27.1 (2000): 7–50.

———. *Off Center: Power and Culture Relations between Japan and the United States*. Cambridge MA: Harvard UP, 1991.

Miyoshi, Masao, and H. D. Harootunian, eds. *Japan in the World*. Durham NC: Duke UP, 1993.

———, eds. *Postmodernism and Japan*. Durham NC: Duke UP, 1989.

Modleski, Tania. "Critical Response 1: 'Fight the Power: A Response to Jane Gallop, James Kincaid, and Ann Pellegrini.'" *Critical Inquiry* 26.3 (spring 2000): 591–600.

Mohanty, Satya P. "The Epistemic Status of Cultural Identity: On *Beloved* and the Postcolonial Condition." Moya and Hames-García 29–66.

Moi, Toril. "'I Am Not a Feminist, But . . .': How Feminism Became the F-Word." *PMLA* 121. 5 (Oct. 2006): 1735–41.

Moraga, Cherríe. "La Güera." Moraga and Anzaldúa 27–34.

———. *Loving in the War Years/Lo que nunca pasó por sus labios*. Boston: South End P, 1983.

Moraga, Cherríe, and Gloria Anzaldúa, eds. *This Bridge Called My Back: Writings by Radical Women of Color*. New York: Kitchen Table: Women of Color P, 1981.

Morrison, Toni. *Playing in the Dark: Whiteness and the Literary Imagination*. New York: Vintage Books, 1992.

Moya, Paula M. L., and Michael R. Hames-García, eds. *Reclaiming Identity: Realist Theory and the Predicament of Postmodernism*. Berkeley: U of California P, 2000.

Mura, David. *A Male Grief: Notes on Pornography and Addiction*. New York: Crown, 1990.

———. *Turning Japanese: Memoirs of a Sansei*. New York: Anchor Books, 1991.

———. *Where the Body Meets Memory: An Odyssey of Race, Sexuality, and Identity*. New York: Anchor Books, 1995.

Musashi, Miyamoto. *The Book of Five Rings: The Classic Guide to Strategy*. New York: Gramercy, 1988.

Newitz, Annalee, ed. *White Trash: Race and Class in America*. New York: Routledge, 1997.

Nguyen, Minh T. "It Matters to Get the Facts Straight': Joy Kagawa, Realism, and Objectivity of Values." Moya and Hames-García 171–204.

Nixon, Rob. *Dreambirds: The Strange History of the Ostrich in Fashion, Food, and Fortune*. New York: Picador, 1999.

Noddings, Nell. *Caring: A Feminine Approach to Ethics and Moral Education*. Berkeley: U of California P, 1984.

———. *The Challenge to Care in Schools: An Alternative Approach to Education*. New York: Teachers College P, 1992.

Noey, Christopher, dir. *Creating Shangri La: The Doris Duke Collection of Islamic Art*. Video. Honolulu Academy of Arts, 2002.

Nussbaum, Martha C. *For Love of Country?* Ed. Joshua Cohen. Boston: Beacon P, 1996, rpt. 2002.

———. "Introduction: Cosmopolitan Emotions?" J. Cohen ix–xiv.

———. "Narrative Emotions: Beckett's Genealogy of Love." *Love's Knowledge: Essays on Philosophy and Literature*. New York: Oxford UP, 1990. 286–313.

———. "Patriotism and Cosmopolitanism." J. Cohen 3–20.

———. "Reply." J. Cohen 131–44.

O'Brien, Sharon. *The Family Silver: A Memoir of Depression and Inheritance*. Chicago: U of Chicago P, 2004.

Okada, John. *No-No Boy*. Seattle: U of Washington P, 1978.

Okimoto, Daniel I. *American in Disguise*. New York: Walker/Weatherhill, 1971.

Ong, Aihwa. "'Flexible Citizenship among Chinese Cosmopolitans." Cheah and Robbins 134–62.

Osorio, Jonathan Kay Kamakawiwoʻole. *Dismembering Lāhui: A History of the Hawaiian Nation to 1887*. Honolulu: U of Hawaiʻi P, 2002.

Otte, George. "In-Voicing: Beyond the Voice Debate." *Pedagogy*. Gallop 147–54.

Ouchi, William. *Theory Z: How American Business Can Meet the Japanese Challenge*. New York: Avon Books, 1983.

Parry, Benita. "Overlapping Territories and Intertwined Histories: Edward Said's Postcolonial Cosmopolitanism." Sprinker 19–47.

Patai, Daphne. "Galloping Contradictions: Sexual Harassment in Academe." *Gender Studies* 16.1/2 (winter/spring 1998): 86–106.

Payne, Michael, and John Schad, eds. *Life after Theory*. London: Continuum International Publishing Group, 2003.

Perloff, Marjorie. *The Vienna Paradox: A Memoir*. New York: New Directions, 2003.

Pfister, Joel, and Nancy Schnog, ed. *Inventing the Psychological: Toward a Cultural History of Emotional Life in America*. New Haven CT: Yale UP, 1997.

Phelan, James. *Beyond the Tenure Track: Fifteen Months in the Life of an English Professor*. Columbus: Ohio State UP, 1991.

Pratt, Mary Louise. *Imperial Eyes: Travel Writing and Transculturation*. London: Routledge, 1992.

Price, Reynolds. *A Whole New Life: An Illness and a Healing*. New York: Scribner, 2000.

Pritchard, William H. *English Papers: A Teaching Life*. St. Paul MN: Graywolf P, 1995.

Qureshi, Emran. "Misreading 'The Arab Mind.'" *Boston Globe* (May 30, 2004). <http://www.boston.com/news/globe/ideas/articles/2004/05/30/misreading_the_arab_mind>, accessed July 18, 2008.

Rafael, Vicente. "Cultures of Area Studies in the U.S." Talk. U of Hawai'i. Honolulu, Hawai'i. Oct. 2, 1998.

Rapaport, Herman. "The New Personalism." *Biography* 21.1 (winter 1998): 36–49.

Readings, Bill. *The University in Ruins*. Cambridge MA: Harvard UP, 1997.

Reddy, Maureen T. *Crossing the Color Line: Race, Parenting, and Culture*. New Brunswick NJ: Rutgers UP, 1997.

———, ed. *Everyday Acts against Racism: Raising Children in a Multiracial World*. Seattle: Seal P, 1996.

Reddy, Maureen T., Martha Roth, and Amy Sheldon, eds. *Mother Journeys: Feminists Write about Mothering*. Minneapolis: Spinsters Ink, 1994.

Robbins, Bruce. "Introduction Part 1: Actually Existing Cosmopolitanism." Cheah and Robbins 1–19.

Rodrigues, Valerian, ed. *The Essential Writings of B. R. Ambedkar*. London: Oxford UP, 2002.

Roediger, David R. *Towards the Abolition of Whiteness: Essays on Race, Politics, and Working Class History*. London: Verso, 1994.

Rooney, Ellen. "A Semiprivate Room." *Differences: A Journal of Feminist Cultural Studies* 13.1 (2002): 128–56.

Rosenbloom, Stephanie. "The Professor as Open Book." *New York Times* (March 20, 2008). <http://www.nytimes.com/2008/03/20/fashion/20professor.html?_r=1>, accessed July 23, 2008.

Rothenberg, Paula. *Invisible Privilege: A Memoir about Race, Class, and Gender*. Lawrence: UP of Kansas, 2000.

Rowe, John Carlos. "Edward Said and American Studies." *American Quarterly* 56. 1 (March 2004): 33–47.

Ruddick, Lisa. "Critical Response 2: Professional Harassment." *Critical Inquiry* 26.3 (spring 2000): 601–09.

Said, Edward W. *Beginnings: Intention and Method*. New York: Columbia UP, 1975, rpt. 1985.

———. "Defamation, Zionist Style." *Al-Ahram Weekly* 444 (Aug. 26–Sep. 1, 1999). <http://www.zmag.org/saidreply.htm>.

———. *The Edward Said Reader*. Eds. Moustafa Bayoumi and Andrew Rubin. New York: Vintage Books, 2000.

———. *Humanism and Democratic Criticism*. New York: Palgrave Macmillan, 2004.

———. "An Interview with Edward W. Said (1999)." *Edward Said Reader*. Said 419–44.

———. *Orientalism*. Sprinker 63–113.

———. *Out of Place: A Memoir*. New York: Alfred A. Knopf, 1999.

———. "Punishment by Detail," *Al Ahram Weekly* (Aug. 13, 2002). <http://aljazeerah.info/Opinion%20editorials/2002%20Opinion%20editorials/Aug.%202002/Punishment%20by%20detail,%20by%20Edward%20Sa'id.htm>, accessed July 15, 2008.

———. *Representations of the Intellectual: The 1993 Reith Lectures*. New York: Pantheon, 1994.

———. *Traveling Theory*. Sprinker 195–217.

———. *The World, the Text, and the Critic*. Cambridge MA: Harvard UP, 1983.

———. *Zionism from the Standpoint of Its Victims*. Sprinker 116–48.

Said, Edward W., with photographs by Jean Mohr. *After the Last Sky: Palestinian Lives*. New York: Pantheon Books, 1986.

Sanger, Carol. "The Erotics of Torts." *Michigan Law Review* 96.6 (May 1998): 1852–83.

Scarry, Elaine. "The Difficulty of Imagining Other People." J. Cohen 98–110.

Schneider, Alison. "Jane Tompkins's Message to Academe: Nurture the Individual, Not Just the Intellect." *Chronicle of Higher Education* (1998). <http://chronicle.com/colloquy/98/tompkins/background.shtml>, accessed July 14, 2008. Responses, <http://chronicle.com/colloquy/98/tompkins/re.shtml>, accessed July 14. 2008.

Schnog, Nancy. "On Inventing the Psychological." Pfister and Schnog 3–16.

Sedgwick, Eve Kosofsky. *Between Men: English Literature and Male Homosocial Desire*. New York: Columbia UP, 1985.

———. "Breast Cancer: Issues and Resources." *Lesbian and Gay Studies Newsletter* 22.3 (fall 1995): 10–15.

———. *A Dialogue on Love*. Boston: Beacon P, 1999.

———. *Epistemology of the Closet*. Berkeley: U of California P, 1990.

———. *Fat Art, Thin Art*. Durham NC: Duke UP, 1994.

———. "Gosh, Boy George, You Must Be Awfully Secure in Your Masculinity!" *Constructing Masculinity*. Ed. Maurice Berger, Brian Wallis, and Simon Watson. New York: Routledge, 1995. 11–19.

———. *Tendencies*. Durham NC: Duke UP, 1993.

Sedgwick, Eve Kosofsky, Stephen M. Barber, and David L. Clark. "This Piercing Bouquet: An Interview with Eve Kosofsky Sedgwick." Barber and Clark 243–62.

Sedgwick, Eve Kosofsky, and Adam Frank. "Shame in the Cybernetic Fold: Reading Silvan Tomkins." *Shame and Its Sisters: A Silvan Tomkins Reader*. Ed. Eve Kosofsky Sedgwick and Adam Frank. Durham NC: Duke UP, 1995. 1–28.

Sen, Amartya. *The Argumentative Indian: Writings on Indian History, Culture and Identity*. New York: Farrar, Straus & Giroux, 2005.

Shankar, S. "Edward Said, Critical Humanist." *Journal of Contemporary Thought* 18 (winter 2003): 175–80.

Shohat, Ella. "Antinomies of Exile: Said at the Frontiers of National Narrations." Sprinker 121–43.

Shor, Ira. *Empowering Education: Critical Teaching for Social Change*. Chicago: U of Chicago P, 1992.

Showalter, Elaine. *Faculty Towers: The Academic Novel and Its Discontents*. Philadelphia: U of Pennsylvania P, 2005.

Shumway, David. "The Star System in Literary Studies." *PMLA* 112.1 (Jan. 1997): 85–100.

Silva, Noenoe K. *Aloha Betrayed: Native Hawaiian Resistance to American Colonialism*. Durham NC: Duke UP, 2004.

Simpson, David. *The Academic Postmodern and the Rule of Literature: A Report on Half-Knowledge*. Chicago: U of Chicago, 1995.

———. "Speaking Personally: The Culture of Autobiographical Criticism." Veeser 82–96.

Singal, Daniel J. "The Other Crisis in American Education." *The Atlantic* 268.5 (1991): 59–74.

Slaughter, Joseph R. "Enabling Fictions and Novel Subjects: The *Bildungsroman* and International Human Rights Law." *PMLA* 121.5 (Oct. 2006): 1405–23.

Slaughter, Shelia, and Larry L. Leslie. *Academic Capitalism: Politics, Policies, and the Entrepreneurial University*. Baltimore: Johns Hopkins UP, 1999.

Smith, Barbara, ed. *Home Girls: A Black Feminist Anthology*. New York: Kitchen Table/Women of Color P, 1983.

Smith, Patrick. "What Memoir Forgets." *Nation* 268.4 (July 27–Aug. 3, 1998): 30–33.

Smith, Paul. "Pedagogy and the Popular-Cultural-Commodity-Text." *Popular Culture, Schooling, and Everyday Life.* Ed. Henry A. Giroux and Roger I. Simon. New York: Bergin, 1989. 31–46.

Smith, Sidonie. *Moving Lives: Twentieth-Century Women's Travel Writing.* Minneapolis: U of Minnesota P, 2001.

Smith, Sidonie, and Julia Watson. *Reading Autobiography: A Guide for Interpreting Life Narratives.* Minneapolis: U of Minnesota P, 2001.

Snyder, Don J. *The Cliff Walk: A Memoir of a Job Lost and a Life Found.* Boston: Little, Brown, 1997.

Snyder, Sharon L., Rosemarie Garland-Thomson, and Brenda Jo Brueggemann, eds. *Disability Studies: Enabling the Humanities.* New York: Modern Language Association of America, 2002.

Snyder, Sharon L., and David T. Mitchell. "Re-engaging the Body: Disability Studies and the Resistance to Embodiment." *Public Culture* 13.3 (2001): 367–90.

Solomon, Melissa. "Flaming Iguanas, Dalai Pandas, and Other Lesbian Bardos (A Few Perimeter Points)." Barber and Clark 201–16.

Sone, Monica Itoi. *Nisei Daughter.* Seattle: U of Washington P, 1979.

Spitzer, Leo. *Hotel Bolivia: The Culture of Memory in a Refuge from Nazism.* New York: Hill & Wang, 1999.

Spivak, Gayatri Chakravorty. *Death of a Discipline.* New York: Columbia UP, 2003.

Sprinker, Michael, ed. *Edward Said: A Critical Reader.* Oxford UK: Blackwell, 1992.

Stannard, David. "The Hawaiians: Health, Justice, and Sovereignty." Fujikane 161–69.

Stanton, Donna. "Foreword: ANDs, INs, and BUTs." *PMLA* 121.5 (Oct. 2006): 1518–25.

———. "Human Rights and the Humanities." President's column. *MLA Newsletter* 37.4 (winter 2005): 3.

Stepto, Robert B. *Blue as the Lake: A Personal Geography.* Boston: Beacon P, 1999.

Suleri, Sara. *Meatless Days.* Chicago: U of Chicago P, 1989.

Sullivan, Patricia A., and Donna J. Qually, eds. *Pedagogy in the Age of Politics: Writing and Reading (in the Academy).* Urbana IL: National Council of Teachers, 1994.

Talbot, Margaret. "A Most Dangerous Method." *Lingua Franca* 1 (Jan./Feb. 1994): 24–40.

Tan, Kok-Chor. *Justice without Borders: Cosmopolitanism, Nationalism, and Patriotism.* Cambridge: Cambridge UP, 2004.

Tanigawa, Donna Tsuyuko. "Interventions." Paper for Contemporary Autobiography: In and Against the Academy, Prof. Cynthia Franklin, U of Hawai'i, Mānoa, spring 1999.

———. "Premature." Anzaldúa and Keating 267–77.

———. "Premature Prologue." Paper for Contemporary Autobiography: In and Against the Academy, Prof. Cynthia Franklin, U of Hawai'i, Mānoa, spring 1999.

Tengan, Ty P. Kāwika. *Native Men Remade: Gender and Nation in Contemporary Hawai'i.* Durham NC: Duke UP, 2008.

Thomson, Rosemarie Garland. "Disability and Representation." *PMLA* 120.2 (March 2005): 522–27.

———. *Extraordinary Bodies: Figuring Physical Disability in American Culture and Literature.* New York: Columbia UP, 1997.

———. "Theorizing Disability." *Disability Studies Reader.* L. Davis 30–44.

Tobin, Joseph J., ed. *Re-made in Japan: Everyday Life and Consumer Taste in a Changing Society.* New Haven: Yale UP, 1992.

Tompkins, Jane. "'Indians,' Textualism, Morality, and the Problem of History." *Critical Inquiry* 13.1 (autumn 1986): 101–19.

———. *A Life in School: What the Teacher Learned.* Reading MA: Perseus Books, 1996.

———. "Me and My Shadow." *New Literary History* 19 (1987): 169–78.

———. *Sensational Designs: The Cultural Work of American Fiction, 1790–1860.* New York: Oxford UP, 1985.

———. *West of Everything: The Inner Life of Westerns.* New York: Oxford UP, 1992.

Torgovnick, Marianna De Marco. *Crossing Ocean Parkway: Readings by an Italian American Daughter.* Chicago: U of Chicago P, 1994.

———. *Gone Primitive: Savage Intellects, Modern Lives.* Chicago: U of Chicago P, 1990.

———. "On Being White." *Best American Essays 1991.* Ed. Joyce Carol Oates. New York: Ticknor & Fields, 1991.

———. *Primitive Passions: Men, Women, and Quest for Ecstasy.* New York: Alfred A. Knopf, 1997.

———. *The War Complex: World War II in Our Time.* Chicago: U of Chicago P, 2005.

Torrance, Robert M. "The Radical Tradition of Humanistic Consciousness." *Humanism in the Humanities in the Twenty-first Century.* Ed. William S. Haney II and Peter Malekin. Lewisburg PA: Bucknell UP, London: Associated U Presses, 2001. 164–84.

Trask, Haunani-Kay. *From a Native Daughter: Colonialism and Sovereignty in Hawai'i.* Honolulu: U of Hawai'i P, rev. ed. 1999.

Treat, John Whittier. *Great Mirrors Shattered: Homosexuality, Orientalism and Japan*. New York: Oxford UP, 1999.

Tswei, Suzanne. "Rancor Grows as Cayetano Stands Pat on UH Faculty Pay." *Honolulu Star Bulletin* (Feb. 2, 2001), 28.

Uchida, Yoshiko. *Desert Exile: The Uprooting of a Japanese-American Family*. Seattle: U of Washington P, 1984.

The Vapors. "Turning Japanese." Song. 1980.

Veeser, H. Aram, ed. *Confessions of the Critics*. New York: Routledge, 1996.

Vertovec, Steven, and Robin Cohen, eds. *Conceiving Cosmopolitanism: Theory, Context, and Practice*. New York: Oxford UP, 2003.

Villanueva, Victor, Jr. *Bootstraps: From an American Academic of Color*. Urbana IL: National Council of Teachers of English, 1993.

Vitanza, Victor J., mod. PreText Conversations. "A Re/INter/View with Jane Gallop on *Feminist Accused of Sexual Harassment*." Jan. 22–Feb. 10, 1998. Parts 1–12: <http://www.pre-text.com/ptlist/gallop1.html> through <http://www.pre-text.com/ptlist/gallop12.html>, accessed July 14, 2008.

Wall, Susan. "Rereading the Discourses of Gender in Composition: A Cautionary Tale." Sullivan and Qualley 166–82.

Wallace, Michelle. "Art for Whose Sake?" *Women's Review of Books* 13.1 (Oct. 1995): 8.

Wallerstein, Immanuel. "Neither Patriotism nor Cosmopolitanism." J. Cohen 122–24.

Warner, Michael, ed. *Fear of a Queer Planet: Queer Politics and Social Theory*. Minneapolis: U of Minnesota P, 1993.

Washburn, Jennifer. *University, Inc.: The Corporate Corruption of American Higher Education*. New York: Basic Books, 2005.

Weed, Elizabeth, Ellen Rooney, and Naomi Schor, eds. *Differences: On Humanism*. Durham NC: Duke UP, 2003.

Wendell, Susan. "Toward a Feminist Theory of Disability." *Disability Studies Reader*. L. Davis 260–78.

Wexler, Alice. *Mapping Fate: A Memoir of Family, Risk, and Genetic Research*. Berkeley: U of California P, 1996.

Wicke, Jennifer, and Michael Sprinker. "Interview with Edward Said." Sprinker 221–64.

Williams, Jeffrey. "Writing in Concert: An Interview with Cathy Davidson, Alice Kaplan, Jane Tompkins, and Marianna Torgovnick." Veeser 156–76.

Williams, Patricia J. *The Alchemy of Race and Rights*. Cambridge MA: Harvard UP, 1992.

———. *The Rooster's Egg*. Cambridge MA: Harvard UP, 1997.

Williams, Raymond. *Marxism and Literature*. New York: Oxford UP, 1977.

Wolfe, Alan. "Suicide and the Japanese Postmodern: A Postnarrative Paradigm?" Miyoshi and Harootunian, *Postmodernism and Japan* 215–34.

Wong, Sau-ling Cynthia. "Denationalization Reconsidered: Asian American Cultural Criticism at a Theoretical Crossroads." *Amerasia* 21.1,2 (1995): 1–27.

Woodward, Kathleen M. "Statistical Panic." *Differences: A Journal of Feminist Cultural Studies* 11.2 (1999): 177–203.

Yap, Allison. "An Absence Ever Present." Paper for Contemporary Autobiography: In and Against the Academy, Prof. Cynthia Franklin, U of Hawai'i, Mānoa, spring 1999.

Yoneyama, Lisa. "Traveling Memories, Contagious Justice: Americanization of Japanese War Crimes at the End of the Post–Cold War." *Journal of Asian American Studies* 6.1 (2003): 57–93.

Yoshihara, Mari. *Embracing the East: White Women and American Orientalism.* New York: Oxford UP, 2003.

Zandy, Janet. *Hands: Physical Labor, Class, and Cultural Work.* New Brunswick NJ: Rutgers UP, 2004.

Zhou, Xiaojing. "Race, Sexuality, and Representation in David Mura's *The Colors of Desire*." *Journal of Asian American Studies* 1.3 (Oct. 1998): 245–67.

Zuern, John. "Ask Me for the Moon: Working Nights in Waikīkī." *Iowa Review Web* 7.1 (Aug. 2005). <http://www2.hawaii.edu/~zuern/ask/>, accessed July 19, 2008.

INDEX

Printed in the United States
146020LV00002B/3/P